Religious Crisis and Civic Transformation

Brandeis Series on Gender, Culture, Religion, and Law

SERIES EDITORS: LISA FISHBAYN JOFFE AND SYLVIA NEIL

This series focuses on the conflict between women's claims to gender equality and legal norms justified in terms of religious and cultural traditions. It seeks work that develops new theoretical tools for conceptualizing feminist projects for transforming the interpretation and justification of religious law, examines the interaction or application of civil law or remedies to gender issues in a religious context, and engages in analysis of conflicts over gender and culture/religion in a particular religious legal tradition, cultural community, or nation. Created under the auspices of the Hadassah-Brandeis Institute in conjunction with its Project on Gender, Culture, Religion, and the Law, this series emphasizes cross-cultural and interdisciplinary scholarship concerning Judaism, Islam, Christianity, and other religious traditions.

For a complete list of books that are available in the series, visit www.upne.com

Kimba Allie Tichenor, *Religious Crisis and Civic Transformation: How Conflicts over Gender and Sexuality Changed the West German Catholic Church*

Margalit Shilo, *Girls of Liberty: The Struggle for Suffrage in Mandatory Palestine*

Mark Goldfeder, *Legalizing Plural Marriage: The Next Frontier in Family Law*

Susan M. Weiss and Netty C. Gross-Horowitz, *Marriage and Divorce in the Jewish State: Israel's Civil War*

Lisa Fishbayn Joffe and Sylvia Neil, editors, *Gender, Religion, and Family Law: Theorizing Conflicts between Women's Rights and Cultural Traditions*

Chitra Raghavan and James P. Levine, editors, *Self-Determination and Women's Rights in Muslim Societies*

Janet Bennion, *Polygamy in Primetime: Media, Gender, and Politics in Mormon Fundamentalism*

Ronit Irshai, *Fertility and Jewish Law: Feminist Perspectives on Orthodox Responsa Literature*

Jan Feldman, *Citizenship, Faith, and Feminism: Jewish and Muslim Women Reclaim Their Rights*

Religious Crisis and Civic Transformation

*How Conflicts over Gender and Sexuality
Changed the West German Catholic Church*

KIMBA ALLIE TICHENOR

Brandeis University Press
WALTHAM, MASSACHUSETTS

Brandeis University Press
An imprint of University Press of New England
www.upne.com
© 2016 Brandeis University
All rights reserved
Manufactured in the United States of America
Designed by Dean Bornstein
Typeset in Adobe Jenson Pro by The Perpetua Press

For permission to reproduce any of the material in this book, contact Permissions, University Press of New England, One Court Street, Suite 250, Lebanon NH 03766; or visit www.upne.com

Library of Congress Cataloging-in-Publication Data

Names: Tichenor, Kimba Allie, 1959– author.
Title: Religious crisis and civic transformation: how conflicts over gender and sexuality changed the West German Catholic Church / Kimba Allie Tichenor.
Description: Waltham, Massachusetts: Brandeis University Press, 2016. | Series: Brandeis Series on gender, culture, religion, and law | Includes bibliographical references and index. | Description based on print version record and CIP data provided by publisher; resource not viewed.
Identifiers: LCCN 2015040835 (print) | LCCN 2015040190 (ebook) | ISBN 9781611689709 (epub, mobi & pdf) | ISBN 9781611689082 (cloth) | ISBN 9781611689099 (paper)
Subjects: LCSH: Sex—Religious aspects—Catholic Church. | Celibacy—Catholic Church. | Gender identity—Religious aspects—Catholic Church. | Religion and civil society—Germany (West) | Catholic Church—Germany (West) Classification: LCC BX1795.S48 (print) | LCC BX1795.S48 T534 2016 (ebook) |
DDC 282/.4308109045—dc23
LC record available at http://lccn.loc.gov/2015040835

5 4 3 2 1

Contents

Foreword · ix
Lisa Fishbayn Joffe

Acknowledgments · xi
List of Abbreviations · xiii

Introduction · 1

Part I. The Male Celibate Priesthood and
Woman's Place in the Church
1. Celibacy for the Kingdom of Heaven and Earth · 29
2. Women's Ordination: Sacramental and Gendered Bodies · 62

Part II. The Catholic Church and Reproductive Politics
3. Artificial Contraception: German Angst and Catholic Rebellion · 99
4. The Abortion Debate: Hidden Tensions and New Directions · 136
5. Assisted Reproduction: Changing Bedfellows · 174

Epilogue · 208

Appendixes · 217
Notes · 235
Selected Bibliography · 275
Index · 291

Foreword

Lisa Fishbayn Joffe

Kimba Allie Tichenor notes that the challenge of reconciling women's rights and religious law is often raised in discussions of Islam in Europe but is rarely explored in connection with Christian denominations. The Brandeis Series on Gender, Culture, Religion, and Law is committed to publishing work that deepens our understanding of the dynamics surrounding women's struggle for gender equality under religious law across a broad range of traditions. Much can be learned from comparing the struggles for ritual inclusion, interpretive authority, and equality under law in different religious traditions and different nations.

Some of the works in this series are directly comparative, such as Jan Feldman's study of religious women's advocacy in Israel and Kuwait in *Citizenship, Faith, and Feminism* and our anthology *Gender, Religion, and Family Law*. Others present an in-depth analysis of a single religious tradition. Jewish law is explored in Ronit Irshai's *Fertility and Jewish Law*, Susan Weiss and Netty Gross-Horowitz's *Marriage and Divorce in the Jewish State*, and Margalit Shilo's *Girls of Liberty: The Struggle for Suffrage in Mandatory Palestine*. Islam is the focus of Chitra Raghavan and James Levine's book *Self-Determination and Women's Rights in Muslim Societies*, and Janet Bennion's *Polygamy in Primetime* looks at the changing face of Mormonism in America.

Tichenor's book on struggles over women's rights in Catholicism provides a detailed and incisive analysis of the decline and reemergence of the Catholic Church as a potent political force in postwar Germany. She demonstrates how the worldwide Catholic Church responded to women's demands by developing and emphasizing theological norms that made achievement of gender equality more difficult.

The Catholic Church has faced the dual challenge of declining interest among men in becoming celibate priests and of women's increasing demands to be allowed to take on a priestly role. Tichenor describes how the German Catholic Church resisted claims that it afford equality in achieving access to ritual roles and in shaping religious doctrine on contraception, abortion, and assisted reproduction. As in other religious traditions, Catholicism confronted the "feminization" of the community of congregants filling the pews and available to do the work of creating and maintaining communal religious life. As women took on much of the day-to-day work in churches (and synagogues), they began to ask why they should continue to be excluded from the more highly valued ritual roles of rabbi in the synagogue and altar server or deacon in the Catholic Church. Tichenor describes how this challenge was viewed by the Catholic Church as an attack not just on male dominance in the Church but also on the theological underpinnings of priestly power. Recognizing equality between men and women would necessitate recognizing equality between clergy and laity.

In other religious traditions, the creation of opportunities for advanced learning about religious doctrine has enabled women to become qualified to fulfill positions of religious leadership and to become informed challengers of doctrines that purport to exclude them on the basis of their sex. Over the course of the twentieth and twenty-first centuries, women have become eligible for ordination in other Christian denominations and in the more liberal branches of Judaism. In 2015 a small cohort of Orthodox Jewish women in America and Israel were ordained with authority to decide questions of law. Women have been recognized as pleaders in rabbinical and Islamic courts, as Islamic court judges, and as authorized interpreters of some branches of Jewish law, as *yoatzot halacha*.

Tichenor's elegant and comprehensive work helps us understand how and why the Catholic Church has been able to resist similar demands and the implications its stance has had. She shows how even widespread demands for gender equality among members of a religious community may not translate into transformation of discriminatory religious norms. Many women and moderates have left the Church. The reconstituted body is even more conservative and punitive toward those seeking gender equality than the old Church.

Acknowledgments

This book would not have been possible without the input and assistance of many persons and organizations. First I would like to thank the members of my dissertation committee—Michael Geyer, Leora Auslander, and John Boyer. To Michael Geyer I owe an immense debt for his unwavering support and wise counsel throughout my time at the University of Chicago and since. I would also like to thank him for pointing me in the direction of this project when I came to him looking for a topic for a seminar paper. Out of that paper emerged this book. I also wish to thank Leora Auslander, who encouraged me to consider the gender dimensions of politics in the West German Catholic Church. To John Boyer, I express my gratitude for providing me feedback and advice throughout the writing process.

I also thank Dagmar Herzog, Till van Rahden, Mark Ruff, Christine Stansell, and Benjamin Ziemann, who all read early drafts of my proposal and provided comments that helped me fine-tune my project at an early stage.

The research behind this book could not have been completed without the generous funding of the University of Chicago, the German Academic Exchange Service (DAAD), the Institute for European History in Mainz, and the Notre Dame Institute for Advanced Study. For their assistance in negotiating German Catholic archives and their constructive criticism of the project during my stay in Germany, I wish to thank Wilhelm Damberg and Thomas Schulte-Umberg. I also owe Martin Geyer a huge debt for the assistance he provided in a time of crisis during this project.

I would like to thank my friends and colleagues at the Notre Dame Institute for Advanced Study for their feedback during the revision stage. In particular, I am grateful to the following institute fellows for their encouragement and feedback: Thadious Davis, Sabine Doering, Lewis Ayers, Susannah Monta, and Margaret Abruzzo. It would not have been possible to finish this book without the technical, logistical, and moral support provided by the institute's directors and staff: Robert Sullivan, Don Stelluto, Carolyn Sherman, and Grant Osborn. I also thank Don Kommers, Mary Ellen Konieczny, and Tom Kselman of the University of Notre Dame for their insightful suggestions about how to revise the work for publication.

I wish to thank my dear friend and colleague, Inna Shtasker, who suffered through every chapter draft and served as taskmaster of the project, never allowing me to lose sight of the final goal.

And saving the best for last, I thank Loree, whose love and support provided me with the motivation to see this project through to its completion.

Abbreviations

ACDP	Archiv für Christlich-Demokratische Politik, Konrad-Adenauer Stiftung
AEK	Historisches Archiv des Erzbistums Köln
AI	Artificial insemination
AID	Artificial insemination by donor sperm
AIH	Artificial insemination by husband's sperm
B	Bundesarchiv
BDKJ	Bund der Deutschen Katholischen Jugend (League of German Catholic Youth)
BGHZ	Entscheidung des Bundesgerichtshofes in Zivilsachen (Decision of the Federal Court of Justice in Civil Matters)
BMFT	Bundesministerium für Forschung und Technik (Federal Ministry for Research and Technology)
BverfGE	Entscheidung des Bundesverfassungsgerichts (Decision of the Federal Constitutional Court)
CAJ	Christliche Arbeiterjugend (Association of Young Christian Workers)
CCE	Congregation for Catholic Education
CDF	Congregation for the Doctrine of the Faith
CDU	Christlich Demokratische Union (Christian Democratic Union)
CDWDS	Congregation for Divine Worship and the Discipline of the Sacraments
CSU	Christlich-Soziale Union (Christian Social Union)
DBK	Deutsche Bischofskonferenz (German Bishops' Conference)
dpa	Deutsche Presse-Agentur (German News Agency)
EKD	Evangelische Kirche in Deutschland (Evangelical Church in Germany)
ESchG	Embryonenschutzgesetz (Embryo Protection Act)
FAZ	*Frankfurter Allgemeine Zeitung*
FDP	Freie Demokratische Partei (Free Democratic Party)
FINNRET	Feminist International Network on New Reproductive Technologies

FINRRAGE	Feminist International Network of Resistance to Reproductive and Genetic Engineering
FMG	Fortpflanzungsmedizingesetz (Reproductive Medicine Bill)
FU	Frauen Union (CDU) (Women's Union)
IMWAC	International Movement We Are Church
IVF/ET	In vitro fertilization/embryo transfer
JHD	Jugendhaus Düsseldorf-Bundeszentralle für katholische Jugendarbeit (National Office for Catholic Youth Work)
KDFB	Katholischer Deutscher Frauenbund (League of German Catholic Women)
kfd	Katholische Frauengemeinschaft Deutschlands (Catholic Women's Association in Germany)
KNA	Katholische Nachrichten-Agentur (Catholic News Agency)
NRTs	New reproductive technologies
NYT	*New York Times*
PGD	Preimplantation genetic diagnosis
SPD	Sozialdemokratische Partei Deutschlands (Social Democratic Party of Germany)
StGB	Strafgesetzbuch (Criminal Code)
SZ	*Süddeutsche Zeitung*
WOC	Women's Ordination Conference
ZDF	Zweites Deutsches Fernsehen (Second German Television)
ZdK	Zentralkomitee der deutschen Katholiken (Central Committee of German Catholics)
ZKBS	Zentrale Kommission für Biologische Sicherheit (Central Commission for Biological Safety)

Religious Crisis and Civic Transformation

Introduction

On September 22, 1968, *Stern* proclaimed, "Grandpa's Church Is Dead."[1] The week before at the biennial Catholic Congress in Essen, three thousand ordinary West German Catholics voted in favor of a statement calling upon the pope to rescind *Humanae Vitae*, the encyclical upholding the Church's ban on artificial contraception. The era in which German Catholics publicly acquiesced to the Vatican's moral authority, while perhaps privately rebelling, had ended; and as the motto of the 1968 Essen Catholic Congress proclaimed, West German Catholics now lived "in the midst of this world" (*Mitten in dieser Welt*).[2] The insulated subculture that had organized Catholic life from cradle to grave since Bismarck's *Kulturkampf* in the 1870s had collapsed, and the so-called golden age of political Catholicism had ended. But what would replace the Catholic milieu remained unclear in 1968. What was certain was that West German Catholics had stepped out into a rapidly changing world—one in which issues of gender and sexuality often took center stage.

This book focuses on the West German Catholic Church's engagement in post-1950s religious and secular debates on gender and sexuality. It argues that the Church's engagement in these debates led to a theological and political transformation within Catholicism. In Germany, this transformation facilitated the Church's ability to exercise significant influence on national debates concerning women's reproductive rights and the defense of life long after the collapse of the Catholic milieu. As Vatican pronouncements on sexuality became more stringent, moderate and progressive West German Catholics distanced themselves from the Church, leaving a unified conservative core to promote the Church's sexual mores in the religious and public spheres. By the 1980s, this conservative core had embraced new arguments and new issue-specific alliances with political parties other than the two self-identified Christian parties—the Christian Democratic Union (Christlich Demokratische Union, CDU) and the Christian Socialist Union (Christlich-Soziale Union, CSU)—that proved remarkably successful. As the historian Dagmar Herzog has noted, the Catholic Church in Germany remains to this day a "formidable" political force on questions concerning the defense of life and women's reproductive rights.[3] This influence persists despite a dramatic decline in traditional indices of faith, such as membership in the Church. Yet this seeming paradox—continued political influence, on the one hand, and declining membership, on the other—has received little scholarly or media attention. Instead, most historians and pundits assume that after a brief Christian cultural and political resurgence in the 1950s, a secularized Germany emerged and the Christian churches lost their political influence. Consequently, recent victories by moral conservatives in a reunified Germany, such as the 2009 revision of Paragraph 218 mandating a three-day waiting period for late-term abortions when a fetal disability has been diagnosed, seemed for many scholars a surprising development in a nation known for its liberal attitudes on sexuality.

Yet as this book shows, these victories are inextricably linked to the moral crisis of authority of the 1960s and 1970s; from this crisis, a new Catholic theological and political identity emerged for a postsecular age. In the religious sphere, this meant a move away from the feminized piety of the nineteenth century aimed at filling the pews with women toward a gendered theology aimed at preserving the Church's teachings on the male celibate priesthood and on marriage. It also aimed at rallying the Church's conservative core. In the secular sphere, it meant promoting an interventionist and theologically informed agenda, particularly concerning reproductive politics. At first glance, this political strategy appears to be a return to *Kulturkampf* politics; it is in fact fundamentally different. Neither the German hierarchy nor the faithful harbored any delusions that they could turn back the hands of time. They understood that the German political climate had changed and that new arguments and strategies would be required if they were to succeed in promoting the Church's message in the secular or religious sphere.

From Triumph to Crisis

During the Allied occupation and in the early years of the Federal Republic, the CDU and CSU emerged as the dominant political force in West Germany. Although both parties identified themselves as Christian rather than Catholic, they had their origins in political Catholicism. The CDU had its roots in the prewar Catholic Center Party. The CSU, a regional Christian party, traced its origins to the Bavarian Catholic People's Party. Consequently, in the immediate postwar era, Catholics held the vast majority of leadership positions in both parties. In 1949, the CDU-CSU candidate, Konrad Adenauer (Catholic), became the first chancellor, thanks in large part to Allied support and the widespread belief among the populace that a return to Christian values represented the only viable path forward.

For Adenauer, Germany's economic and political recovery required the restoration of the hierarchical and moral discursive order. As Elizabeth D. Heineman noted in *What Difference Does a Husband Make?*, Adenauer feared that the gender and age imbalance in West Germany, along with the disequilibrium in class relations, made the new state vulnerable to the triple threat of fascism, communism, and Americanism. As part of his campaign to safeguard the country against these threats, Adenauer prioritized the restoration of Christian values and the reconstruction of the bourgeois family, instituting programs designed to remove women from the workplace and promote domesticity.[4] The Catholic Church and the Evangelical Church in Germany (Evangelische Kirche in Deutschland, EKD) supported this agenda. In particular, the West German Catholic Church, "through its many informal contacts with Catholic legislators," lobbied extensively to defend the Church's legal status and to incorporate Christian values into the Basic Law (Grundgesetz).[5] Although the Catholic Church did not succeed in having all its proposals inserted into the Basic Law, it did succeed in many spheres. The Basic Law included an invocation to God in the preamble; affirmed a right to life; ensured religious instruction in the schools; guaranteed the protection of marriage and family; and acknowledged the validity of past concordats between the Catholic Church and the German state.[6] In fact, the Catholic Church proved so successful in its efforts that the Protestant theologian Martin Niemöller remarked in 1949 that the Federal Republic had been "sired by the Vatican and born in Washington."[7]

Yet despite the successes of political Catholicism and its policies of restoration, signs of discontent with the status quo already existed in the 1950s; *Halbstarke* and rock 'n' roll girls, influenced by American cultural imports, challenged the gender, racial, and sexual norms of their parents. Between 1955 and 1957, *Halbstarke*—made up mostly of young working-class males donning "tight blue jeans" and "ducktail haircuts"—engaged the police in street battles, sparking widespread fear among German officialdom of Americanization and moral degeneration, which in turn prompted a rash of youth protection laws. However, as Uta Poiger detailed in *Jazz, Rock, and Rebels*, by the late 1950s West German authorities had largely succeeded in confronting this challenge by pushing "the issues of popular culture and sexuality into arenas defined as nonpolitical."[8] Still, depoliticization was incomplete. The youth culture of the 1950s opened new avenues of individual expression and sexual openness, which in the 1960s young people politicized anew.[9]

But the challenges posed by a relatively small number of rebellious West German youth were perhaps not the most disturbing sign of changing values in 1950s West Germany. As early as 1951, in letters to the editor of the Catholic women's journal *Frau und Mutter*, mainstream Catholic women voiced dissatisfaction with patriarchal marriage, demanding more autonomy and authority for women within marriage. One Catholic woman declared that she should be free to make decisions about household purchases without having to get her husband's approval. Another woman complained that her husband treated her like a "servant," because he provided her with no "pocket money." To the delight of many female readers, the *Frau und Mutter* editorial staff supported demands for a more collaborative partnership between husband and wife.[10] However, as will be discussed in Chapter 3, the editorial staff did not support the concomitant desire of some Catholic women to limit family size. Ordinary German Catholics—male and female—were already voicing their discontent with Church teachings on marriage and family in the 1950s.

Between 1955 and 1965, statistics indicated a slow decline in Church attendance and participation in Easter Communion. For example, in the Diocese of Cologne in 1954, 39.7 percent of Catholics attended mass; by 1960, this number had fallen to 38.7 percent. Easter Communion figures for the Diocese of Trier revealed a similar trend. In 1954, fully 65 percent of Catholics participated, but in 1960 the number had dropped to 64 percent (see Appendixes B and C).[11] These figures certainly did not suggest a steep decline in religiosity; however, Church leaders worried that the temptations of modern life were leading Catholics, particularly young Catholics, astray.

As Mark Ruff documented in *The Wayward Flock*, in the mid-1950s Catholic youth leaders of the League of German Catholic Youth (Bund der Deutschen Katholischen Jugend, BDKJ) complained that many Catholic youth no longer paid their organizational dues and could not name their local youth group leader; some BDKJ leaders responded to this threat by integrating leisure activities associated with the secular sphere into the religious sphere, creating, for example, film, book, and music clubs. But the overt religious tone in which many Church leaders framed discussions of leisure activities increasingly alienated many West German Catholic youth.[12] Like their secular counterparts, these youth began experimenting with new forms of community—ones that centered on generational interests rather than confessional or class ones. On the eve of the Second Vatican Council (Vatican II) and the sexual revolution, genuine fears existed in the secular and religious spheres about the moral and spiritual degeneration of German youth. In the case of the Catholic Church, a worsening shortage of priests exacerbated these fears—who would lead the Catholic youth of tomorrow?

Vatican II, called by Pope John XXIII on January 25, 1959, for the stated aim of modernizing the Church, generated genuine enthusiasm among West German Catholics, who believed that renewal in the Church depended on reform. However, this positive response did not develop immediately. Curial cardinals dominated the preparatory commissions; consequently, West German Catholics doubted that any real reform would result. Instead of the Vatican Council, West German Catholics were preoccupied with the 1961 World Eucharist Conference in Munich, the construction of the Berlin Wall, and the 1962 Catholic Congress in Hanover.[13]

Following conciliar developments on October 13, 1962, West German Catholics took notice of the council. On this date, Achille Cardinal Liénart of France rose from the president's table (the panel of ten cardinals chairing the session) to request a postponement of elections for the council commissions in order for the bishops to get acquainted with each other and for the episcopal conferences to submit lists of candidates. Josef Cardinal Frings of West Germany seconded the motion. The assembled Church fathers greeted the motion with prolonged applause, and the president's table affirmed the postponement. For Catholics around the world, the intervention signaled that the bishops did not plan to rubberstamp the documents prepared by the curial cardinals. For conservative Italian cardinals, such as Giuseppe Cardinal Siri of Genoa, the actions of the Northern European delegates represented something more sinister: "The devil has had his hand in this."[14] In either case, the postponement sparked an unprecedented upsurge in the circulation of Catholic newspapers in West Germany, as the faithful eagerly awaited the latest news on council developments.[15]

The sixteen documents approved by the council had, in the words of John XXIII, opened "the windows of the Church . . . so that we can see out and the people can see in."[16] Unlike past councils, Vatican II did not reject modernity, offering no condemnation of errors. Instead, it highlighted the Church's obligation to engage in dialogue with the modern world. The specific theological innovations that the council introduced—for example, a more positive valuation of the laity, a new emphasis on the missionary function of priests, tolerance for other systems of belief, and collegiality—led secular and religious commentators to describe Vatican II as a watershed in Catholic history.

But the euphoria surrounding council achievements soon disappeared, as a struggle developed within the Church over the meaning of the documents and the future direction of the Church. This battle encompassed many of the Church's fundamental teachings, including the interrelated subjects of marital morality and women's place in the Church. Although these two entangled subjects were by no means the only sites of confrontation in the post–Vatican II Church, they played a leading role in the transformation of Roman Catholicism.

Contextualizing the Crisis of Authority

Without doubt, the West German Catholic Church was not alone in experiencing a moral crisis of authority beginning in the mid-1960s. Throughout Western Europe and the United States, Catholics began questioning the Church's teachings on women's place in church and society, the relationship between the sexes, and women's reproductive rights. The Second Vatican Council's more positive assessment of the laity and its message of religious tolerance led many ordinary Catholics to ask if in an increasingly pluralistic society their Church had the right to impose its moral vision on the general public. Some Catholics even publicly challenged the Church's right to dictate the sexual morality of its congregants. This challenge did not go unnoticed by the Catholic hierarchy or the secular media. On March 19, 1965, an article in *Time*, "Roman Catholics: Authority under Fire," quoted Father Joseph Gallagher, an editor of Baltimore's archdiocesan weekly, as saying that a "crisis of obedience" existed in the Church.[17] Three years later the French archbishop, Marcel Lefebvre, attributed this crisis to Vatican II reforms: "How well I understand the desire on the part of many Catholics who are left stunned, indignant, or dismayed as they see spreading within the Church—through the voice of its ministers—doctrines casting doubt on truths heretofore regarded as the immutable foundations of the Catholic Faith."[18] Even those who supported Vatican II reforms, such as the French theologian Yves Congar, recognized that a "deep-seated malaise in large areas of the faithful" had developed since the council.[19]

It was not just the Catholic Church that experienced a crisis of authority in the 1960s and 1970s. Throughout Europe and the United States, social and political movements emerged that challenged established social hierarchies and secular institutions. As with the crisis in Catholicism, gender and sexuality took center stage in this secular crisis.

The two crises' shared focus on gender and sexuality was no coincidence. As the historian Sybille Steinbacher noted in *Wie der Sex nach Deutschland kam*, in the late nineteenth century, nation-states and the Christian churches in the West developed an increased interest in controlling sexuality and the relationship between the sexes as a means of maintaining the established order. In June 1900, the German Reich passed a law banning obscene literature in an attempt to protect German youth from its deleterious effect (Lex Heinze). In 1926, the Weimar Republic passed the Gesetz zur Bewahrung der Jugend vor Schund- und Schmutzschriften (Law to Protect Youth from Trashy and Filthy Writings);[20] and Paragraph 175, which had been in effect since the establishment of a unified German state in 1871, criminalized homosexual relations.[21] In 1920, the French government outlawed the sale and use of contraceptive devices and in 1923 imposed stiff prison terms on anyone who underwent, helped procure, or performed an abortion. Similarly, in 1923, the Belgian legislature prescribed prison terms for anyone who displayed, distributed, or advertised contraceptive devices, and Italy followed suit in 1926.[22] On the eve of the turbulent 1960s, this governmental practice of regulating obscenity, sexual relations, and reproductive practices remained intact, despite multiple challenges advanced in earlier decades.[23] Moreover, the Christian churches remained powerful allies in this endeavor.

But by the late 1960s, the pendulum in most Western European nations had swung in the direction of reform, as "the gap between what people were doing in private and what they were willing to declare in public narrowed dramatically."[24] Although the exact causes of the transformation of the European sexual landscape in the mid-1960s and early 1970s remain a topic of scholarly debate, an undeniable shift toward the liberalization of the legal sexual order had begun.[25] In 1967, the French legislature approved the so-called Loi Neuwirth, which made contraception available with a doctor's prescription.[26] That same year, Denmark decriminalized pornography, and the tiny nation became the world's largest exporter of pornography. In 1967, Britain passed a bill that legalized abortion in the first two trimesters.[27] Across Europe, the sexual legal order, championed by the educated bourgeoisie and church leaders since the nineteenth century, became subject to revision.

But for many young Western Europeans, reforming the sexual order within the existing liberal democratic, capitalist framework did not suffice.

They wanted a social revolution, and sexual politics became one of the primary focal points for theorizing and giving voice to all that was wrong with the existing order. During the 1968 student revolt in Paris, a popular protest sign read, "The more I make love, the more I make revolution." A 1968 German poem put it more bluntly: "If the state wants to spoil your / dancing and fucking, / then smash the state!"[28] Secular and religious authorities throughout Europe faced a crisis of authority as the younger generations increasingly rejected the moral values and social order that had been codetermined by church and state.

In Germany, this religious and secular crisis of authority had "a distinctive force and fury" that, as Dagmar Herzog noted in *Sex after Fascism*, imparted "a heightened drama to the resulting social transformations."[29] This "heightened drama" resulted in part from the ever-present subtext of the West German debate, namely the need to redefine what it meant to be German in the wake of the recent National Socialist past. Germans anxiously debated questions such as: Had the sexual conservatism of the bourgeoisie contributed to Nazism's success in Germany? Did the liberalization of sexuality represent a path toward democratization? Or was the opposite the case? For example, did proposed changes to West Germany's abortion law lead the way back to Auschwitz? Had "free love" in fact liberated women? Or had it introduced new forms of female oppression, as the Catholic Church and many feminists claimed, albeit for different reasons?

Creating a distinct, non-Nazi German identity also required distinguishing West Germany from its past American occupiers and from Communist East Germany. As Uta Poiger detailed in *Jazz, Rock, and Rebels*, West German authorities wanted to find a "fourth way, between the threat of Bolshevism, the self-destructive sexualizing, and emasculating powers emanating from American-style consumer culture, and finally the dangerous secularism and materialism that according to many contemporary commentators had led to National Socialism."[30] In the immediate postwar period, with the support of the two largest religious communities, the Catholic Church and the EKD, the CDU-CSU championed the creation of a Christian occident as a distinctly German path forward. In 1951 and 1953, the West German parliament passed two youth defense laws. The first law regulated adolescent access to dances, movies, and alcohol. The second law regulated printed matter, such as pulp fiction and pornography. In addition to protecting youth, these 1950s laws aimed at preserving the existing gender hierarchy: "Measures against violent gangster and western stories, in films or fiction, were geared toward curtailing male overaggression, and the restrictions on dancing were supposed to prevent the oversexualizing of women."[31]

By the late 1960s, the CDU-CSU coalition had lost its power, and a new government led by the Social Democratic Party (Sozialdemokratische Partei Deutschlands, SPD) set out to give the West German Criminal Code a modern orientation. By 1973, the category "Offenses against Morality" had been replaced by "Offenses against Sexual Autonomy." The new code decriminalized consensual homosexual acts, adultery, and the distribution of pornography among adults.[32] In 1976, West German women gained legal access to abortion under certain conditions.

Not all Germans welcomed these changes. Abortion, in particular, had been a topic of heated debate throughout the history of the Federal Republic, and all sides invoked the tropes of Americanization, the Communist menace, and the specter of National Socialism. Such hyperbolic and emotionally charged language ensured that for both secular and religious actors the interrelated topics of sexual ethics, women's reproductive rights, and gender equality remained inextricably linked to questions of German identity, democratization, and social justice long after the secular crisis of authority reached a peaceful resolution in the Federal Republic in the late 1970s.

In the case of German Catholic actors, the lack of resolution of the religious crisis of authority in the universal Church gave these debates an even greater urgency, as the future of Catholicism seemed tied to their successful negotiation at the national and transnational levels: What roles should women fill in church and society? Should the Church protest the liberalization of the sexual order? Should Catholic couples be free to make decisions of conscience about using artificial contraception? Did the maintenance of a male celibate priesthood constitute a form of discrimination against Catholic women? If not, how could the Church justify women's exclusion from clerical office? Did greater democratization of the Church represent the path to renewal, or alternatively did renewal depend on the centralization of authority in the office of the papacy? Should Church authorities take steps to preserve Church teachings on gender and sexuality, even at the expense of losing its most loyal constituency—women? These questions polarized the Catholic Church and led to a contraction and intensification of faith in Germany.

From Feminized Piety to Gendered Church

For centuries the Catholic Church had taken for granted the loyalty of its female congregants. In Germany, Catholic women could be counted on to fill the pews every Sunday and to vote as male Catholic leaders directed. As late as 1965, when some CDU officials expressed concern about the upcoming election, Konrad Adenauer reassured them: "But you have forgotten the most important thing. The good Catholic housewives will never forget us when the chips are down."[33] Yet seven years later the CDU's "women's bonus" (i.e., the greater number of votes cast by women than men) dropped from 10 percent to 3 percent (see Appendix M), and by the early 1980s West German bishops, such as Wilhelm Kempf of Limburg, expressed alarm at the growing number of young women leaving the Church.

In an effort to stanch women's exodus from the Catholic Church, in 1972 West German Catholic hierarchs supported the creation of a female diaconate and in 1981 issued the "Declaration on the Position of Women in the Church and Society"—a document that even SPD women praised. But time passed, and no real changes materialized. Instead, Paul VI and John Paul II replaced moderate bishops with more conservative ones who had little or no patience with the demands of reform-oriented women.

Moreover, with his ascension to the papacy in 1978, John Paul II promoted a gendered theology with the dual aim of preserving the male celibate priesthood and the Church's embattled marital morality. Increasingly, the symbolic representation of the Church as the Bride of Christ eclipsed other representations of the Church (e.g., the Church as the people of God and the sheepfold) in papal pronouncements.[34] As discussed in Chapters 1 and 2, it also served to justify a male celibate priesthood and to support the papal call for a new Catholic feminism—one that emphasized sexual difference, glorified women's essential role as mothers, and championed papal loyalty. Although this new feminism found few adherents among the disenchanted, it rallied members of the conservative core, such as the German theologian Simone Twents. In her 2002 book, *Frau sein ist mehr: Die Würde der Frau nach Johannes Paul II* (To be woman is more: The dignity of woman according to John Paul II), she called on women to employ their "own particular genius and orientation to love" in order to help heal humankind and "not adopt male characteristics."[35] Archbishop Joachim Meisner of Cologne wrote the foreword to the book, offering effusive praise for Twents's appreciation of the "fundamental anthropological dimensions of femininity" and for her delineation of a "feminine theology" that rested on the "Catholic image of woman."[36] The feminized Catholic Church of the eighteenth and nineteenth centuries, documented by numerous historians,[37] had given way to a Church in which a gendered ideology provided the conservative core with a rallying cry against attacks from within and without. The ideology itself was not new, but in the late twentieth century it acquired a new emphasis and function, as the battle over the future direction of the Church reached feverish heights and neoconservatives worked out new political strategies for promoting official Church teachings in the secular sphere.

Historiography
The Catholic Church in Secular Histories

As already noted, the dominant narrative of postwar West Germany assumes a dramatic decline in the political influence of the West German Catholic Church after 1965. As proof of this declining influence, many studies have highlighted either the CDU's increasing corporatist orientation beginning in the 1970s or the diminishing influence of the CSU within the CDU-CSU coalition. For example, in *The CDU and the Politics of Gender in Germany*, Sara Elise Wiliarty traced the CDU's transformation from a Catholic-controlled party to a "corporatist catch-all" party in response to new demands from women. By the 1970s, female voters were increasingly dissatisfied with the CDU's view of the proper role of women, summed up by the three Ks —*Kinder, Küche, Kirche* (children, kitchen, church)—and no longer voted overwhelmingly for the CDU. This development did not go unnoticed by CDU party strategists; in an effort to bring women back into the party, the CDU distanced itself from the Catholic Church and developed a "corporatist catch-all" model in which "important societal interest groups [were] represented within a party" and party policy was determined by balancing diverse interests after allowing all constituencies a voice.[38] Increasingly those who promoted Catholic interests within the party lost power to other internal interest groups. Wiliarty's study provides valuable insights into the evolution of a political party and its gender policies; however, because of its focus on the CDU, the political strategies of Catholics disenchanted with the CDU's more moderate stance lie beyond its scope.

The uniqueness of Wiliarty's study—its focus on gender politics within the conservative Christian Democratic Union—highlights another feature of German gender studies. Overwhelmingly, they concentrate on leftist groups, such as the Weimar sexual reform movement, the 1960s student movement, and the feminist movement; consequently, little attention has been paid to the political projects of Catholic women.[39] The historiography reflects the feminist origins of gender studies and the dominant narrative of a secularized Europe. As Ann Taylor Allen noted in a historiographical essay on gender and religion, most German gender histories ignore religion, writing off those women "who did not follow men in their flight from the churches."[40]

This tendency to ignore Catholic women as important political actors is reinforced by the tradition of equating Catholic political interests with those of the CDU-CSU coalition. Yet by the late 1970s, many Catholics recognized that the CDU no longer always prioritized traditional Catholic interests. This realization led some Catholic organizations to pursue issue-specific alliances with political parties other than the Christian parties. As we shall see in Chapter 5, the largest Catholic women's organization in West Germany allied with Green Party women and radical feminists in the battle against new reproductive technologies (NRTs) and stem cell research. This alliance contributed to the Bundestag's adoption of stricter regulations than those initially proposed by the CDU government. At the time, supporters of biotechnology, such as the Free Democratic Party (Freie Demokratische Partei, FDP) legal expert, Detlef Kleinert, bristled at this "unholy alliance."[41] Yet historians of gender have taken little notice of new Catholic political strategies.

Even scholars interested in gender and religion in Germany have rarely ventured past 1950. Allen did not cite a single work on the post-1965 period in her historiographical essay. Moreover, in outlining future research directions, she limited her discussion to the period between 1830 and 1950.[42] Although Allen acknowledged that the Christian churches "have not disappeared" from contemporary Germany, she largely dismissed them: "Their chief role is now to dispense various forms of social assistance and to champion weak and vulnerable members of society."[43]

Only recently, with the resurgence of religious issues in European headlines—for example, the headscarf debate in France, the Danish cartoon controversy, and the question of Christian heritage and European integration—have scholars begun rethinking religion's place in European history of the late twentieth and early twenty-first centuries. However, the new attention accorded religion has concentrated primarily on the challenges to European multiculturalism posed by Islamic fundamentalism or in some cases the rise of Pentecostalism. Developments within mainstream Christian churches remain largely unincorporated into the history of late-twentieth-century Europe, and those works that do reference the Catholic Church typically depict it as a monolithic actor.

Dagmar Herzog's pathbreaking work, *Sex after Fascism*, constitutes a notable exception. In this study of postwar German sexuality, she details how the Christian churches, particularly the Catholic Church, shaped immediate postwar debates on gender equality and reproductive rights by exercising significant control over the way in which the Nazi past was narrated. Rather than depicting a monolithic Church, she highlights the diverse opinions on sexuality held by lay Catholics, theologians, and even Church hierarchs in the late 1950s and early 1960s. She rightly identifies how this diversity contributed to a Catholic crisis of moral authority, which made it vulnerable to attacks by the student movement in the 1960s and the feminist movement in the 1970s. Not only did these two groups attack the Church's narrative of the past, they equated Christian views on sexuality with fascism.[44]

However, in focusing exclusively on changing narratives of the National Socialist past and who controlled this narration, Herzog lost sight of internal developments within West German Catholicism in the late 1970s and early 1980s—specifically the upsurge in the political power of Catholic moral conservatives and their cultivation of new arguments and political alliances in an effort to protect unborn life. Consequently, in a 2010 article, "Post coitum triste est . . . ? Sexual Politics and Culture in Postunification Germany," on post-unification debates on abortion law, Herzog had difficulty accounting for Germany's recent conservative turn.[45]

Another exception was Eva-Maria Silies's monograph, *Liebe, Lust und Last*, a nuanced study of German political debates on artificial contraception in the 1960s and on women's experience with the pill.[46] In one chapter Silies highlighted the diversity of views Catholic theologians held on artificial contraception and their interventions in the secular debate. However, because the chapter was dedicated to Catholicism, it seemed divorced from the main narrative. Moreover, the author's analysis did not extend far past *Humanae Vitae*'s release in 1968. Thus, her narrative did not address how this debate redefined the West German Catholic community, influenced Catholic women's perception of mandatory clerical celibacy, and generated a small women's ordination movement.

Gender and Sexuality in Histories of German Catholicism

Until very recently, histories of German Catholicism also seldom ventured past 1965. In part, the absence of post-1965 studies reflected the difficulty of gaining access to Catholic archival materials on the recent past. As noted later in this introduction, in the section on sources, few diocesan archives have been willing to grant critical scholars access to materials that involve ongoing controversies.

The absence of such studies also derived from the tremendous influence exercised by the Commission for Contemporary History (Kommission für Zeitgeschichte) in shaping postwar histories of the Catholic Church. Founded in 1962, the commission served as a "nexus for historical research" on German Catholicism.[47] Scholars affiliated with the commission pursued individual and collaborative projects addressing the Church's role under Nazism, the formation of the Catholic milieu in the nineteenth century, and the milieu's collapse with the encroachment of modernity on its sphere of influence. To date, the commission has published more than 175 monographs in its "Blue Series," exploring institutional, political, and social developments in the Catholic Church. In doing so, it has provided a rich history of German Catholic political and associational life. However, until recently, this scholarship has had two significant shortcomings: a tendency to equate modernization with religious decline and a resistance to new approaches and methodologies, including gender studies.

For most of its history, the commission advanced the milieu model as the master narrative of German Catholicism. In 1966, M. Rainier Lepsius first used the term "socio-moral milieus" to describe political and social divisions within Germany between 1871 and 1933. Lepsius argued that Socialists, bourgeois Protestants, Catholics, and aristocrats developed their own subcultures. Each subculture or milieu promoted distinct cultural values and provided a carefully coordinated set of organizations and associations in which members participated.[48]

Within the framework of Catholic scholarship, the milieu described the Catholic subculture that emerged in response to Bismarck's *Kulturkampf* in the 1870s. Otto von Bismarck, chancellor of the German Empire, wanted to curtail the influence of the Catholic Church in the newly formed German Imperial Reich, enacting a series of laws that placed the state in control of religious and educational affairs. The German Catholic community responded by circling the wagons, creating an insulated cultural-religious sphere that organized Catholic life from cradle to grave. The elements of this milieu included (1) political Catholicism—its primary representatives being the Catholic Center Party and the Catholic Bavarian People's Party; (2) the Church's institutional framework—bishops, priests, diocese, and parish; (3) social and religious associations; (4) youth groups and Catholic schools; (5) workers' and professional associations; and (6) popular piety—Marian devotion and pilgrimages. A few historians, such as Wilfried Loth, pointed to diversity and fragmentation within this subculture, positing the existence of multiple milieus within German Catholicism.[49] However, most historians emphasized that shared religious belief gave the Catholic milieu social, cultural, and political cohesiveness in Imperial and Weimar Germany. Within the milieu, the antimodern message of traditional Catholicism flourished.

The dominance of the milieu model had two consequences for Catholic scholarship. First, it resulted in a plethora of studies that sought to pinpoint the exact moment of the milieu's collapse. Although some historians dated the collapse to as early as the Weimar era, no historian suggested that the milieu survived past 1965.[50] In focusing on an insulated Catholic milieu, historians of Catholicism isolated Catholic history from mainstream German history. Second, in positing religion's inevitable decline as a consequence of modernization and secularization, Catholic historians validated profane historians' assumption that, in a secularized Germany, religion did not matter.

Challenges to the milieu model have recently gained momentum. In 2000, Benjamin Ziemann argued that the model could not account for what came after the milieu, because it emphasized religious decline at the expense of religious transformation. A new paradigm was needed for German Catholic history.[51] In 2007, Ziemann utilized the paradigm of "functional differentiation" to describe the postwar Church's transformation in his pioneering work, *Katholische Kirche und Sozialwissenschaften, 1945–1975*. He detailed how West German Church officials embraced techniques of polling, statistics, sociology, and even psychotherapy in an effort to mitigate the exodus from the Catholic Church.[52] In focusing on Church leaders' active engagement with scientific techniques, Ziemann pointed to the immense mental and cultural transformations taking place within the German Catholic Church.

Ziemann's rejection of the milieu model initially encountered resistance. In a review of his book, Mark Ruff noted that Ziemann's focus on the scientification (*Verwissensschaftlichung*) of religion did not have "the weight to replace the erosion of the Catholic milieu as an alternative master narrative."[53] While recognizing the pioneering character of Ziemann's work, Ruff rightly pointed out that engagement with the social sciences proved a double-edged sword for the Catholic Church. Although it allowed Church officials to identify accurately the attitudes and needs of congregants, its reliance on empiricism also threatened to desacralize Church institutions and "render the transcendent immanent."[54] Ruff concluded that Ziemann's study had left "open the possibility that there might be some validity to traditional narratives of secularization and milieu erosion."[55]

Ziemann was not alone in challenging the milieu model; a new generation of historians affiliated with the Commission for Contemporary History also criticized the model.[56] Slowly, a paradigm shift in describing post-1965 Catholicism began to emerge in scholarship on German Catholicism. In 2011, *Soziale Strukturen und Semantiken des Religiösen im Wande*, edited by Wilhelm Damberg, co-chair of the commission, and Frank Bösch, was published. Instead of religious decline, the contributors employed the frame of religious transformation to detail the efforts of Catholic and Protestant actors to adapt to a postconfessional rather than post-Christian world. For example, Thomas Mitmann's essay described the new strategies that Church leaders developed for marketing the Church to a public that demanded increased participation and interaction in worship. Andreas Henkelmann and Katherine Kunter's essay analyzed the transformation of women's religious charitable work, paying attention to the complex interaction between changes in societal structures and changes in ideological beliefs. Rosel Oehmen-Vieregge investigated the formation of women's synods from the 1970s to the first decade of the twenty-first century. In emphasizing religious transformation, the authors did not downplay secularization. Instead, as Lucian Hölscher's explained in the concluding essay, secularization and transformation constituted interrelated processes.[57] The commission's new focus on religious transformation was underscored at a conference in September 2012 celebrating the commission's fiftieth anniversary. The conference also acknowledged the need for more studies on gender.[58]

As Mark Ruff respectfully noted in 2005, the commission has shown a reluctance to adopt "new approaches that have gained favor in the secular historical world."[59] This reluctance has meant that until very recently few postwar histories of German Catholicism have addressed gender or sexuality. This failure has resulted in a significant thematic gap between scholarship on late-twentieth-century German Catholicism and that on nineteenth- and early-twentieth-century German Catholicism. There are numerous histories, particularly from the Anglophone world, that emphasize Catholic concerns about the feminization of religion during the Imperial and Weimar eras. For example, Derek Hastings described Catholic efforts on the eve of World War I to create a "more manly" Church. Members of the Munich-based Catholic cultural association, Krausgesellschaft, feared that the Catholic Church was "becoming a Church for women and children only" and consequently an irrelevant institution.[60] David Blackbourn, in his study of nineteenth-century Marian apparitions in Germany, emphasized the class and gender dimensions of internal Catholic debates on the authenticity of these sightings. Typically women and children of the lower classes reported these sightings; once reported, the sightings generated spontaneous expressions of popular devotion that male Church authorities frequently had difficulty controlling. As a result, Church leaders perceived these sightings as potential threats to authority and supported only those sightings whose interpretation they could control.[61] Yet women have been curiously absent from most studies of late-twentieth-century Catholicism, leaving one to wonder what happened to all those Catholic women who filled the pews every Sunday.

Ignoring gender and sexuality is also problematic because the Catholic Church, in conjunction with the state, had a vested interest in regulating sexuality. As already noted, discursive battles on sexual morality were commonplace in the religious and secular spheres, and the churches were active participants in these debates. Yet Catholic historians have largely ignored the role of late-twentieth-century debates on gender and sexuality in transforming the German Catholic community. For example, Damberg's 1997 comparative study of German and Dutch Catholicism between 1945 and 1980 included no mention of the 1968 "pill encyclical," despite the massive protests it prompted among Catholics and non-Catholics. Similarly, the study did not cover the West German celibacy debate that unfolded at the Würzburg Synod (1972–1975), although it did cover the celibacy debate at the Dutch Pastoral Council (1967–1970).[62]

Lukas Rölli-Alkemper's *Familie im Wiederaufbau* (2000), Petra von der Osten's *Jugend- und Gefährdentenfürsorge* (2003), and Mark Ruff's *The Wayward Flock* (2005) represented the first efforts to incorporate gender into Catholic histories of the postwar era. Lukas Rölli-Alkemper explored the growing chasm between Catholic ideology concerning marriage and the realities of West German Catholic family life in the immediate postwar era. Petra von der Osten detailed the transformation of the Catholic women's charitable organization Katholischer Fürsorgeverein für Mädchen, Frauen und Kinder from a volunteer confessional organization concerned with its clientele's salvation to a professional organization renamed Sozialdienst katholischer Frauen that focused on serving its clientele. In *The Wayward Flock*, Mark Ruff discussed how questions of gender influenced the decision of many young girls to leave Catholic organizations.[63]

All three studies suggested the valuable insights to be gained from incorporating gender into the study of German Catholicism. However, these early studies emphasized decline and attributed changing attitudes toward gender and sexuality to forces outside the Church. This characterization oversimplified the dynamics of institutional change, which involve more than a reactionary response to exogenous forces. While reform-oriented Catholics certainly borrowed from non-Catholic ideologies and were influenced by external events, this borrowing was "as much a result as a cause of political and ideological processes internal to the Church."[64] Multiple traditions have always existed within Catholicism. When Catholic conservatives, progressives, and feminists in the postwar era chose to emphasize different aspects of these traditions, they exposed latent tensions in values, beliefs, and ideas, catalyzing internal forces of change that interacted with external ones.[65]

These early studies also assumed a unidirectional flow of influence from the secular to the religious sphere. In fact, as we shall see, changes in Catholic gender ideology reshaped profane discourses on gender and sexuality. This study examines the dynamic interplay between processes of transformation in the Catholic community and in postwar German society. It does not deny the validity of secularization, but rather focuses on the dynamics that allowed an admittedly much smaller German Catholic Church to exercise significant influence on profane debates concerning gender and sexuality.

Methodology

Analyzing the evolution of Catholic discourses on gender and sexuality (popular, theological, and political) that are in dialogue with secular discourses and are situated within the broader cultural, social, and political context has multiple advantages over writing the history of a particular Catholic organization or interest group. First, focusing on the entanglement of Catholic and secular discourses provides a means of reintegrating Catholic history into the historical mainstream. Second, it underscores the diversity of views that Catholic bishops, theologians, and lay Catholics held on gender and sexuality. Mapping this multifaceted theological landscape reveals the latent contradictions in ideas, values, and beliefs that led to ideological and political clashes within the Catholic Church. Thus, my study highlights the dynamic interplay between endogenous and exogenous forces in transforming Catholic identity, organizational structures, and power dynamics in the late twentieth century. Finally, this approach allows me to bridge the gap between histories of nineteenth- and late-twentieth-century Catholicism by demonstrating the centrality of the *Frauenfrage* (the woman question) for both.

Incorporating theological discourse into one's investigation constitutes a risky enterprise for a historian. However, without an analysis of theological discourse, we cannot understand the ideological changes taking place within Catholicism. As already noted, Catholic actors who challenged Vatican authority on issues such as celibacy, birth control, and abortion did so within the framework of a multifaceted Catholic legacy. They did not simply import ideas from outside the Church, that is, from the student movement, feminism, socialism, and Protestantism. Moreover, Catholic actors—the pope, the Roman Curia, bishops, theologians, priests, and committed lay Catholics—understood the secular and religious worlds from a perspective learned and developed within the Church. Without an understanding of this perspective, it is impossible to accurately assess the motivations and actions of religious actors. For example, the Vatican's refusal to compromise on artificial contraception, given the crisis it provoked, makes sense only if we take into account the debate's theological stakes. As Norbert Lüdecke's thought-provoking essay on *Humanae Vitae* as a Catholic *lieu de mémoire* demonstrated, the encyclical represented for the Church hierarchy a critical reassertion of power and of the Church's mission:

> The encyclical is also more than the transcultural determination of the correct configuration of the sexual act willed by God. In this address, the correct notion of marriage is safeguarded as well as the identity of the sexes and their prescribed roles; in fact, the hierarchical structure of the Church becomes visible and affirmed—how the pope conveys God's holy plan and in doing so preempts and forestalls the insight of the people; the corporate structure of the Church and its teaching office clearly and authoritatively shape and nurture the conscience in all human affairs.[66]

In upholding the Church's ban, Paul VI and his successors believed that the Church "is and remains as Christ wanted it."[67] From this perspective, "the defection of individuals is not critical because the Church has won the struggle for truth."[68]

Detailing the changing ideological, institutional, and political contours of the German Catholic Church also cannot be divorced from developments in the universal Catholic Church. The Church's hierarchical structure limited the responses available to the West German episcopate in dealing with disgruntled congregants and clergy. For example, the German episcopate supported the creation of a female diaconate in 1975 and received praise for its 1981 declaration on women in church and society. However, papal pronouncements and Church doctrine constrained the German episcopate's ability to implement these measures. Still, German bishops were not helpless vis-à-vis the Vatican. The 1968 Königstein Declaration affirmed the German episcopate's loyalty to the pope, while at the same creating an autonomous space in which Catholic couples could reach their own decision about contraception. Even fringe Catholic groups, such as the Society of Saint Pius X and the women's ordination movement, could exercise power in a negative sense, forcing through their actions a response from the official Church.

In addition to universal Church structures, one must also factor in the West German legal, social, cultural, historical, and even geographic frames. Church–state relations, the role of media, the history of feminism, and West Germany's geographic position on the front lines of the Cold War all differed dramatically from what existed in the United States and elsewhere; these German frames both created opportunities and placed constraints on the German Catholic Church that differed from those in the United States and other national contexts. For example, although West Germany, like the United States, recognized no state religion, the Basic Law accorded "the established churches an important role in the nation's public life, investing them with various institutional guarantees, including privileges flowing from their constitutional status as 'religious bodies under public law.'"[69] This status conferred on the churches powers normally reserved for the state, such as the power to employ officials and levy a church tax. As Don P. Kommers and Russell A. Miller concluded in *The Constitutional Jurisprudence of the Federal Republic of Germany*, Articles 4 and 140 of the Basic Law emphasized "a cooperative" rather than a strict "separationist model" of church–state relations that anticipated "a limited partnership between church and state."⁷⁰ Under this system, the West German Catholic Church came to administer a substantial share of the German welfare system, meaning that the impact of Catholic doctrine, for example on abortion, extended far beyond its congregation.

Sources

In detailing the sources for this book, I must acknowledge certain limitations. Because of the time period under investigation and the topics covered, gaining access to archival sources proved challenging. Four diocesan archives, on learning the subject of the study, denied access—Fulda, Mainz, Münster, and Paderborn. Only the diocesan archive of Cologne allowed access to materials prior to 1972, as well as to the archival records for the Würzburg Synod (1972–1975). However, three Catholic lay organizations—the Central Committee of German Catholics (Zentralkomitee der deutschen Katholiken, ZdK), the National Office for Catholic Youth Work (Jugendhaus Düsseldorf-Bundeszentrale für katholische Jugendarbeit, JHD), and the Catholic Women's Association in Germany (Katholische Frauengemeinschaft Deutschlands, kfd)—granted access to their collections. The ZdK, the highest-ranking lay organization in Germany, allowed access through 1981. Jugendhaus Düsseldorf did likewise. The central office of the kfd, the largest Catholic women's organization in Germany, granted access to its archives for the entire time period under investigation. In referring to this organization by its acronym, I have chosen to use lowercase letters (kfd), in keeping with the way it appears on member publications, rather than the uppercase letters (KFD) often used in scholarly monographs. Given that an orthographic change in the title of the organization's magazine in January 1988 precipitated a heated debate on the organization's attitude toward abortion (see Chapter 4), I believed it important to duplicate the organization's use of the lowercase. As tensions escalated between Catholic hierarchs and Catholic women leaders, such mundane choices became sites of contention.

In addition to Catholic archives, I drew on the archival collections of the German Federal Republic (Bundesarchiv) and the Christian Democratic Union (Archiv für Christliche-Demokratische Politik). Unlike the debates on celibacy and women's ordination, discussions of birth control regulation, abortion, and assisted reproduction entailed substantial interactions between state actors and religious actors.

Beyond these archival sources, I made extensive use of official Church statistics on attendance at mass, frequency of Communion, the number of Catholics who officially separated from the church, and the number of priests in Germany. I also utilized the results of three surveys commissioned by the German Bishops' Conference (Deutsche Bischofskonferenz, DBK) and conducted by the Allensbach Institute of Public Opinion Research. The first two surveys were conducted in preparation for the General Synod of Dioceses in the Federal Republic of Germany (1972–1975), commonly referred to as the Würzburg Synod. The DBK sent questionnaires to all lay Catholics over the age of sixteen; another questionnaire was sent to all priests. Roughly 25 percent of German Catholics returned the surveys inquiring about how they perceived their relationship to the Church, as well as their stances on various Church doctrines, including celibacy, birth control, and Marian devotion. Seventy-five percent of priests returned the survey asking about their experience of office and their views on mandatory celibacy. The third survey, conducted in 1993, focused on Catholic women's attitudes toward the Church. It asked a thousand Catholic women how they felt about Church teachings, including those on birth control, celibacy, and abortion. In addition to official Church statistics and surveys, I utilized surveys conducted by Emnid and by Infratest on German voting patterns, attitudes toward abortion, clerical celibacy, and women's ordination. The quantitative data pointed to the key role played by gender politics in redefining West German Catholics' relationship to the official Church, which I explored through an in-depth qualitative analysis of secular and religious discourses on celibacy, women's ordination, birth control, abortion, and NRTs.

Vatican II proclaimed the Catholic Church's openness to modernity, and West German Catholics took this message seriously. Consequently, public discourse took on new meaning for West German Catholics in the post–Vatican II era. In open letters published in the religious and secular press, as well as in monographs and public declarations, dissenting theologians, priests, and laypersons took their message of reform to the court of public opinion. The institutional Church responded in kind, issuing public condemnations of dissenting views and launching its own public morality campaign. For example, the DBK issued declarations appealing to Catholics and non-Catholics to defend unborn life. Given the public nature of these appeals and the widespread media attention they received, analyzing public discourse was a key component of my investigation. To do so, I made extensive use of published primary sources, such as Vatican documents, declarations issued by the DBK and various German Catholic organizations, articles and letters to the editor that appeared in the secular and religious press, as well as essays and books published by members of the institutional Church and concerned lay Catholics.

With reference to Vatican documents (e.g., encyclicals, apostolic constitutions, *motu proprio*, declarations by the various congregations, and papal speeches), all citations were taken from the official Vatican website, with the exception of four documents: the 1917 Code of Canon Law, *Lamentabili Sane*, and two documents issued by the Congregation for Divine Worship and the Discipline of the Sacraments (CDWDS)—*Inaestimabile Donum* and "Vatican Communication on Female Altar Servers" of March 15, 1994. At the time of the writing of this book, these documents were not available on the Vatican website, and other sources were consulted.[71] However, the Vatican website provides an official English version of most documents, which I utilized for citations. For a few texts, no official English version existed, and, depending on availability, citations were taken from the official German, Spanish, or Italian versions of the texts; in these cases, all translations are my own.[72]

Organization

This book is divided into two parts. Part I, "The Male Celibate Priesthood and Woman's Place in the Church," focuses on German debates concerning mandatory clerical celibacy. The priestly coalition—pope, bishops, priests, ordained theologians—dominate the institutional Church. Since most Church offices with decision-making power are open only to priests, lay Catholics, particularly female Catholics, are effectively excluded from positions of power. This exclusion increasingly became a source of contention among German Catholics in the post–Vatican II era. Because in Catholic theology the celibate priest is understood to be both bride and bridegroom in a nuptial relationship between Christ and Church, any challenge to celibacy also constituted a challenge to Catholic marital and sexual morality. Thus, Chapter 1, "Celibacy for the Kingdom of Heaven and Earth," focuses on the changing meanings assigned to the celibacy debate between 1959 and 1989. It highlights how Church efforts to preserve the discipline of celibacy informed its gender politics in the religious and secular spheres.

The second chapter in Part I, "Women's Ordination: Sacramental and Gendered Bodies," continues the discussion introduced in the first chapter concerning the symbolic and sacramental marriage between the Church and Christ. This chapter fulfills two functions. First, it traces the growing interest of mainstream Catholic women's organizations in women's ordination, as well as the emergence of subaltern communities within the Catholic Church in response to the women's ordination debate. Second, through an analysis of the theological discourses that underpinned this debate, it underscores the interpenetration of the Church's rationales concerning celibacy, artificial contraception, abortion, and women's ordination and thus why the Church found itself trapped in a cascading series of crises that cannot be explained by exogenous forces alone. These internal crises, in turn, shaped Catholic responses to profane discourses on women's reproductive rights. Thus, without an understanding of these "internal" debates, which in fact witnessed significant engagement by non-Catholics, one cannot understand Catholic actions in the secular sphere.

In Part II, "The Catholic Church and Reproductive Politics," the focus shifts from "internal" Catholic debates on sexual morality and women's place in the Church to secular debates on women's reproductive rights. Chapter 3, "Artificial Contraception: German Angst and Catholic Rebellion," expands on several themes introduced in Part I, specifically the changing theological landscape and its relationship to Catholic interventions in secular debates on reproductive rights. The controversy concerning birth control in late 1950s West Germany began as a debate among experts on the new oral form of contraception. The "pill" became the prism through which politicians, doctors, university professors, and members of the clergy outlined and dictated what constituted acceptable public sexual mores. However, by the mid-1960s, most West Germans had rejected the public discourse of sexual conservatism from the 1950s. Experts (overwhelmingly male) lost control of the debate, and the Catholic Church became marginalized in the public discussion. The Vatican's intransigence on artificial contraception fueled widespread disillusionment with the official Church in West Germany, and the concept of loyal disobedience took hold. A plethora of newly formed protest communities—liberal and conservative—struggled with each other and with the institutional Church over the future direction of the Church and of German society.

Chapter 4, "The Abortion Debate: Hidden Tensions and New Directions," focuses on Catholic engagement in West German abortion debates. In 1960, the recently elected SPD-FDP coalition government announced plans to reform Paragraph 218, the law regulating women's access to abortion. This announcement prompted a public debate in West Germany on the state's obligation to protect unborn life—a debate that continues to this day. Analyzing key events in that debate between 1969 and 1989, the chapter argues that despite West Germany's growing secular orientation, the Catholic Church exercised significant political influence with respect to abortion policy throughout the history of the Federal Republic. In addition, it argues that the West German Church's participation in these debates exposed deep rifts in the Catholic community, which in turn contributed to the formation of a smaller, more activist and conservative Church.

The final chapter, "Assisted Reproduction: Changing Bedfellows," compares and contrasts three debates on reproductive technologies—the first began in 1905, the second in 1958, and the third in the early 1980s. It highlights the confluence of events that shaped these debates—changing perceptions of gender relations, technology, National Socialism, and Germany's relationship to the United States. In doing so, the chapter points to continuities and discontinuities in the arguments for and against reproductive technologies, as well as shifts in the actors involved. It details how the German Catholic Church first gained and then maintained political influence over questions concerning reproductive technologies. It demonstrates that as German society became more secular, the Church's influence did not dwindle but in fact increased, as Catholic theological arguments and political strategies evolved in dialogue with secular discourse and changing public sentiment.

The epilogue looks ahead to the post-1989 era; it pays particular attention to the rise and fall of Benedict XVI's papacy, the new pastoral approach of Francis I, and the Third Extraordinary General Assembly of the Synod of Bishops on the topic of the family. It shows how conflicts concerning gender and sexuality continue to shape the battle between conservative and progressive Catholics over the future direction of both the German Church and the universal Church.

PART I

The Male Celibate Priesthood and Woman's Place in the Church

CHAPTER I

Celibacy for the Kingdom of Heaven and Earth

The postwar debate on mandatory clerical celibacy in the Catholic Church did not begin in earnest until 1968. Against the backdrop of the release of the papal encyclical *Humanae Vitae* banning artificial contraception and calls for liberalizing the legal sexual order in West Germany, an internal Catholic debate on the charismatic nature of celibacy metamorphosed into a public debate, in which non-Catholics took an active role. For reform-minded Catholics and non-Catholics in the 1970s, the clerical celibacy requirement became emblematic of the Church's intransigence on artificial contraception and more generally of its negative valuation of sexuality. Resentful of the Church's active resistance to ecclesial and secular reforms concerning sexual morality, Catholic reformers and non-Catholics utilized the issue of celibacy to challenge the religious and secular authority exercised by the institutional Church in West Germany. In this challenge, the media played a critical role.

For the Church hierarchy, the celibacy debate posed multiple theological and practical challenges. Theologically, as we shall see, any challenge to the celibacy requirement had the potential to destabilize the priesthood, the relationship between clergy and laity, and marital morality. But maintaining clerical celibacy was fraught with peril for practical reasons. The immediate postwar era witnessed a dramatic increase in the shortage of priests. Initially, few Church or secular experts associated this shortage with the celibacy requirement. However, by the late 1960s, this link had been made; moreover, as Germans embraced more liberal attitudes about sexuality, they began to view the celibate priesthood as unhealthy, even perverse. This assessment was given credence by the secular media's coverage of the debate, which centered on titillating stories about the sexual exploits of priests and behind-the-scene political intrigues involving celibacy. The Church found itself caught in a public relations nightmare, despite the valiant efforts of some bishops and theologians to utilize psychology to show that celibacy constituted a viable choice that did not compromise the health of its adherents. But fewer and fewer Catholics and non-Catholics found these arguments convincing as a growing number of dissident priests and theologians aired the Church's dirty laundry in public. These insider accounts of sexual intrigue reinforced public perceptions of a corrupt, patriarchal church whose influence on mainstream society should be curtailed. For the West German Catholic Church, these exposés made attracting new candidates to the priesthood even more difficult.

The Church's public image was further damaged when Catholic women entered the debate in the 1980s. For reform-minded Catholic women, the maintenance of a male celibate priesthood reinforced women's oppression in the Church and in society. They demanded that women be given more offices in the Church; in particular, they called for the creation of a female diaconate. When the West German episcopate would not or could not institute the desired changes because of universal Church doctrine, many women stopped engaging in Church life or created niches within the Church where they could voice discontent. Alternatively, conservative women saw the celibacy debate as indicative of moral collapse in the Church and in German society; for these women, the maintenance of clerical celibacy in conjunction with Church doctrine on marriage, birth control, and abortion became a rallying point; an embattled German hierarchy would choose to support this conservative core, as did the universal Church beginning with John Paul II's papacy. Under John Paul II, disciplinary actions against dissident theologians and priests increased dramatically, and the theological arguments advanced to support celibacy and to reject women's ordination, artificial contraception, abortion, and NRTs became more entangled. This interpenetration of theological arguments meant that the Church found itself embroiled in an escalating series of crises from the 1960s onward, as increasingly its views on sexual morality no longer coincided with secular views.

Clerical Celibacy's Significance for Catholicism

To understand the post–World War II celibacy debate, some information on the meaning the Catholic Church assigns to clerical celibacy is required. The word "celibacy" simply refers to the state of living unmarried.[1] But in Catholicism, celibacy means much more than bachelorhood. Since the Catholic Church considers all sexual activity outside of marriage sinful, celibacy also implies chastity. Celibacy is a requisite of clerical office, but it is also considered an eschatological sign of and stimulus for the call to ministry. The celibate priest is understood to be both bride and bridegroom in the suprasexual nuptial relationship between Christ and Church. He is a chaste bride of Christ and a "living sign" of the world to come in which "the children of the resurrection neither marry nor take wives."[2] He is also the bridegroom of the Church, "his bride," with whom he has entered into an indissoluble marriage contract. Thus, as Tina Beattie pointed out, the female body is excluded from the suprasexual relationship between Christ and the Church.[3] This exclusion informs both the Church's understanding of marriage and the exalted status accorded the celibate priesthood.

For centuries, the Church taught that celibacy, as a form of spiritual marriage with God, constituted a state superior to that of earthly marriage.[4] Although marriage represented a gift from God, in its sexuality it was tainted by original sin and consequently intended for those Christians who could not practice continence. In the teachings of Thomas Aquinas, sexual intercourse prior to the Fall was a function of reason. Afterward, sexual intercourse became corrupted by lust, and the emphasis shifted to man's loss of control over the sexual organs.[5] Eve's role as temptress and instigator of human suffering meant that marriage was intended not only as a means of controlling human sexuality, but more specifically as a means of controlling women.[6] To this end, the Catholic Church taught that the primary purpose of marriage was the generation and rearing of offspring.[7] This conception of marriage as an inferior form of Christian life defined by parturition helped justify the celibate male clergy's authority over the laity, particularly in the bedroom.

Untainted by sexual intercourse, the priest was a man apart from and above his congregation. Franz Franken, a laicized priest, described the pre–Vatican II public image of the priest: "A priest was not seen as a collaborator or mediator, but as a magical numinous being with special hidden access to God, a being to which one could attach one's most secret wishes and hopes, like the devotional objects of pilgrimage sites . . . so that at the time of Vatican II, a priest who no longer lived a celibate life was frequently branded and condemned in the Catholic public sphere as the most terrible disgrace of the Holy Catholic Church."[8] The Church went to great lengths to safeguard the sexual purity of its priests. Both codes of canon law valid during the time span covered by this monograph—those of 1917 and 1983—advised priests to avoid persons who might jeopardize their celibacy. The 1917 Code of Canon Law identified such persons specifically as women. In Germany, the 1954 Cologne Diocesan Synod established detailed rules governing interactions between priests and women. For example, young priests on vacation were prohibited from swimming with groups of young girls, and seminary students were not allowed to have any contact with girls during holidays.[9] One priest reported that, during his seminary training, he was advised to avoid interactions with his sister because this too could be fraught with danger![10] The priest's authority was based on his otherness, and the most visible manifestation of that otherness was his celibacy.

In addition to establishing rules regulating interactions between priests and women, both codes delineated punitive measures to be taken against those who broke the celibacy vow. Under these codes, the celibacy vow was binding for life. A priest who was removed from office or resigned from office remained obligated to practice celibacy. A priest could be released from his celibacy vow only if he applied for and received a dispensation from the Apostolic See; dispensation from celibacy did not automatically accompany laicization. Prior to the 1983 code, a former priest who married without dispensation was automatically excommunicated, as was his wife. Under both codes, such priests were removed from office, returned to the lay estate, and barred from holding any future office in the Church—including most offices open to the laity.

The Pre–Vatican II Era: Celibacy and the Clerical Shortage

The Latin Church has not always demanded celibacy or continence of its priests. There is evidence that, beginning in the third century, many bishops and priests were married and had children. In fact, until the fourth century, no law was promulgated by Church authorities concerning clerical marriage or continence. The Council of Elvira in roughly AD 305 would be the first to decree that married priests practice continence; however, it did not exclude married men from the priesthood. Celibacy became mandatory for priests in the Latin Church only after the Second Lateran Council in 1139. Between the twelfth and the sixteenth centuries, the celibacy requirement in the Latin Church was subject to multiple challenges; this state of affairs ended when Pius V (1566–1572) made it clear that the matter was closed. Although the issue surfaced from time to time, particularly during the French Revolution, the celibacy requirement and the elevated status assigned to the celibate state had been largely quiescent within the Latin Church from the late eighteenth century until the late 1960s.[11]

That said, this renewed celibacy debate did not develop overnight; it had its origins in the dynamic interplay between theological innovations, latent contradictions in existing Church doctrine, and social changes reshaping

Europe in the early twentieth century. In the late 1920s, the elevated status assigned to celibacy by the Latin Church experienced a significant challenge when theologians such as Dietrich von Hildebrand, Herbert Doms, and Norbert Rochol began reconsidering the Church's gendered and hierarchical understanding of marriage in response to the emergence of more companionate models of marriage in late-nineteenth-century Europe.[12] Instead of emphasizing the primary and secondary purposes of marriage, these theologians focused on the primacy of the human subject. Although they reserved a central role in marriage for procreation and childrearing, the development of the relationship between the man and woman took precedence. In *The Meaning of Marriage*, Herbert Doms, perhaps the most influential critic of the scholastic understanding of matrimony, denied that marriage entailed subservience to a purpose outside the spouses: "It consists in the constant vital ordination of husband and wife to each other until they are one."[13]

As Susan A. Ross has argued, in making the relationship between husband and wife one of mutuality and one in which gender roles were of minimal importance, Doms inadvertently called into question clerical authority. Marriage is one of the primary lenses through which the Catholic Church defines itself. Repeated references are made to the Church's nuptial relationship to God; the priest's nuptial relationship to the Church; the Christ-like authority of the husband; and the receptive character of the wife and the laity. An understanding of marriage that did not include a gendered conception of primary and secondary purposes jeopardized the masculine power of a celibate clergy to lead and instruct a receptive laity—if marriage was between two equals, the implication was that the relationship between clergy and laity was also between equals.[14]

In 1944, the Rota Romana banned the continued publication of Herbert Doms's *On the Meaning of Marriage* because the book placed the secondary ends of marriage on the same level as its primary ends. But personalism did not disappear. In fact, Pope Pius XI incorporated a modified version of this approach into his encyclical on marriage, *Casti Connubii*—as will be discussed in greater detail in the chapter on birth control.[15] Suffice it to say for now that a more positive valuation of the institution of marriage led some Catholics to challenge the pronouncements of a celibate clergy on marriage and reproduction. In a 1968 interview with Auxiliary Bishop Walther Kampe of Munich, some young Catholics went so far as to make the following analogy: "You can compare the advice of a celibate priest on marriage to that of a swimming instructor who gives instructions from the shore, without ever having swam himself."[16]

Theological innovation was not the only internal dynamic that informed renewed debates on clerical celibacy in the 1960s. Critics also pointed to latent contradictions in current Church policy. For example, to this day, other churches in union with the Latin Church (Ukrainian, Melkite, and others) allow clergy to marry with certain restrictions.[17] Moreover, the Latin Church has always made exceptions to the celibacy requirement. Both the 1917 and 1983 Codes of Canon Law outlined conditions under which exceptions could be made and stipulated that the pope alone could approve such exceptions.[18] As we shall see later in this chapter, in the 1950s and 1960s, the German Catholic Church assimilated numerous married Protestant ministers unhappy with their church's response to Communism. For many German Catholics, awareness of married priests working in their parish made the celibacy requirement seem arbitrary and suggested an alternative model for the priesthood, especially as the clerical shortage became more acute and scandals involving celibate priests received more attention.

In addition to these internal factors, social changes in Europe had an impact on the Catholic priesthood as well. The shift from an agrarian to an urban, industrialized society in the early twentieth century decimated the population from which the Church filled its clerical ranks. Traditionally most priests came from farming communities. As the 1958 International Enquête into the Priesthood in Europe concluded, the Church had to find ways of attracting the sons of laborers and white-collar employees to the priesthood in order to combat the devastating effects of this historic trend on the practice of Catholicism.[19] If it failed to do so, the Catholic Church in Western Europe would cease to be able to fulfill its threefold mission: to provide for the spiritual needs of Catholics in Europe, to offer assistance to "brethren in the Church of Silence behind the Iron Curtain," and to witness for Christ throughout the world.[20]

The importance of this shortage of priests cannot be underestimated. According to Catholic doctrine, priests are the only persons who may officiate at the Eucharist celebration—described in the Catholic catechism as the "sum and summary of our faith."[21] The sociologist Richard A. Schoenherr argued convincingly in *Goodbye Father* that there is "no group of members more central to the technical core of the Roman Catholic Church than its ordained clergy. Therefore, the priest drain represents the continual loss of its most critical 'economic' resource and, as such, is the most powerful force for structural change within contemporary Catholicism."[22] By the late 1950s, this "drain" had become a major preoccupation in Western Europe.

Yet participants at the 1958 enquête did not cite celibacy as a primary cause of the priest shortage. In addition to the demographic shift already mentioned, participants attributed the shortage to the decimation and dislocation of priests as a consequence of World War II, the de-Christianization of Europe, and the perceived collapse of traditional family values that accompanied these events. Other reasons sometimes cited for the shortage included insufficient prayer on the part of priests, the unwillingness of young people to make sacrifices, and an eroticization of public life.[23]

In West Germany, statistical studies from the late 1950s indicated an increase in the ratio of parishioners to priests (see Appendix C). Moreover, the German bishops increasingly expressed concern about the decline in the number of candidates for the priesthood. In a 1959 letter, Archbishop Johann Dietz of Fulda wrote Josef Cardinal Frings, chair of the Fulda Bishops' Conference (precursor of the post–Vatican II German Bishops' Conference) concerning the priest shortage in the dioceses of North Rhine-Westphalia. In particular, he expressed concern about the newly created Diocese of Essen, noting that in 1959 only twenty-seven students had enrolled in theological studies, as compared with seventy-four in Münster, fifty-nine in Paderborn, fifty-four in Cologne, and forty-eight in Aachen. He attributed Essen's more pronounced shortage to the demographic makeup of the new diocese. Unlike other German dioceses, Essen consisted primarily of "large cities and diaspora areas" rather than rural communities from which the Church traditionally drew its clergy. To combat this development, he stressed the importance of fostering traditional family values.[24] The bishop of Essen, in a 1959 pastoral letter, also highlighted the connection between the preservation of traditional family values and the future of the priesthood: "There is the expression that the family is the first priestly seminar; and it is rightly so . . . if the child is accepted as a gift from God; if the family does not deny God as the source of all life; if a religious spirit dominates in the family; if through the celebration of Sunday mass, feast days and daily prayer father, mother and children are joined before God; if the children are brought up prepared to make sacrifices happily and resolutely; then the priestly and religious vocations will grow out of such families."[25] In short, the growing concern about the shortage of priests did not yet center on the issue of celibacy—not at the International Enquête in Vienna, not among the Church hierarchy, not even among young German priests and seminarians. In a 1960 survey of priests and seminarians in the Diocese of Essen, celibacy was conspicuously absent from the responses of those who expressed discontent with their vocation. Instead, disgruntled priests complained about the overcentralization of church life. Seminary students believed that more prayer on the part of priests and positive modeling of clerical life by parish priests held the solution to the clerical shortage.[26]

However, silence on the topic of celibacy should not be interpreted to mean that prior to Vatican II mandatory celibacy was not troublesome for some priests and seminarians; rather it reflects the fact that the topic was taboo within the Church. In 1973, Fritz Leist published *Zum Thema Zölibat*, in which priests and former priests described the "oppressive silence" engulfing the topic of celibacy in the Church. Repeatedly, the anonymous contributors referenced the absence of any comprehensive discussion during their seminary training. Several priests complained that, prior to ordination, only the value of celibacy, not its problems, was mentioned. One priest lamented, "They let us enter helplessly into the life of a priest."[27] Another priest described the sudden entrance of women into his life upon leaving the seminary—an event for which he was totally unprepared.[28] Admittedly, the anonymous testimonies found in Fritz's study offered a one-sided account of the experience of celibacy. However, the multiple references in official Church documents concerning the need to adequately prepare seminarians for a celibate life would suggest that the Church itself recognized this deficiency.[29]

Clerical celibacy was never totally absent from public discourse on the priesthood. In a 1960 interview with the French Catholic philosopher Étienne Gilson, Pope John XXIII inadvertently fueled the fires of the post–Vatican II debate when he expressed compassion for priests who struggled with celibacy: "For some of them it is martyrdom. Yes, a sort of martyrdom. It seems to me that sometimes I hear a sort of moan, as if many voices were asking the church for liberation from the burden. What can I do? Ecclesiastical celibacy is not a dogma. It is not imposed in the Scriptures. How simple it would be: we take up a pen, sign an act, and priests who so desire can marry tomorrow. But this is impossible. Celibacy is a sacrifice, which the church has imposed upon herself—freely, generously and heroically."[30] Despite the affirmation of celibacy contained herein and in his 1959 encyclical *Sacerdotii Nostri Primordia*,[31] opponents of celibacy employed these words as a rallying cry for their cause. It became a common tactic of Church reformers and of the secular media to contrast the "good pope"—John XXIII—with the "bad popes"—Paul VI, John Paul II, and Benedict XVI.

Pope John XXIII's comments were not the only sign before Vatican II that some clergy members no longer embraced celibacy. On June 16, 1962, the Central Preparatory Commission for Vatican II considered the schema *De Sacerdotibus Lapsis* concerning priests who abandoned their office. The schema assumed that most clerical offenders did so because of the celibacy requirement. Although none of the sixty-eight prelates at the meeting challenged the validity of the discipline of celibacy for priests in the Latin Church, Cardinals Josef Frings of Germany, Augustin Bea of Germany, Leo Joseph Suenens of Belgium, Paul-Émile Léger of Canada, and others wanted to ease the ecclesiastical situation of "lapsed" priests, who faced automatic excommunication if they married without dispensation.[32] But supporters of liberalization represented the minority position; the majority position is best summed up by the petition submitted by Karol Wojtyla, auxiliary bishop of Krakow and the future pope John Paul II: "A priest who has married without the blessing of the Church relinquishes claim to divine aid, as does his wife."[33] The Central Preparatory Commission resolved that the issue of "lapsed priests" would not be broached by the Vatican Council, but left to the discretion of the Holy See. Thus, no Vatican II text addressed the topic of "lapsed priests."[34]

Meanwhile in the German-speaking sphere, Josef Cardinal Frings (Cologne) and Franz Cardinal König (Vienna) received a letter from Dr. Alfred Sztuka, a lay Catholic who in his youth had considered the priesthood. The letter contained a scathing critique of clerical celibacy that foreshadowed the vehemence of the post–Vatican II debate. Sztuka compared the tactics used by the Church to recruit young men to the priesthood to those of the Nazis and accused the Church of hypocrisy: "You were angry with Third Reich authorities when they abused youthful passion and enthusiasm for their own political purposes and ends. But what does the Church do? You obligate young men at the age of 25, and sometimes even younger, to practice celibacy, men who often have had a very truncated education and who frequently have grown up without a clear understanding of marriage. . . . What you denounced in the Nazi regime, you do in the name of God."[35]

Sztuka's heated intervention represented the exception to the rule in the pre–Vatican II era. Most German Catholics, at least in the public discourse, upheld an idealized image of the priesthood. The idea that priests might be secretly violating their celibacy vows or even engaging in criminal sexual offenses (both alluded to in Sztuka's letter) the German Catholic public rarely entertained. Even in 1970, self-identified Catholic readers of *Der Spiegel* reacted across the board negatively to the magazine's cover story about priests who rejected celibacy, describing these cases as rare exceptions. One female reader wrote: "Why should the Church abolish celibacy because of a few renegades? With devilish joy, you drag out some examples and then kick the dirt about everywhere, thereby defaming the large army of priests who are pure and faithful to their oath."[36] This positive assessment of a celibate priesthood, particularly among women—the backbone of the Church— eroded gradually as the clerical shortage became more pronounced, the negative press coverage escalated, and Catholic women embraced new concepts of womanhood that were developing both inside and outside the Church in the 1970s and 1980s.

Vatican II and Its Impact on the Celibacy Debate

Paul VI removed celibacy from the Vatican II agenda in October 1965. During the fourth seating of the council, Brazilian bishops wanted to discuss modifying the requirement (at least in geographic regions where the shortage of priests was most pressing) and tried to enlist the support of Leo Joseph Cardinal Suenens of Belgium—one of the four council moderators appointed by Paul VI. This situation prompted Paul VI's intervention. On October 11, 1965, Cardinal Tisserant read a papal letter to the assembly in which Paul VI asserted that public debate "is not opportune on this subject."[37] In the letter, the pope also made clear his intention to safeguard the tradition of compulsory celibacy in the Latin Church; however, he gave the bishops the option to communicate their concerns to the Council of Presidents, who would transmit these concerns to him.[38]

Although a few council fathers expressed reservations about the celibacy requirement, the council affirmed the high valuation accorded celibacy by the Latin Church in four of the sixteen documents of Vatican II—*Lumen Gentium, Perfectae Caritatis, Optatam Totius,* and *Presbyterorum Ordinis*.[39] However, in the last two documents, the council fathers introduced two significant innovations, one procedural and one theological.

In *Optatam Totius*, the council fathers encouraged bishops to consider the results and methods of psychology in the recruitment and pedagogical training of young priests. They envisioned the deployment of scientific methods in the service of a healthy priesthood. But the new willingness to embrace the social sciences had unanticipated consequences. The findings of psychology and psychoanalysis became critical elements in the attack against celibacy from within the Church. Catholic critics such as Fritz Leist, Hubertus Mynarek, and Eugen Drewermann called attention to the Church's suppression of what they considered a fundamental human drive (the sex drive) and cast suspicion on the type of man attracted to a celibate priesthood, whom they labeled psychologically suspect.[40] In the context of the sexual revolution of the late 1960s and early 1970s, this critique found a receptive public audience and gave credibility to the countless rumors circulating in the secular press after 1968 of priests leading secret sexual lives. Since the Church had called for openness to the social sciences, it could not simply ignore these charges.

In *Presbyterorum Ordinis*, the council fathers departed from Pius XII's 1954 characterization of clerical celibacy as "doctrine" (a truth revealed by God and therefore not subject to revision).[41] Instead, they described celibacy as a matter of Church law: "Indeed it is not demanded by the very nature of the priesthood, as is apparent from the practice of the early Church and from the traditions of the Eastern Churches, where besides those who with all the bishops, by a gift of grace, choose to observe celibacy, there are also married priests of highest merit."[42] Although John XXIII had alluded to the nondoctrinal quality of priestly celibacy in his 1963 interview with Étienne Gilson, *Presbyterorum Ordinis* was the first official post–World War II Church document to do so.

The characterization of celibacy as a gift rather than a doctrine opened the door to public challenges of compulsory celibacy, because it allowed the following question to be raised: If celibacy is a gift, how can it be imposed? The council fathers offered an answer to this question. As Michael Schmaus and Rudolph Lange explained, they believed that celibacy was "so appropriate" and "so consonant" with the priesthood that God would not "deny to those whom he called to the priesthood this other grace also."[43] In the post–Vatican II atmosphere of crisis, however, few Catholics found this explanation satisfactory.

The new emphasis on the charismatic nature of celibacy was not the only theological innovation of the council fathers that influenced the postconciliar celibacy debate. There were four others—the reintroduction of a permanent diaconate; the new theological understanding of the priesthood; the more positive valuation of the laity; and the reduced importance assigned to Marian devotion.

The diaconate had not been a permanent office in the Catholic Church for approximately twelve hundred years. The reintroduction of a permanent diaconate had been proposed at the Council of Trent (1545–1563) but had not been approved. Instead, admission to the diaconate was understood to be a preparatory step for the priesthood. The campaign for the revival of a permanent diaconate to which married men might be admitted began in Germany. In 1953 a Paderborn priest, Father Wilhelm Schamoni, authored *Familienväter als geweihte Diakone*, in which he advocated the restoration of the permanent diaconate and the admission of married men to this order. Interest in this proposal soon spread beyond Germany, and three years later at the First International Congress for Pastoral Liturgy in Assisi, Italy, Bishop Wilhelm van Bekkum, the apostolic vicar of Ruteng Island, Indonesia, called for the restoration of a permanent diaconate; he was the first bishop to do so publicly. Then, in October 1957 at the World Congress of the Lay Apostolate, Pius XII set a precedent by broaching the subject. Although Pius XII did not believe the time was right for its reintroduction, he did not rule out the possibility.[44]

At Vatican II, the time proved ripe. The Central Preparatory Commission received many comments from bishops, theologians, and laypersons who favored the restoration of a permanent diaconate. Still, the first draft of *De Ecclesia*, the Dogmatic Constitution of the Church, included no reference to a permanent diaconate.[45] However, a revised draft of the Dogmatic Constitution, now designated by its opening words, *Lumen Gentium*, called for the reinstatement of the diaconate as a permanent office and the possible admission of married men to this major clerical order. The latter proviso sparked heated debate among the council fathers. Cardinals Francis Spellman of the United States, Ernesto Ruffini of Italy, Alfredo Ottaviani of the Roman Curia, and Antonio Bacci of the Roman Curia all feared that admitting married men to the diaconate would devalue the virtue of celibacy; Cardinal Bacci asserted that the number of priests would decline, because young men would be tempted by "the easier way."[46] Despite these objections, on September 29, 1963, the council fathers approved Paragraph 29 of *Lumen Gentium*, allowing for the creation of a diaconate to which married men of mature age and proven as family men and good husbands might belong. The council fathers did not make the reinstatement compulsory, but left it up to the discretion of the national bishops' conferences with the approval of the pope. Although married men of mature age were exempted from the celibacy requirement, younger candidates for the diaconate remained obligated to practice celibacy in perpetuity.[47] In the post–Vatican II era, the seeming coexistence of two diaconates (one for married men and one for celibate men) with the same duties sparked questions: If celibacy was no longer uniformly required of all members of the diaconate (a clerical order), why must it be uniformly applied to the priesthood and the bishopric?[48]

The council fathers also introduced significant changes in the theological foundations of the priesthood, believing that renewal in the Church required a comprehensive theology of office. Until Vatican II, the decrees formulated at the Council of Trent (1545–1563) had shaped the theological understanding of the priesthood. The council fathers of Vatican II believed that Trent had failed to provide a complete theology of office. Trent focused exclusively on the sacramental dimension of the priesthood and on the necessity of a hierarchy of office. This focus reflected the Catholic Church's primary concern at the time—the condemnation of Protestant heresies and clarification of its teachings in response to the objections of reformers to the Catholic understanding of the sacraments. The Church wanted to make it clear that all believers did not have the same access to the Gospel and to the sacraments. In drawing a distinction between the priest and the laity, the Council of Trent emphasized the priest's role in the sacrificial mass.[49] Only through the priest was the eternal priesthood of Christ realized:

> And forasmuch as, in this divine sacrifice which is celebrated in the mass, that same Christ is contained and immolated in an unbloody manner, who once offered Himself in a bloody manner on the altar of the cross; the holy Synod teaches, that this sacrifice is truly propitiatory and that by means thereof this is effected, that we obtain mercy, and find grace in seasonable aid, if we draw nigh unto God, contrite and penitent, with a sincere heart and upright faith, with fear and reverence. For the Lord, appeased by the oblation thereof, and granting the grace and gift of penitence, forgives even heinous crimes and sins. For the victim is one and the same, the same now offering by the ministry of priests, who then offered Himself on the cross, the manner alone of offering being different.[50]

Priests controlled the layperson's access to redemption; bishops controlled access to the priesthood; and the pope controlled access to the episcopate.

To buttress its hierarchical understanding of office and the Church, the Council of Trent utilized the Scholastic approach.[51] In *What Happened at Vatican II*, John O'Malley argued convincingly that the council fathers of Vatican II largely eschewed Scholastic language in favor of a more patristic/

biblical approach that emphasized reconciliation rather than the defining of concepts, the winning of arguments, or the enforcement of laws. This shift in style introduced a parallel new vocabulary in conciliar documents. Instead of issuing condemnations, Vatican II council fathers employed words of reciprocity, such as "cooperation," "partnership," and "collaboration." In terms of the priesthood, this stylistic change translated into a deemphasis on hierarchy.[52]

Although the Vatican II council fathers reaffirmed the sacrificial and hierarchical character of the priesthood, they no longer placed the ordination and authority of the priest in the foreground; instead, they highlighted the priest's status as co-participant in Christ's mission along with the laity. In short, the priest was no longer characterized as intrinsically different from his congregants. The council fathers also emphasized the missionary aspect of the priestly vocation, calling upon the priest to go out among the people and proclaim the word of God.[53]

The altered relationship between priest and laity was most visible in the discussion of the common priesthood of all believers. Although the Council of Trent had not explicitly rejected the common priesthood, it focused almost exclusively on the ministerial priesthood. In contrast, the Vatican II council fathers spoke at length about the significance of the common priesthood, thereby augmenting the vertical conception of the Church (from God to pope, through the bishops to the priests and finally to the laity) with a horizontal one (the Church as the "people of God"). In *Lumen Gentium*, the council fathers no longer referred to the laity as "subjects," nor did they describe the structure of the Church as "monarchical."[54] Striving for holiness was not just a clerical obligation, but the responsibility of all. A universal priesthood, identified with the "people of God," whose authority was not derived from the ministerial priesthood but from baptism, signified a new, more positive valuation of the laity. This more positive assessment promoted a new appreciation of nonclerical offices; the priesthood ceased to be the only Church office held in high esteem. Catholics, wanting a more active role in the Church, now argued that they could and should perform many duties previously reserved for the priesthood.[55]

Vatican II also made possible a more positive valuation of women in the Church. At the end of the second session of the council, Cardinal Suenens of Belgium provocatively asked his fellow council fathers: "Women too should be invited as auditors: unless I am mistaken, they make up half of the human race?"[56] As a result, the council invited fifteen women to serve as official auditors. Never before in the history of the Catholic Church had women participated in a council; now thanks to Cardinal Suenens and a suggestion by the German theologian Bernhard Häring, some of these women collaborated on commissions responsible for formulating documents.[57] Their participation contributed to a new understanding of women's place in church and society: "With respect to the fundamental rights of the person, every type of discrimination, whether social or cultural, whether based on sex, race, color, social condition, language or religion, is to be overcome and eradicated as contrary to God's intent."[58] At least in theory, the Roman Catholic Church now recognized women as equal participants in the common priesthood of all believers.

The council fathers had aimed for consensus; consequently, many documents contained ambiguous or even contradictory passages that in the years to come would be subject to multiple interpretations. The nature of the relationship between this priesthood of all believers and the ministerial priesthood became a major source of contention in the post–Vatican II era. Advocates of greater democratization of the Church asserted that authority in the Church belonged to the people of God, not the clergy. This reform movement reached its culmination in 1996 with the founding of the International Movement We Are Church (IMWAC), whose manifesto demanded the co-participation of the laity in all aspects of ministry and Church governance.[59]

However, this new understanding of the ministry and of the relationship between clergy and laity first found expression in an identity crisis among priests. Vatican II highlighted the missionary function of the priesthood, which brought priests into more intimate contact with married couples and their families; for some priests, contact with happily married couples led to a new appreciation of married life—one that contradicted the negative model of obligation and sin taught to them at the seminary. These priests began imagining the possibility of establishing new relationships, including ones with women. More intimate contact with families also inspired greater sympathy for married couples who failed to adhere to some Church doctrine, such as the ban on artificial forms of contraception. Increasingly, priests found themselves torn between their loyalty to the pope and their sympathy for their congregants; these divided loyalties led many to leave office. The Dutch sociologist Walter Goddijn explained: "He [the priest] is expected to proclaim truths behind which he no longer stands or no longer completely stands because he is expected to communicate values that he believes are outdated, because he is supposed to transmit teaching statements and ecclesial positions that he personally does not accept, because he is expected to carry out actions in whose efficacy he no longer believes and because he must represent an authority with whose positions he cannot agree."[60] In some nations, this identity crisis preceded the Second Vatican Council. But in the politically charged post–Vatican II climate, priests were no longer willing to suffer in silence.[61]

Finally, the conciliar debate on Marian devotion influenced the postconciliar debate on celibacy. Devoid of all connotations of sexuality, Mary had long served a twofold purpose in maintaining the discipline of celibacy. First, she provided a justification for a celibate priesthood. The medieval monk Petrus Damiani argued that because Jesus was born of a virgin, he could be touched only by virgin hands, thereby establishing a connection between sexual purity and the Eucharist celebration.[62] Second, she served as a chaste role model and mother figure for priests. Mary, Pius XII wrote, provided the priest solace in his daily struggles against the temptations of the flesh: "When you meet very serious difficulties in the path of holiness and the exercise of your ministry, turn your eyes and your mind trustfully to she who is the Mother of the Eternal Priest and therefore the loving Mother of all Catholic priests."[63]

Many bishops and theologians wanted the council to expand Marian doctrine; some supported conferring on Mary a new title, "Mother of the Church." However, not all council fathers shared this view. Some preferred that piety be more centered on the Bible and the liturgy and less on devotional practices, including Marian worship. They felt that Marian devotion often diverged from the message found in scripture and in the liturgy. They also feared that any elaboration of Marian devotion would undermine the ecumenical movement. Thus, the seemingly innocent question of where to locate a statement on Mary had far-reaching theological and political ramifications. On August 29, by a margin of only forty votes, the council fathers decided in favor of incorporating a statement on Marian piety into *Lumen Gentium*.[64]

Although Paul VI later preempted the decision of the council fathers and bestowed upon Mary the title they had denied her, "Mother of the Church,"[65] the popularity of Marian devotion continued to decline in Western Europe. In the survey of all West German Catholics conducted for the Würzburg Synod in 1970, only 8 percent of Catholics between the ages of sixteen and twenty described the veneration of Mary as an important dimension of faith, as opposed to 24 percent of Catholics over the age of seventy.[66] Among theologians and lay congregants, scripture increasingly took precedence. Unlike Marian devotion, scripture provided no unequivocal justification for mandatory clerical celibacy; many of Jesus's apostles had been married men, including Peter, the rock upon whom the Church was built.

In the 1980s, Marian piety came under vehement attack by European feminist theologians, such as Catherina Halkes and Uta Ranke-Heinemann. They argued that Marian piety provided the means by which celibate priests sublimated their sexuality into a sexually safe relationship with a virgin mother, untainted by original sin; the hostility caused by this sublimation was then projected onto real women, who could never realize the unattainable feminine ideal represented by Mary. The Church's exaltation of Mary did not speak to the dignity of women, but rather served as a counterpoint to real women, who in Church teachings remained the daughters of the sexual temptress Eve.[67]

The Post–Vatican II Celibacy Debate in the Church

Many council fathers interpreted Paul VI's invitation to submit remarks on clerical celibacy as an invitation to continue the discussion in a different venue, one not subject to such intense media coverage. However, according to the five-volume history of Vatican II edited by Giuseppe Alberigo, this discussion never materialized prior to Paul VI's affirmation of mandatory celibacy for priests in the 1967 encyclical *Sacerdotalis Caelibatus*.[68]

In the encyclical, Paul VI enumerated seven objections voiced by critics of celibacy: (1) Jesus did not require celibacy of his apostles, nor did the apostles later require it of priests. (2) The celibacy requirement had its origin in values and historical circumstances that no longer existed. (3) A vocation to the priesthood was not synonymous with a vocation to celibacy. (4) Celibacy exacerbated the shortage of priests. (5) Allowing priests to marry would eliminate infidelity and defections from the priesthood. (6) Celibacy injured the human psyche because it required repressing a fundamental biological drive. (7) A young man was incapable of appreciating the seriousness of the obligation. To these objections, Paul VI responded that the difficulties associated with celibacy could be "penetrated and resolved by the light of divine revelation." He stressed the authority of the Church to admit to the priesthood "those whom she judges qualified: that is, those to whom God has given, along with other signs of an ecclesiastical vocation, the gift of consecrated celibacy."⁶⁹

In West Germany, the publication of *Sacerdotalis Caelibatus* triggered only mild protests among some clergy members and a few laypersons. Protesters claimed the encyclical was an affront to the post–Vatican II emphasis on collegiality and greater openness to the world. Only a few bishops and no priests had been consulted in the writing of the encyclical. For some theologians, such as Hans Küng, Vatican II made silent obedience impossible: "After the Council, is one to accept such solitary decisions, again made in the authoritarian style of the *ancien régime*, moaning, grumbling and despairing or hoping for better times? No, after the Council, the role of the theologians isn't the same as it was before. Theologians have a responsibility for their fellow men and women. But they can exercise it only by making public statements. Public opinion in the church has a right to that. At the same time a signal has to be sent to Rome that such uncollegial proceedings in the spirit of pre-conciliar absolutism will not be accepted without resistance."⁷⁰ Several German newspapers published Küng's call for a plebiscite on celibacy in conjunction with a summary of the encyclical.⁷¹

However, not all Vatican II supporters of collegiality and openness in the Church reacted negatively to the encyclical. Karl Rahner, professor of dogmatics at the University of Münster and one of the architects of Vatican II reforms, published a defense of mandatory celibacy. His intervention quickly became the most frequently discussed text in the immediate post-encyclical West German celibacy debate. Rahner wrote his defense in the form of a letter to an anonymous brother who was struggling with his vow of celibacy. He expressed sympathy for those who struggled with celibacy; their difficulties, however, did not change his support of celibacy. He dismissed those "enemies of celibacy, acting as if its abandonment would open the gates of paradise to the poor clergy whom nothing but an antiquated, unnatural ecclesial law holds back from happiness and development of 'personality.'"⁷² Rahner countered that no proof existed that a priest who failed at celibacy would be any more successful in marriage. He contended that the virtues that allowed one to succeed in marriage were the same ones needed to succeed in celibacy—solitude and self-denial. He suggested that if the Church permitted priests to marry, the bishops might have as many broken marriages on their hands as they now had "scandals" over celibacy.⁷³

To counter the claim that celibacy signaled a psychological or physical defect in priests, Rahner drew on a study by Marc Oraison, a French Freudian psychoanalyst and Catholic priest, who viewed celibacy as a viable alternative "offered man by his nature." Rahner affirmed Oraison's position; he claimed, "Sexuality is not a fixed quantity but a task, a challenge, an opportunity, a riddle."[74] For those critics who argued that the Church had turned the charisma of celibacy into a coercive institution, he responded that a commitment "until further notice" equaled no commitment at all: "A man who expects to be sustained by God's grace without soberly and inflexibly demanding the utmost from himself will never discover that virgin roads into the unknown do lead to our destination in the end."[75] Rahner acknowledged that a time might come when the Church must abandon celibacy to ensure a sufficient number of priests for the community. Yet he concluded: "I do not await the 'future' like that gargoyle on the cathedral at Freiburg, an old nun pointing to her last tooth to show that she may yet marry. I have already made my choice. I am sticking to the vocation that is my own."[76]

Like Küng's response, Rahner's letter received extensive coverage in the religious and secular media. The Austrian and German bishops distributed copies to all clergy members. *Der Spiegel* assessed Rahner's position as both the more realistic one and the one endorsed by the majority of the clergy.[77] In the wake of Küng's declaration and Rahner's letter, no mass movement against clerical celibacy materialized. Only a few titillating reports of celibacy scandals appeared in the popular press. Most German Catholics gave clerical celibacy little thought.

With the publication on July 25, 1968, of the papal encyclical *Humanae Vitae* condemning artificial contraception, this relative state of calm ended. Although public outrage focused on Paul VI's condemnation of all methods of birth control, except rhythm, as contrary to natural and divine law, the floodgates of protest unleashed by *Humanae Vitae* had profound consequences for the celibacy debate in Germany. Traditionally, German Catholics supported the pope. Policies instituted by the new German state in 1871, intended to curtail the influence of the Catholic Church in Germany, not only resulted in the creation of an insulated Catholic subculture, but also made most German Catholics reluctant to speak out against the pope, on whose support they depended in the so-called *Kulturkampf*.[78] But unconditional public support of the pope ended with the publication of *Humanae Vitae*; ordinary middle-class West German Catholics lashed out against the encyclical.[79] In an effort to diffuse the situation, the West German bishops released "Wort der deutschen Bischöfe zur seelsorglichen Lage nach dem

Erscheinen der Enzyklika *Humanae Vitae*" (the Königstein Declaration) on August 30, 1968; the declaration affirmed the right of married couples to make their own decisions of conscience about the use of artificial birth control.[80]

The Königstein Declaration dissipated tensions in Germany; however, it did not extinguish the spirit of protest. Anticipating controversy at the biennial Catholic Congress in September 1968, an unprecedented 424 journalists converged on the congress in Essen (Essener Katholikentag), resulting in 2,538 print stories, sixty-three radio broadcasts, and seventeen hours of television coverage.[81] As the motto of the congress proclaimed, the West German Catholic Church found itself "in the midst of this world" (*Mitten in dieser Welt*). Under the watchful eye of the international press, German Catholics created a new type of congress. The triumphal reviews of a receptive and obedient laity by the hierarchy were replaced by a host of forums in which West German Catholics debated the doctrines and practices of their faith.

Essen inaugurated a time of great excitement, trepidation, and conflict in the German Catholic Church.[82] Headlines such as "Conscience versus Obedience" and "3000 Catholics Demand Revision of the Pill Ban" captured the new mood in the West German Church.[83] Franz-Maria Elsner, a participant at the Essener Katholikentag, concluded that *Humanae Vitae* launched "a new period in the history of the German Catholic Church," one in which "participants at Catholic congresses could discuss the most difficult problems in open and democratic forums."[84] Official representatives at the forum on marriage voted in favor of a resolution calling on the pope to revise his position on artificial birth control. Outside the forum, Catholic youth carried banners that boldly declared: "The people of God betrayed—by Roman prelates"; "Everybody talks about the pill, we take it!"; and "Christ spoke with whores, not with bishops' frocks!"[85] The Vatican's credibility had suffered a serious blow among West German Catholics.

In West Germany, this loss of credibility did not translate into an immediate attack on the institution of celibacy. The conference of priests held on September 4, 1968, as part of the Essener Katholikentag received minimal media coverage. What coverage it did receive was largely neutral; only a few mildly negative reports appeared. The theme of the conference was the modern priesthood, but neither of the two keynote speakers—Karl Rahner or the Munich moral theologian Alois Müller—addressed clerical celibacy. Instead, spiritual and abstract rhetoric carried the day. The *Ruhr-*

Nachrichten labeled the conference "disappointing," because the "concrete burning issues for the most part were excluded from the discussion."[86] Other accounts emphasized Rahner's efforts to bridge the gap between the Left and the Right. In his presentation, Rahner rejected "orthodox spiritual inertia," on the one hand, and "modernistic theological non-conformism," on the other.[87] According to press reports, some protesters attended the conference carrying banners condemning the "nebulous imagery of the celibacy encyclical," but their protests were described as "tentative."[88]

The lack of outcry at the conference of priests did not indicate an absence of clerical unrest. Instead, clerical protests at this point also focused on the birth control ban. Press accounts described how priests and nuns applauded the resolution rejecting the papal position on birth control.[89] But when it became clear that the Church would not revise its position on artificial birth control, many German Catholics and non-Catholics turned a critical eye toward celibacy. They blamed the preservation of a male celibate priesthood for the Church's intransigence on birth control and, more generally, for its negative valuation of sexuality. One man went so far as to describe the abolition of celibacy as necessary for human progress: "Taboos would collapse; prejudices and opinions of a negative nature would be dismantled; the number of uptight, inhibited Catholics would decline (everything being a matter of education); the sanctimonious philistinism would shift rapidly from frustration to joy; the way to a happier society would be open."[90]

By the time the German bishops announced the General Synod of the Dioceses of West Germany (Würzburg Synod) in February 1969, celibacy had replaced birth control as the most pressing issue facing the West German Catholic Church. In November 1969, the editorial department, "Kirche und Leben," of the Second German Television (Zweites Deutsches Fernsehen, ZDF) asked viewers to send in their opinions concerning the upcoming synod. Thirty-two hundred letters arrived by the deadline of June 1, 1970.[91] Preliminary results released in February 1970 indicated that celibacy was the primary concern of respondents. Of these letters, 36 percent referenced clerical celibacy, more than twice the number received on any other topic; by May 1970, the proportion of letters on celibacy had risen to 45 percent, with the vast majority of respondents rejecting mandatory celibacy.[92]

This small survey was not the only indication of changing West German Catholic attitudes toward celibacy. The official survey of all West German Catholics over the age of sixteen commissioned by the DBK showed that 62 percent of West German Catholics no longer supported a celibate priesthood. Among Catholics who identified themselves as having a strong connection with the Church, this number dropped to 31 percent (see Appendix D).[93] A survey of priests also conducted for the Würzburg Synod revealed that 28 percent of priests believed the celibacy requirement should be abolished, and 51 percent considered it worthy of consideration. However, these numbers did not tell the whole story; the survey exposed a sharp generational divide. Among priests ordained before 1921, only 6 percent supported the abolition of mandatory celibacy, as opposed to 54 percent of priests ordained between 1966 and 1970 (see Appendix E).[94] Younger priests, like their nonclerical counterparts, were rethinking Catholic moral doctrine.

Developments in the Dutch Catholic Church also shaped West German interest in the topic of clerical celibacy. While West Germans were preparing for their General Synod, the Dutch National Pastoral Council was under way. In the Netherlands, the clerical shortage was particularly acute. In 1962, there were 388 seminary students; by 1968, that number had dropped to 68. Even more alarming, 400 Dutch priests had abandoned office in order to marry between 1968 and 1970. Moreover, it was widely anticipated that delegates to the Dutch council would reject compulsory celibacy if allowed to vote on the issue.

In an effort to block that vote, Paul VI intervened. He wrote Bernardus Johannes Cardinal Alfrink, chair of the Dutch Episcopal Conference, asking him to remove celibacy from the Dutch council's agenda. Cardinal Alfrink never informed the council of the letter, although he acknowledged the letter's existence to delegates who via the media had read rumors of it. In response, Alfrink described the letter as private correspondence. He stated that the Vatican position was well known, and the council's task was to make the Dutch position known to the Vatican. On January 5, 1970, the delegates voted to abolish the celibacy requirement for future priests (ninety votes in favor, six against, and two abstentions).[95]

Immediately, the Vatican launched a counterattack. On January 12, 1970, *L'Osservatore Romano* (the semiofficial Vatican newspaper) published Paul VI's letter to Cardinal Alfrink. Two weeks later, Jean Daniélou, a member of the Roman Curia and prominent Church historian, raised the stakes of the debate: "For some among the proponents, the campaign against celibacy represents merely a pretext. Through this campaign, they want to strike at the authority of the pope."[96] Shortly thereafter, Paul VI summoned Cardinal Alfrink to Rome. Rumors circulated in the European and American press that the pope would excommunicate the Dutch Church. Some news reports predicted a schism in the Church; others believed that the pope would back down in order to preserve his own credibility.[97]

Ultimately it was the Dutch Church that lost the battle; however, events in the Netherlands had drawn attention to the topic in Germany and elsewhere. In a show of solidarity with the Dutch Church, eighty-four theologians, led by the Tübingen professors of theology Hans Küng, Norbert Greinacher, and Johannes Neumann, presented a declaration to the Bishops' Conferences of West Germany, Austria, and Switzerland. The declaration also appeared in the press:

> The question of celibacy for the Latin Church has become an extremely serious problem not only in the Netherlands but also in our countries and threatens to lead to a split in the Catholic Church. We cannot and may not look on this development without taking action. Even those who don't reject a law of celibacy outright regard the unity of the Church as a greater good than the preservation of a disciplinary law which has neither applied for all times nor applies everywhere today.... Given the present heightening of the issue, the situation outside of the Netherlands is also very much more threatening than might appear at first sight. We therefore call on our bishops, in accordance with the shared responsibility of the bishops for the whole church which was endorsed again at Vatican II, as individuals and through their conferences to intercede publicly for the substantive conversation about this question in Rome which is long overdue and has often been called for.[98]

The DBK received at least three other petitions in response to the Dutch controversy—two of which rejected any further discussion of clerical celibacy. A group of 134 theologians led by the Munich theologian Michael Schmaus and the Essen prelate Gerhard Fittkau asked the German bishops "in the interest of clarity" to issue a statement reaffirming the discipline of celibacy.[99] A petition sent by the Association of German Catholic Women Teachers (Verein katholischer deutscher Lehrerinnen) denounced clergy members who broke their vow of celibacy and made a "spectacle of themselves in the media." They called upon the German bishops not to waiver in their support of the pope.[100] A fourth petition, submitted by a group of nine theologians acting as official DBK consultants for the upcoming Würzburg Synod (1971–1975), urged continued dialogue; Josef Ratzinger, the future pope Benedict XVI, numbered among its signers. Although this last petition recommended continued discussion, it refrained from making any statement about the desired outcome.[101] Against this backdrop, the German bishops released the list of topics for the synod. Many Catholics had criticized the German bishops for failing to take into account topics favored by German Catholics; however, the celibacy debate—at least indirectly—made the list. On the agenda of Subcommission VII, "Charismas, Ministries, Offices," was the issue of the admission of married men (*viri probati*) to the priesthood.

Subcommission VII had many issues on its agenda besides celibacy; however, celibacy was the most divisive. The shortage of priests and the lack of candidates for the priesthood in Germany created a sense of urgency. As already noted, canon law allowed for exceptions to the celibacy requirement. In the 1950s and early 1960s, Germany experienced a relatively large influx of former Protestant ministers into the Catholic priesthood. In a 1959 letter to Josef Cardinal Frings of Cologne, the archbishop of Paderborn referenced ten to twelve former Protestant priests engaged in the conversion process. The letter stated that most of these men had lost their trust in the EKD because its leadership acquiesced to too many Communist demands. Although exactly how many former Protestant ministers joined the Catholic clergy is unknown, the number was sufficient for the German bishops to develop a systematic plan for the education and assimilation of these married men into the Catholic priesthood.[102] This influx of married Protestant men into the Catholic Church as a result of the postwar ideological divide between Western and Eastern Europe contributed to a growing belief among many West German Catholics that the ordination of married men held the answer to the priest shortage. The post–Vatican II establishment of a married diaconate in West Germany, the celibacy debate in the Netherlands, and lay dissatisfaction with a celibate Church's decision on birth control gave further credence to this belief.

Meanwhile in Rome, the Second Ordinary General Assembly of the World Synod of Bishops began in September 1971. The ministerial priesthood was one of two topics on the agenda. Under the watchful eyes of Paul VI, the bishops affirmed celibacy by an overwhelming majority.[103] Only a few bishops spoke out in favor of liberalizing the celibacy requirement. Two familiar motifs—the superiority of the celibate way of life and the exclusion of the female body from the suprasexual relationship between the Church and God—served as rationales: "While the value of the sign and holiness of Christian marriage is fully recognized, celibacy for the sake of the Kingdom nevertheless more clearly displays that spiritual fruitfulness of generative power of the new law by which the apostle knows that in Christ he is the father and the mother of his community."[104] The World Synod of Bishops also rejected the admission of married men to the clergy.[105]

The decision of the synod placed the West German bishops in a no-win situation. Prior to the Second Ordinary General Assembly, they had approved discussion of *viri probati* at the Würzburg Synod, and Subcommission VII had already commenced discussion. The West German bishops must have realized that any reversal of their earlier decision would not be well received by synod members, the West German Catholic community, or the media. The disproportionate representation of clergy at the synod, the underrepresentation of women and youth, and the lack of relevance of many topics chosen for the Würzburg Synod had already generated harsh criticism in the Catholic community. A small but vocal minority in the Catholic Church went so far as to accuse the bishops of deliberately manipulating the Würzburg Synod's agenda.[106] If the DBK took no action and the German synod approved *viri probati*, the West German Catholic Church would find itself in direct conflict with the Vatican, and the West German bishops would face having to make a very public choice between the wishes of the people of God and those of the supreme pontiff in Rome. In the immediate aftermath of the World Bishops' Synod in Rome, the DBK remained silent, and members of Subcommission VII resolved to continue its discussion of *viri probati*, despite news of the Rome synod.[107]

But members of Subcommission VII could reach no consensus on the wisdom or efficacy of admitting married men to the priesthood. Some members supported abolishing the celibacy requirement; they argued that priests should be free to choose between celibacy and marriage, and they envisioned celibate and married priests working side by side in the ministry. Others advocated the introduction of *viri probati* only as an extraordinary measure in areas where the clerical shortage was most acute. Still others wanted no changes to the existing law, insisting that the Church focus its efforts on developing the lay ministry and creating strategies for recruiting young men to the celibate priesthood. All participants recognized that each solution posed problems: If clerical celibacy was no longer required, how was celibacy as a charisma to be maintained? Would the introduction of a married clergy result in the ghettoization or even extinction of the celibate priesthood? If the introduction of *viri probati* was limited to extraordinary cases, how was its exceptional character to be maintained? If no changes were made, what concrete steps could be taken to develop a more positive valuation of celibacy among the clergy and the laity? To facilitate discussion, the subcommission requested that the DBK provide statistical data on the number of candidates for the priesthood, the age structure of the priesthood, the number of priests who left office, and a breakdown of their reasons for leaving office.[108]

In addition to statistical data and treatises generated by subcommission members and approved by expert consultants, Subcommission VII took under advisement numerous unsolicited petitions submitted by various clerical and lay groups. It appointed a member to act as the contact person for the group Priests without Office (Priester ohne Amt). Initially, the subcommission nominated a member of this group to act as an official adviser, but the central commission rejected the nomination on the grounds that "the category 'priests without office' is only the negative dimension of vocation or estate in the Church."[109] Through the designated contact person, Priests without Office lobbied for improvements in the status of laicized priests. They demanded that such priests have access to any Church office open to the laity. They also asked that priests not be forced to leave their home diocese as a condition of laicization.[110]

Interaction between this group of former priests and commission members gave a human face to abstract data on defections from the priesthood, as did the announcement by Bishop Tenhumberg on June 14, 1972, that a member of Subcommission VII had requested laicization and consequently had been removed as a member of the synod.[111] According to a paper submitted to the subcommission by Speyer theological students, Rome received 3,800 requests for laicization in 1970, as opposed to 167 in 1963.[112] The "talent drain" meant that the remaining priests had to take on responsibility for larger congregations. This phenomenon coincided with a growing expectation on the part of West German congregants that priests would take an active role in contemporary life. In the Würzburg survey, 76 percent of West German Catholics expected the active support of priests in dealing with personal problems, such as marital strife and conflicts between parent and child.[113] Clearly a solution to the priest shortage had to be found in order for the clergy to fulfill old and new expectations.

Yet Subcommission VII was still deadlocked when on April 17, 1972, the DBK prohibited further discussion of *viri probati:* "Based on the detailed discussion about the acceptance of married men of mature age to the priesthood that has already taken place within the Bishops' Conference and in the general public, as well as the results of the Roman synod, the German Bishops' Conference considers it neither in order nor meaningful for the

General Synod of the Dioceses of the Federal Republic of Germany to address anew this question. In accord with previous experiences, it is unlikely that further discussion will provide new arguments."[114] Given the deadlock, the DBK's conclusion may have seemed reasonable. However, neither commission members nor the Catholic public nor the media reacted positively to the announcement. Few accepted the bishops' assertion that they did not want to "restrict freedom of discussion."[115]

The decision sparked a "crisis of confidence" at the synod. Approximately one-third of the delegates threatened to resign. When the synod presidents attempted to explain the decision on May 13, 1972, a "lively debate" erupted. And shortly thereafter, a "rumor" circulated concerning "name-calling of bishops." In fact, the rumor gained so much credence that the authors of the official text of the synod felt obligated to deny it. No one, they asserted, challenged the authority of the bishops to make the decision; criticism centered on the manner in which the prohibition had been communicated. A large-scale walkout was averted when several bishops offered public apologies. In his apology, Bishop Stein of Trier spoke of a learning process for the bishops, and Auxiliary Bishop Moser of Rottenburg-Stuttgart also apologized for the manner of communication. At the June meeting of Subcommission VII, Bishop Tenhumberg clarified the decision to the satisfaction of participants.[116]

Removing *viri probati* from the Würzburg Synod's agenda, however, did not bring an end to debate on the topic. Subcommission VII continued to discuss related topics, such as the appropriate role of laicized priests in the Church, strategies for motivating young men to embrace a celibate way of life, and the point at which candidates for the priesthood should take the vow of celibacy. As we shall see in the next chapter, the removal of *viri probati* from the agenda created a new sense of urgency concerning the need to develop the lay ministry in order to alleviate the pastoral emergency. In doing so, it brought the question of a female diaconate into the foreground.

The Escalating Stakes of the Debate

By the mid-1970s, the scope of the celibacy debate had expanded. The discussion among Church officials about the continued relevance of celibacy, given the shortage of priests, had evolved into a debate on the structure and moral character of the Catholic Church. The media played a crucial role in the escalation of the celibacy debate, as did the entry of Catholic women into the debate in the 1980s. Although Catholic women also understood the debate in terms of a crisis in the structure and moral character of the Church, their critique centered on how preserving a celibate male priesthood reinforced hierarchical and patriarchal structures that oppressed women. In particular, they associated the clerical celibacy requirement with women's exclusion from office in the Church.

During the Würzburg Synod, the secular press paid little attention to the deliberations of Subcommission VII on celibacy and *viri probati*. Instead, reporters focused on behind-the-scenes political intrigue and celibacy scandals. The sheer number of news stories detailing the alleged sexual exploits of priests and cases of political intrigue must have weighed heavily on the West German Catholic Church. From the time of *Humanae Vitae*'s publication in 1968 until the end of 1979, *Der Spiegel* published forty-five stories on clerical celibacy in the Catholic Church. A 1970 cover showed a priest standing at the altar with his bride. During this same period, *Die Zeit* published forty-one articles with provocative titles such as "Only the Courageous Still Protest" and "Is Sex of the Devil?" Given the plethora of stories, it would be impossible to cover all of them. However, two scandals exemplified how media coverage contributed to the escalation of the debate. The first scandal pitted the German hierarchy against the former Catholic theologian Hubertus Mynarek. The second scandal centered on the efforts of the papal nuncio Cardinal Bafile to remove Bishop Wilhelm Kempf of Limburg from office because of his appointment of a married priest to a pastoral position.

On November 2, 1972, Hubertus Mynarek, a German theologian and professor at the University of Vienna in Austria, wrote an open letter to the pope. He sent copies of the letter to Cardinal König of Vienna and to the press. In the twenty-two-page letter, he announced his resignation from the priesthood and his separation from the Church: "After long and careful consideration and in the wake of numerous disappointing confrontations with the negative realities of the Roman Catholic Church, I have arrived at the decision, demanded by my conscience, to separate from this institution, composed as an absolute monarchy, its power structure quintessentially authoritarian."[117] The Austrian and German press reprinted extensive excerpts of the letter. Mynarek's decision to leave the priesthood and the Catholic Church created a small stir. Most Catholic priests who surrendered office endeavored to maintain a continued presence in the Church and thus did not publicize their decision. The separation of such a prominent clergyman from the German Church had not happened since 1953.[118]

Yet Mynarek's very public separation from the Church marked only the beginning of the controversy. Following his resignation, several publishers approached Mynarek about writing a book on his experiences in the Church. In the resulting book, *Herren und Knechte der Kirche*, Mynarek named five prominent German and Austrian theologians whom he alleged had secret sex lives. Anticipating a best seller, the Catholic publishing house of C. Bertelsmann sent advance copies to the news media. In their book reviews, *Der Spiegel* and *Stern* reprinted the names of the five accused theologians. All five theologians issued disclaimers, which both magazines carried. At this point, on the recommendation of its attorneys, C. Bertelsmann announced that it would not proceed with publication. The DBK initiated legal action against Mynarek. A Munich court ordered him to pay between 10,000 and 20,000 DM per theologian, plus court costs.[119]

Mynarek's case was not the first civil suit instigated by the West German Catholic Church against a former priest because of statements on celibacy. In 1969, Cardinal Höffner sued Edmund Steffensky for telling the *Kölner Anzeiger* that priests were married "to a thousand things from good food and drink, moving on up to masturbation, female friends, and homosexuality." However, unlike that against Mynarek, the case against Steffensky was dropped by the Church.[120]

But the drama did not end there. In 1978, Mynarek published a second book on sexual exploits of clergy—*Eros und Klerus*. The new book did not name names but depicted "typical" cases of clerical sexual encounters. These typical cases included rape and child abuse. The book also described incidents in which priests pressured women to have abortions in order to keep their sexual exploits secret. The Katholische Nachrichten-Agentur (KNA) sued Mynarek and lost. In fact, a Bonn court ordered the KNA editor, Konrad W. Kraemer, to desist from referring to Mynarek as a scoundrel (*Schmutzfink*).[121]

Media coverage of the Mynarek affair diverged widely. *Der Spiegel* championed Mynarek as a reformer fighting against an antiquated, authoritarian Church; *Die Zeit* denounced Mynarek's two books as "trashy," "self-serving," and "hypocritical."[122] Despite their very different conclusions, both newsmagazines framed their narratives as moral indictments—in the former case against the Catholic Church and in the latter case against Mynarek.

The second incident generated greater public outrage. In August 1973, the papal nuncio Cardinal Bafile sent two confidential letters to the Vatican state secretary, Jean Villot. In the first letter, Bafile advocated appointing a coadjutor for the Diocese of Limburg. In the second letter, he made the "humble suggestion" that Bishop Kempf be pressured to resign for reasons of health and that an apostolic administrator be appointed in his place. Bafile cited Otto Franzmann's recent appointment to a leading pastoral role in the parish of Maria Hilf in Frankfurt as a justification. Franzmann, a former priest in the Old Catholic Church (Alt-Katholische Kirche), was married and the father of two children.[123]

In 1971, the Congregation for the Doctrine of the Faith (CDF) had authorized Bishop Kempf to assimilate three married priests into his diocese. However, the authorization stipulated that the priests not be assigned to posts that placed them in regular contact with the Catholic public. Bafile believed Kempf's actions set a dangerous precedent: "It cannot be taken lightly what effects this measure will have—not only in Germany—on the opponents of celibacy."[124]

Neither Bishop Kempf nor Cardinal Döpfner, chair of the DBK, knew of Bafile's plan when the press broke the story. According to press reports, an anonymous Vatican official had sent a copy of Bafile's letter to a group of priests in Kempf's diocese. In an accompanying letter, the Vatican official stated that he wanted to expose the methods of papal nuncios, which he labeled "more terrible than those of the Soviets." The Limburg priests gave the letters to the press. The ecclesial and secular media published excerpts, unleashing widespread protests in the West German Catholic Church. Prominent theologians, such as Norbert Greinacher, publicly denounced Bafile's actions.[125] The DBK and ZdK issued public declarations supporting Bishop Kempf.[126]

Bafile's surreptitious move to remove Kempf from office had backfired. While press coverage of the Mynarek affair had been divided, the German press overwhelmingly condemned Bafile's actions. Both *Der Spiegel* and *Die Zeit* compared Kempf favorably to John XXIII. In contrast, they depicted Paul VI as an "ascetic prince" whose ruling style was reminiscent of the Grand Inquisition.[127]

As charges of authoritarianism and moral depravity saturated the headlines, enrollment at seminaries declined, lay confidence in Church leadership diminished, and the number of priests abandoning office increased. According to official Vatican statistics, roughly 13,000 priests in the world church were laicized between 1963 and 1970. However, this number did not include priests who left office without requesting laicization. Factoring in this second group, experts estimated the total number of priests who left office at somewhere between 22,000 and 25,000.[128]

Under John Paul II, the liberal dispensation policy came to an abrupt end. Shortly after taking office in 1978, John Paul II appointed a special CDF commission to investigate laicization and celibacy dispensations. As a result, the Vatican released new guidelines on October 14, 1980. Henceforth, dispensations would be granted only to priests who had surrendered their office years ago and thus no longer could abandon their current life situation but wished to reconcile with the Church and to priests who never should have been ordained (coerced into office or lacked sufficient psychological maturity to accept the celibacy vow). Additionally, dispensation now required extensive documentation and examination under oath in order to establish that the applicant met the criteria. The new guidelines also stressed that dispensation from celibacy did not constitute "a right which the Church must recognize indiscriminately as belonging to all its priests."[129] With the introduction of the new rules, dispensations from celibacy once again became rare. As a result, priests who were unhappy with their vow of celibacy either abandoned office without the blessing of the Church or opted to have secret sexual liaisons.

In the 1980s, women directly affected by the ban on celibacy added their voices to the debate. In April 1983, Anne Dördelmann-Lueg published an advertisement in the German Catholic journal *Publik Forum* for a solidarity group for women in intimate relationships with priests. The advertisement led to the founding of the Initiative Group for Women Affected by Celibacy (Initiativgruppe vom Zölibat betroffener Frauen). One year later, an association for married priests and their wives was founded in Germany—Vereinigung katholischer Priester und ihrer Frauen. Shortly thereafter, a series of books appeared in Germany detailing the celibacy debate from the perspective of the women in intimate relationships with priests and the children of these relationships.[130]

The emergence of this new voice in the debate coincided with growing discontent among young West German Catholic women with the Catholic Church. Many of these women resented the Church's teachings on sexuality, the inferior status assigned to women, and the role of the male celibate clergy in fostering these views. Vatican II had proclaimed women's equal status in the common priesthood, yet twenty years later few women held positions with decision-making power in the Church. Instead, their positions accentuated traditional female virtues—caretaking and household work. Influenced by the emancipatory rhetoric of religious and secular feminists and by new options in the secular sphere, many young Catholic women no longer accepted their exclusion from the decision-making bodies of the Church. For these women, the Church's preservation of a male celibate clergy fostered a negative valuation of female sexuality and by extension a pejorative assessment of women.[131]

By the early 1980s, this discontent led women to join the inner migration already taking place within the Church. This migration took two forms. Some Catholics, who disagreed with elements of the Church's teachings but did not wish to separate from the Church, created solidarity groups. These groups often focused on one issue, such as celibacy, liturgical reform, or women's ordination; all of them envisioned their protests as part of a larger grassroots effort to redefine the theology and structure of the Catholic Church. Paradoxically, Catholics involved in this form of inner migration became more engaged in religious life, while at the same time distancing themselves from the official Church. Other Catholics simply distanced themselves from the Church. They stopped attending mass and participating in Catholic organizations. Although they did not officially separate from the Church, the Church ceased to play a significant role in their lives.

This inner migration did not go unnoticed by the official Church. When it became apparent in the early 1980s that Catholic women were not immune to this trend, the German hierarchy became alarmed; Catholic women's loyalty could no longer be assumed. In response, the DBK attempted to work with the two largest West German Catholic women's organizations, the Katholische Frauengemeinschaft Deutschlands (kfd) and the Katholischer Deutscher Frauenbund (KDFB) to stem the tide.[132] However, the Vatican's refusal to change its position on celibacy, on issues of reproduction, and on women's ordination limited the efficacy of any efforts undertaken at the national or local level in West Germany.

. . .

In this chapter, we have seen how the celibacy debate began as a relatively small component of a larger concern among Church officials about the post-1945 shortage of priests. In the late 1960s and early 1970s, the issue of clerical celibacy took center stage, and an internal Catholic debate escalated into a public debate on the moral and structural authority of the Church. Via the media, Catholics and non-Catholics took an active role, and the Church became trapped in a public relations nightmare that further undermined its efforts to recruit new priests. The debate metamorphosed again in the early 1980s when Catholic women entered the fray. Influenced by new theological and secular conceptions of womanhood, Catholic women drew connections between the preservation of a male celibate priesthood and women's oppression in the Church and in German society. In this context, the debate on clerical celibacy became inextricably linked to women's exclusion from Church office, including the priesthood. However, not all Catholic women supported change. Conservative women's groups received the support of an increasingly conservative German episcopate, further alienating moderates and progressives. For conservative Catholics, the Church's theological understanding of earthly marriage and of the suprasexual marriage between Christ and the Church became the lynchpin of Catholic identity and Catholic politics. In closing, it is important to note that widespread, substantiated allegations of child abuse by clergy did not surface in the German Church until 2010. Consequently, the clerical celibacy debate in Germany played out very differently during this time period than in the United States, where charges of child abuse surfaced in the 1980s, reminding us that although the clerical celibacy debate was transnational in scope, its articulation had distinctly national features.

CHAPTER 2

Women's Ordination
Sacramental and Gendered Bodies

The issue of women's ordination cannot be understood in isolation from that of the male celibate priesthood and the symbolic nuptial relationship between the Church and Christ. The idea of the Church as a maternal body and the bride of Christ has always existed within Catholicism, and theologians trace its origins back to the Old and New Testaments.[1] However, in the late twentieth century, this nuptial relationship gained added significance when for the first time it became one of the primary rationales for excluding women from the priesthood.

In Catholicism, the nuptial relationship between the Church and Christ is seen as paralleling the marital relationship between a husband and wife; thus, the theory of sexual complementarity is also applied to this divine marriage. Sexual complementarity defines men and women as equal in their humanity but having gender-specific roles to fulfill in life based on their natural inclinations. According to this theory, motherhood and virginity demarcate woman's contribution to the Church as receptive, passive, and subordinate, whereas man's role is active and authoritative. As the German theologian Manfred Hauke explained in 1986, "The superiorities of men, to express things pointedly, lead to a position of authority, but the superiorities of women to a position of subordination."[2] Similarly, the Church as bride is subordinate to her bridegroom, Christ.

In 1976, the CDF applied the nuptial metaphor to the priesthood. The CDF argued that a woman could not serve as a priest, because she could not embody the relationship between Christ the bridegroom and his bride, the Church: "Christ is the Bridegroom; the Church his Bride, whom he loves because he has gained her by his blood and made her glorious, holy and without blemish, and henceforth he is inseparable from her.... That is why we can never ignore the fact that Christ is a man."[3] *Inter Insigniores* introduced a new and explicitly sexualized argument against women priests—one that described "the relationship between Christ and the Church in often floridly extravagant metaphors of sexuality and procreation."[4] Unlike previous arguments, it did not assume women's inherent inferiority.[5] In the 1980s, this new argument grew in popularity among opponents of women's ordination, and John Paul II employed nuptial symbolism to the exclusion of other symbolic representations of the Church in order to condemn women's ordination, as well as birth control, abortion, homosexuality, and NRTs.

This new inflection of the argument against female priests emerged because of growing pressure in the secular and religious spheres to recognize women's equality with men. As discussed in the preceding chapter, the post-1945 clerical shortage necessitated the laity's taking over many functions typically reserved for priests. Given the disproportionate representation of women in congregations, this lay ministry proved overwhelmingly female. As Catholic women gained greater responsibility, competency, and confidence in the secular and religious spheres, some challenged the Church's centuries-old gender divide advanced in the early twentieth century by eminent moral theologians such as Joseph Mausbach: "The existing association of woman with marriage and motherhood is a completely valid explanation of her humble, sum contribution to culture."[6]

Developments in other religious communities also placed pressure on the Catholic Church to change its teachings on ordination. In 1958, the General Synod of the Swedish Lutheran Church allowed women to serve as pastors;[7] that same year some member churches of the EKD in Germany endorsed ordaining women, so long as these women remained unmarried.[8] Within Christianity, attitudes toward women were gradually shifting under the dual influence of changing theological and secular conceptions of womanhood. Yet these early ordinations posed no serious issues for Rome. Unlike the Roman Catholic Church, the Eastern Orthodox Church, and the Anglican Communion, none of the aforementioned Protestant churches associated ministry with a claim to apostolic succession (a lineage dating back to Jesus's twelve apostles). Then, in 1975, the Anglican Church of Canada authorized the ordination of women, capturing the Catholic imagination: Did theological or biblical justifications, in fact, exist for excluding women from the apostolic priesthood? If the Anglican Church allowed women priests, might the Catholic Church also do so?[9]

That same year, twelve hundred Catholics gathered in Detroit, Michigan, for the Women's Ordination Conference (WOC), sponsored by Priests for Equality; the following year the WOC was established as a separate organization.[10] In Canada and the United States, the Catholic women's ordination movement grew rapidly in the 1970s, and by the early 1980s it had made some headway in Western Europe, including West Germany. The number of Anglican churches endorsing women's ordination also continued to multiply, despite the pressure Paul VI and John Paul II placed on the archbishop of Canterbury, the figurehead of the Anglican Communion. In 1985 the Church of England accepted women into the diaconate, and in 1992 it joined the ranks of those permitting women priests.[11]

The Catholic Church's resistance to the ordination of women, like its positions on celibacy, artificial contraception, abortion, and NRTs, intensified its isolation from other Christian communities. In its staunch defense of a gendered division of labor and the values associated with it, the Church's arguments in favor of a male celibate priesthood and against birth control, abortion, and reproductive technologies became increasingly entangled in the second half of the twentieth century. Against this backdrop, a theological and pastoral neoconservatism developed at the highest levels of the Church hierarchy that exacerbated tensions within the Church and polarized the Catholic lay community in West Germany and elsewhere.

Vatican II, the Priesthood, and Women in the Church

Long before John XXIII championed the dignity of women in his 1963 encyclical, *Pacem in Terris*, papal attitudes toward women had been changing.[12] Pius X (1903–1914) approved of women attending universities and engaging in some professional activities; Benedict XV (1914–1922) favored extending the vote to women.[13] Yet on the eve of Vatican II, canon law still viewed women as inferior to men. In addition to denying women the right to act as altar servers, readers, deacons, and priests,[14] Canon 133 required priests to avoid "women upon whom suspicion might fall."[15] Canon 702 stated that women could not be full members of religious orders. Canon 1262 required women to wear veils in church; it also specified that they "should dress modestly, especially when they approach the table of the Lord."[16] No corresponding admonishments existed for men.

For the Swiss Catholic lawyer Gertrud Heinzelmann, Vatican II represented an opportunity for the Church to abandon Thomist teachings and introduce full equality for women. On May 23, 1962, she submitted a petition to the Preparatory Commission of the Second Vatican Council: "I want this petition to point an accusing finger as it were, for half of mankind, the feminine half which has been oppressed for thousands of years. By its wrong concept of women the Church has aided and abetted in this oppression, and it still does, in a way that grievously offends the Christian conscience."[17] Heinzelmann attacked the Church's continued reliance on "antiquated Thomist opinions" that represented "a slur on the value and dignity of half of mankind and a sore wound to their spiritual dignity."[18] She argued that although some contemporary theologians endeavored "to interpret women in a different light," these efforts remained inconsequential so long as they continued to be "repudiated by clearly contrary formal pronouncements."[19] She then reasoned that if the Church must cling to Thomist doctrine, it should heed Aquinas's assertion that women also possessed a rational soul and could be baptized in the Church. Aquinas acknowledged that "man and woman receive Baptism in the same way" and that "the effect of Baptism is the same in both."[20] For Heinzelmann, this acknowledgment demonstrated that Thomist principles did not support denying women admission to the priesthood: "The opposite conclusion should have been reached from the Thomist doctrine on the faculties of the human soul and the sacramental character. For the sacramental has its seat in the faculty of knowing and this faculty is in woman in the same way as in man, inherent in the incorporeal reason."[21]

The council fathers received petitions from three other German women, all academically trained in theology, advocating women's ordination—one submitted jointly by Ida Raming and Iris Müller and one from Josefa Theresia Münch. Raming and Müller opened their petition by enumerating eight typical arguments against women's ordination: (1) In the order of creation, woman was subordinate to man. (2) The essential qualities of womanhood (passivity and receptivity) disqualified her. (3) Christ appeared on earth as a man. (4) Christ chose only men as apostles. (5) The apostle Paul admonished women to remain silent in the Church. (6) The mother of Jesus was never recognized as an apostle. (7) Women's ordination would disturb the sexual polarity of the sacramental space. (8) It would violate Church tradition.[22] In their rebuttal, they focused on the argument that Christ came into the world as a man. They argued that Christ's maleness was not the essential dimension of his incarnation: "The sexual component is irrelevant, since the male gender of Christ does not make Christ a Redeemer, only his incarnation as a human being."[23] Since Christ's redemptory power is not determined by his male gender, the essential semblance between priest and Christ is not maleness but rather the "grace-filled personality of a human being."[24] In contrast, in her petition, Münch underscored the devastating impact of the clerical shortage on Catholic communities. In fact, her petition was prompted by news of Heinzelmann's emphasis on gender equality, which she feared would do more damage than good: "Up to now I had been afraid that an un-polemic, theological, pastoral justification for the ordination of women would only unleash increased resistance among the competent circles in Rome; now I tried to imagine how much more vehement a resistance would be provoked if the question were approached from the aspect of women's rights as in the Council contribution of this Swiss lawyer."[25]

Münch also gained notoriety for asking Auxiliary Bishop Walther Kampe of Limburg, Germany, at the first conciliar press conference for German-speaking journalists if women would also be invited to the council. Kampe responded, "Perhaps to the Third Vatican Council!"[26] According to Münch, "roaring laughter like applause to a successful joke" greeted his response, and Ferdinand Örtel explained to readers of the German Catholic journal *Feuerreiter*, "Many of the journalists are not Catholics and so ask questions that Catholics take for granted."[27] As Münch noted wryly in 1991, it seemed "the writer could not imagine that such a question could stem from the mouth of a Catholic theologian who knew very well, and regretted very much, that no women had been invited."[28] But once the issue of women's place in the Church had been broached, Church officials proved unable to silence discussions.

In 1964, Heinzelmann published the edited volume *Wir schweigen nicht länger!* (We won't keep silent any longer!), which included the three conciliar petitions advocating women's ordination, as well as essays by the American feminist theologian Mary Daly and the American Catholic philosopher Rosemary Lauer. The book also reprinted the resolutions of the St. Joan's International Alliance from 1963 and 1964 advocating women's equal participation in all Church spheres. The book sparked a heated reaction from *L'Osservatore Romano*, which published a four-part series defending the male-only priesthood by Italian theologian Gino Concetti. Concetti's defense emphasized Church tradition and implied that the book's authors were guilty of heresy: "The Rubicon, the insurmountable wall, has its origins in Christ. Not without reason have the fathers on the authority of St. Ephanius, St. Ambrosius, St. Augustinus, and St. Irenaeus specified as heresy the doctrine whereby women are granted priestly authority."[29]

But *L'Osservatore Romano* had overreacted to what it described as the "blossoming" tendency since Vatican II to recognize women as capable of priestly authority.[30] In 1964, most Catholic women did not support women's ordination; in fact, they were largely uninterested in the topic. Of the

106 West German Catholic women who responded to *Frau und Mutter*'s invitation to express their hopes for Vatican II, not one referenced women's ordination. Instead, the reforms that they wanted included removing the ban on married couples' use of artificial contraception; allowing divorced and remarried persons to participate in Communion; and introducing the vernacular mass. They also voiced their preference for more ecumenical dialogue and a new understanding of confession—one that emphasized forgiveness rather than guilt. A few readers mentioned that they wanted the Church to abandon its teaching that stillborn children went to hell because they had not been baptized.[31] The Austrian journal *Wort und Wahrheit* also surveyed readers about expectations for the upcoming council. Of the eighty-one respondents, only five were women. Ida Friederike Görres, the Church historian, argued against the council addressing the woman question. Three female respondents did not mention it and only one proposed a partial revision of Thomist teachings on women.[32]

In short, the council fathers faced no serious pressure from mainstream Catholic women's groups to discuss women's ordination, and the topic was never broached at Vatican II, although Archbishop Paul J. Hallinan of Atlanta, Georgia, filed a written opinion with the council's General Secretariat recommending that women be allowed to serve as readers and acolytes and, after appropriate instruction, as ordained deacons.[33] However, the other American bishops did not support his motion, and it was never read in the aula. Thus, most council fathers were unaware of its existence.[34]

Yet Vatican II did introduce three theological innovations that would inform subsequent debates on women's ordination. First, Article 29 of *Gaudium et Spes* disavowed all forms of discrimination in church and society, including discrimination based on gender.[35] Thus, woman's exclusion from Church offices could no longer be justified by the claim of female inferiority; a new rationale would have to be found. Second, although no conciliar document mentioned minor orders, the new accent on lay participation in the liturgy, introduced at Vatican II, suggested that minor orders had no place in the Church's future. The Council of Trent had recognized three major orders (priest, deacon, and subdeacon) and four minor orders (porter, acolyte, exorcist, and lector).[36] The 1917 Code of Canon Law restricted minor orders to candidates for the priesthood.[37] In 1972, Paul VI abolished minor orders, noting that the Constitution on the Sacred Liturgy had made them "obsolete" because it clearly demonstrated that baptism gave laypersons the right to participate in liturgical celebrations. In lieu of minor orders, Paul VI established two ministries—acolyte and lector; he opened these new ministries to laymen, but not laywomen.[38] Since the new offices did not require ordination, women's exclusion seemed theologically unjustified and exposed the Church to charges of misogyny. Third, Article 29 of *Lumen Gentium* reinstated the permanent diaconate to which married men could be admitted. As discussed in the preceding chapter, the coexistence of two diaconates (one for married and one for unmarried men) fueled the post–Vatican II celibacy debate. It also had implications for the women's ordination debate. If the diaconate no longer constituted a stepping-stone to the priesthood, why not ordain women as deacons, even if the priesthood remained restricted to them? The Bible and early Church documents contained multiple references to female deacons. Unlike the priesthood, the ordination of female deacons had a potential historical precedent.[39] By encouraging lay participation in the liturgy, introducing a more positive valuation of women, and opening the diaconate to married men, Vatican II had created the foundation for a reevaluation of women's roles in the Church.

Inspired by Vatican II, mainstream West German Catholic women's organizations cautiously pursued the offices of deacon, altar server, and lector as options for women wanting a more active role in ministry. Marianne Dirks, president of the kfd, noted in 1967 that the council fathers no longer limited women "to the sphere of caritas and welfare and to their maternal role as in countless earlier ecclesial official statements, but accepted and called for them in the entire scope of human and spiritual competencies."[40] Although canon law still excluded women from these offices, many Catholics believed that the Pontifical Commission for the Revision of Canon Law, charged with updating the code in light of conciliar principles, would lift some or all of these restrictions. In 1967, the kfd leader Hildegard Harmsen opined, "Since no theological reasons exist for excluding women from the priesthood, a legal action that allowed for women's ordination as deacons should be considered so as to realize the repeatedly underscored 'equality' found in conciliar decrees."[41]

The new Code of Canon Law, however, did not materialize until January 1983. For Catholics who wanted the Church to open more offices to women, the new code was a disappointment. The restriction against women being officially installed as lectors or acolytes remained intact, although it allowed for "the temporary deputation" of women if no qualified male was available.[42] The diaconate also remained closed to women. Admittedly, the new code employed more gender-neutral language and did not explicitly ban female altar servers.⁴³ But in the twenty years that had elapsed since the commission's establishment, Catholic women's expectations had changed and many viewed these revisions as merely cosmetic.

Reconceptualizing Catholic Womanhood in West Germany

Until 1968, the kfd had been known as the Central Association of Catholic Communities of Women and Mothers (Zentralverband der katholischen Frauen- und Müttergemeinschaften). Yet as early as the 1950s, the kfd president, Marianne Dirks, recognized that the organization's name posed problems: "They [young women] will not join our communities if they are named mothers' associations."⁴⁴ In making this statement, Dirks was not disavowing motherhood as central to women's identity. In fact, as late as 1960, she equated women's ministry in the Church with motherhood: "For every obedient service of the woman amounts to her saying yes to her innermost calling—motherhood."⁴⁵ Like those of most West German Catholic women, Marianne Dirks's views on gender evolved slowly—influenced by Vatican II, subsequent theological innovations, and changes in mainstream society.

By 1967, Dirks no longer accepted the well-worn Catholic image of the "eternal woman" as self-sacrificing wife and mother: "We know today that much of what seemingly belonged to the essential being of woman—greater capacity for sacrifice and lesser ability for abstraction—is historically determined on the basis of necessary accommodation and conventional definition, and it can and has changed in various cultures."⁴⁶ After Vatican II, Dirks championed a collaborative partnership between women and priests, asserting that the time when priests acted authoritatively in the name of a women's organization had passed.⁴⁷ However, she did not support council petitions advocating women's ordination.⁴⁸

Leaders of mainstream West German Catholic women's organizations such as Dirks rejected the petitioners' approach to improving women's position in the Church. Heinzelmann, Müller, and Raming believed that female equality in the Church required women's admission to the priesthood and rejected any compromise solution. In *Die getrennten Schwester*, published in 1966, Heinzelmann described women's ordination as "the litmus test" through which "the sincerity of council statements about the equality of humans in Christ had to be proved."⁴⁹ In the same publication, Heinzelmann expressed frustration with mainstream Catholic women's organizations, attributing their failure to support women's ordination to an absence of the "psychical preconditions" for resisting the "traditional orientation to subordination and obedience."[50]

In contrast, kfd leaders advocated an incremental approach to reform, believing it unwise to pressure German bishops and priests, because they were ill prepared for the "upsurge of women" (*Frauenaufschwung*) sparked by Vatican II. As Dirks explained, "The fact is, as a woman, one cannot escape the impression that some priests cannot see us impartially as human beings, but only as female beings who could be dangerous to them."[51] Given this clerical mentality, Dirks contended that the tactics of Heinzelmann, Raming, and their followers were counterproductive, because they generated a clerical "allergic reaction" to the "woman question."[52]

Dirks had experienced this "allergic reaction" firsthand in 1967 when she wrote the chair of the DBK, Julius Cardinal Döpfner, concerning a female diaconate. His negative reaction surprised Dirks.[53] In 1966, Döpfner had supported the resolution of the European Congress of the Lay Apostolate, in which Dirks took part, asking the pope to approve the use of artificial contraception by married couples.[54] Yet in 1967, Döpfner's willingness to embrace reform did not include an acceptance of a female diaconate. In two letters to Hildegard Harmsen, Dirks reconstructed her exchange with Döpfner, who reacted to the topic "as if it were a thorn in his flesh."[55] Despite this negative reaction, Harmsen believed that the kfd should officially broach the topic with the DBK, as the conservative Catholic leaders with whom she had spoken had expressed no strong objections, though most had given the topic little thought.[56] However, neither woman considered the creation of a female diaconate the most pressing issue for women in the Church. Dirks explained, "In my view, the call for a female diaconate is somewhat forced; admittedly we must make our position fundamentally clear and we have done that."[57]

This tentative dialogue with the German hierarchy made significant advances at the Würzburg Synod, when Subcommission VII—the same subcommission handling the topics of clerical celibacy and *viri probati*—included the creation of a female diaconate on its agenda. Upon hearing the news, a Catholic career woman wrote the chair of the subcommission, Bishop Tenhumberg, highlighting the topic's significance for the future of the Church: "First I want to express my joy that this topic is being addressed; it was so disappointing when the survey did not mention it. This theme is of great importance to the Church today, because the Church's credibility before the world depends upon it. In a world in which equality has by no means been realized, should not the Church lead by example? ... I know of no cogent reason to refuse women the priestly office."[58] Tenhumberg dismissed the topic of female priests as impractical; however, in his response, he supported a female diaconate: "I believe that your concerns are well represented—that is, to secure for women their due place in the Church. However, the issue of ordaining women as priests is still so theologically unclear that on this matter any practical decision can hardly be expected. However, it seems to me that accepting women as deacons is a very real possibility."[59] The DBK had revised its position since Döpfner's 1967 exchange with Marianne Dirks.

The Würzburg Synod's final report described the creation of a female diaconate as "one of the most controversial" issues discussed, since "dogmatic and historical-dogmatic issues" were at stake.[60] Three theological experts had been consulted—Professor Yves Congar of France and Professors Peter Hünermann and Herbert Vorgrimler of West Germany. All three experts had supported the creation of a female diaconate. According to the report, two issues dominated discussions at the synod. The first was whether a historical precedent existed for a female diaconate and, if so, whether female deacons in the early Church took the same vows as their male counterparts. The subcommission concluded that the New Testament in conjunction with early Church documents such as the *Didascalia* provided sufficient evidence that a female diaconate constituted a common practice in the early Church;[61] moreover, until the medieval era, the ordinations of male and female candidates had the same character. The second major issue, which the report mentioned, concerned the expedience of creating a female diaconate. Would reinstating a female diaconate enrich the life of the Church? Synodal delegates agreed that the continued exclusion of women from the diaconate did not serve the Church's best interests and called on the pope to accept women as deacons.[62]

Interestingly, the final report did not mention two themes that permeated Subcommission VII's discussions of the female diaconate: the "crisis in the priestly career"[63] and the fear that theologically trained women would settle for nothing less than the priesthood. As noted in Chapter 1, members of the subcommission reviewed multiple documents detailing the growing severity of the clerical shortage in the post-1945 era (see Appendixes C and F). In 1946, the German bishops had opened the study of theology to laymen and laywomen because there were not enough priests to provide religious instruction in the schools. By 1950, women constituted 20 percent of

Catholic theological students at the University of Münster; in the 1960s, women's presence in West German Catholic theological faculties continued to grow, so that by 1983, women constituted 40 percent of the student body at the Faculty for Catholic Theology at the University of Münster.[64]

The increase in lay theologians, particularly female theologians, alarmed some clergy members serving on the subcommission, and this fear found expression in discussions about creating a female diaconate. Klaus Fritz, a priest and secondary school instructor, predicted that if the Church did not find opportunities to engage lay theologians in the ministry, "intentionally or unintentionally" these theologians would "incite anti-Church sentiments." Bishop Tenhumberg reported that in the Diocese of Münster, lay theological students (male and female) were advised to pursue a second field in addition to their religious studies. In response, Theresia Hauser, leader of the Arbeitsgemeinschaft Frauenseelsorge in Bavaria, demanded to know "why the Church feared the collaboration of academically trained women in pastoral service," and Barbara Albrecht asserted that employing women as pastoral assistants was not an acceptable alternative to ordaining women as deacons.[65]

Although the women serving on Subcommission VII refused to compromise on a female diaconate, they chose not to broach the topic of ordaining women priests. Barbara Bredlow underscored this point in a letter to Bishop Klaus Hemmerle: "In my opinion, with the exception of the priestly ministry, there is no pastoral duty that the woman could not perform. . . . As far as the priesthood, I have deliberately omitted this topic, because I believe the time is not ripe."[66] Like the kfd leadership, female participants at the synod were sensitive to the possibility of a clerical backlash. They acknowledged that the diaconate was no substitute for the priesthood and that "Church governance theologically could not be separated from priestly ordination"—a point insisted on by their male colleagues.[67]

But the cautious approach of mainstream Catholic female leaders did not change the fact that a growing number of West German Catholic women questioned women's exclusion from the priesthood. In 1973, the KDFB, the second-largest Catholic women's association, surveyed its members on women's roles in church and society and published a synopsis of "representative responses" in its magazine, *Die christliche Frau*.[68] On the question of women's ordination, the editors claimed that young and middle-age members criticized the taboo nature of the topic and challenged the theological justification for excluding women from the priesthood. For example, they quoted one young woman as follows: "The rationale, namely that Christ called no women as apostles, is not substantive. He did not come to change historical conditions."[69]

However, the results of this survey should not be exaggerated; the editors provided no statistical data, so the actual percentage of young KDFB members who were dissatisfied with the Church's position on ordination remains unknown. Moreover, that same year, kfd members indicated their support for the papal ban on women's ordination in countless letters to *Frau und Mutter*, the kfd journal. One woman wrote, "It is serendipitous that Pope Paul VI clearly delineated in his decree that women should be excluded in perpetuity from the liturgical ministry." Another woman wrote, "Catholic women should stand behind the Holy Father; there are already enough opportunities for women to work in the Church." A third woman dismissed the idea of expanding women's ministries, asserting, "Today there is too much talk and not enough prayer."[70] The different perspectives of kfd and KDFB women can be explained in part by the divergent histories of the two organizations. Unlike the kfd, the KDFB promoted the participation of married and unmarried women from its inception; founded in 1903, it supported the liberal and socialist concepts of the secular women's movement of that era, and its early programs mirrored that commitment. Traditionally, the KDFB drew its members from the ranks of the educated bourgeoisie, while kfd members came from the petty bourgeoisie.[71]

But slowly Catholic women from all social strata were beginning to reconceptualize womanhood and their relationship with the Church. Change was incremental, however, and West German Catholic women's organizations lagged far behind their North American counterparts. Although German-speaking women had voiced their dissatisfaction with women's exclusion from the priesthood as early as the 1920s, the epicenter of the women's ordination movement had shifted from Europe to North America by the 1970s.[72]

International Developments and German Reactions

The Würzburg Synod coincided with the 1971 World Bishops' Synod in Rome. The themes of this international synod were justice in the world and the priesthood. During discussions on justice in the world, Archbishop Flahiff of Winnipeg, speaking on behalf of the Canadian bishops, recommended establishing a commission to study women's role in the ministry: "Despite a centuries-old social tradition against the ministry of women in the Church, we are convinced that the signs of the times (and one of these is that women already perform many pastoral services with great success) strongly urge at least a study both of the present situation and of the possibilities for the future."[73] The Third World Congress of the Lay Apostolate in 1968 and the Dutch National Pastoral Council in 1969 had made similar appeals.[74] With pressure mounting on Rome to address women's position in the Church, Paul VI announced on May 3, 1972, the creation of the Papal Study Commission on Women in the Church and Society. The study commission had twenty-five members, thirteen of whom were women.[75] That same year, Paul VI granted an audience to Betty Friedan, author of *The Feminine Mystique* and former president of the National Organization for Women.[76]

Friedan had requested an audience with the pope, believing despite some "implacable die-hard statements issuing from the Pope" that the creation of the papal commission and Flahiff's remarks signaled a more positive valuation of women at the highest levels of the Church hierarchy. To her surprise, Paul VI agreed to meet with her.[77] At their meeting, Friedan presented the pope with a gift, a pendant, and told him: "This is the symbol of the women's movement—the sign of the female, in biology, crossed by the sign of absolute equality. As Your Holiness can see, when women are completely equal to men, it becomes a different kind of cross."[78] She told the pope that she hoped that the Catholic Church would become "a force for the liberation of women."[79] Through his interpreter, Paul VI responded, "We want you to know that it will not be a radical approach because the Church has always upheld the dignity of women."[80]

Paul VI and Betty Friedan, as representatives of the Catholic hierarchy and the American women's movement, respectively, had fundamentally different understandings of gender equality. The pope believed that the Church's esteem for the Virgin Mary constituted an avowal of women's dignity. Since Mary embodied the feminine essence, any discussion of equality had to stem from the emulation of Mary. On November 6, 1974, in response to the United Nations' designation of 1975 as "International Women's Year," Paul VI underscored how Mary defined the feminine sphere and equality:

> Equality can only be found in its essential foundation, which is the dignity of the human person, man and woman, in their filial relationship with God, of whom they are the visible image. But this does not exclude the distinction, in unity, and the specific contribution of woman to the full development of

society, according to her proper and personal vocation. . . . As we stated in our recent Exhortation *Marialis Cultus*, our age is called upon to verify and to "compare its anthropological ideas and the problems springing therefrom with the figure of the Virgin Mary as presented by the Gospel."[81]

For Paul VI, equality did not mean that men and women shared the same vocation. Women priests had no place in "the economy of the mystery of Christ and the Church," because the emulation of Mary defined women's role as virgin and mother.[82] Thus, shortly after establishing the study commission, Paul VI informed commission members that they were not to broach the topic of women priests, birth control, or abortion.[83]

Removing women's ordination from the study commission's agenda did not dampen Catholic interest in the topic, which was fueled in part by developments in the Anglican Communion. In 1974, many Catholic feminists attended the irregular ordination of eleven Episcopalian women in Philadelphia.[84] These ordinations inspired Catholic feminists and threatened to derail the ecumenical talks of the Anglican-Roman Catholic International Commission, established in 1969.[85] On July 9, 1975, Donald Coggan, archbishop of Canterbury, informed Paul VI of "the slow but steady growth of a consensus of opinion within the Anglican Communion, that there are no fundamental objections in principle to the ordination of women to the priesthood."[86] Paul VI replied by reiterating the Catholic position and warning that ordaining women jeopardized continued ecumenical dialogue between the two churches: "We must regretfully recognize that the new course taken by the Anglican Communion in admitting women to the ordained priesthood cannot fail to introduce into this dialogue an element of grave difficulty which those involved will have to take seriously into account."[87] But the number of Anglican churches ordaining women continued to grow, and the newly ordained women became regular speakers at Catholic feminist gatherings in the United States and Canada.[88]

In 1975, inspired by their Anglican sisters and by Bishop Flahiff's entreaty at the 1971 World Bishops' Synod, American Catholic feminists with the support of Priests for Equality held the first Catholic Women's Ordination Conference in Detroit, Michigan. The conference was a huge success, attracting more participants than could be accommodated; an estimated five hundred people had to be turned away. Of the twelve hundred participants, two-thirds belonged to religious communities.[89] Unlike nuns in West Germany, American nuns played a leading role in the Catholic feminist movement. Ida Raming, the founder of the first German group dedicated solely to women's ordination, attributed German nuns' noninvolvement in the ordination movement to two factors—differences in the education and indoctrination of North American and German nuns and the greater dependence of German female orders than their American and Canadian counterparts on male supervision. Whatever the explanation, Norbert Sommer, editor of the book *Nennt uns nicht Brüder! Frauen in der Kirche durchbrechen das Schweigen*, noted in 1983 that he could find only one German nun willing to contribute to his book, and *Der Spiegel* observed in 1984 that nuns dissatisfied with religious life in West Germany opted to resign rather than protest.[90]

But so-called new nuns in North America joined female lay theologians at the conference in calling for a renewed priestly ministry free of the corruption brought about by "two thousand years of patriarchal traditions."[91] Elisabeth Schüssler-Fiorenza, a West German lay theologian who moved to the United States after failing to secure an academic position in her homeland, spoke about the leadership roles exercised by women in the early Church as missionaries, prophets, evangelists, and apostles and claimed that the Church had systematically suppressed their history in order to exclude women from office.[92] Rosemary Radford Ruether emphasized the oppressive character of patriarchal symbolism: "Patriarchy not only pervades specific dictates about women, but also creates an entire symbolic edifice of reality that reflects the social hierarchy of male dominance and female submission."[93] Yet according to one witness, it was Sister Margaret Farley's plea that women pursue ordination "without bitterness," never abandoning the Church despite its failure to recognize woman's full humanity, that brought many participants to tears.[94] In 1976, the WOC was established as an independent entity (no longer under the auspices of Priests for Equality); it was the first Catholic organization dedicated soley to women's admission to the priesthood.[95]

The Vatican viewed the conference and developments in the Anglican Church with grave concern. However, the Church's worries did not end there. In 1976, news leaked that the Pontifical Bible Commission had concluded that biblical evidence did not suffice to settle "in a clear way and once and for all" the question of ordaining women.[96] The leak of the commission's findings exacerbated ecumenical and feminist pressures on Vatican authorities to provide theological justification for excluding women from the priesthood. Against this backdrop, Paul VI instructed the CDF to explain the Church's teachings on the male-only priesthood. On October 15, 1976, the CDF released *Inter Insigniores*, but the declaration proved anything but *Roma locuta, causa finita*. Instead, as Leonard Swidler noted in the introduction of the edited volume *Women Priests: A Catholic Commentary on the Vatican Declaration*, in which forty-four North American Catholic scholars offered scathing critiques of the declaration, *Inter Insigniores* had the opposite effect, stimulating discussion and attracting more individuals to the cause.[97] The German theologian Karl-Heinz Weger echoed this opinion in an article for the Swiss Catholic journal *Orientierung*.[98]

Inter Insigniores opened with an acknowledgment that the ordination of women within other Christian faiths posed ecumenical and internal problems for the Church, sparking demands for the Catholic Church to "modify her discipline."[99] These initiatives required the Church to "make her thinking known"—that "the Church, in fidelity to the example of the Lord, does not consider herself authorized to admit women to priestly ordination."[100] The primary rationale was that women were incapable of acting in the person and role of Christ, because they did not resemble Jesus in his maleness. The CDF supported this assertion by citing the constant tradition of the Church, Jesus's actions, the practices of the apostles, and the symbolic nuptial relationship between the Church and Christ.

Inter Insigniores asserted that with the exception of a "few heretical sects in the first centuries," the Church had never permitted women priests.[101] The document conceded that early Church fathers had been influenced by contemporary social prejudices against women; however, these prejudices "hardly had any influence on their pastoral activity, and still less on their spiritual direction."[102] Thus, the exclusion of women from the priesthood had been "willed by the Lord Jesus Christ and carefully maintained by the apostles."[103]

The CDF then turned its attention to the actions of Christ, specifically to the fact that Jesus chose no women as "part of the Twelve."[104] This choice, the CDF asserted, could not be dismissed as a concession to the customs of the time, since on other occasions Jesus had "deliberately and courageously" broken with those customs.[105] Although the document admitted that a "purely historical exegesis" could not by itself justify the all-male priesthood, it contended that there were "a number of convergent indications that make all the more remarkable the fact that Jesus did not entrust the apostolic charge to women."[106]

As convergent indications, the CDF cited the apostles' actions and nuptial symbolism in the New Testament. According to the CDF, the apostles, following Jesus's example, allowed women an active role in spreading the word of God. However, despite the important role "played by women on the day of Resurrection, their collaboration was not extended by Saint Paul to the official and public proclamation of the message, since this proclamation belongs exclusively to the apostolic mission."[107] The CDF concluded that although the Church possessed some power over the sacraments, in that it could modify a sacramental sign to accommodate "circumstances, times and places," it had no authority to alter the basic "substance" of a sacrament established by Jesus.[108]

The CDF next extended the nuptial metaphor to the ministry, arguing that the nuptial relationship defined human identity, salvation, and the life of the Church: "For the salvation offered by God to men and women, the union with him to which they are called—in short, the Covenant—took on, from the Old Testament Prophets onwards, the privileged form of a nuptial mystery. . . . It is through this Scriptural language, all interwoven with symbols, and which expresses and affects man and woman in their profound identity, that there is revealed the mystery of God and Christ, a mystery which of itself is unfathomable. . . . That is why we can never ignore the fact that Christ is a man."[109] In other words, the priest needed to be a biological copy of Christ, because "the Incarnation of the Word took place according to the male sex . . . and this fact . . . cannot be disassociated from the economy of salvation."[110] Although the CDF underscored that women's exclusion from the priesthood did not imply inferiority, it asserted that sexual differences exercised "an important influence, much deeper than, for example, ethnic differences; the latter of which do not affect the human person as intimately as the difference of sex, which is directly ordained both for the communion of the persons and for the generation of human beings."[111] The nuptial metaphor as used by the CDF established a gendered and hierarchical relationship between the different levels of the Church—Christ and Church at the top level of the bridegroom/bride hierarchy, followed by priest and laity, and finally man and woman.

Supporters and opponents of *Inter Insigniores* immediately mobilized their resources, and a flood of articles—pro and con—inundated the Catholic world. In January 1977, *L'Osservatore Romano* launched a five-part series by prominent theologians defending and expanding on the declaration's arguments, particularly its use of nuptial symbolism. In the opening article, the Italian theologian Raimondo Spiazzi praised the declaration for clarifying the relationship between the male priest and the community by elucidating the "nuptial mystery": "The declaration clarifies and completes this traditional doctrine, explaining that it is a question of a reflection of Christ as 'author of the covenant, bridegroom and head of the Church,' the eternal Word who, to carry out God's plan historically, became incarnate in our human nature according to the male sex, certainly not to affirm a natural superiority of man over woman, but raising to the summit of creation—where the mystery of incarnation is placed—the duality, complementarity, and correlativity of the sexes."[112] By recognizing the divinely sanctioned distinction between the sexes, a woman could advance herself "as a woman, and not according to other considerations."[113]

However, Hans Urs von Balthasar's article ultimately garnered the most attention because of his subsequent influence on John Paul II's theology of the body, in which nuptial symbolism played a prominent role.[114] Balthasar argued that the Church "must accept herself, as she was born." In his estimation, sexual difference reproduced the divine relationship between the Church and Christ: "The redemptive mystery 'Christ-Church' is the superabundant fulfillment of the mystery of creation between man and woman, as Paul affirms very forcefully, so that the fundamental mystery of creation is called 'great' precisely in view of its fulfillment in the mystery of redemption. . . . The natural sexual difference is charged, as difference, with a supernatural emphasis. . . . It is only from the indestructible difference between Christ and Church (prepared, but not yet incarnate in the difference between Yahweh and Israel) that there is reflected the decisive light about the real reciprocity between man and woman."[115] For Balthasar, reciprocity meant that woman represented the counterimage of man. Man, "as a sexual being, only represents what he is not and transmits what he does not actually possess, and so is, as described, at the same time more and less than himself; woman rests on herself," having nothing to represent that is not herself.[116] Although Balthasar exalted women because "in the virgin-mother Mary—is the privileged place where God can and wishes to be received in the world," he denied her ability to represent Christ, because she was incapable of transcending her gender.[117]

For opponents of *Inter Insigniores*, Plato's admonishment that a "man should above all be on guard against resemblances" seemed apropos.[118] In the German-speaking world, the Swiss Jesuit Albert Ebneter underscored the contradictions and dangers embedded in the gendered "acrobatics" of *Inter Insigniores*: "When for example it is stated in the text that Christ was and remains a man, for many it makes no sense because then Christ 'represents' only a man in the Annunciation and in the sacraments. If it is then claimed that the priest also represents the Church, but the Church is depicted in the text and by the Church Fathers as 'bride' and 'mother,' then it requires a bit of conceptual acrobatics in order to show that nevertheless it is the man and not the women who represents the corresponding symbolic figure."[119] If women could not represent Christ, then Christ could not represent women; the salvation of half of humanity could no longer be assumed. Moreover, in arguing that the priest also represented the Church—that is, the "bride" and "mother" of Christ—the CDF effectively denied women any gender-specific role, since the male priest could embody both the female Church and the male Savior.[120]

In *Theologische Quartalschrift*, Hans Küng and Gerhard Lohfink employed a *reductio ad absurdum* argument: "Are we to think that only married and gainfully employed Jews (whenever possible fishermen from Lake Gennesaret) will now be considered for the office of priest or bishop in the Catholic Church?"[121] Karl Rahner also challenged claims that the male-only priesthood was divinely willed, stating the declaration had not proved "that the actual attitude of Jesus and the apostles in the strict sense of the word implies a norm of divine revelation."[122] Rahner also noted that "the declaration, despite papal approval, is not a definitive statement; it is fundamentally reformable; it can (which does not *a priori* mean 'must') be erroneous."[123]

In fact, the CDF declaration did not categorically ban women's ordination. As the biblical scholar Carroll Stuhlmueller pointed out, the declaration's language exhibited "a low profile of authority."[124] For example, it admitted that "classical theology scarcely touched upon" the topic and thus "the current argumentation runs the risk of neglecting essential elements."[125] The declaration's hesitancy reflected the newness of the challenge: "The Church's tradition in the matter has thus been so firm in the course of the centuries that the Magisterium has not felt the need to intervene in order to formulate a principle which was not attacked, or to defend a law which was not challenged."[126] For the moment, continued discussion and loyal dissent remained open to Catholics.

Growing Unrest: Mainstream and Alternative Catholic Women's Organizations

In 1963, Gertrud Heinzelmann predicted that when modern Catholic women finally grasped the Church's official teachings on womanhood, this knowledge would have "a disenchanting effect" on their attitude toward the Church.[127] By 1979, Heinzelmann's 1963 prediction appeared to have become a reality.

Mainstream Catholic Organizations: Expanding Women's Sphere

In May 1979, the kfd approved a new "Orientation and Work Program," which provided guidelines for the organization's future mission based on the "identified situation." This situation included the growing disillusionment of many women and youth with the Catholic faith: "Approximately sixty percent of Catholic women attend mass irregularly or not even at all. Faith and the Church for some women [are] of so little importance to their life that they look upon [them] with indifference."[128] Bishop Wilhelm Kempf of Limburg lamented in his 1981 Lenten letter that the Church had already lost workers and soon would lose women if it did not find new ways to include them in Church ministry.[129] The West German bishops had supported the creation of a female diaconate in 1975, but the pope had refused to heed this recommendation.

In 1980, the German bishops faced a crisis when the CDWDS declared that "women are not permitted to act as altar servers."[130] For years, girls had acted as altar servers in West Germany. The congregation's 1980 announcement shocked and angered many West German Catholics, particularly because Vatican officials gave no reason for the exclusion. Thus, many saw it as an arbitrary assertion of patriarchal authority. This time, letters to the editor indicated that kfd members overwhelmingly disapproved of the Vatican's actions. One woman wrote to *Frau und Mutter*, "Once again, the affected are women, and this time even girls. Women and girls have reacted with consternation, bewilderment, and yes, even desperation."[131] A second woman demanded resistance: "Should women give up? We say no! We finally live in the twentieth century, and we want to be accepted as full-fledged human beings."[132] Another woman recommended a boycott: "How much time, work, and money have we women given to the Church? Why don't we withdraw for a year from all ministries and also from Church services? Then, the bishops would have to become very respectful and concrete!"[133] Passive acceptance was slowly giving away to active resistance among German Catholic women.

The kfd leadership launched a petition drive against the ban on altar girls. At the 1980 Catholic Congress, they collected more than twenty-four hundred signatures, including those of prominent Catholic politicians and leaders, such as Irmgard Karwartzki (CDU) and Rita Weschbüsch (CDU), and the president of ZdK, Dr. Hans Maier. International visitors to the congress also signed the petition. The kfd wrote the chair of DBK, Joseph Cardinal Höffner:

> We ask you urgently and sincerely not to stop the positive, lively development of women's collaboration in the liturgy, including girls as altar servers. We cannot understand why the Church would characterize the participation of faithful, qualified, and engaged women in the liturgical space as dangerous for the Church. In fact, we see a real danger in the coming generations if the Church does not give clear signs of abandoning its rejection of women's participation in the Liturgy and from other duties in the Church. As such a sign, we ask you, venerable Cardinal, to take this matter up with the standing council and the complete assembly of the German Bishops' Conference.[134]

Yet in demanding action, kfd leaders made no reference to feminist theology.

Feminist theology was conspicuously absent from the pages of *Frau und Mutter* in the early 1980s. For one reader, this absence was unconscionable: "Why are the works of female Catholic theologians missing from Church publications? Women's dissatisfaction with the Church is mushrooming into a much-lamented silent exodus. Why do we withhold the truth about what feminist theologians are saying?"[135] Members of the kfd who wanted to know what Catholic feminist theologians were saying about the Church had to turn to sources other than the kfd member magazine—for example, liberal Catholic theological journals like *Stimmen der Zeit*, *Concilium*, and *Orientierung*, ecumenical feminist journals like *Schlangenbrut* (established in 1983), or even secular publications like *Stern*, *Der Spiegel*, and *Emma*. In these publications, they could find scathing critiques of the Church's oppression of women. For example, during the altar girl controversy, the West German feminist theologian Hildegard Lüning wrote in *Orientierung*: "Silent, listening, obeying—so three generations of Catholic women closest to me exercised a subordinate role in church, family and society.... What is willed by God has been determined by men. Only they do theology; they determine our life in the Church: men at the altar; women in the pews; men in the episcopate; women governed; men in teaching posts; women instructed; men in the leadership of diaconal work and caritas; women in the care of the sick and disabled. This gender division of roles we women in the Church have endured."[136] Such critiques rarely appeared in mainstream Catholic women's journals. Most Catholic women's organizations still distrusted feminism, painstakingly distinguishing their reform efforts from those of religious feminists. In a 1987 letter to the kfd president, the Kreis katholischer Frauen in Heliandbund underscored the need to differentiate between the kfd's "legitimate concerns" and the "ideological aims" of religious feminists.[137] Leaders of the kfd also worried that rapprochement with feminist circles might alienate their more conservative members. Despite widespread support for the altar girl petition, many kfd members resented the organization's new orientation: "I find the emancipatory carrying-on about the position of women in the Church just for the aggrandizement of women to be embarrassing.... I belong to the kfd and I herewith declare my separation."[138]

In the years after Vatican II, the West German Church had experienced a proliferation of small but vocal conservative Catholic groups: Una Voce Deutschland (1964), Traditionalisten-Bewegung (1965), Bewegung für Papst und Kirche (1969), Priesterbruderschaft St. Pius X (1970), Katholische Pfadfinderschaft Europas (1976), Marienkinder (1983), Medjugorje Deutschland (1988), and Jugend 2000 Deutschland (1998), to name only a few. These groups rejected most Vatican II reforms, stressed the adulation of Mary, and supported the Church's teachings on marriage and the priesthood.[139]

Still, most German Catholics, including women, did not endorse the views of these ultraconservative organizations; they supported the modernization of the Church, including a more active role for women in the ministry. Yet even liberal Catholics, such as the kfd member and CDU politician Hanna-Renate Laurien, believed that the battle for women's equality in the Church should not concentrate on the priesthood, because "the introduction of a priesthood of women would lead to a schism among Catholics."[140] Incremental change in the Church's position on women remained the strategy of mainstream, reform-minded Catholics.

The West German bishops were willing to entertain some changes; they realized that the Church could ill-afford to alienate its core constituency, women. With reference to the ban on female altar servers, Auxiliary Bishop Walther Kampe of Limburg wrote Cardinal Höffner, "In a time when the Church must wrestle so hard for the souls of women and make such concerted efforts to preserve women's loyalty to the Church, we should avoid anything that without good cause imposes a great burden on our ministry to women."[141] He proposed that the DBK petition the Vatican for a special provision to allow female altar servers: "Since the instruction unequivocally forbids altar girls, we should not attempt any sleight-of-hand interpretation."[142] Kampe noted that the use of female altar servers had become so commonplace that the ban was unenforceable in West Germany. Moreover, he believed that "the pastoral damage" caused by any attempt to enforce the ban "would be disproportionate to the weight of the matter," given that the position of altar server was no longer a stepping-stone to priesthood.[143] Fourteen years passed before the CDWDS granted conditional approval of female altar servers, but by then the mass exodus of young women from the Church had accelerated.[144]

In the early 1980s, however, the kfd had cause for optimism. On September 25, 1981, the DBK released *Zu Fragen der Stellung der Frau in Kirche und Gesellschaft* (On the question of the position of woman in Church and society)—a declaration that garnered widespread praise, including that of the SPD. Dr. Brunhilde Peters, a member of the executive board of the Study Group of Social Democratic Women (Arbeitsgemeinschaft sozialdemokratischer Frauen), noted that the German bishops demonstrated "a surprising level of understanding" about the daily challenges women faced.[145] In particular, Peters praised the bishops' call to end discrimination against women in the workplace and to provide more social assistance to single mothers. She contrasted the bishops' progressive position with that of the ZdK, which had denounced paid maternity leave as an "unfair disadvantage for housewives."[146] The kfd also praised the declaration, because it "did not block the path to a female diaconate and gave unprecedented recognition to women's freedom to shape their own lives."[147] They hoped that the declaration would result in the installation of more women as consultants on episcopal commissions.[148]

Three years later, hope had turned to disappointment. On December 19, 1984, the BDKJ reported in its member magazine that the 1975 request for the creation of a female diaconate by the Würzburg Synod remained unanswered by Rome.[149] That same year, the kfd called for another general synod, citing the failure to implement the Würzburg Synod decisions and the lack of any real progress toward including more women in decision-making bodies since the DBK had released *Zu Fragen der Stellung der Frau in Kirche und Gesellschaft*. In fact, the kfd complained that the Church had imposed more restrictions on women's service and noted that their representative with the DBK remained a male priest.[150] One frustrated woman wrote, "What Catholic men's association allows a woman to represent it?"[151] By 1987, the BDKJ regularly reprinted open letters and petitions addressed to the pope that voiced the hopes, fears, and disappointments of young people: "In the Church, old men determine young people's appropriate way of life. The Church dies because it offers no space for the young, for women, and for those who think differently.... We want a church in which the power structures and hierarchy are transparent, in which women have the opportunity for leadership offices, in which women are not third-class citizens (priests—men—women)."[152] The patience of reform-minded, mainstream Catholic women and youth was wearing thin. Whereas 60 percent of young women attended mass regularly in 1953, that number had dropped to 7 percent by 1985.[153] Yet feminism and women's ordination still faced an uphill battle in the West German Catholic Church.

German Catholic Feminism: Internal Strife and Limited Appeal

The first Catholic feminist theological study group in West Germany, Arbeitsgemeinschaft Feminismus und Kirche, was formed in 1981. Its stated aims included the study of feminist theology and the advancement of gender equality in the Catholic Church. But the topic of women's ordination proved unpopular with most German feminist theologians. Ida Raming, who had fought for women's ordination since the early 1960s and written her habilitation on the subject, wanted the new group to endorse the admission of women to the priesthood as one of its primary aims.[154] She argued that admission to the priesthood guaranteed women a voice in the decision-making bodies of the Church and thus the power to end women's legal discrimination under canon law. In contrast, Angelika Strotmann, Magdalene Bußmann, Cheryl Benard, and Edith Schlaffer reasoned that until fundamental changes were made in the structure of the Church, the danger existed that women would become complicit in patriarchal rule.[155] Raming denounced this form of "inner migration" in *Frauenbewegung und Kirche*, citing J. M. Potter, an American Catholic activist: "One does not change a system by remaining pure, clean and idealistic, safely criticizing from a distance, but by stepping in and rolling up one's sleeves and working and sharing and being."[156] Raming accused her opponents of using "unfair methods" to keep women's ordination off the group's program—a charge that Angelika Strotmann denied.[157]

Raming and her supporters split with the group; yet as Raming acknowledged, few West German Catholic feminists supported her position: "Since most female theologians in this work group rejected solidarity in the struggle for women's ordination ... ultimately there was no basis for [my] further collaboration."¹⁵⁸ In 1986, Raming and Iris Müller cofounded Maria von Magdala: Initiative Gleichberechtigung für Frauen in der Kirche, the first West German Catholic group dedicated to women's admission to the priesthood. On April 3, 1987, the two cofounders and six other Catholic women (Regina Bittner, Gertrud Tacke, Annegret Laakmann, Bärbel Sinnsbeck, Irmgard Jansen, and Hild Schmitt-Maercker) held the group's first meeting.¹⁵⁹ This meeting of eight women received substantial media coverage, including articles in the secular Hamburg newspaper *Die Zeit* and the liberal Catholic journal *Publik-Forum* and coverage on several television news broadcasts.¹⁶⁰ *Die Zeit* published an interview with the group's spokesperson, Gertrud Tacke, under the provocative title "Papst und Päpstin" (Pope and Pope Joan)—an allusion to the legend of a female pope who reigned briefly during the medieval era.¹⁶¹

Media coverage provided the small group with badly needed publicity, and its membership soon grew. Regional chapters were created, and in 1988 the group established ties with the United States–based woc. Still, the group found it difficult to garner support for women's ordination among West German Catholic women. Instead, many Catholic women continued to seek out spaces within the Church where they could meet and exchange ideas free from patriarchal interference. Alternatively, they became active in ecumenical feminist groups. Since ordination was not an issue for Protestant women, these groups devoted little time to the issue. Instead, they focused on topics of shared concern, such as the dominant representation of God as male and sexist liturgical language.¹⁶²

Ecumenical feminism, in turn, generated calls for a "women-church." The women-church movement began in the United States in 1983 as a feminist-oriented movement within Roman Catholicism that emphasized community over hierarchy.¹⁶³ Mary Hunt, one of the American founders, provided the following definition: "My definition of women-church is a global, ecumenical movement made up of local feminist communities.... They seek to change social structures and personal attitudes, to stop oppression."¹⁶⁴ In West Germany, the movement first appeared in the late 1980s and early 1990s.¹⁶⁵ Still, other German women, like their North American counterparts, opted for the Goddess movement, believing that the Christian churches were incapable of reform.¹⁶⁶ In short, a growing number of German Catholic women were seeking spiritual fulfillment outside the Church. As the DBK noted in its report for the 1987 World Synod of Bishops, "It is an obvious symptom of crisis when the percentage of West German women participating in Church life has decreased by half, as indicated by a survey conducted last year."[167]

A Church Divided

In October 1987, a total of 232 members of the Catholic hierarchy met for the World Synod of Bishops on the topic "Vocation and Mission of the Laity."[168] Only 64 laypersons attended; of those, 60 were nonvoting auditors. In his opening homily, the pope reminded the bishops that in addressing the mission of the laity, they were examining the Church's fundamental identity, particularly its post–Vatican II modern identity.[169]

Probing the Church's modern identity included tackling the woman question. The bishops introduced more than thirty proposals addressing women's role in the Church. Archbishop Rembert G. Weakland of the United States called on bishops to accept women as lectors, altar servers, and acolytes. He described this as the first step toward achieving full equality of the sexes in the Catholic Church. Weakland also proposed that decision-making and administrative positions at all levels be opened to women, including positions in the diaconate and high offices in the Curia and diplomatic corps.[170] Bishop Gerhard Schwenzer of Norway recommended that religious women be given "equal responsibility and decision-making" authority in the Curial Congregation for Institutes of Consecrated Life and Societies of Apostolic Life.[171] Yet the final report, *Christifideles Laici*, written by John Paul II at the request of the bishops, made no reference to these proposals.

Ostensibly, *Christifideles Laici* supported a more active role for women in the Church ministry. However, it offered no specific proposals for expanding women's role in the Church and reiterated the ban on women priests. Instead, it called attention to women's "often lowly and hidden work" that contributed to humanizing social relations.[172] For reform-minded Catholics, such as Irmgard Jalowy, president of kfd, the synod was "very disappointing."[173]

That same year, John Paul II released the apostolic letter *Mulieris Dignitatem* in response to the synod's call for "further study of the anthropological and theological bases" of the "dignity of being women and of being man."[174] Using Mariology and nuptial symbolism, *Mulieris Dignitatem* framed the feminine mystique, the indissolubility of marriage, the celibate male priesthood, and indirectly the Church's condemnation of homosexuality, artificial contraception, abortion, and NRTs as one cohesive argument. As noted by critics, supporters, and skeptics, *Mulieris Dignitatem* constituted the key document for understanding John Paul II's call for a new pro-life feminine theology—one that privileged the "feminine genius" as well as a gendered and hierarchical division of labor.[175]

Mulieris Dignitatem opened by asserting Mary's centrality to the Catholic faith: "A woman is to be found at the centre of this salvific event. The self-revelation of God, who is the inscrutable unity of the Trinity, is outlined in the Annunciation at Nazareth."[176] For John Paul II, Mary represented the "humanity which belongs to all human beings, both men and women," while at the same time modeling the archetypal ideal of women.[177] Mary, as the new Eve, was tainted neither by original sin nor by sexual intercourse and consequently embodied the feminine virtues to which women should aspire: "Mary means, in a sense, a going beyond the limit spoken of in the Book of Genesis (3:16) and a return to that 'beginning' in which one finds the 'woman' as she was intended to be in creation, and therefore in the eternal mind of God: in the bosom of the Most Holy Trinity. Mary is 'the new beginning' of the dignity and vocation of women, of each and every woman."[178] By emulating Mary, John Paul II asserted, women avoided the danger of "masculinization." In his estimation, any pursuit of equality that elided sexual difference threatened woman's "fulfillment" and "deform[ed]" her.[179] He defined the two essential dimensions of womanhood as virginity and motherhood, which achieved "their loftiest expression" in the mother of Jesus.[180]

Having established Mary's centrality to the Catholic faith and the importance of women emulating her, John Paul II turned to the interrelated themes of sexual complementarity and the spousal relationship: "*The woman is another 'I' in a common humanity.* From the very beginning they appear as a 'unity of the two,' and this signifies that the original solitude is overcome, the solitude in which man does not find 'a helper fit for him' (Gen 2:20)."[181] Woman is defined in relationship to man and man in relationship to woman; their subjugation is mutual, since the husband is now called upon also to obey his wife. Additionally, marriage is described as "an indispensable condition for the transmission of life." Thus, marriage and conjugal love are "by their nature ordered: 'Be fruitful and multiply, and fill the earth and subdue it' (Gen 1:28)." Although John Paul II did not explicitly reference artificial contraception, abortion, or reproductive technologies in *Mulieris Dignitatem*, this statement implied condemnation of all three. In fact, John Paul II cited *Mulieris Dignitatem* in his subsequent explicit condemnation of artificial contraception, abortion, and NRTS in *Evangelium Vitae* (1995), noting that their practice inflicted a mortal wound on the family and the dignity of woman.[182] Moreover, conservative theologians and "new feminists"[183] subsequently argued that implementing *Mulieris Dignitatem* required the unconditional renunciation of artificial contraception and reproductive technologies, since they compromised the sexual union of the spouses.[184]

John Paul II also utilized the emphasis on "the unity of the two" to affirm heteronormativity and a gendered division of labor. The complementarity of man and woman precluded homosexual relations, because communion with God was tied to the male–female spousal relationship: "Moreover, we read that man cannot exist 'alone' (cf. Gen 2:18); he can exist only as a 'unity of the two,' and therefore in relation to another human person. It is a question here of a mutual relationship: man to woman and woman to man. Being a person in the image and likeness of God thus also involves existing in a relationship, in relation to the other 'I.' This is a prelude to the definitive self-revelation of the Triune God: a living unity in the communion of the Father, Son and Holy Spirit."[185] Conjugal love between a man and a woman represented a physical reenactment of the unity of the two sexes as well as that of the divine Trinity.

But "unity of the two" did not mean abandoning the doctrine of sexual complementarity. Although John Paul II affirmed that "man and woman are human beings to an equal degree," the declaration contained multiple statements distinguishing between masculine and feminine biological and psychological traits.[186] For example, he argued that physical and spiritual motherhood complemented one another and defined woman's vocation: "And does not physical motherhood also have to be spiritual motherhood, in order to respond to the whole truth about the human being, who is a unity of body and spirit? Thus there exist many reasons in these two different paths—the two different vocations of women—a profound complementarity, and even a profound union with a person's being."[187]

Spiritual motherhood also accounted for the celibacy of priests and female members of religious orders: "In the teachings of Christ, motherhood is also connected with virginity, but also distinct from it." John Paul II noted that in the context of explaining to his disciples the indissolubility of marriage, Jesus took the opportunity to explain the "value of celibacy." Celibacy for the kingdom of heaven, John Paul II asserted, represented a free choice on the part of the individual as well as a grace bestowed on the individual by God. John Paul II granted that this understanding of celibacy applied equally to men and women choosing to live a consecrated life. However, he distinguished between the nature of celibacy as practiced by men and women. The celibacy of women, as a path to realizing womanhood, could be understood only with reference to Christian anthropology and the complementary spousal relationship: "At the same time they realize the personal value of their own femininity by becoming 'a sincere gift' for God who has revealed himself in Christ, a gift for Christ, the Redeemer of humanity and the Spouse of souls: a 'spousal' gift. One cannot correctly understand virginity—a woman's consecration in virginity—without referring to spousal love. It is through this kind of love that a person becomes a gift for the other. Moreover, a man's consecration in priestly celibacy or in the religious state is to be understood analogously."[188] Women's consecration in virginity was defined in terms of the woman's role as wife.

The same logic was used to exclude women from the priesthood: "The Bridegroom—the Son consubstantial with the Father as God—became the son of Mary; he became the 'son of man,' a true man, a male. *The symbol of the Bridegroom is masculine.*"[189] However, men could embody the symbolic role of bride: "In the Church every human being—male and female—is the 'Bride,' in that he or she accepts the gift of the love of Christ the Redeemer, and seeks to respond to it with the gift of his or her own person."[190]

For John Paul II, understanding the nuptial relationship between Church and Christ as well as between man and woman made clear the reasons for Christ's selection of twelve male apostles; it had not been the product of social constraints, but the expression of the gendered division of labor willed by God:

> Meditating on what the Gospels say about Christ's attitude toward women, we can conclude that as a man, a son of Israel, he revealed the dignity of the daughters of Abraham (cf. Lk 13:16), *the dignity belonging to women* from the very "beginning" on an equal footing with men. At the same time Christ emphasized the originality which distinguishes women from men, all the richness lavished upon women in the mystery of creation. Christ's attitude towards women serves as a model of what the Letter to the Ephesians expresses with the concept of "bridegroom." Precisely because Christ's divine love is the love of a Bridegroom, it is the model and pattern of all human love, men's love in particular. Against this broad background of the great mystery expressed in the spousal relationship between Church and Christ, it is possible to understand adequately the calling of the "Twelve."[191]

Mulieris Dignitatem received mixed reviews. The German Canadian theologian Gregory Baum noted in the international theological journal *Concilium* that John Paul II's hermeneutical approach to biblical texts led him to "interpretations that differ[ed] strikingly from the interpretations given by the Church Fathers and traditional teachings."[192] Baum applauded the letter's recognition that "God is father and mother, that generativity has no gender, and that according to God's creation the man–woman relationship is not patriarchal."[193] However, the letter also contained contradictory statements. For example, in equating feminine genius with motherhood and the emulation of Mary, John Paul II seemingly excluded women from participating in church or society "as thinkers, inventors, initiators, presiders, and leaders."[194] Moreover, it made femininity a characteristic shared by women and men, but masculinity a trait possessed only by men.

The German Japanese feminist theologian Elisabeth Gössmann cautioned that scripture did not support John Paul II's one-sided application of nuptial symbolism: "The text does not argue from a biological perspective for the maleness of Christ, though of course this is implied, but argues symbolically—without distinguishing between the historic Jesus and the risen Christ, whom Paul declared the head vis-à-vis the 'body of the Church,' making him, together with his followers, a symbolic collective person, where sexuality has no role. Here it is clear that symbols and allegories have no absolute validity, but can be reciprocally imposed and even excluded. An obstruction of the Church's developmental potential through a one-sided attachment to such a symbol consequently is extremely alarming."[195] Other West German women also questioned John Paul II's biblical exegesis. In an article for the KNA, Irene Willig noted: "The symbolic meaning of the twelve apostles is not taken into account. The apostolic twelve and office in the Church are not differentiated; a historically documented development (of office) is not noted. It does not consider that Jesus accepted into the Twelve no Gentiles or others affiliated with any group besides the Jewish community."[196] The women's ordination group Maria von Magdala rejected the pope's historical-exegetical arguments and described women's exclusion from the priesthood as "apartheid at the altar."[197]

The sharpest critiques of *Mulieris Dignitatem* came from theologians of the English-speaking world. Susan A. Ross contended that the nuptial relationship under John Paul II not only elided other symbolic representations of the Church, it had taken on new meanings that undermined gender equality and condemned homosexuality:

> The Church's "feminine character"—as well as that of women human beings—has come to be emphasized far more than it had been before women's ordination became contentious, and when other metaphors such as People of God, field of God, edifice of God, the sheepfold, etc., were used more frequently. The nuptial metaphor has been used frequently in the Christian spiritual and mystical tradition, and it has most often illustrated intimacy and love between partners. It has not, for the most part, served as a prescriptive model for gender roles.... But in the present, femininity no longer has the more fluid meaning that was associated with it in the medieval period. The nuptial metaphor is now defined consciously and purposefully to prescribe gender roles—particularly in relation to the hierarchy and male priesthood—and implicitly to proscribe homosexual relations.[198]

Tina Beattie claimed that this model for a gendered division of labor, which associated a myriad of gender identities with the male body but only one with the female body, constituted an act of violence against women, because "the female body has been effectively annihilated in the symbolic life of the Church."[199] She believed that the female body was eliminated from the suprasexual nuptial relationship between the Church and Christ "not in order to let man be man, but in order to let man be woman,"[200] because "the only 'man' in creation is the priest who vicariously represents the masculine divinity of Christ, while all other men are in fact 'women' and 'brides' in their humanity."[201] Therefore, woman constituted "a threat to man's wholeness and autonomy before God" and must be effaced.[202]

Meanwhile German Catholic feminists continued to struggle to find an audience within the largest Catholic women's organization—the kfd. As one letter to the editor from September 1988 made clear, most kfd members were older and found it difficult to follow the new theological arguments concerning women's place in the Church that had begun appearing in *Frau und Mutter*: "We would like to ask you with respect to the presentation and selection of topics not to forget older readers. The fact is that the majority of our membership is older, and in their youth, they did not receive the education necessary to follow these texts and read them with pleasure and interest." When in February 1989 the editorial staff of *Frau und Mutter* invited members to submit their views on *Mulieris Dignitatem*, roughly three-quarters of the responses sent to the central office supported the papal position on ordination. However, because many letters were group submissions, the exact percentages of supporters and opponents of the papal position cannot be determined.[203]

The letters indicated a generational divide within the organization. Older members lamented the current state of affairs in church and society: "Although the present-day era likes to be so modern and feminist, we must conform to God's commandments and cannot expect the pope (actually an attempt to force the pope to his knees) to give us an alibi or adapt to the *Zeitgeist*."[204] Another older member wrote: "Why would Catholic women fight for an office that Jesus allocated to men. . . . As modern women, we no longer take seriously our mission as guardians of life; we fail to see that in pursuing equality, we act against God and nature (the pill, abortion and unlimited sexual intercourse). . . . I feel that your association, of which I have been a member since 1954, no longer represents me as a Catholic woman."[205] In contrast, younger members often expressed frustration with women's continued exclusion from the priesthood: "I find it shameful, even degrading, that because of my sex I cannot receive one of the seven sacraments."[206] In 1993, a survey of women commissioned by the DBK indicated that 77 percent of young women felt that the Church did not understand the "concerns and problems of women today" (see Appendixes J and K).[207] The Catholic Church could no longer assume the acquiescence of its core constituency—women.

. . .

The women's ordination debate did not end with *Mulieris Dignitatem*. In 1992, the Church of England announced it would accept women as priests. As in 1976, the pope responded to developments in the Anglican Church by reiterating the Catholic Church's ban. *Sacerdotalis Ordinatio*, released in 1994 by John Paul II, offered no new theological arguments for women's exclusion from the priesthood; however, strategically, it differed significantly from *Inter Insigniores* (1976) and *Mulieris Dignitatem* (1988); it argued less from Christ's example and more from papal authority. The new approach had already been evident in the 1993 encyclical, *Veritatis Splendor*, in which the pope declared that the Church's teachings on morality could not be bent to accommodate modernity: "But the negative moral precepts, those prohibiting certain concrete actions or kinds of behaviour as intrinsically evil, do not allow for any legitimate exception. They do not leave room, in any morally acceptable way, for the 'creativity' of any contrary determination whatsoever."[208] *Veritatis Splendor* advised bishops to take "appropriate measures" against dissenters in order to safeguard the faithful against "every doctrine and theory" contrary to the Church's teachings.[209] With *Sacerdotalis Ordinatio*, John Paul II used the same tactic, declaring that women's exclusion from the priesthood constituted Church doctrine that must be "definitively held by all the Church's faithful."[210]

Like *Inter Insigniores*, *Sacerdotalis Ordinatio* only fueled the debate. As Thomas J. Reese noted in *Inside the Vatican*, Paul's attempt to end the discussion only succeeded in angering more women.[211] Feminists quickly mobilized resources, flooding Catholic publications with critiques of *Sacerdotalis Ordinatio*. But they were not alone; the Belgian Bishops' Commission on Women and the Church questioned whether male exclusivity in the priestly office was compatible with equality of the sexes: "Since the power of ordination and the power of government are tied to each other, a reference to Mary does not really help, because the central question is not who can represent which 'persona,' but why the whole power of government has to hang on the representative who acts 'in persona Christi.' Criticism is not only levelled at the fact that men are allowed to lead in the Church because they are physically men, but also at the fact that they are allowed to dominate because they are allowed to lead."[212] As criticism mounted, the CDF took the unprecedented step of issuing a *Responsum* declaring *Sacerdotalis Ordinatio* an infallible teaching: "This teaching requires definitive assent, since, founded on the written Word of God, and from the beginning constantly preserved and applied in the Tradition of the Church, it has been set forth infallibly by the ordinary and universal Magisterium."[213] The CDF statement sparked more controversy, even as the space for loyal opposition contracted.

Still, German opposition was growing. A 1992 Emnid survey commissioned by *Der Spiegel* showed that 70 percent of West Germans and 50 percent of Catholic churchgoers supported women priests (see Appendix M).[214] German rebellion did not go unnoticed by Vatican authorities. In 1999, John Paul II chastised the German Church for blurring the distinction between laity and clergy:

> In your land, there is growing discontent with the Church's attitude towards the role of women. . . . However, too little consideration is given to the difference between the human and civil rights of the person and his rights, duties and related functions in the Church. Precisely for this reason, some time ago, by virtue of my ministry of confirming the brethren, I recalled "that the Church has no authority whatsoever to confer priestly ordination on women and that this judgement is to be definitively held by all the Church's faithful."[215]

Three years later, the frustration of longtime supporters of ordination in Germany gave way to open rebellion. On June 29, 2002, an excommunicated

Catholic bishop ordained seven women from Germany, Austria, and the United States (Christine Mayr-Lumetzberger, Adelinde Theresia Roitinger, Gisela Forster, Iris Müller, Ida Raming, Pia Brunner, and Angela White) aboard a chartered boat on the Danube River near the German–Austrian border.[216]

The event generated banner headlines across the globe and polarized the Catholic women's ordination movement.[217] The WOC enthusiastically supported the women; however, Wir sind Kirche in Austria and Germany, the Initiativ Kirche von unten in Germany, and the New Wine movement in Great Britain distanced themselves from the illegal ordinations. The CDF excommunicated the women and the presiding bishop (for a second time), but the harsh punishments did not act as a deterrent; more illegal ordinations followed in Germany, the United States, and elsewhere.[218]

However, proponents of ordination were no closer to their goal than they had been in 1962, when Gertrud Heinzelmann submitted the first petition advocating women's ordination to the Second Vatican Council. Over the years, the Vatican position hardened, and stiff punishments were imposed for supporting ordination. In addition to the excommunication of women priests, disciplinary actions were taken against theologians who supported women's ordination. For example, Sister Carmel McEnroy, author of *Guests in Their Own Home*, was terminated as professor of systematic theology at St. Meinrad School of Theology in Indiana after signing a petition supporting women's ordination.[219]

Under John Paul II, complementarity of the sexes in human relations and in the Church's understanding of its relationship to Christ gained greater prominence in Church teachings. The allegorical-typological argument against women in the priesthood introduced in *Inter Insigniores* and expanded by John Paul II in *Mulieris Dignitatem* transformed gender from a physical category into a metaphysical and theological category that determined the divine and earthly order. As critics pointed out, the multivalence of nuptial symbolism as found in the Bible was eclipsed in the Church's efforts to defend its traditional teachings on the male-only priesthood and its understanding of human marriage on the basis of sexual complementarity and reproduction.

But with the passage of time, fewer Catholics found the argument convincing. They believed that the Church's teachings on the priesthood and on marriage violated principles of social justice, arguing that subordination necessarily implied a devaluation of the person. In contrast, papal supporters, such as the German theologian Manfred Hauke, argued that the feminist call for "undifferentiated access to every sort of task" led to "a death-dealing barbarism."[220] Feminism, he charged, "has, from the very start, promoted abortion . . . a more brutal form of 'domination of man by man'—the charge brought against patriarchy by feminist theology—can hardly be imagined."[221] The Catholic American journalist Donna Steichen claimed, "Whether or not any given feminist intends to serve the Prince of Lies, every progression more clearly reveals the cause itself as a demonic assault on God, on his creation, on the Church and on the family."[222] The line between the Church's ban on women's ordination and its condemnation of artificial contraception, abortion, and reproductive technologies became increasingly blurred, as conservatives and Vatican officials retrenched.

· PART II ·

The Catholic Church and Reproductive Politics

CHAPTER 3

Artificial Contraception
German Angst and Catholic Rebellion

Like mandatory celibacy for priests, contraception is an issue that has plagued the Church almost since its inception. However, on this matter, unlike celibacy, the official Church has never wavered in its position. At no time in its history has the Catholic Church taught that contraception is a good thing. However, the constancy of the Church's position does not mean that the rationale for this condemnation has always been the same or that there have not been significant revisions of the position over time.[1] In the second half of the twentieth century, the most significant shift in the Catholic position occurred in 1951 when Pius XII approved the rhythm method as a means of natural family planning. This change in the official Catholic stance reflected two theological developments: growing recognition of mutual love as a primary purpose of marriage and a new emphasis on responsible parenthood. It also suggested the Church's growing awareness of the altered realities of contemporary life—the increased cost of raising a family, the longer time required to educate children in technically advanced societies, and world population growth. But as we shall see, in endorsing natural family planning, Pius XII inadvertently opened the door to a religious and secular debate on the moral acceptability of artificial contraception in the 1960s.

In Western Europe in the 1950s, the Christian churches, particularly the Catholic Church, promoted a public discourse of sexual conservatism. In Austria, Belgium, France, Italy, the Netherlands, and West Germany, Christian political parties gained power; these parties promoted sexual conservatism as part of an effort to restore normalcy in war-torn Europe. The war and its immediate aftermath, as Dagmar Herzog noted in *Sexuality in Europe*, provided "the context in which millions of people had experienced premarital and extramarital sexuality, and crossed boundaries or experimented with relationships that might never have been possible in the more closely monitored and stable environments of peacetime towns."[2] Postwar Christian political leaders saw this sexual experimentation as indicative of the very secularization that had allowed fascism to gain a foothold in Europe. They utilized this interpretation of fascism to promote youth defense laws and to block the efforts of those who wanted to liberalize the laws governing sexuality (e.g., contraception and abortion). The onset of the Cold War gave conservative Christian political parties in the West an additional ideological advantage over their opponents. In promoting sexual conservatism and the restoration of traditional gender roles, they contrasted a re-Christianized and democratic West with a godless and Communist East. Communist and Social Democratic parties in the West had to tread lightly, lest they become associated with Stalinism in the mind of the public. As a result, most Social Democratic and Communist parties in 1950s Western Europe endorsed positions on gender and sexuality that did not differ significantly from those of their conservative opponents.[3] But controlling public discourse and legislating morality proved easier tasks for the Christian churches and their political allies than controlling Western European attitudes and behaviors, including those of the Christian faithful.

Among Catholics in West Germany and elsewhere in Europe, the mid-1950s witnessed growing public dissatisfaction with the Church's teachings on marriage and family. The initial relief experienced by Catholic married couples and their confessors following Pius XII's acceptance of the rhythm method in 1951 dissipated quickly. Many Catholics complained that the method was ineffective; others lamented that it took the spontaneity out of sexual intercourse. Still others questioned the distinction that the Church drew between natural and unnatural means of regulating fertility. By the early 1960s, some theologians and bishops also questioned the Church's stance on artificial contraception on theological grounds. This theological debate, in turn, emboldened an already disenchanted laity. Paul VI's attempt in 1968 to end this debate by reaffirming the Church's ban on artificial contraception provoked an unparalleled crisis of authority in the Catholic Church as laypersons, theologians, and even some bishops throughout Western Europe and the United States publicly criticized the encyclical.

In West Germany, mainstream Catholics rejected Paul VI's encyclical at the biennial Catholic Congress in September 1968 and demanded that the pope revise his position. *Humanae Vitae*'s negative reception marked the end of an era; no longer would West German Catholics unconditionally obey papal edicts. Like their non-Catholic counterparts, Catholics in late

1960s West Germany were rethinking their attitudes toward sexual morality and more generally their relationship to secular and religious authorities. In particular, German youth were demanding increased democratization of German society, and this call for greater democratization extended to the religious sphere. Unlike their elders, many German youths did not see Christianity as an antidote to fascism. Instead, they pointed to church leaders' complicity in the Nazi past. They also condemned the sexual conservatism promoted by the churches and legislated by the West German government under CDU-CSU leadership. Because Catholic politicians and religious leaders had played a dominant role in shaping the family/youth policy of the 1950s, against which protesters now directed their ire, the concurrent debate within the Catholic Church on artificial contraception attracted the attention of rebellious youth, the secular media, and the broader West German public.

German Catholic leaders were acutely aware that the Catholic faithful no longer lived in an insulated milieu. They knew that many Catholic couples practiced some form of family planning and that a reiteration of the ban would be ill received in Germany. Most German bishops supported revision, and when revision did not materialize, they issued the Königstein Declaration to ease tensions within the West German Catholic community. The declaration called for obedience to the pope, while also affirming spouses' right to make their own decision of conscience on artificial contraception. The declaration succeeded in diffusing tensions in the German Catholic Church and preserved the credibility of the German bishops with their lay congregants.

However, the Königstein Declaration also had negative consequences. The declaration set a precedent for so-called loyal disobedience, whereby Catholics acknowledged papal authority while opting to disregard certain nonfallible teachings. In the West German context, loyal disobedience increasingly characterized the lay response to many Church teachings that the laity deemed outdated. Moreover, as we have seen in the chapters on celibacy and women's ordination, German Catholics now expected their bishops to issue documents comparable to the Königstein Declaration on controversial topics such as clerical celibacy and women's position in the Church. When the German bishops did not or could not countermand Vatican teachings through such documents, the credibility that they had preserved with the Königstein Declaration was seriously compromised. Many reform-minded

German Catholics ceased to believe in the Church's ability to reform itself. Still other German Catholics redoubled their efforts to bring about desired reforms.

In the late 1970s and early 1980s, the birth control debate acquired a new dimension when new concepts of womanhood began permeating Catholic women's organizations. These new concepts came from religious feminist circles and the secular feminist movement. Mainstream West German Catholic women's organizations now perceived the Church's intransigence on artificial contraception as indicative of the Church's negative attitude toward women. They demanded that the Church recognize women's intrinsic worth rather than define women exclusively as wives and mothers. Additionally, some feminist theologians demanded women's admission to the priesthood. For these women, a Church ruled by celibate men was incapable of representing women's interests. When concrete changes failed to materialize despite the promulgation of multiple ecclesial documents proclaiming women's dignity, the West German Catholic Church experienced both an alarming drop in the number of women engaged in Church life and increased engagement by those women who stayed.

The interrelated debates on birth control and celibacy in the 1960s and early 1970s sparked a cascading series of crises that came to encompass among other things women's ordination, abortion, and NRTs. These new controversies, in turn, accelerated the dual processes of exodus from the Church and inner migration within the Church. This inner migration manifested itself not only as indifference to the Church, but also in the formation of subaltern communities with radically opposing and irreconcilable visions of the future of the Catholic Church. By the 1980s, reconciliation of these diverse views appeared unrealistic. The issue ceased to be one of reconciliation or compromise; instead, the focus shifted to the acceptable limits of dissent. By the beginning of the twenty-first century, many who believed the Church could be saved only through greater centralization of authority advocated a "smaller but purer Church."[4]

Natural Law, Marriage, and Contraception

On October 29, 1951, Pius XII introduced a significant modification of the Church's teachings on contraception. In an address to the Italian Catholic Society of Midwives, Pius XII became the first Roman authority to endorse the rhythm method as a means of controlling family size: "Serious motives may exist, such as those frequently mentioned in so-called medical, eugenic, economic, and social 'indications' that may exempt married couples from carrying out their positive and obligatory duty [to beget and rear children] for a long time or perhaps even for the duration of their marriage. From this it follows that the observance of natural sterile periods may be lawful, from the moral viewpoint: and it is lawful in the conditions mentioned."[5] One month later, in an address to the Congress of the Family Front and the Association of Large Families, Pius XII reaffirmed the rhythm method as a licit means of regulating births.[6]

Pius XII's endorsement of the rhythm method reflected two developments in the Catholic Church. First, Catholic authorities increasingly recognized that a real tension existed between the two primary purposes of marriage—procreation and the education of children. As the American Jesuit John Lynch explained in a 1963 address to the Catholic Theological Society, until Pius XII's allocution, Catholic authors failed to recognize the inadvisability of promoting large families for all Catholic couples: "This maxim is not universally applicable to each individual marriage; it obtains, in truth, only in circumstances wherein the decent raising of a large family is reasonably possible."[7] Providing an adequate education for children might require regulating the time between births. Second, as noted in Chapter 1, in the 1920s a growing number of Catholic philosophers and theologians, such as Dietrich von Hildebrand and Herbert Doms, were reconsidering the nature of the marital relationship in response to the emergence of a more companionate model of marriage in late-nineteenth-century Europe. Both Hildebrand and Doms rejected elements of the Augustinian/Thomist conception of marriage that had shaped Church teachings on marital morality for centuries.

Augustine of Hippo and Thomas Aquinas advanced a hierarchical and patriarchal conception of marriage in which the primary purpose was procreation. Neither Augustine nor Aquinas acknowledged a connection between marital love and marital intercourse.[8] With the emergence of a more companionate model of marriage, many Catholic laypersons and some theologians no longer accepted this view. In a 1925 lecture, Dietrich von Hildebrand, a professor of philosophy in Munich, rejected a strictly biological approach to marital sex. Sexual intercourse, he argued, had two primary purposes: procreation and the expression and fulfillment of marital love.[9] In his 1935 book, *Vom Sinn und Zweck der Ehe*, Herbert Doms discarded the language of primary and secondary purposes and redefined marital intercourse as an ontological act in which the spouses attained completion in their union with each other. He also shifted the frame in which marital sexual pleasure was understood; he no longer treated it as an animalistic drive that fueled procreation; instead, Doms saw sexual pleasure as reflective of the metaphysical change that occurred when the married couple found completion in one another.[10] Although Doms did not reject traditional gender roles, he seldom referenced them. The absolute difference between man and woman, which the Church justified through the language of complementarity of the sexes, did not play a central role in his analysis.

Doms's theology of marriage represented a comprehensive alternative to the natural law approach. It had the advantage of providing a coherent rationale for many common practices in Church life, which the Augustinian/Thomist theory could not. For example, if the primary purpose of marriage was ontological completion rather than procreation, then the Church's teaching on the moral permissibility of sexual intercourse between sterile married partners and its rejection of artificial insemination made sense.[11] But the Rota Romana condemned Doms's theory in 1944.[12]

However, a modified version of the personalist approach did gain currency in the Catholic Church during this period. The modified approach merged the new positive conception of marital intimacy with the traditional language of sexual complementarity, thereby preserving the Church's emphasis on the hierarchical ends of marriage. For example, Pius XI took this approach in his 1930 encyclical *Casti Connubii*, which described marriage as an intimate life partnership sanctioned by God, affirmed the primary and secondary purposes of marriage, and condemned birth control.[13] According to this approach, sexual complementarity unified the couple in marriage and in sexual intercourse by bringing the masculine and feminine biological and psychological elements into an undivided whole. The masculine elements were understood to be greater strength, physicality, and orientation to the secular world. The feminine elements were receptivity, domesticity, and motherhood. Through the joining of these two elements, the married couple fulfilled their true vocation to receive and to care for new human life. Although this approach gave a more positive valuation of marital sexual intercourse, it still defined the marital relationship in hierarchical terms. The primary purpose remained procreation, and the husband's final authority was justified by his greater physicality and capacity for reason; he must guide his wife, whose leadership capacity was circumscribed by her narrow focus on children.

Casti Connubii extended no mercy to those who willfully limited family size: "Small wonder, therefore, if Holy Writ bears witness that the Divine Majesty regards with greatest detestation this horrible crime and at times has punished it with death. As Augustine notes, 'Intercourse even with one's legitimate wife is unlawful and wicked where the conception of the offspring is prevented.'"[14] It described birth control as a "grave sin" that constituted "an offense against the law of God and nature."[15] Priests were instructed to inquire about the use of birth control in the confession box. The encyclical warned that priests who exercised tolerance in such cases placed their souls in jeopardy.[16] Pius XI's condemnation of birth control permitted no exceptions. Neither economic nor social hardship justified contraceptive use: "There is no possible circumstance in which husband and wife cannot, strengthened by the grace of God, fulfill faithfully their duties and preserve in wedlock their chastity unspotted."[17]

In light of the Anglican Church's qualified acceptance of birth control by married couples at the Lambeth Conference on August 14, 1930, Pius XI wanted to send a clear message that the Catholic Church would not tolerate contraception or any affront to the patriarchal family: "This order includes both the primacy of the husband with regard to the wife and children, the ready subjection of the wife and her willing obedience, which the Apostle commends in these words: 'Let women be subject to their husbands as to the Lord, because the husband is the head of the wife, and Christ is the head of the Church.'"[18]

Thus, Pius XII's approval of the rhythm method in 1951 represented a major shift in the Church's position. However, in opening the door to one form of contraception while condemning others, Pius XII inadvertently opened a theological Pandora's Box. If the end result was the same (preventing pregnancy), why did the means matter? How could such a position be justified theologically and lay Catholics be made to see the moral distinction between different methods? These theological questions became focal points in the 1960s debate on "the pill."

Ideology versus Reality: Contraception and Morality in 1950s West Germany

In public discourse, the topic of contraception remained taboo in 1950s West Germany, since it explicitly challenged the ideology of marriage and family promoted by conservative Christian politicians and religious authorities. Conservative Christian politicians and the Catholic Church, in particular, argued that only a return to traditional family values could save Germany from the resurgence of a totalitarian state, whether National Socialist or Communist. Whereas in the late 1940s West Germans had engaged in lively discussions of the viability and advantages of alternative family forms, the 1950s saw the emergence of a far-reaching public consensus that "incomplete" families and "mother families" were legacies of war and the National Socialist past—a past that West Germans wanted to move beyond.

In *What Difference Does a Husband Make?*, Elizabeth Heineman detailed the frank discussions of divorce and illegitimacy in the late 1940s that took place in women's journals. For example, in an article entitled "A Dangerous Phrase between Spouses: 'For the Children's Sake,'" *Constanze* urged readers in unhappy marriages to divorce and expressed admiration for those women who did: "We ... want to bow down before the women who—despite the legal codes, which stand on the side of the men—muster up the courage and the strength to end marriages gone awry."[19] In the women's journal *Sie*, Walther von Hollander wrote that the state should amend its laws banning cohabitation by unwed couples: "The days when a woman uncomplainingly dried up into an old maid, a sexless being, are gone and will not come back."[20] He advised married women to support their single sisters by tolerating their husband's affairs or even to befriend their husband's mistresses![21]

Hollander was not alone in endorsing open marriages and extramarital sexual relations. A 1948 survey conducted in Hamburg and Schleswig-Holstein asked, "Is 'free love' immoral?" Sixty-one percent of respondents replied no.[22] Similarly, a 1949 Allensbach survey found that 71 percent of those surveyed approved of premarital sexual relations. The survey also noted that 89 percent of men and 69 percent of women admitted to having had premarital sexual relations. Approximately the same percentage admitted to having had sexual intercourse with someone other than their future spouse (89 percent of men and 70 percent of women).[23]

Although female authors expressed less enthusiasm for short-term and open marriages than male authors, they supported alternative living arrangements for single-mother households. For example, *Constanze*'s female readers suggested communal housing with on-site daycare facilities for single mothers. As Heineman noted, proposing that the state expend substantial funds on housing for single women communicated an acceptance that singlehood was not necessarily a temporary stage of life for women and that single women constituted a population worthy of investment.[24] Both were radical ideas for the time.

By the mid-1950s, this openness to "mother families" and "free love" had disappeared from West German public discourse, a victim of efforts to leave behind the recent Nazi past. As Dagmar Herzog explained, sexual conservatism became a "crucial strategy for managing the memory of Nazism and Holocaust." By emphasizing the very real link between sexual licentiousness and mass murder under Nazism, Christian conservatives could claim with some legitimacy that turning away from sexual pleasure constituted a rejection of Nazi morality.[25] An Allensbach survey from the early 1950s indicated a dramatic reversal in West German attitudes toward extramarital relations. Fifty-two percent of city dwellers and 62 percent of those living in rural regions now rejected extramarital sexual relations. Concomitantly, women's magazines such as *Constanze*, *Brigitte*, and *Das Blatt der Hausfrau* changed their editorial direction. They discouraged discussions of alternative family forms and filled their pages with stories and images that characterized the feminine ideal in terms of women's role as stay-at-home housewife and mother.[26] An editorial in the Catholic women's journal *Frau und Mutter*, the largest women's journal in 1950s Germany with a readership of five hundred to six hundred thousand, deplored the state of West German families, for which it held women accountable: "If the family is shattered today, if it is torn apart, if it is rejected by many as an antiquated way of life, one cannot avoid the following conclusion: the woman, the mother, the wife is in many cases not present and is not what she should be."[27]

This changed attitude also found expression in the political sphere. Although the 1949 Basic Law (Article 3, Paragraph 2) guaranteed the equal rights of men and women, Article 6, Sentence 1 of the Basic Law placed marriage and family "under the special protection of the public order (*staatlichen Ordnung*)." For Christian conservatives, marriage necessarily preceded family, and the CDU-CSU constitutional draft emphasized this connection: "Marriage is the form of communal living between man and woman sanctioned by law. It forms the basis of the family. Marriage and family and the rights and duties associated with it stand under the protection of the law."[28] The SPD successfully prevented this narrow understanding of family from being incorporated into the Basic Law. However, the SPD proved less successful when discussion turned to the legal status of illegitimate children. Article 6, Sentence 3 of the Basic Law safeguarded the physical and spiritual development of children born out of wedlock, but it did not guarantee them legal equality. Marital status still determined the legal standing of women and children.

In revising the Civil Code to align with the Basic Law, Christian conservatives proved adept at using the constitutional protection accorded marriage and family to restore the difference between the sexes. Following the 1953 elections, the CDU-CSU coalition held the majority of parliamentary seats, and in 1954, the new government created the Federal Ministry of Family Affairs under the leadership of Josef Wuermeling—a committed Catholic. Wuermeling believed that strong families provided the best defense against Nazism, Communism, and "a liberal-inspired decline into individualism, materialism, and secularism."[29] He defined family in patriarchal and hierarchical terms and vehemently denounced any conception of women's equality that might undermine "the Christian foundation of the family authority exercised by the father."[30] Moreover, Wuermeling and CDU-CSU parliamentarians, such as Helene Weber and Adolf Süsterhenn, argued that the family was a pre-political unit; women's equality in the family meant moral equality; political equality, they maintained, had no bearing on the familial sphere.[31] For the welfare of the children, someone must have final authority, and that someone should be the father. Although Social Democrats and former Weimar feminists argued that this solution violated women's rights, they lost the battle. Until a 1959 high court decision struck down inequality within marriage, the husband's authority over the children was absolute.[32]

Christian conservatives also advanced pro-natalist policies. Wuermeling drew a close connection between any failure of West German married couples to be fruitful and multiply and a potential takeover by populous "peoples of the east."[33] As Hanna Schissler noted, "Amid the highly charged anticommunism of the 1950s, single women often were accused of being *Flintenweiber*—communist subversives who sought to undermine the sanctity of marriage and family life."[34]

Anti-Communist fervor also influenced SPD policy. Wanting to distance the party from Communism, Social Democrats were as inclined as their conservative Christian colleagues in the 1950s to emphasize women's roles as wives and mothers so as to avoid being tainted by the rhetoric of the "forced emancipation" of East German women. Consequently, throughout the 1950s, consensus existed across the political spectrum that women's ideal roles were those of housewife and mother. The Bundestag imposed measures against households with two wage earners and mandated "money for children" (*Kindergeld*). The CDU-sponsored law attached money for children to the (usually) male wage, rather than making the payment to the mother for use in managing household expenses. Payments began with the birth of the third child. Because female-headed households rarely exceeded two children and many single mothers did not earn regular wages but pieced together an existence from domestic labor, welfare payments, and pensions, few single mothers benefited from the child allowance.[35] Instead, the child allowance awarded "complete families," reinforced married women's dependence on the male breadwinner, and hardened "the symbolic and material divide of marital status."[36] For women, economic security meant marriage, and by the late 1950s, popular discourse inculcated marriage and family as the natural progression for women.

Yet population politics represented a potential political minefield for the newly created West German state, which wanted to distinguish itself from its Nazi predecessor. To broach population politics without risking comparisons to National Socialism, policymakers had to redefine the terms in which the topic was discussed. To this end, they employed the language of capitalism, domesticity, and natural law.

CDU-CSU policymakers contrasted the goals of family politics in a free democratic and capitalist nation with those in totalitarian states—understood nondifferentially to be National Socialist and Communist. Whereas Communists and Nazis attempted to transform the private family sphere into public spaces, conservative Christians maintained that they wanted to protect the boundary between the two spheres by using public policy to buttress the family's ability to resist incursions by the state.[37] In addition to family policies intended "to channel female desire into marriage and childbearing," CDU government officials, such as the Protestant minister of economic affairs, Ludwig Erhard, promoted the housewife as the guardian of consumption, whose thrift and rational consumption served as "the engine" of the economic miracle.[38]

As Erica Carter convincingly argued in *How German Is She?*, the social market became the "displaced space of the nation" in 1950s West Germany.[39] Women, as wives, mothers, domestic laborers, and arbiters of household purchases, were expected to play an active role in the nation's physical and moral reconstruction and in fighting the specter of Communism.[40] However, the consumer aspect of women's domestic identity posed potential dangers. Social commentators warned women against the pitfalls of unlimited materialism, especially when it came to determining family size. In striving for economic prosperity, women should not succumb to the temptation of contraception and abortion, endangering both their health and the existence of future generations of West Germans.[41]

Although the language of capitalism and the free market played a crucial role in distinguishing West German family and population politics from those of so-called totalitarian regimes, Catholic natural law theory provided the moral underpinnings for a family policy that praised large families, frowned on birth control, and consigned women to the role of wife and mother. Immediately following the war, a booklet published by the Düsseldorf CDU declared, "Each family—indeed, this cannot be disputed—each family needs paternal power [*patria potestas*], the master who carries the burden of all-encompassing worry."[42] Similarly, the 1945 Frankfurt Guiding Principles described marriage "according to its inherent law of nature" as a "life covenant" that culminated in the "blessing of children" and over which a benevolent father ruled: "The man must be the head in the fullest sense; he can do that only when he is not the object, but the subject of his life; that means that the state—through its economic and social policies—grants him the possibility to nourish his family in honor; and through its social and state constitution, [it offers him the possibility] to be a true supporter of public responsibility. Only then will the woman as the heart of the family in inner freedom help to carry the responsibility of the man and be able to be the trusted mother of his children."[43] Some Christian Democrats also championed the Catholic Church for its "glorious struggle" against Nazism; this *Kirchenkampf* discourse soon embraced the notion that "the community of Christians" had offered the most serious resistance to Hitler. Jakob Kaiser, a Catholic resistance leader during World War II, noted that Hitler tried to eliminate all vestiges of Christianity because he rightly identified Christianity as "the strongest counterweight against all aberrations and exaggerations of political extremes."[44] These types of claims received the support of the occupying authorities and contributed to the growing credence of the *Kirchenkampf* concept within the West German population. But more important, the concept championed by the CDU-CSU allowed ordinary Germans to identify themselves as opponents of National Socialism, since most belonged to a Christian church.

In addition to the German populace's desire for a return to normalcy and the Catholic Church's claim of being untainted by Nazism, the increased willingness of Germans to endorse, at least publicly, the Catholic view of marriage and family reflected the changed confessional demographics of the newly created Federal Republic. The eastern regions of Germany historically had been strongholds of Protestantism. With their exclusion from the new West German state, Catholics ceased to be a minority group. They now represented roughly half the population, giving political Catholicism a new privileged place in politics.⁴⁵ Although the CDU-CSU did not have a specifically Catholic identity as had its predecessor, the Center Party, Catholics dominated the ranks of the CDU-CSU coalition; from 1949 until 1969, the CDU-CSU controlled or belonged to the ruling coalition.

However, neither public policy nor discourse reflected the reality of the contemporary West German family—Catholic or non-Catholic. In 1963, only 60 percent of the West German population lived in the idealized complete family.⁴⁶ Moreover, the gendered division of labor championed by the Christian parties never materialized in practice. As Christine von Oertzen detailed in *The Pleasures of a Surplus Income*, the number of West German women in paid employment grew significantly between 1950 and 1965, and the employment of married women outside the home skyrocketed in the late 1950s. By 1962, the percentage of female wage earners in West Germany was greater than that of any other labor force in Western Europe.⁴⁷ Many of these women sought employment because they found working pleasurable. It provided relief from the drudgery of housework and gave them an independent income. In the autumn of 1960, *Constanze* devoted an entire issue to women's part-time employment; the articles included quotes from women who described how working outside the home had made them feel young again.⁴⁸ Thus, long before the 1970s feminist movement, West German women were seeking new roles in society beyond that of wife and mother; in fact, they were neither staying home nor having the large families envisioned by the CDU government.

For policymakers who discerned a direct correlation between defeating Communism and increasing German family size, the declining birthrate was perhaps the most disturbing development. Although West Germany experienced a baby boom in the 1950s, it had ended by 1964. A 1950 survey of West German couples showed that 50 percent believed the ideal number of children was two; 21 percent said three; and only 11 percent thought four children were ideal. Despite family and child allowances, West Germans were having fewer children. On average, even Catholic families were becoming smaller.⁴⁹ At least some Catholic and non-Catholic West Germans were practicing some form of birth control, whether natural, mechanical, or abortive, in order to keep families small or to pursue extramarital/premarital sexual relationships.

Yet neither information about contraception nor the means of contraception were readily available in the 1950s or early 1960s. In some West German states, the production, sale, and distribution of contraceptives were prohibited.⁵⁰ However, as Elizabeth Heineman explained in *Before Porn Was Legal*, the mail order erotica industry allowed many Germans in regions with strict regulations to circumvent the law and their neighbors' watchful eyes. The two largest erotica firms in the 1950s and early 1960s, Gisela and Beate Uhse, employed a domesticated language of sexual consumption that stressed how unwanted pregnancies and sexual dissatisfaction could lead to marital ruin. This strategy allowed the two firms to gain the confidence of millions of West Germans. By 1957, an estimated 8 million Germans out of a population of 54 million subscribed to erotica mailing lists, and the most sought-after products were contraceptives, accounting for 30 percent of all sales for the mail order firm Beate Uhse in the early 1960s.⁵¹

Although it is impossible to determine how many of these mail order consumers were Catholic, the trend toward growing dissatisfaction with the Church's conception of marital morality was clear. Readers of *Frau und Mutter* were unhappy when magazine staff members appeared unsympathetic to the hardships suffered by large families. One reader described a woman who had a nervous breakdown when she discovered she was pregnant again. This reader questioned whether having large families compromised one's ability to be a good Christian and parent. The letter engendered a harsh reaction from Aenne Volk, one of the journal's contributors. Volk accused such parents of being unwilling to make the necessary sacrifices to raise children.⁵² The magazine frequently blamed materialism and consumerism for the trend toward smaller families. In a 1953 article, Idamarie Solltmann lambasted a refrigerator advertisement that advised, "Temporarily the stork must wait until you have your home practically and beautifully equipped."⁵³ In a series of articles by a Catholic doctor, Georg Volk, the magazine also refuted the argument that giving birth to a large number of children endangered women's health. Not only did Volk reject the argument, he drew a close correlation between feminine fulfillment and pregnancy.⁵⁴

Despite the magazine's support for the Church's official position on contraception, readers remained unconvinced. Yet to its credit, the editorial staff continued to provide a forum where Catholic women and men could express discontent with official Church teachings. In a 1959 letter to the editor, one female reader captured the financial, emotional, and moral dilemma that the choice between an unwanted pregnancy and using contraception posed for many Catholic women: "We have four children, ranging in age from three to twelve, and have reached the conclusion that our income level makes having another child undesirable. We have tried to limit sexual relations to the infertile days. But my husband often finds abstinence during the fertile period impossible. I resist relations during these times, but my frigidity injures him and creates serious resentments. When I give in to my husband, my reluctant compliance offends him or it aggrieves my conscience; consequently I avoid Communion and in so doing make my life spiritually poorer."[55] For such women, the rhythm method provided little or no relief from unwanted pregnancies, marital strife, or moral qualms.

Couples also complained that it removed all spontaneity from sexual intercourse. The rhythm method (also called the calendar method) required women to painstakingly track their menstrual cycle—the theory being that since ovulation occurred twelve to sixteen days before the anticipated first day of the menstrual cycle, a woman could determine her fertile and infertile days. By avoiding sexual intercourse during fertile days, she could prevent unwanted pregnancies. Success necessitated strict adherence to the dictates of a calendar that many married couples experienced as less than satisfying.[56]

Even more problematic, the method was unreliable, since many women commonly experience irregularities in their cycle. With the rhythm method, any irregularity could result in an unwanted pregnancy. One woman lamented in a 1975 letter to the German moral theologian Bernhard Häring that she had conceived three children on the rhythm method. Out of desperation, she turned to the pill because she and her husband could not afford another child. However, using this illicit form of birth control caused her great moral distress.[57]

To fully appreciate this moral suffering requires an understanding of the idealized conception of womanhood that many Catholic women internalized through constant exposure to its many manifestations at German Catholic congresses, at mothers' schools (*Mütterschule*), in marriage preparation classes operated by Catholic youth groups, in Catholic schools, in marriage manuals, and from families and friends. Catholic leaders counseled women and girls to emulate the Virgin Mary. In *Die ewige Frau*—a text widely used in German Catholic confessional schools in the 1930s, 1940s, and 1950s—Gertrud von Le Fort extolled Marian virtues and assigned eschatological meaning to women's role as mother:

> In motherhood, the existential contact between God and humanity is constantly renewed; it is the only place in the entire creation where God, Regent

and Sustainer, remains always active in his creative Fatherhood, whereby the man as friend of God must cooperate in his intention. Likewise, in her mystical marriage with Christ, the Holy Virgin is sanctified in the birth of new creation. By emulating Mary, the woman recognizes that she receives only for this purpose mystic Grace and thus can pass it on to others.[58]

Le Fort cautioned that women who did not emulate Mary existed outside the realm of spiritual redemption; such women forfeited their feminine identity and succumbed to masculinization. Le Fort described this development as "apocalyptic."[59]

Catholic femininity also implied a willingness to embrace suffering. In his 1961 book, *Die Frau vor der Zukunft*, E. R. Maexie extolled maternal sacrifice and condemned egoistic motherhood. Maexie characterized women who were unwilling to die in childbirth or who even used modern medication to relieve the pain of childbirth as guilty of disobeying God's commandment: "That the woman until now had to use her life for the life of her child, that she had to be prepared to die, if she were to give life, was her induction into the mystery of motherhood.... The possibility of painless birth that the scientific magus gives the modern woman is an emancipation from divine Law (Gen. 2/16) and brings no blessing, because it advances the egoism of the woman, instead of being a radical relief. The fruit of 'egoistic motherhood' is the unloved child who together with the Mother for the most part ends up in need of psychotherapy."[60] Both Le Fort and Maexie assumed that a woman who did not embrace motherhood acted against nature and the will of God.

The burdens of womanhood extended beyond childbirth. Women were also responsible for safeguarding the purity of sexual relations. In 1954 Hans March explained in *Stimmen der Zeit* how the obligation to keep the male libido in check derived from woman's essence: "The natural design of woman ... holds in check not only her own animalism and libidinal urges, but also domesticates and makes ethical the animalism of the man; it channels his natural needs toward a different mode of loving development."[61] For March, the woman who could not control her husband's sexuality suffered from a defect in her natural disposition.

The Catholic Church offered no realistic role model for girls and women. According to the Church's dualistic view of womanhood, one either emulated the Virgin Mother or followed the temptress Eve, whom Church fathers had reviled for centuries.[62] But Mary as a role model posed a dilemma. She established motherhood as women's destiny, but she escaped the sexual intercourse required for mortal women to fulfill that destiny. In *Alone of All Her Sex*, Marina Warner concluded that the unattainable character of the twin ideals (virginity and motherhood) embodied in Mary produced one of two reactions in Catholic girls. They either rebelled or experienced an intensification of "the need for religion's consolation, for the screen of rushes against the perpetual frost of being carnal and female."[63] Although rebellion and renewed religious fervor did characterize women's reaction to the reproductive model of marriage, Warner's dualistic account oversimplifies the phenomenon. As seen in this chapter and other chapters, religious fervor did not always signify affirmation of traditional values. Rebellion could also take the form of intense religiosity, as when women demanded admission to the priesthood.

However, female rebellion first found expression in modest demands. At the 1962 West German Catholic Congress, a group of women and mothers dared to ask for the abolition of the term "abuse of marriage" (*ehelicher Missbrauch*) to describe the actions of "those Christians who in principle do not fail in the service of life but have already proved with 4, 5, or more children that they are prepared to make great sacrifices." The petitioners explained that women with so many children were often too weak to fulfill their duty and consequently should not face condemnation in the confession box. The official account of the congress labeled this modest request "most shocking."[64]

The Pill: Early West German Debates

Against this backdrop of social, political, and religious condemnation of birth control, on the one hand, and the outright practice of contraception, on the other, the Berlin-based pharmaceutical company Schering debated introducing the pill on the West German market. Concerns about bad press and public protest in West Germany prompted Schering to delay the German release. Instead, on February 1, 1961, Schering introduced Anovlar in Australia, where the company anticipated less moral resistance.[65]

Schering wanted to secure the German medical community's support before releasing the pill. However, the company knew that getting that support would be no easy task. A 1961 survey of 1,370 doctors in northern Germany showed that only 13 percent had a strong interest in birth control products; 55 percent expressed little or no interest. This dearth of interest reflected the topic's taboo nature and the fact that few West German doctors received information about contraception during their medical training. On June 1, 1961, after securing the support of several prominent doctors, Schering introduced Anovlar in West Germany. But even with support, the company proceeded cautiously. It limited its initial distribution of brochures to a small group of prescreened doctors. The brochure underscored Anovlar's use in treating menstrual disorders and included only a brief reference to the drug's undesirable contraceptive properties. The brochure advised that Anovlar be prescribed only to married women with three or more children.[66]

However, events soon forced Schering to change its marketing strategy. On June 20, 1961, *Stern* published an article by Dr. Anne-Marie Durand-Wever calling attention to Anovlar's contraceptive properties. Durand-Wever had been active in the Weimar sex reform movement and was one of the founders of Pro Familia (1952). In the article, she offered a qualified endorsement of the new drug for contraceptive purposes and pleaded for an open discussion of the complex issues surrounding contraception. Her cautious support reflected her concerns about the drug's potentially negative moral and medical consequences. She feared that the pill would encourage promiscuous sexual behavior on the part of youth, who would no longer worry about the consequences of their actions. She also felt that the trial period had been too short and feared that there might be unknown long-term side effects. Therefore, she advised prescribing Anovlar only for short-term use by women who had just conceived, and could thereby prevent a second pregnancy too soon after the first, and for long-term use by women "who already have at least three living children and are approaching the change of life."[67]

The publication of Durand-Wever's article meant that a large segment of the general population now potentially knew of Anovlar's contraceptive properties. Schering realized that information about Anovlar would have to be sent to all German doctors and pharmacists. Like the old brochure, the new one emphasized the drug's use in treating menstrual disorders. However, it also included a cautiously worded statement about the drug's contraceptive properties that also underscored the company's disapproval of the *Stern* story: "ANOVLAR can also be prescribed if the prevention of conception under a doctor's control is temporarily desired. In recent days, this property has gained unwanted publicity, which has induced us to offer scientific information to all German doctors."[68]

The pill became the prism through which West Germans debated socially acceptable sexual mores. The cautious approach of Durand-Wever and of Schering typified early West German public discourse on the pill. Doctors, politicians, university professors, and church officials dominated a discussion that focused on both the moral and medical ramifications of the pill. The general consensus among supporters was that contraceptive use belonged exclusively within the confines of marriage. They saw the pill as a solution for spouses who already had more children than they could support financially. They also recommended it for women who were too sick or too weak to give birth. Some experts saw the pill as a means of reducing the number of illegal abortions in Germany. No one spoke in favor of the pill as a means of sexual liberation. Instead, supporters and critics shared concerns about the risk of increased promiscuity among young people and the development of a "contraceptive mentality."[69]

At first, no Catholic theologians supported even this qualified endorsement of the pill for contraceptive purposes. Until the end of 1961, Catholic theologians concurred that oral contraception constituted a deliberate act of direct sterilization and consequently was illicit.[70] As Pius XII made clear in a 1958 speech to the Seventh International Congress of Hematology, the individual's intentions determined the morality of ingesting anovulatory medications: "If the woman takes the pill with no intention of preventing contraception, but solely for a medical purpose, as a necessary remedy for a disease of the uterus, she brings about an indirect sterilization, which is permissible according to the general principle concerning actions that have a double effect.[71] But a direct sterilization, and consequently an illicit one, is brought about whenever ovulation is impeded with the goal of protecting the uterus and the body from a pregnancy that it cannot support."[72] If the aim was contraceptive, the Church condemned the use of the pill.

December 1961 witnessed the first significant modification of this position. In response to reports of multiple rapes of nuns stationed in the Congo, the Italian Catholic theological journal *Studi Cattolici* posed the following theoretical question: Could an unmarried woman (particularly a nun) who had reason to fear being raped take the pill as a means of protection? The journal published the affirmative responses of three prominent theologians—Pietro Palazzini, Franz Hürth, and Ferdinando Lambruschini. Although Palazzini relied on the doctrine of double effect, the other two theologians introduced new theological principles that potentially allowed the pill to be used in other scenarios.

Hürth distinguished between absolute and relative sterilization. He defined absolute sterilization as any act that produced sterilization in the subject. Hürth contended that sterilization became a sin only if the individual's motivation was lust. In other words, a woman who made herself sterile without any intention of associating her sterility with a sexual act committed no sin. Thus, a nun who used the pill because she feared being rape acted in good faith. This rationale could be applied to a married woman whose husband compelled her to submit to his sexual advances when her duty as a responsible parent called for abstinence. Hürth acknowledged that a close parallel existed between the two cases, although he still maintained a distinction.[73]

Lambruschini's response had even broader implications. He acknowledged that a deliberate act of sterilization had taken place in the scenario just described. He affirmed the Church's position that sterilization for reasons of health was illicit. The reason for this condemnation, he argued, was that a married couple had at their disposal a more radical method of avoiding procreation—namely, abstinence. In the case of the nun, no such radical alternative existed. Sterilization was her only option. Moreover, he asserted that grave reasons existed for her actions—namely, to act otherwise jeopardized her physical and spiritual well-being. Therefore, Lambruschini concluded that the Church could not deny her access to anovulatory interventions because "when a physical and physiological process is in opposition to a pre-existent moral and spiritual right, precedence must be given to the latter."[74]

Lambruschini's prioritization of the subject's moral and spiritual well-being in conjunction with the Church's more positive teachings on marriage raised new questions about contraception: Could married couples use artificial contraception if serious reasons existed for counseling against abstinence? Could they use artificial contraception if their spiritual well-being depended on a more reasonable approach to procreation? If spiritual well-being took precedence over physiology, did the couple's right to express their love via sexual intimacy without fear of an unwanted pregnancy justify an intervention in the wife's ovulation cycle? By the end of 1962, these questions met with an affirmative response by some theologians and Church officials, including German theologians, such as Bernhard Häring and Franz Böckle, who had previously rejected the use of the pill for contraceptive purposes.[75]

Joseph Reuss, auxiliary bishop of Mainz, was the first German bishop to support married couples using artificial forms of contraception. Like

Herbert Doms, Reuss argued that marital sexual intercourse could not be reduced to its biophysiological aspects; as an expression of marital love, it represented an act of communion. However, the two men reached different conclusions about the use of artificial forms of contraception by married couples. In 1935, Doms argued that artificial contraception destroyed "the natural inner harmony of marriage" and thus reduced marital intercourse to an egoistic act.[76] In contrast, Reuss endorsed natural and artificial contraceptive methods. He asserted that stipulating acceptable methods went beyond the competence of the theologian, who could "merely stipulate that the intervention took place in such a way as to safeguard the personal dignity of the married couple for the sake of increasing their mutual love."[77] The German moral theologian Alfons Auer agreed in substance with Reuss's argument; however, he did not think that all contraceptive forms (i.e., natural, hormonal, chemical, mechanical, and surgical) were equally acceptable. Other Catholic theologians, such as Dietrich von Hildebrand, remained steadfast in condemning artificial contraception.[78] Thus, on the eve of the third session of Vatican II (September 14–November 21, 1964), the Catholic theological community was deeply divided.

On October 28, 1964, Cardinal Agagianian announced to the commission responsible for revising the schema that became *Gaudium et Spes* that "some points" had been reserved for the pope's special commission on birth control. The following day, Archbishiop John Dearden of Detroit, chair of the subcommission responsible for revising the chapter on marriage and family, made it clear to its members that the progesterone pill in particular and birth control in general were no longer topics open for discussion; those wishing to make their views known should submit them in writing to the papal commission. Dearden assured the subcommission members that the papal special commission would give serious consideration to their recommendations.[79]

The full commission opened debate on Article 21, "The Sanctity of Marriage and the Family," on October 29, 1964. Despite the removal of the topic of birth control from the agenda, the commission did not ignore the issue completely. Cardinal Suenens of Belgium, Cardinal Döpfner of Germany, and Cardinal Léger of Canada wanted the Church to move away from the language of primary and secondary purposes of marriage. They believed the Church had placed too much emphasis on the biblical call to "be fruitful and multiply" and paid insufficient attention to the words "and the two become one flesh." By rejecting the language of primary and secondary purposes,

Cardinals Suenens, Döpfner, and Léger paved the way for their second proposal—married couples should be given primary responsibility for determining family size.[80] They believed that this proposal was in keeping with the council's higher valuation of the laity as the people of God: "These faithful are by baptism made one body with Christ and are constituted among the People of God; they are in their own way made sharers in the priestly, prophetical, and kingly functions of Christ; and they carry out for their own part the mission of the whole Christian people in the Church and in the world."[81]

However, this shift in emphasis was not well received by all council fathers. Alfredo Cardinal Ottaviani, pro-prefect of the Magisterium (CDF) and president of the Theological Commission, objected to the proposal because it implied that for centuries the Church had erred: "Does this mean that the inerrancy of the Church will be called into question? Or was not the Holy Spirit with his Church in past centuries to illumine minds on this point of doctrine?"[82] Ottaviani was not alone in his concerns about the proposed draft's implications. Cardinals Giovanni Colombo and Carlo Colombo also objected, citing the draft's failure to link sexual intercourse with procreation and the lack of direction for priests in the confession box.[83] As close associates of Paul VI since the 1930s, these three men were in a unique position to influence Paul's views on birth control.[84] Thus, it should have come as no surprise to members of the commission when on November 25, 1965, during the fourth session of the council, Father Sebastian Tromp read a letter from Amleto Cardinal Cicognani, the Vatican secretary of the state, stating that the pope required four *modi* (amendments) to the chapter on marriage and family, including an explicit reference to Pius XI's *Casti Connubii*: "Secondly, it is absolutely necessary that the methods and instruments used to make conception ineffectual—that is to say the contraceptive methods which are dealt with in the encyclical *Casti Connubii*—be openly rejected; for in this matter admitting doubts, keeping silent or insinuating that such opinions may perhaps be admitted can bring about the gravest dangers in public opinion."[85]

Paul VI's call for revisions provoked heated protests at a meeting of the full commission. The text on marriage and family had already received the necessary two-thirds approval by the entire council. According to council rules, no amendments could be introduced that substantially altered a text once it had been affirmed by a two-thirds majority. However, Cardinals Brown, Parente, and Ottaviani and other Roman Curia members championed the amendments, proclaiming, "The pope has spoken. Causa finita! Contradiction is inadmissible."[86]

Commission members who favored greater democracy in the Church feared that the request for amendments signaled an increasingly autocratic approach to the papacy and the council by Paul VI. They believed the amendments were designed to preempt any decision made by the papal commission on birth control. Alarmed lay auditors at the council wrote the pope warning him of the danger of alienating Catholics throughout the world if he simply reiterated *Casti Connubii*'s ban on all forms of artificial birth control. The next day the pope replied by letter, stating that the commission members did not have to insert the amendments verbatim into the chapter on marriage and family; they were free to express the essence of the amendments in their own language.[87] Thus, the goal of some bishops and their *periti* (theological advisers) became that of neutralizing the amendments' effect. Paul's reference to the "contraceptive arts" was changed to "illicit practices against human generation." On the "ends of marriage," the commission remained deliberately vague, avoiding any direct references to primary and secondary purposes. It did cite *Casti Connubii*, but in a footnote. The same footnote mentioned the ongoing investigation of the papal commission.[88]

For the council fathers, the birth control debate had ramifications beyond marital doctrine; the principle of collegiality was also at stake. Whereas Vatican I underscored papal primacy,[89] Vatican II highlighted episcopal collegiality. Collegiality is the doctrine which asserts that the worldwide episcopate together with the pope, albeit never separate from the pope, possesses supreme authority and thus bears joint responsibility for the universal Church. Although the term "collegiality" never appeared in any Vatican II document, both *Lumen Gentium* and *Christus Dominus* described Church governance as "collegial" and characterized the hierarchy as unified in a "collegium."[90] However, neither document provided a concrete plan for implementing collegiality. In the years after the council, heated debates erupted on what collegiality entailed. In a nutshell, the debate centered on which council's teaching took precedence—Vatican I's teaching on papal primacy or Vatican II's emphasis on collegiality. With *Humanae Vitae*'s release on July 25, 1968, many European bishops believed that Paul VI had violated the principle of collegiality, for two reasons. First, Paul VI ignored the recommendations of the Pontifical Study Commission on Family, Population, and Birth Problems, which he had charged with investigating the moral and doctrinal aspects of contraception. Second, Paul VI had not consulted the bishops. Cardinal Suenens of Belgium explained that "although no one could say that he had no right to produce *Humanae Vitae* on his own, it would have been more credible if it had been collegially prepared."[91]

The study commission had been created by Pope John XXIII and expanded by Pope Paul VI.[92] Its members included bishops, theologians, social scientists, and laypersons. The theological discussions of the commission focused on three questions: Was artificial birth control intrinsically evil? Did *Casti Connubii* constitute an infallible teaching? And could the Church revise its position without harming its credibility in the eyes of the faithful?[93] For some members, *Casti Connubii* constituted an infallible teaching that clearly condemned artificial contraception: "This is the doctrine of Holy Scripture; this is the constant tradition of the Universal Church; this the solemn definition of the sacred Council of Trent, which declares and establishes from the words of Holy Writ itself that God is the Author of the perpetual stability of the marriage bond, its unity and its firmness."[94] However, Auxiliary Bishop Reuss of Mainz, Cardinal Döpfner's leading expert on the question, argued that a pope who wished to speak *ex cathedra* explicitly declared his intention to do so. He reminded commission members, "The church has not always taught the same things about what is licit in marriage."[95] Furthermore, Reuss argued, the Church's authority would not suffer, because believers understood the difference between infallible teachings and other doctrinal pronouncements subject to reform.[96]

The commission also considered Catholic married couples' experiences with the rhythm method. Patricia and Patrick Crowley, an American Catholic couple serving on the commission, had sponsored a survey of three thousand Catholic couples from eighteen nations; their survey showed that most couples did not experience the "tonic effects" attributed to the rhythm method by celibate clergy.[97] On June 28, 1966, the commission sent its final report to the pope.[98] The report offered a qualified endorsement of married couple's use of artificial birth control if financial, social, or psychological conditions existed that made having a child unwise. The report argued that this position did not constitute a break from earlier Church teachings on regulating birth. It maintained that this qualified acceptance of artificial contraception was the natural outgrowth of Pius XII's acceptance of the rhythm method.[99] The Vatican intended for the report to remain secret; however, it was leaked to the international press. The *National Catholic Reporter* (United States), the *Tablet* (Great Britain), and *Le Monde* (France) all published the full report.¹⁰⁰ News of the commission's recommendations guaranteed widespread public outcry when Paul VI reaffirmed the Church's ban in *Humanae Vitae*. Most Catholics assumed that the pope would not ignore the advice of his commission.

Turning Point: *Humanae Vitae* and the Sexual Revolution

The publication of *Humanae Vitae* on July 25, 1968, unleashed a firestorm of protests throughout the world. Laypersons, theologians, bishops, and even cardinals numbered among the protesters. Nor were these protests limited to Catholics. In West Germany, non-Catholics voiced their views in letters to the editor of secular magazines and even in letters to the federal government.¹⁰¹ Although *Humanae Vitae* had some supporters in West Germany, the overwhelming majority of Germans rejected the encyclical's conclusions, and German Catholics demanded that the pope rescind the encyclical.

Since Anovlar's release in 1961, West Germany's social and political climate had changed dramatically. While experts continued to debate the moral and medical ramifications of the pill, the general public was slowly overcoming its initial reservations about oral contraception. In 1964, only 300,000 packets of the pill were sold monthly, leading the Düsseldorf financial newspaper, *Handelsblatt*, to note wryly that the pill was much discussed but not much used.¹⁰² However, by 1968, the Deutsche Presse-Agentur reported on an international study that ranked West Germany third in pill use, with an estimated 12 percent of all women between the ages of fifteen and forty-five taking the pill.¹⁰³ By 1972, almost one-third of all German women took oral contraceptives, making it the most popular form of birth control in West Germany.¹⁰⁴

The initial lack of enthusiasm for the pill was the product of several interrelated and overlapping events. First, shortly after Anovlar's release in West Germany, reports began to trickle in from the United States and England that some women had developed thrombosis after taking the pill. Some cases of death had even been reported. This news coincided with the thalidomide scandal in Germany. Following a short clinical trial period, the German pharmaceutical company Grünenthal put Contergan (thalidomide) on the market. The company championed the drug as a safe and effective treatment for anxiety, insomnia, and morning sickness in pregnant women. In December 1961, Grünenthal pulled the drug from the market after its use by pregnant women was linked to catastrophic birth defects. By 1962, newspapers and magazines had carried countless stories underscor-

TABLE 3.1. WEST GERMAN WOMEN BETWEEN THE AGES OF
15 AND 44 USING THE PILL, 1964–1972.

Year	West German Women Using the Pill (%)
1964	1.7
1965	2.4
1966	3.7
1967	6.5
1968	11.9
1969	16.3
1970	18.7
1971	25.6
1972	29.6

Source: Ralf Dose, *Die Durchsetzung der chemisch-hormonellen Kontrazeption in der Bundesrepublik Deutschland* (Berlin: Wissenschaftszentrum Berlin, 1989), 17.

ing the gross negligence of Grünenthal. The federal government launched a criminal investigation of the company.[105]

Given the ongoing thalidomide scandal, it is not surprising that Germans were reluctant to embrace the new oral contraceptive; news magazines contained countless reports of the dangerous side effects experienced by women in other countries who had used oral contraceptives, and German medical experts offered conflicting views on the pill's safety. This uncertainty prompted some Germans to turn to the federal government for a definitive answer. But no such answer was immediately forthcoming. The Federal Ministry of Health responded to one woman's inquiry by shifting the burden back to the pharmaceutical company: "Legislators addressed this question at length before passing the pharmaceutical law on May 16, 1961; they decided not to relieve pharmaceutical companies from responsibility for the drugs they produced, that before bringing a drug to market the company must carry out all tests and trials in an objective manner based on the current state of scientific knowledge."[106] Given Grünenthal's culpability in the thalidomide debacle, Germans more than likely did not find this response reassuring.

Some women also had difficulty finding doctors willing to prescribe oral contraceptives, particularly in predominantly Catholic regions. In November 1967, *Stern* reported that a Munich law student had published a list of doctors who would prescribe the pill without asking "dumb or humiliating questions."[107] The list itself represented nothing new; many student committees had published such lists. However, until now, no mainstream publication had supported such endeavors.

Stern's endorsement was indicative of Germans' changing attitudes toward sexuality. The younger generation, in particular, increasingly rejected the bourgeois conformity of their parents. Between 1967 and 1973, the number of unmarried women between the ages of eighteen and twenty-nine who believed that it was morally acceptable to live with a man outside of wedlock increased from 24 percent to 92 percent.[108] Instead of seeing Christianity as an antidote to fascism, many West German youths underscored similarities between fascism and Christianity; they drew parallels between the sexual conservatism promoted by the churches and sexual repression under Nazism.[109] By 1968, German university campuses had been transformed into sites of protest against the political, social, economic, and sexual norms of the 1950s. For students, lifestyle revolt and political protest became intricately linked. "Make love, not war" became the defining idea behind the movement.[110]

Against the backdrop of this new political and cultural climate, Germans reacted negatively to the encyclical. In addition to having believed that the pope would not reject the advice of his own commission, many German Catholics could not fathom why using the pill contradicted Church teachings. They endorsed the argument made by John Rock, an American Catholic doctor and one of the pill's creators. Rock claimed that by preventing ovulation rather than intervening directly in the sex act (as was the case with condoms and IUDs), the pill constituted a hormonal rhythm method. Moreover, as early as 1965, the chair of DBK, Julius Cardinal Döpfner, instructed priests in the Diocese of Munich not to exclude from Communion all married couples who practiced contraception: "Responsible partners who see themselves obliged to contraceptive marital intercourse, not lightly and habitually, but rather as a regrettable emergency solution, may take it that by doing so they do not exclude themselves from communion at the Eucharist table." Although Döpfner did not go so far as to approve artificial contraception, by allowing such couples to receive Communion, he did contravene the instructions of *Casti Connubii*.[111] Thus, many West German Catholic married couples felt that they had the implicit if not explicit support of the Church to use artificial contraception.

So when *Humanae Vitae* contravened this implicit support, West German Catholics and non-Catholics expressed shock and anger. In the press, on the radio, and on television, the encyclical encountered widespread resistance and ridicule. *Der Spiegel* printed multiple letters to the editor from Catholics and non-Catholics concerning the encyclical. Although a few writers praised the encyclical, the vast majority did not. One male reader satirically proposed the following solution to the Catholic moral dilemma: "As a way to relieve the conscience, a Catholic man should marry a Protestant girl. So long as the woman does not accept the Catholic faith, she could without further ado use the pill for family planning."[112] This cynicism was not limited to non-Catholics. Walter Dirks, a prominent Catholic journalist and husband of the kfd president, Marianne Dirks, wrote in the *Frankfurter Hefte*, "The pope speaks of love as the blind speak of color."[113]

While lay Catholics responded swiftly, German bishops and theologians initially kept silent. Most found themselves in an awkward position; they had overwhelmingly supported revising the Church's teachings on birth control. Now it appeared that they had led their flock astray. In *Strukturkrise einer Kirche* (1969), Thomas and Gertrude Sartory described German Church leaders' early reactions: "From some apologetic radio broadcasts, one heard in the first days after the appearance of the encyclical that whether one looked high or low, no moral theologian could be found to comment. It was as if they vanished from the face of the earth."[114] But the official Church in West Germany could not remain silent indefinitely.

Priests, congregants, and the ZdK demanded to know how *Humanae Vitae* should be interpreted in Germany. Could Germans dissent without jeopardizing their souls? What were priests to say to their congregants? According to a *Deutsche Tagespost* report of August 17, 1968, one hundred Münster priests were refusing to do an about-face; they argued that in keeping with the "Majority Report," they had not misled their parishioners. The prominent Catholic author Luise Rinser published an open letter to Döpfner in which she pleaded for him to take action against the encyclical because it violated the spirit of Vatican II.[115] Most significantly, the president of ZdK, Karl Furst zu Löwenstein, wrote Döpfner to make it clear that it was "not about the corruption of our times" if young married couples "earnestly question how many children their family can rear responsibly before God." Löwenstein noted that Vatican II had affirmed responsible parenthood, as did *Humanae Vitae*. Yet the encyclical forbade married couples to use reliable methods of contraception. Löwenstein concluded by mentioning the upcoming Catholic Congress, at which he believed a discussion of birth control must take place, not in order to tell the pope what he must do, but to "give him a picture of our situation—as families, as modern married persons, as astute, responsible Church members, as German Catholics, with perhaps problems different from those in other continents, so that the Mother Church realizes that we are adult children of God who can be given more trust."[116] German Catholics were no longer willing to accept unconditionally papal pronouncements and expected German hierarchs to support their decisions.

On August 30, 1968, the German bishops gave their qualified support for the continued use of artificial contraception. But like Vatican II documents, the so-called Königstein Declaration was a document of compromise, since not all German bishops supported reform. Bishops Hermann Schäufele of Freiburg and Rudolf Graber of Regensburg sent personal messages of gratitude to the pope for the encyclical. Lorenz Cardinal Jaeger of Paderborn accused believers of having "misguided consciences" and argued that public outrage against the encyclical demonstrated "how weak the belief of many Catholics was in the truths that merited obedience."[117] The Königstein Declaration's language of compromise led a more conservative Church leadership in the 1980s to try to limit or even rescind the declaration's tacit approval of artificial contraception. However, in 1968, its cautious acknowledgment of married couples' right to make informed decisions of conscience about contraception significantly reduced tensions in the German Catholic Church and safeguarded the credibility of the German bishops. Catholic couples chose to hear only the affirmation of their right to decide; the document's admonishment that such couples must face the judgment of God alone received little attention, and its assertion that even nonfallible teachings of the Church deserved obedience went unheeded.[118] Lay endorsement of contraception would carry the day at the upcoming Catholic Congress in Essen.

The issue of birth control dominated press coverage of the Essen congress. On September 3, 1968, the Catholic extraparliamentary opposition group, Kritischer Katholizismus, demanded Paul VI's resignation, as well as that of two German cardinals who openly supported the encyclical. This announcement garnered banner headlines in the secular and religious press. The press also highlighted the close link that Kritischer Katholizismus drew between the Church's condemnation of birth control and its complicity in National Socialist crimes, its postwar failure to de-Nazify ecclesiastic bureaucracies, and its support of remilitarization.[119] The Tübingen paper, *Schwäbisches Tagblatt*, gave credence to the group's accusations that the Church acted like a police state when it confirmed that plainclothes officers had been instructed to prevent group members from attending official forums; congress organizers denied the charge.[120] Other newspapers, such as *Westdeutsche Allgemeine Zeitung*, countered that it was the Catholic extraparliamentary opposition whose tactics mirrored those of the Nazis.[121] Everyone agreed that the Catholic unified front no longer existed.

But Kritischer Katholizismus's shock tactics were not the real story of the Catholic Congress in Essen. As Reinhold Noll, the editor of *Fränkische Nachrichten*, astutely noted, such tactics distracted from the real revolution; ordinary middle-class German Catholics were demanding fundamental changes in the Church's structure and organization.[122] At the official forum on marriage, numerous speakers enumerated the encyclical's flaws to loud applause. One speaker explained that the encyclical's condemnation of artificial contraception was based on natural law, not on evidence from the Bible. Given that modern science had demonstrated natural law's shortcomings, the encyclical's authority was dubious. Another speaker simply asserted that he had no need for "cheap" absolution given by priests in the confession box. In the end, the participants voted overwhelmingly in favor of demanding the encyclical's revision (three thousand in favor, ninety against, and fifty-eight abstentions).[123]

Although theological debate on *Humanae Vitae* continued long after the Essen congress, the general Catholic population ceased to follow such debates closely. Catholics had reached their decision, and the Königstein Declaration affirmed that decision. By the time of the Würzburg Synod (1972–1975), the controversy over marital morality in West Germany had shifted from birth control to celibacy and interfaith marriage.[124] Using birth control became a nonissue for German Catholics. Consequently, when John Paul II gave a series of addresses on marital morality beginning in 1978, Germans paid little attention to his condemnation of artificial contraception or his effort to redefine *Humanae Vitae* as an infallible teaching. The Königstein Declaration provided them a framework in which they could express loyal dissent.

In addition to undermining German Catholic confidence in Vatican leadership of the universal Church, the *Humanae Vitae* crisis had two other significant ramifications in Germany. First, many prominent Catholics believed that affirming the birth control ban undermined the Church's stance on abortion. In a 1972 *Der Spiegel* interview, the Bonn moral theologian Franz Böckle noted, "So long as we have no credible answer for family planning, it is difficult to provide a convincing rule for abortion."[125] Similarly,

TABLE 3.2: SURVEY OF WEST GERMAN CATHOLICS ON *HUMANAE VITAE*.

West German Catholics on *Humanae Vitae*	All Surveyed(%)	Churchgoers(%)
I believe the pope has acted according to divine inspiration and we must comply.	6	14
I have doubts about whether the pope in this case was well advised, but I will comply with his instruction.	17	25
I believe the pope has erred; consequently I will act according to my conscience.	68	57
In my opinion, the pope is so far removed from reality on this that I am seriously considering separating from the Church.	8	3
No opinion	1	1

Source: Institut für Demoskopie Allensbach, *Katholische Ehepaare über Humanae Vitae*, BA, ZSg. 132/1542.

a German priest opined in a letter to the president of the ZdK that many Catholics now would be "unable to resist the temptation to limit the number of children through abortion."[126]

Humanae Vitae also compromised the German Catholic Church's credibility as a partner in formulating government policy on sex education, family planning, and abortion. On October 2, 1968, two German Catholic organizations—Katholisches Zentral Institut für Ehe- und Familienfragen (Catholic Central Institute on Marriage and Family) and Katholische Ehe- und Familienberatung (Catholic Marriage and Family Counseling Service)—found themselves in an awkward position when their continued involvement on the Committee on Sex Education and Family Planning organized by the Federal Ministry for Family and Youth was called into question by other members. Dr. G. Struck, a representative of the Katholisches Zentral Institut für Ehe- und Familienfragen, explained that neither organization agreed with the encyclical. In keeping with a statement released by the national organization of Catholic doctors, Katholische Ärztearbeit Deutschlands, they believed that the distinction the encyclical drew between natural and artificial means of contraception was itself artificial.[127] Copies of this statement were provided to all committee members. Struck also emphasized that his organization had the German bishops' support.[128]

Unfortunately, the minutes of the meeting provide no indication of the committee members' responses. But German attitudes on sexuality were changing, and Catholic organizations that objected to government-sponsored sex education and family planning programs increasingly encountered stiff resistance from women's groups and even from some government officials. For example, in a 1980 internal memo, a government official sharply criticized the Catholic social welfare organization, Caritas, for its stance on abortion: "'Help' according to Caritas means only assistance in preserving the life of the unborn child. The interests of the woman, acknowledged by the Constitutional Court, are ignored."[129] This attitude was not confined to secular actors; by the early 1980s some Catholic women were also questioning whether the Church had their best interests at heart.

Catholic Women, Birth Control, and the Church

Although prominent German Catholic women, such as Luise Rinser and Marianne Dirks, participated in the early birth control debate, they did so either as individuals or as members of male-dominated groups. Despite the topic's obvious relevance to women's lives, most mainstream Catholic women's groups did not take up the cause of birth control in the 1960s or early 1970s. The editors of *Frau und Mutter* made no reference to *Humanae Vitae* in the months immediately following its release. Moreover, at the meeting of the World Union of Catholic Women's Organizations in November 1968, opinions on the encyclical were so varied that the organization concluded that no statement in the name of its member organizations could be issued.[130] Catholic women were deeply divided on the question of artificial contraception.

In West Germany, the influence of religious and secular feminism on mainstream Catholic women's organizations developed at a much slower pace than was the case in the United States. In fact, prior to 1971, women did not hold a majority of the leadership positions in the kfd, the largest West German Catholic women's organization.[131] Although a shift in emphasis could be detected by the mid-1970s in *Frau und Mutter*, the kfd did not adopt a new mission statement calling for the recognition of women's fundamental right to equal treatment in church and society until 1979.[132]

The 1979 kfd mission statement did not have the universal support of its members. The national kfd leadership knew that deep divisions existed among German Catholic women: many rejected feminism and clung to traditional notions of Catholic femininity; others questioned or rejected the Church's traditional teachings on gender and sexuality. At the 1980 Catholic

Congress in Berlin, the kfd general secretary, Anneliese Lissner, described her role as one of guiding the organization toward a more progressive future, while "making sure that the steps are not too large for the traditionalists or too small for the feminists."[133]

The national kfd leadership did not have to wait long to discover just how difficult negotiating a middle way would be. On November 18, 1980, Barbara Engl, the designated BDKJ youth spokesperson, confronted Pope John Paul II during his Munich visit:

> In your sermons, you have said many things that move us. Yet many youth in the Federal Republic find the Church difficult to understand. They have the impression that the Church anxiously tries to maintain existing relationships and emphasizes confessional differences, instead of seeking common ground. It reacts to issues of youth, friendship, sexuality, and partnership with prohibitions, and too often offers no response to young people's search for understanding and dialogue. Many cannot understand why the Church holds so axiomatically to celibacy, given the clerical shortage. Currently there are insufficient youth pastoral care workers and many want to know if it might not be possible for more women to hold offices in the Church.[134]

Engl's statement sparked widespread controversy in the German Catholic Church, particularly in the kfd. When the national kfd leadership publicly expressed its support for Engl's statement, most members reacted negatively. One kfd member wrote: "In fact, the Pope has addressed topics like premarital relations and birth control . . . and given clear answers! It is just that Barbara Engl and other youths prefer different answers. Christ's representative on earth and the successor of Peter, however, has proclaimed the truth of Christ. He cannot say 'yes' to an immoral way of life. That would be against God's divine order (= natural law)."[135] Entire local chapters also voiced their objections: "The St. Maria Magdalena Rheinbreitbach kfd chapter was outraged when it heard of your radio broadcast from the 14th of this month, declaring your support—hopefully incorrect—for Barbara Engl's remarks during the papal mass in Munich; we expect an immediate retraction. Our sense of faith and of ethics was effectively destroyed when the kfd abandoned its previous positions on questions of partnership and sexuality as well as on clerical celibacy; we cannot work within a Catholic women's association that thinks this way."[136]

Increasingly, the national kfd leadership found itself torn between two realities. On the one hand, young women were leaving the Church in alarming numbers because of its teachings on sexuality and femininity. A 1985 survey conducted by Renate Köcher of the Allensbach Institute for Public Opinion Research revealed that only 22 percent of Catholic women under the age of thirty identified themselves as faithful members of the Church, down from 50 percent in 1968. Only 38 percent believed that the Church could assist them in resolving moral questions.[137] On the other hand, those who remained active in the Church, particularly within Catholic women's organizations such as the kfd, were largely conservative in their orientation. Consequently, efforts by the kfd central office to stanch young women's exodus from the Church by incorporating into their mission statement a more liberal approach to questions of sexuality often alienated their most active members.

Yet despite the persistence of traditional beliefs within Catholic women's organizations, new ideas about sexuality and women's place in the Church were gaining favor among some German Catholic women. Press coverage of the 1982 Catholic Congress in Düsseldorf noted the growing dissonance between the hierarchy's perception of women's place in church and society and that of Catholic women. *Die Zeit* reported:

> The gentlemen of the hierarchy probably see that the role of women has changed. Nevertheless, their daily official bulletins depict an image of woman as housewife and mother that is consistent with their fanciful opinions about marriage and family. For them *Kinder*, Küche, *Kirche* is no worn-out formulation....
>
> Many women, however, have begun to feel the wounds inflicted upon them by the Church. They applaud appreciatively the Dutch professor Catharina Halkes.... [M]any women dream of a Church in which the divorced are accepted; in which more female altar servers are allowed ... a Church in which women can speak out without fear when they are beaten and maltreated; one in which the responsibility for sexual morality and family planning, and the associated feelings of guilt and conflicts of conscience, will no longer be the burden of women alone.[138]

The old ideology of *Kinder*, Küche, *Kirche* no longer rang true for many West German Catholic women. For these women, the Church's attitude toward artificial contraception was indicative of a larger problem—the Church's refusal to recognize women's equality.

In 1985–1986, the topic of artificial contraception suddenly reappeared in German headlines. Several articles noted that Cardinal Höffner was underscoring the "almost dogmatic" character of *Humanae Vitae* and that he had described the pill as a form of "private abortion at the earliest possible point in time."[139] In an interview with *Rheinischer Merkur/Christ und Welt*, Höffner declared that the Königstein Declaration supported only natural family planning methods. Citing the conclusions of the Fifth Ordinary General Assembly of the Synod of the Bishops (1980) on "The Duties of the Christian Family in Today's World" and the teachings of John Paul II, Cardinal Höffner associated the acceptance of artificial birth control with increased acceptance of other "manipulations" such as artificial fertilization, sterilization, and abortion.[140]

Like John Paul II, Höffner was moving beyond Paul VI's characterization of the use of artificial contraception as a violation of moral chastity, labeling it instead a violation of faith. For two decades, West German Catholics had believed that the German episcopate supported married couples' right to use artificial contraception within marriage if good reasons existed for not having more children. Thus, Höffner's statement shocked many German Catholics who had taken for granted that the Königstein Declaration shielded them from John Paul II's growing insistence on *Humanae Vitae*'s infallibility.

The president of the Katholischer Deutscher Frauenbund (KDFB), Rachel Pechel, wrote Höffner, "We feel compelled to make you aware that a high percentage of Catholic women are uninterested in your definition of the Königstein Declaration and are apathetic toward it." Pechel asserted that German Catholic women were "no longer willing to acquiesce to any restriction on their freedom to make decisions of conscience or to turn away from the Second Vatican Council."[141] Similarly, the kfd president wrote, "Precisely because we want to prevent the growing dissonance on issues of marriage and family between German Catholics, particularly women, and official Church representatives, we believe a general consultation is urgently needed on these questions."[142]

In response to the letters, the DBK agreed to a meeting with representatives of the two largest German Catholic women's organizations. In July 1987, the first of a series of meetings took place in which Höffner's remarks on birth control served as the entry point into a broader discussion about women's place in the Church. The KDFB and kfd representatives stressed: "Patriarchal society has reached its end. There has to be a conversation in the Church about new forms of collaboration between men and women in the family, in society, and in the Church."[143] Despite the DBK's 1981 declaration, *Zu Fragen der Stellung der Frau in Kirche und Gesellschaft*, German Catholic women believed that little had changed in practice. Catholic women had begun the difficult process of redefining their relationship with the Church.

. . .

The birth control debate in postwar West Germany began as a debate among experts about the new oral form of contraception. Politicians, doctors, university professors, and clergy members discussed the pill and by extension what constituted acceptable public sexual mores. As the new form of contraception gained in popularity, experts lost control of the debate. Despite the official rhetoric of sexual conservatism in 1950s Germany, West German attitudes toward family size and more generally toward sexuality were changing. The introduction of the pill accelerated this process, because the pill constituted a reliable and minimally invasive form of contraception, and it gave women control over their fertility. But West German acceptance of the pill was not accompanied by a parallel acceptance by the universal Catholic Church. When Paul VI reaffirmed the traditional ban on artificial contraception in 1968, many West Germans—non-Catholic and Catholic—reacted angrily. Mainstream Catholics rebelled. The Königstein Declaration, in which the DBK recognized the right of married couples to make informed decisions of conscience about birth control, mollified them to some extent. However, the declaration could not change the fact that, increasingly, official Catholic doctrine on gender and sexuality did not reflect the values of most Germans, including Catholics. This development had multiple consequences. First, it compromised the ability of Catholic officials in West Germany to influence government policy on questions of sexual mores; by the early 1970s, the Church found itself marginalized in policy discussions on sex education and abortion. Second, within the Catholic Church, it raised questions about the Church's unconditional rejection of abortion. Third, the Vatican position on artificial contraception left many German Catholics disillusioned. This disillusionment, in turn, took multiple forms. For some West German Catholics, it represented the last straw; they separated from the Church or simply distanced themselves from it. For others disillusionment led to increased engagement in the Church. As members of either alternative or traditional organizations, they advocated for change in official Church teachings on artificial contraception and more generally for a revision of the Church's negative assessment of sexuality. They associated this negative assessment of sexuality with the persistence of a male-dominated celibate clergy and the lack of democracy in the Church.

By the late 1970s and early 1980s, the connection drawn between celibacy and a negative assessment of sexuality and contraception developed a new dimension, as mainstream Catholic women slowly internalized ideas promoted by religious and secular feminists. Increasingly, they perceived the Church's rejection of artificial contraception as symptomatic of the Church's low valuation of women. Slowly, mainstream Catholic women's organizations joined alternative women's groups in demanding that the Church acknowledge their worth as human beings, not just as wives and mothers. However, not all West German Catholic women welcomed this change; many remained loyal to the Vatican's position. Consequently, mainstream Catholic women's organizations, such as the kfd, found that they were torn between two realities. Young women were abandoning the Church because of its position on gender and sexuality. However, kfd efforts to prevent their departure by endorsing artificial contraception and championing more roles for women in Church governance alienated the organization's conservative base. Many conservative women left the kfd and joined small fundamentalist/evangelical groups. Fragmentation within mainstream organizations made it clear that the Church could no longer count on the unconditional support of women, but it also meant that women often worked at cross-purposes with one another in their efforts to renegotiate their traditional relationship with the Church. The interrelated debates on celibacy and artificial contraception produced a series of crises that continue to redefine modern piety. On the one hand, these crises accelerated the exodus from and the inner migration within the Church. On the other hand, they catalyzed an intense engagement with and defense of the Vatican's positions on sexuality by those Catholics who remained active in the Church.

CHAPTER 4

The Abortion Debate
Hidden Tensions and New Directions

In 1969, the newly elected SPD-FDP coalition government announced plans to reform Paragraph 218, the law that regulated women's access to abortion. This announcement prompted a public debate in West Germany on the state's obligation to protect unborn life—a debate that continues today in reunified Germany. In analyzing key events in that debate between 1969 and 1989, this chapter makes a twofold argument. First, it argues that despite West Germany's increasingly secular orientation, the Catholic Church exercised significant political influence with respect to abortion policy throughout the history of the Federal Republic. Second, it argues that the West German Church's participation in these debates exposed deep rifts within the Catholic community, which in turn contributed to the formation of a smaller, more activist, and conservative Church. By the early 1980s, this smaller Church began developing new arguments, strategies, and issue-specific alliances in response to Germany's changed social, cultural, and political climate.

This transformation of the Catholic community did not take place overnight, nor did all Catholic leaders embrace the need for change at the same time. Catholic women's organizations, painfully aware of women's growing alienation from the Church because of its stance on issues such as birth control and abortion, led the charge. They introduced new strategies for protecting unborn life as part of a larger campaign to expand women's roles in the Church. However, the episcopate and the ZdK initially resisted these efforts. In 1988, Archbishop Johannes Dyba of Fulda went so far as to suggest that the kfd had "nothing against the mass killing of children," because it changed its magazine title from *Frau und Mutter* (Woman and Mother) to *Frau & mutter*. With this accusation, the debate on abortion and on women's place in the Church reached a new crescendo, and the exodus of women from the Church accelerated. Given women's greater engagement in the Catholic community than that of their male counterparts, the Church could not indefinitely ignore women's growing disillusionment. It also could not ignore that the CDU's position on the defense of life no longer coincided with that of the Church. If the Church wanted to remain politically relevant, it would have to cultivate new political allies, as well as new tactics. This awareness first translated into political success in the context of the debate on NRTs and embryonic research in the late 1980s; however, it was the new stance taken by CDU women and the kfd leadership on abortion in 1984 that created the space in which new strategies and new alliances with political actors other than the Christian parties could develop.

The Theological and Legal Framework of the Debate

Although most West Germans equated the Catholic position on abortion with a unilateral condemnation, the theological framework in which Catholics approached abortion reform in 1969 was much more complex. In fact, many Catholics, including several prominent theologians, numbered among the early supporters of abortion law reform. In supporting reform, they did not repudiate Catholic doctrine; they drew upon it, catalyzing a heated theological and political debate that polarized the West German Catholic community and had long-term consequences for reproductive politics in Germany.

The Theological Context

The Catholic Church has always considered abortion immoral; however, it has not always considered all abortions murder. In fact, for centuries two theological traditions on abortion coexisted—one that advocated a limited pro-choice position and one that supported a rigid condemnation. Only with the publication of the 1917 Code of Canon Law did the latter tradition achieve complete dominance in official Vatican teachings.[1]

As with contraception, the Bible provides little guidance on the subject of abortion. The most explicit biblical condemnation of abortion concerns miscarriages in cases of violence: "When men have a fight and hurt a pregnant woman, so that she suffers a miscarriage, but no further injury, the guilty one shall be fined as much as the woman's husband demands of him. . . . But if injury ensues, you shall give life for life."[2] In AD 100 the Didache, one of the earliest Church documents, made no distinction between the killing of an unborn child and the murder of a living child. However, by the fourth century, the Church fathers offered differing views on whether abortion was equivalent to murder.[3] Consequently, in some early Church documents, the

Church fathers emphasized the sins of fornication and adultery over the sin of abortion. For example, the Synod of Elvira in AD 306 addressed abortion only in cases of adultery, and in the eighth century the Irish canons declared sterilization a more serious offense than abortion, except in cases where the fetus was fully formed. Since sterilization permanently broke the connection between procreation and sexual relations, the penitent had to fast for seven years, whereas only three years of fasting were required for abortion.[4] Similarly, the *Decretum Gratiani* (1151), the first comprehensive code of canon law accepted as authoritative by the Church, concluded that abortion was homicide "only when the fetus was formed."[5] Many Catholic theologians at this time endorsed a delayed hominization theory, according to which the fetus did not possess a rational soul at the time of conception and consequently did not yet constitute a human life. Augustine of Hippo, Jerome, and Thomas Aquinas all propagated this view. According to Aquinas, the fetus is first endowed with a vegetative soul, then an animal soul, and finally a rational human soul. The fetus acquired a human soul once it reached full development—approximately forty days after conception for a male and eighty days for a female.[6]

In addition to concerns about the moment of ensoulment, early theologians grappled with the question of therapeutic abortion. In the fifteenth century, Antoninus of Florence, later canonized by the Church, approved early abortions in order to save a mother's life. And in the sixteenth century, Antonius de Cordoba argued that the mother could take abortive medication even late in pregnancy if required for health, insisting that the woman had a *jus prius*.[7] As late as 1872, the Vatican refused to give a definitive answer when consulted about an abortion requiring dismemberment of a formed fetus in order to save the mother's life.[8]

Yet in 2009 the Catholic Church excommunicated Sister Margaret McBride, an administrator at a Catholic hospital in Phoenix, Arizona, for approving an abortion in order to save a woman's life and rescinded the excommunication only after she agreed to serve penance for her transgression.[9] That same year the Church became entangled in controversy when a Brazilian archbishop excommunicated the doctors who performed an abortion on a nine-year-old girl who had been raped by her stepfather. The archbishop also excommunicated the mother, who approved the procedure in order to save her child's life. Neither the child nor the rapist was excommunicated.[10]

Like the limited pro-choice position, this unilateral condemnation also had a long history in the Church. In 1220, the Decretals of Gregory IX treated contraception and abortion as homicide. In 1588, Pope Sixtus rescinded the distinction made in the Gratian Code between aborting an animated and a nonanimated fetus; all abortions were designated homicides, and no exception was made for therapeutic abortion. Similarly, the 1917 Code of Canon Law implicitly endorsed immediate hominization and prescribed excommunication for the mother and any person who abetted an abortion. From this point forward, the official Church moved in the direction of rejecting delayed hominization, declaring abortion a sin against life.[11] In 1974, the CDF acknowledged in *On Procured Abortions* that the point of ensoulment could not be established definitively, but emphasized the human potentiality of the fetus: "From a moral point of view this is certain: even if a doubt existed concerning whether the fruit of conception is already a human person, it is objectively a grave sin to risk murder: 'The one who will be man is already one.'"[12]

Yet this seemingly clear-cut condemnation is more complicated than it first appears to be. The Church permits some therapeutic abortions, based on the distinction it draws between direct and indirect abortion. The former is illicit and the latter is licit. A direct therapeutic abortion is defined as the intentional killing of the fetus in order to save the mother's life. An indirect abortion is one in which the death of the fetus is an unintended secondary effect. The acceptability of the latter is based on the principle of double effect (explained in Chapter 2). A woman diagnosed with aggressive uterine cancer or an ectopic pregnancy may have an abortion because treatment requires the removal of a diseased uterus or fallopian tubes or both. The removal of the uterus or fallopian tubes is not intended to bring about the death of the infant; death is an unintended side effect of removing the diseased organ, albeit a known one.[13] However, the decision to abort was that of the doctor, not the pregnant woman. The West German Catholic feminist theologian Uta Ranke-Heinemann noted in 1988 with reference to the 1976 German bishops' directive, which stated that they would respect the doctor's decision in cases where the mother's life was in jeopardy: "This letter is directed to the physicians. . . . The mothers are simply shifted from one alien jurisdiction to another. The decision about their life or death is transferred from the almighty gentlemen in black to the almighty gentlemen in white."[14] Yet even this concession deviated from the Vatican position; it implied that the German bishops would not take action against physicians who in good conscience performed a direct therapeutic abortion when the mother's life was in jeopardy. When on June 29, 1986, ZDF aired a program suggesting that the German bishops supported direct therapeutic abortion, the DBK chair immediately clarified their position, stating that respecting the doctor's decision should not be conflated with approving it.[15]

Because Catholic teachings emphasized safeguarding the unborn child's soul and motherly sacrifice, they potentially placed the mother's physical well-being in jeopardy. As late as 1961, Bernhard Häring argued that willingness to die in childbirth defined motherhood: "The very essence of motherly love and of the maternal spirit of sacrifice demands that the mother be willing to forfeit her own life rather than presume to intervene in the life of her child."[16] Ensuring the baptism of the dying child also took precedence over safeguarding the mother's health: "If there is no other way to save the life of the child, above all no way to ensure its baptism, the mother is obliged to submit to an operation of this kind. In cases where the child is in extreme danger, the surgeon is permitted to perform a cesarean section without her consent in order to rescue the child in its 'necessity.'"[17] These types of statements led Uta Ranke-Heinemann in 1988 to conclude acerbically that "the only good mother is a dead mother, for the only mother who does not 'betray her conscience' is the one who is ready to go under with the fetus."[18]

Yet despite the prominence of the "right-to-life" argument in twentieth-century Catholicism, some Catholic theologians defended the morality of direct abortion in certain circumstances. These theologians took one of three approaches—that of delayed hominization based on modern scientific knowledge about fetal development; the relational approach; or a broader interpretation of the principle of double effect.[19] Modern proponents of delayed hominization, such as Joseph Donceel, argued that since the nervous system and the cortex of the brain were not fully formed in early pregnancy, the fetus was not yet a person. Although the fetus deserved consideration because it was in the process of becoming human, it could not command the same respect as fully formed life; consequently, in some limited circumstances abortion might be permissible. Other proponents of this view simply insisted that theologians could not presume to know the point of hominization. In 1962, Karl Rahner wrote: "It cannot be inferred from the Church's dogmatic definitions that it would be contrary to faith to assume that the leap to spirit-person happens only during the course of the embryo's development. No theologian would claim the ability to prove interrupting pregnancy is in every case the murder of a human being."[20] The relational approach emphasized the centrality of the parents' acceptance of the child. By their acceptance of the fetus, particularly by naming it, the parents gave the fetus its place in the world. The fetus did not become a child until its parents accepted it as such. If this relationship did not exist, one had a duty to discuss the legitimacy of continuing the pregnancy. Anton Antweiler, a Swiss theologian teaching in Germany, endorsed this view in a 1971 *Stern* article, which then received prominent coverage in *Der Spiegel*.[21] Finally, some theologians supported a broader interpretation of the principle of double effect. They argued that direct abortion to save the mother's life should be allowed if the fetus was not viable and failure to remove it would result in serious injury or death for the mother. Bernhard Häring (after 1968) and Franz Böckle endorsed this view.[22]

Additionally, many Catholics considered the Church's unconditional condemnation of birth control and abortion hypocritical because of the Church's role in Germany's Nazi past and its postwar support of rearmament. The inferior status assigned to illegitimate children by canon law until 1983 also made the Church vulnerable to accusations of hypocrisy. The canon law expert Horst Hermann noted that the Church demanded that the state extend protection to unwanted illegitimate children, while the Church itself did not guarantee such children equal rights. The 1917 Code of Canon Law, in effect until 1983, dictated that an illegitimate child could not join a religious order or become a priest without receiving dispensation from the official Church. Nor could an illegitimate child inherit property.[23] Although some critics highlighted Church hypocrisy in the early debates on abortion, this viewpoint did not dominate media coverage until the late 1970s, when the moral credibility and authority of the Church came under heavy attack.

Abortion's status as a moral and political issue also reopened the theological and political debate on the separation of church and state. At Vatican II (1962–1965), the council fathers emphasized the separation of church and state, as well as the freedom of lay Catholics to formulate their own political opinions, albeit with Christian principles in mind: "It is very important, especially where a pluralistic society prevails, that there be a correct notion of the relationship between the political community and the Church, and a clear distinction between the tasks which Christians undertake, individually or as a group, on their own responsibility as citizens guided by the dictates of a Christian conscience, and the activities which in union with their pastors they carry out in the name of the state."[24] The council fathers did not rule out all political interventions, but they disavowed the close association of church and state that typified the Adenauer era (1949–1963), when Catholic priests held prominent political positions in the CDU-CSU, and many bishops explicitly told the faithful how to vote. In 1969, the DBK reaffirmed its commitment to nonintervention in the political sphere unless "the foundations of our democracy are at risk."²⁵ For conservative West German Catholics, the proposed liberalization of Paragraph 218 constituted such a threat. However, as we shall see, most German Catholics disagreed and interpreted the institutional Church's interventions in the political debate on abortion as a violation of the spirit of Vatican II—a violation for which West German Catholics had little tolerance, especially after the 1968 papal condemnation of artificial contraception. Increasingly, West German Catholics, even some who rejected abortion law reform, disapproved of the Church's intervention into the political debate on abortion.

The Legal Context

Like the ecclesial/theological debate on abortion, the legal debate on abortion in West Germany had a long history, predating the formation of the German state in 1871. The 1871 penal code defined abortion as a felony punishable by up to five years' imprisonment. By the late nineteenth century, feminists and some social reformers demanded support for unwed mothers, recognition of women's right of self-determination, and the removal of restrictions on abortions. These efforts occurred in the context of a broader movement to put contraception, population control, and women's rights on the political agenda. In 1926, the Weimar government approved revisions that decriminalized abortions performed to save the mother's life. The National Socialist government introduced two new provisions that reflected the distinction it drew between worthy life and "life unworthy of life" (*Lebensunwertes Leben*). The 1935 Law for Hereditary Health approved abortion and enforced sterilization for members of so-called alien races and inferior persons, while the 1943 amendment to Paragraph 218 made abortion a capital offense for Aryan women.²⁶

In 1949, determined to distinguish itself from its predecessor, the new Federal Republic of Germany adopted the Grundgesetz, which established a hierarchy of rights—the most important of which was the government's duty to safeguard "human dignity" and the "right to life."²⁷ It also reinstated the Weimar Criminal Code, including the 1926 version of Paragraph 218.

Although revisions of Paragraph 218 had been proposed in the 1950s, efforts to reform the West German Criminal Code did not take off until the late 1960s and early 1970s. As Dagmar Herzog noted in *Sex after Fascism*, the post–World War II abortion reform movement became possible only because of fundamental shifts in social and political perspectives: "In the reconfigured social and political climate of the late 1960s, under the quadruple impact of the 'sex wave,' the Social Democrats' ascension to participation in power in the Grand Coalition (1966–1969), the rise of the student movement, and the growing popular conviction that the morality of the Christian churches was hypocritical, there was a far greater willingness across the political spectrum to liberaliz[e] sex-related law."[28]

In 1969, the SPD in coalition with the FDP defeated the CDU-CSU coalition. For the first time in the history of the Federal Republic, the Christian parties did not control or share control of the federal government. Almost immediately, the new coalition government announced its intentions to reform Paragraph 218. A commission appointed by the government presented two proposals. The majority of commission members recommended the *Fristenlösung* (term solution) that decriminalized abortion during the first trimester after the woman had received counseling. A minority of the commission recommended the *Indikationslösung* (indication or legal justification solution) that prohibited abortion unless there was a justification for it, such as rape. The two reform models quickly spurred a heated public debate in which the West German media, secular feminist groups, the political parties, the two Christian churches, the medical community, and the general public became embroiled.

The abortion reform battle was by no means limited to West Germany. The West German debate occurred in the context of widespread efforts to liberalize or abolish abortion laws throughout Western Europe and the United States.[29] Moreover, in 1972, East Germany quietly legalized abortion in the first trimester.[30] Proponents of reform employed multiple rationales for liberalizing or abolishing abortion laws: the inefficacy of criminal punishment, class inequities in the application of the law, the danger that illegal abortion posed to women's health, women's right to self-determination, and the right to privacy. However, the choice of rationales as well as the emphasis placed on different rationales and the discursive frame in which they were presented varied from one nation to another. Both reformers and their opponents adapted their approach to the cultural and political traditions of each nation in order to garner widespread support. For example, the idea that women possessed a special competency to speak on abortion had wide acceptance in Germany. Consequently, German feminists utilized this frame to publicize problems with the existing law in the 1970s and to demand additional reforms in the 1990s. In contrast, feminists in the U.S. abortion debate strategically chose to downplay the gender dimension. Instead, they underscored the right to privacy, taking advantage of American mistrust of government intervention in the private sphere.[31] Thus, despite the international scope of the debate, the articulation was decisively national. However, this should not be taken to mean that nations acted in isolation. Not only were transnational actors involved in national debates, opponents and proponents of abortion reform closely followed developments in other nations and tried to use these developments to their advantage.

Early Interventions: Frauenaktion 218, the Vatican, and Cardinal Höffner

The altered social and political climate of the late 1960s and early 1970s did not translate into an easy victory for proponents of abortion law reform; instead, reformers confronted stiff resistance from the Christian churches and the medical community. On December 10, 1970, a group of Catholic and Protestant writers published a thirty-page brochure, "Das Gesetz des Staates und die sittliche Ordnung," with a foreword coauthored by the chair of the DBK, Cardinal Julius Döpfner, and the chair of the Council of the EKD, Bishop Hermann Dietzelbinger. The document condemned abortion as an immoral act that required criminal prosecution: "Not every infringement of a moral obligation requires criminal prosecution. However, the commandment against killing human life as a moral axiom is of such fundamental significance for the human community that it must likewise be anchored in the law of the state."[32] In 1970–1971, the DBK, ZdK, and BDKJ also issued condemnations.[33]

The medical community joined the churches in opposing reform. On June 24, 1971, the Association of Established Doctors in Germany (Verband der niedergelassenen Ärzte Deutschlands) declared that "every abortion is a destruction of new life and thus an act of killing." It warned that an abortion should not be likened "to the removal of an appendix or blastoma."[34] Similarly, the president of the Professional Association of Gynecologists (Berufverband der Frauenärzte) wrote, "In our opinion, the obligation of the doctor to weigh meticulously the risks (i.e., the justifications) must be preserved; in accordance with this obligation is the right of professional freedom, which can never be qualified or coerced."[35]

Although the liberal press and some prominent Protestant and Catholic theologians criticized these interventions, government officials and politicians reacted cautiously. With national elections fast approaching, they were reluctant to antagonize either the churches or the medical community. In 1971, Justice Minister Gerhard Jahn (SPD) withdrew his support for the *Fristenlösung*, as did some SPD legislators. Immediately, the editor in chief of *Der Spiegel*, Rudolf Augstein (a former Catholic), attacked Jahn and the Christian churches, particularly the Catholic Church: "But whether a two-month-old embryo is a 'someone' who already has the right to its nascent life is now the controversial question, which the minister, at least, has decided in agreement with the pope."[36] Augstein also accused Jahn and other politicians of pursuing selfish interests at the expense of the concerned women—both parties, he contended, wanted to control the outcome of the upcoming 1972 Bundestag elections.[37]

Efforts by politicians to place abortion law reform on the back burner until after 1972 failed. On June 3, 1971, a coalition of three grassroots feminist organizations from West Berlin, Frankfurt, and Munich (Sozialistischer Frauenbund Westberlin, Frankfurter Frauenaktion 70, and Münchener Weiberrat) launched a national campaign of self-incrimination modeled on a similar 1970 French campaign; 374 women, many of them celebrities, announced in *Stern* that they had aborted illegally: "Women with means can abort without danger in Germany and in foreign countries. Paragraph 218 forces women without means onto the kitchen tables of quacks. It stamps them as criminals and threatens to imprison them for up to five years. Nevertheless one million women abort under degrading and life-threatening circumstances. I am one of them."[38] Liselotte Funcke, the FDP vice president, numbered among the signers. That evening, Funcke and Maria Henze (CDU) debated abortion reform on national television.[39] Shortly thereafter, the "Infratest-Politikbarometer" printed the results of a survey on German Catholic attitudes toward abortion. Of the 2,000 Catholics polled, 51 percent said they believed women should have the right to terminate a pregnancy. The number rose to 70 percent if extenuating social or economic circumstances existed. It increased to 80 percent if it was highly probable the child would be born with serious mental/physical disabilities and to 84 percent if the mother's life was in jeopardy. Despite official Church condemnation, most West German Catholics supported broader parameters for legalized abortion (see Appendix H).[40] German feminists had captured the undivided attention of the West German public. Within one month of publication of the *Stern* article, feminists had collected 90,000 signatures of those supporting the abolition of Paragraph 218.[41] However, the feminist movement in West Germany, unlike that in the United States, had no national-level organization; without centralized leadership, the movement could not create sufficient organized political pressure to influence legislative proceedings.[42] Instead, the political parties, the Constitutional Court, and interests groups, such as the Catholic Church and the medical community, with strong national-level organizations determined the direction of reform.

Pro-life Catholic organizations immediately launched a counteroffensive in response to the feminist campaign. In July 1971, the Association of Young Christian Workers (Christliche Arbeiterjugend, CAJ) and the Münster Youth Community (Münster Junge Gemeinschaft) published an open letter that criticized the "dishonest and manipulative methods" of *Stern*, *Der Spiegel*, and Aktion 218.[43] Similarly, in North Rhine-Westphalia, the CAJ distributed flyers attacking *Stern* for "celebrating a series of celebrities as saints because they killed human beings." The CAJ also wrote the federal chancellor and the leaders of the CDU, SPD, and FDP to declare their opposition to reform.[44] Several kfd chapters also pursued letter-writing campaigns and petition drives, as did smaller Catholic groups such as The Lady of All Nations (Die Frau aller Völker).[45]

The German bishops and the Vatican also entered the fray. In a pastoral letter, Cardinal Jaeger of Paderborn characterized efforts to abolish Paragraph 218 as the "new euthanasia program."[46] Cardinal Döpfner of Munich admonished the SPD for prioritizing women's interests over the life of the unborn child.[47] No Catholic intervention generated as much controversy, however, as those of *L'Osservatore Romano* and of Joseph Cardinal Höffner of Cologne.

On February 12, 1972, the *L'Osservatore Romano* published an article on the proposed liberalization of West German abortion law. The article began by reiterating remarks made by Paul VI on January 12, 1972, in connection with the Italian abortion debate: "It is only a small step from legalized abortion to sterilization and from there to the elimination of 'unworthy life.'" It then suggested that the West German government had placed "indirect and direct pressure" on some individuals to be sterilized.[48] That same weekend, German newspapers reported that the Milanese Catholic newspaper, *Avvenire*, had made similar claims in an article entitled "Worse Than Hitler." The article charged, "The hospitals that performed abortions then were called Auschwitz, Dachau, and Mauthausen. It seems to us a unique schoolhouse for socialists and social democrats."[49]

The apostolic nuncio in Bonn quickly issued a disclaimer stating that the comments represented the views of the author, not the Vatican. The German press challenged the disclaimer. The Hamburg newspaper *Die Welt* pointed out that the statement appeared without a byline. The most likely author, therefore, was the chief editor of the Vatican newspaper, who answered directly to the Vatican state secretary.[50] *Die Welt* also reprinted the *L'Osservatore Romano* article in German translation. Other German editorial columns lambasted the Vatican for stooping to such low tactics and questioned the appropriateness of any religion that would make a political intervention in a pluralist society.

On February 21, 1972, Cardinal Joseph Höffner added more fuel to the fire. In an interview with the KNA, Höffner described any legislator unwilling to safeguard the sanctity of life, including that of an unborn fetus, as unelectable by observant Catholics. The Düsseldorf state secretary, Dr. Ulrich Klug (FDP), called Höffner's comments "an attempt at political coercion."[51] Bundestag member Lenelotte von Bothmer (SPD) described them as "a despicable undemocratic incitement."[52] Heinz Kühn, the SPD minister of North Rhineland-Westphalia and a former Catholic youth group member, accused the bishop of trying to exercise undue influence over the political decisions of Catholics.[53]

Höffner's comments placed the Church on the defensive. The newly elected president of the ZdK, Bernhard Vogel, attempted damage control. In an interview with *Der Spiegel*, Vogel reassured the West German public that Catholics were free to vote for whomever they chose: "Cardinal Höffner holds a high office in the Catholic Church and Catholic Christians expect bearers of high office to state positions when fundamental issues are concerned. Höffner has done so. Catholic Christians are free to accept this position or have a different opinion for reasons of conscience. But it is also the obligation of the cardinal of the Roman Church to express his opinions clearly on decisive issues."[54] While Vogel did not condemn Höffner's statement, he made it clear that he did not think it was a "good idea when the Church, even the Catholic Church, recommend[ed] a particular party to voters."[55] Other prominent Catholics issued stronger statements. In an interview with the journal *konkret*, Norbert Greinacher, a Catholic priest and professor of theology at the University of Tübingen, described Höffner's remarks as symptomatic of the Church's centuries-old negative attitude toward sexuality. He also called Cardinal Höffner's unconditional defense of life hypocritical, alleging that in 1959 Cardinal Höffner wrote a paper supporting the use of the atomic bomb against Japan. The Arbeitsgemeinschaft der Priester- und Solidaritätsgruppen in der Bundesrepublik Deutschland, with approximately two thousand members, condemned Höffner's statement, as did Dr. Lengsbach, a professor of moral theology at the University of Münster, who actively campaigned for the SPD's reform initiative.[56]

Not all prominent Catholics took offense at Höffner's statements, however. Otto Roegele, an editor of the international Catholic journal *Communio*, contended that Höffner's only crime was holding an unpopular position. He pointed out that no one had accused Lengsbach or Greinacher of meddling when they campaigned for the SPD wearing clerical garb. Roegele also characterized *konkret* as a "political-pornographic magazine."[57]

The results of the 1972 election demonstrated that most Catholics did not feel obliged to honor the cardinal's recommendation. The CDU-CSU coalition did not regain power, and voter patterns revealed an upsurge in Catholic defections from the CDU-CSU. In the city of Kleve in North-Rhine Westphalia—where 45.5 percent of Catholics attended mass every Sunday and one SPD legislator once joked, "Even the potatoes are Catholic"—the SPD experienced a 6.6 percent increase in votes.[58] Defections from the CDU were equally dramatic among women voters. In the 1950s and 1960s, women overwhelmingly cast their ballots for the two Christian parties. In the 1969 national election, 10 percent more women than men voted for the CDU (see Appendix L). In 1972, the "woman bonus" dropped to 3 percent, prompting some CDU officials "to explore changing the party's stance on women's issues."[59] Elisabeth Noelle-Neumann, an executive at the Allensbach Institute of Demography, attributed the 1972 SPD victory "primarily to Catholic women" who defected from the Christian parties.[60]

The Vatican's intervention and Cardinal Höffner's remarks divided the German Catholic community; they also obfuscated a complicated and nuanced debate within the Catholic Church. Most Catholic leaders did not endorse such extreme tactics. Although many feared that the liberalization of abortion law would set a dangerous precedent given Germany's National Socialist past, they recognized that drawing such analogies marginalized the Church and alienated many West German Catholics. Not one speaker at the 1973 public rally "Für das Leben," organized by the Consortium of Catholic Associations in Germany (Arbeitsgemeinschaft der katholischen Verbände Deutschlands) in conjunction with the ZdK, referred to Germany's Nazi past.[61] In fact, when quoting a British doctor who opposed abortion reform in England, speakers at the rally excised the doctor's references to parallels between Nazism and contemporary British support for abortion.⁶² No speaker recognized the legitimacy of abortion except in cases of an imminent danger to the mother's life, of course, but all stressed that both church and state had a duty to provide assistance to pregnant women in crisis. Several underscored the need to end discrimination against unwed mothers within the Church and to hold fathers accountable.⁶³

The 1972 election exposed the growing isolation of the institutional Catholic Church on abortion. It also generated concerns among some prominent Catholics about the West German Church's future. In *Strukturwandel der Kirche*, Karl Rahner asserted that if the Church continued down its current path, it would become "a historically and socially meaningless sect."⁶⁴ Rahner argued that "the Church should be a church that courageously and clearly defends morality, but without moralizing."⁶⁵ The Catholic Church, he declared, needed to embrace pluralism in West German society and within Catholicism. Although he did not refer to Höffner by name, Rahner made apparent his disapproval of the cardinal's positions: "It is not so clear where the boundaries for open Communion lie; it is not clear that remarried divorced persons should not be allowed the sacraments in every case. . . . It is also not clear what possibilities exist for a Christian conscience with reference to the state penal code on the termination of pregnancy. . . . It is not so simple to say that a party is no longer electable for a Christian or a Catholic."⁶⁶ For Rahner, issuing unilateral moral condemnations did not serve the best interests of the Church or its members. Instead, the Church needed to foster a moral framework where Catholics could learn to make responsible decisions of conscience.⁶⁷ Rahner worried that the institutional Church would opt for a "comfortable traditionalism and pseudo-orthodoxy," noting that many Church leaders did not regret the "drifting of restless and questioning people from the Church, because then peace and order could be restored and everything in the Church could be as it was previously."⁶⁸

In fact, the seeming unity and lack of stormy protests at the 1974 Catholic Congress, noted with optimism by many conservative Catholic commentators and some German bishops, concealed a mass exodus from the Church. In the *Stuttgarter Zeitung*, Hannes Burger called attention to the decline in the number of Catholics participating in congress forums. Although the very young and the old were well represented, college students and the middle generations seemed almost completely absent. Burger noted wryly that in their critical engagement with the Church, high school students lacked "the frustration and aggression of the 20- to 30-year-olds who had been strongly represented at Essen [the 1968 congress] and whose anger had been palpable because all discussions about reform in the Church have hardly changed anything."⁶⁹ Many reform-minded Catholics, Burger concluded, had simply given up: "Above all more and more Catholics, particularly the middle generations, make their own arrangements on issues of faith and life problems, such as on marital morality and ecumenical contact in the community, and no longer bother struggling with the Church."⁷⁰ The decline in Catholic protest actions did not result from a resolution of the issues; instead, it resulted from the resignation of reformers and moderates, which in turn created a smaller, more conservative West German Church.

The Bundestag, the Constitutional Court, and Reaction to the *Indikationslösung*

On April 26, 1974, the Bundestag passed the Fifth Statute to Reform the Penal Law, endorsing the *Fristenlösung*. The vote was so close that individual votes had to be tallied for the first time in the Bundestag's history (247–233). Given the intensity of the debate leading up to the vote, the initial reaction of opponents was relatively mild. The two most outspoken opponents—the Catholic Church and the German Medical Association—expressed only mild regrets about the parliamentary decision. A few Christian opponents, such as the former president of the Evangelical Congress, Heinz Zahrnt, worried that the vehemence of the two churches' campaign may have been counterproductive—and thus garnered support for the opposition.⁷¹

A more likely explanation for the mildness of the response was that opponents of the *Fristenlösung* knew that for the measure to become law, it required the approval of the Bundesrat, the legislative body that represented the ten German states (*Länder*) at the federal level. In 1974, representatives of the Christian parties dominated the Bundesrat; opponents thus believed the bill had little chance of becoming law. As expected on May 10, 1974, the Bundesrat rejected the *Fristenlösung* approved by the Bundestag and called for the mediation committee (*Vermittlungsausschuß*) to negotiate a compromise. The SPD-FDP coalition government led by Helmut Schmidt now faced a decision. As the *Frankfurter Allgemeine Zeitung* explained, "Whether it comes down to an effort at a compromise in the mediation committee or a confrontation essentially depends on how the Schmidt government appraises the issue of abortion, whether it is appropriate to demonstrate flexibility or whether it is an occasion to demonstrate the will of the new government to prevail even against the Bundesrat."⁷²

To pass the *Fristenlösung* without Bundesrat approval, supporters needed an absolute majority in the Bundestag, meaning that at least two of the eighteen SPD legislators who previously supported the *Indikationslösung* had to change their votes. When efforts at compromise with the Bundesrat failed, a new vote on the *Fristenlösung* was scheduled in the Bundestag for June 15, 1974. With nine of the eighteen SPD supporters of the *Indikationslösung* switching sides, supporters of the *Fristenlösung* now had an absolute majority (260–218).[73]

Catholic opponents reacted vehemently to the new vote. The ZdK president, Bernhard Vogel, declared, "We accept the challenge, as so often in the past, we will tirelessly fight and advocate with all available means, so that the current decision of the German Bundestag is countermanded."[74] Cardinal Döpfner vowed that the Church "never will resign itself" to the *Fristenlösung*.[75]

Catholic conservatives had not accepted defeat. On June 21, 1974, *Die Zeit* reported that Hans Filbinger, a committed Catholic and the prime minister of Baden-Württemberg, announced that his government would file an injunction to prevent the new law from going into effect before the German Constitutional Court could rule on its constitutionality.[76] The court granted the injunction; however, it did not recommend reverting to the status quo. Instead, it stipulated that Paragraph 218b and Paragraph 219 of the new statute, which imposed the *Indikationslösung* for late-term abortions, apply to all abortions. In addition to the two justifications recognized by the new statute for late abortions (medical and eugenic), the court stipulated a third justification (rape).[77]

Concomitant with the action of the government of Baden-Württemberg, 193 CDU-CSU Bundestag members submitted an application for an abstract control of norms (*abstrakte Normenkontrolle*) to the Federal Constitutional Court.[78] The state governments of Bavaria, the Saarland, Baden-Württemberg, Schleswig-Holstein, and the Rhineland-Palatinate submitted similar motions. According to Article 14 of the Federal Constitutional Court Act, the First Senate had jurisdiction; unlike the Second Senate, judges affiliated with the two Christian parties held the majority of seats.[79] In mid-November 1974, the court began hearing oral arguments.

The primary issue at stake was the legal status of unborn life: Was it entitled to protection under Articles 1 and 2 of the Basic Law? If so, did the state's duty to safeguard fetal life include protecting it from actors other than the state (e.g., the mother)? Legal representatives for the CDU-CSU argued that the word "everyone" (*Jeder*) found in Article 2, Paragraph 2, Sentence

1 of the Basic Law allowed no exceptions; the state could not distinguish between prenatal and postnatal life.[80]

Speaking for the federal government, the minister of justice did not dispute the state's constitutional obligation to protect unborn life; he instead argued that the new law, in conjunction with other measures, protected unborn life by providing counseling and social assistance to pregnant women and families in crisis. This form of protection, the minister contended, was more effective than criminal punishment.[81]

The legal representative for the Bundestag, Dr. Horst Ehmke, took a different approach, questioning the legal status of unborn life. In the court verdict reiterating the oral arguments made by all parties, Ehmke's position was represented as follows: "The use of the word 'everyone' speaks against the acceptance of a fundamental right for unborn life, since both in colloquial speech and in legal parlance a human person clearly is identified with 'everyone.' Also in the legal sense, personhood begins at birth. Thus it is not yet decided whether and to what extent unborn life represents a legal good protected under Article 2, Paragraph 2, Sentence 1 of the Basic Law."[82] Ehmke turned the tables on his Catholic opponents and supported his claim by underscoring the Catholic Church's past acceptance of delayed hominization: "According to Church law up until the end of the nineteenth century, only the aborting of an 'animated' fetus was punishable; in practice the eightieth day after conception was recognized as the point in time of animation."[83] He added that in recognizing the potential validity of justifications other than a threat to the mother's life, his opponents implicitly acknowledged a distinction between prenatal and postnatal life.[84]

On February 25, 1975, the court ruled by a vote of six to two that the new statute was unconstitutional. In rejecting the arguments made by representatives of the federal government and parliament, the court emphasized the history and origins of the Basic Law. It pointed out that the inclusion of a provision acknowledging "the self-evident right to life" was a "reaction to the extermination of 'life unworthy of life'" under National Socialism. In affirming a right to life, the Basic Law distinguished the new state from the old. The court argued, moreover, that current scientific knowledge did not support a clear demarcation between prenatal and postnatal life.[85] "Everyone" included developing life:

> Contrary to the objection that "everyone" in colloquial speech and legal language denotes a "completed" human person and that a pristine interpretation

of the wording therefore speaks against the inclusion of unborn life in the scope of Art. 2, Par. 2, Sentence I of the GG [Basic Law], it should be stressed that in any case, the meaning and purpose of this provision of the Basic Law require that the protection of life extends to developing life. The security of human existence against state encroachment would be incomplete if it did not also comprise the preliminary stage of unborn life.[86]

The court also noted that the authors of the Basic Law advanced a definition of life that included unborn life.

The court did not deny women's constitutional right to self-determination; the Basic Law established a hierarchy of values that gave precedence to the fetus's right to life over the mother's right to self-determination: "The opinion expressed in the Bundestag during the third reading of criminal law reform, which underscored the primacy of the woman's right to self-determination derived from human dignity over [the right] of all others for a certain time period, including the child's right to life, is not compatible with the constitutional order of values."[87] The court did not claim that abortion was acceptable only if the pregnancy endangered the mother's life; the legislature could establish an *Indikationslösung* balancing the constitutional claims of the mother against those of the unborn child.[88] Abortion could not be decriminalized, however. Independent of the actual effectiveness of criminal sanction, "the unjust character" of the act demanded "legal condemnation."[89]

The judgment incensed feminists and the liberal media. Feminists were furious that the court had not unequivocally affirmed women's right to make decisions concerning their bodies. They staged mass protests at Catholic churches in Berlin, Munich, and Frankfurt[90] and organized bus tours to the Netherlands, where no legal restrictions were placed on abortions during the first trimester of pregnancy.[91] The liberal media charged that the decision owed its reasoning to Catholic natural law; some critics even alleged a Vatican conspiracy. In an editorial in *Die Zeit*, Hans Schueler described the verdict as an "apodictic shibboleth from the command post on high (*Feldherrhügel*) of natural law."[92] A headline in the *Frankfurter Rundschau* rechristened the decision "the Karlsruhe Encyclical."[93] Rudolf Augstein accused the CDU of exercising undue control over the Constitutional Court's composition.[94]

Although West German allegations of a Vatican conspiracy had no factual foundation, equally erroneous was the 1976 assessment of the U.S. legal expert John D. Gorby, who claimed that religion played no role in the decision. The reasoning of the verdict, as well as the history of the Basic Law to which it alluded, indicated that Christian moral principles, particularly Catholics ones, shaped the decision. In the dissenting opinion, Justices Helmut Simon and Wiltraut Rupp-von Brünneck (the only female justice) objected to the court's insistence on an independent ethical condemnation: "Our essential objection is directed against the fact that the majority did not demonstrate from where they constitutionally derived a requirement of condemnation as an independent duty. In our opinion, nowhere does the Constitution stipulate that ethically objectionable or criminal behavior must be condemned per se with the help of statutory law without regard to its desired effect. In a pluralist, ideologically neutral and free democratic community, it remains entrusted to the forces of society to determine postulates of ethics."[95] In effect, the majority decision inserted an absolute moral value into a modern criminal code; in doing so, the decision recalled earlier West German court decisions that explicitly affirmed a theory of supraconstitutionality and prescribed criminal sanctions for all moral offenses. For example, in its decisions on the redrawing of borders between the southwest states in October 1951 and on the equality of husband and wife within marriage in December 1953, the Constitutional Court declared that the court had a duty to strike down any law that contradicted higher principles.[96] A decision of the Federal High Court of Justice (Bundesgerichtshof, BGH) in 1958 specified that natural law established the limits of state law.[97]

By referring to the Parliamentary Council debates, the court incorporated earlier defense-of-life arguments that drew on natural law. In the immediate post–World War II era, natural law theory experienced a revival in Europe, particularly in Germany. As Gottfried Dietze explained in 1956, "The negative revolution of 1945 was negative indeed . . . insofar as it was mainly a reaction against juristic positivism, which under the dictatorships had been carried to extremes. Quite naturally refuge was sought in natural law, which promised to assure the restoration of human dignity."[98] This receptivity to natural law and concomitant disillusionment with legal positivism placed the Christian parties at a distinct advantage in promoting their vision of the new West German Constitution.[99] In discussions of Article 2, conservative Christian leaders, such as Hans-Christoph Seebohm and Helene Weber, pressured for including the defense of "germinating life" in the right to life clause.[100] The 1975 decision noted that Theodor Heuss (FDP) had agreed that life included prenatal life; however, he also argued that the topics of prenatal life and the death penalty belonged in the criminal code, not the Constitution. The verdict also acknowledged that Dr. Heinrich Greve (SPD) objected to extending the right to life to prenatal life. Still, the court concluded that irrespective of political affiliation, most constitutional authors believed that the right to life extended to unborn life, since only one objection appeared in the minutes.[101]

The court's assessment was accurate up to a point; with the exception of Greve, SPD members made no objections to this understanding of the right to life during plenary discussions. But as Michael Gante pointed out in § 218 in der Diskussion, the Constitutional Court referred only to plenary discussions. The court did not mention the discussions of the main committee of the Parliamentary Council. By the time of the plenary discussions, the SPD had abandoned its earlier objections, recognizing that the prevailing consensus within the population with respect to values made it inopportune to pursue its previous position.[102] Strategic silence, not consensus across the political spectrum, explained the absence of objections in 1949. This silence came back to haunt the SPD in 1975; the Christian political parties had won an important, albeit qualified, victory in the abortion debate. In framing all future discussions of abortion, opponents would have to acknowledge the right to life of the unborn fetus.[103]

On learning of the decision, Catholics celebrated. Bernhard Vogel, the president of ZdK, announced, "Now the legislators must revise the criminal stipulations on abortion in accordance with the limits imposed by the Federal Constitutional Court—a revision that is in accord with the Basic Law and that excludes a blanket approval of abortion."[104] But the celebration proved short-lived. The revised law recognized four justifications—medical, eugenic, criminal, and social. Opponents attacked in particular the new social justification that allowed women with a doctor's approval to have an abortion during the first trimester if for financial or psychological reasons they were unable to care for the child.

Many Catholic organizations, including the BDKJ, kfd, and ZdK, condemned the new law, as did the German bishops. On March 13, 1976, the KNA quoted Cardinal Döpfner: "The Church will not accept the new abortion law and will do everything in its power to ensure that the law is revised."[105] On May 7, 1976, the DBK published its official condemnation. It also released two directives—one addressed to pastoral care providers and religious instructors and one directed to the Catholic medical community.

In the directive to pastoral care providers and religious instructors, the bishops emphasized the importance of providing religious instruction that underscored the immorality of abortion. The bishops also advocated creating a climate of openness and understanding toward women in crisis.[106] The directive to the Catholic medical community assumed a more negative tone, focusing on the moral and contractual obligation of Catholic hospitals and doctors to enforce Catholic values. Doctors at West German Catholic hospitals could perform an abortion only if the pregnancy jeopardized the mother's life. The directive also clearly stated that this restriction applied to Catholic doctors and nurses working at non-Catholic facilities.[107] In response, the federal minister of justice, Hans-Jochen Vogel—a member of SPD, a Catholic, and brother of the former ZdK president, Bernhard Vogel[108]—expressed his regrets that the German bishops focused on Paragraph 218 to the exclusion of all other reforms introduced by the government intended to create a family-friendly environment in West Germany: "It remains regrettable that the German bishops have passed over in silence such praiseworthy laws like the reform of the penal system, the victim compensation law, the reorganization of adoption and the tenancy law."[109] On June 21, 1976, the new law went into effect, and proponents and opponents settled into an uneasy truce.

But conservative Catholics, who viewed the new law as indicative of the nation's moral collapse, found the truce intolerable. The Militia Sanctae Mariae pleaded with the ZdK to petition for another constitutional review: "The declaration concerning the new formulation of § 218 made by Cardinal Döpfner in the name of the German bishops at the national press conference remains empty rhetoric if all means for changing this law are not employed."[110]

Other conservative Catholics, frustrated by the failure of the ZdK and the German bishops to block reform, resorted to personal attacks or lashed out against a liberal Catholic conspiracy for which they held Vatican II responsible. One Catholic doctor wrote Bernhard Vogel, "Until now, I believed that you were different from your SPD brother, who disloyally turned his back on his family."[111] A priest complained that the ZdK had lost its credibility as a Catholic organization because two ZdK members serving in the Bundestag voted for the *Fristenlösung*.[112] Another Catholic linked the Church's failure to block abortion law reform to its failure to support the traditionalist, Archbishop Marcel Lefebvre:

> For many Catholics, Lefebvre is perhaps the Church's only hope today. No one defends the faith like him; no one sustains the Church like him.... Do you not

see where the present path of the Church leads? Into the abyss! Do you not see the destruction everywhere? Can you tell me just one thing that has improved in the Church since the Council [Vatican II]?

One more thing, declarations like the one on Lefebvre will not improve the CDU's electoral prospects. If we conservatives no longer have a home in the CDU because liberals like you dominate it, then we will stay home on Election Day.[113]

Given the strong objections of conservative Catholics and changing West German moral norms, the truce had little chance of long-term success.

International Year of the Child (1979) and Escalating Tensions

Conservative Catholics saw the "International Year of the Child" as the ideal occasion for renewing their campaign against legalized abortion. On January 22, 1979, the Standing Council of the DBK drafted a declaration that presaged the upcoming antiabortion campaign:

> For some years a trend has existed toward the consciously chosen childless marriage and even toward a community of man and woman living out of wedlock, in which, without exception, the child has no place. Contrary to this attitude, the Christian understanding of the sexual community between man and woman stresses the complete turning of both partners to one another in a valid marriage and, at the same time, the shared devotion of both spouses to the children—the gift and the task of their encompassing love.[114]

Three years after the *Indikationslösung*'s passage, the institutional Church had not admitted defeat. Instead, government statistics showing an almost 30 percent increase in the number of abortions revitalized Catholic resistance.

On February 10, 1979, the *Abendzeitung München* printed a declaration by the Catholic group Cartell Rupert Mayer: "The 'Year of the Child' begins with numerous news reports about the number of abortions registered last year. After examining these appalling numbers, one asks whether the 'Year' should more appropriately be called the 'Year of Killing Unborn Life.'"[115] The national Catholic newspaper *Neue Bildpost* ran a banner headline that read, "For murder, large sums of money exist! Government—how you lied to us!" The first allegation referred to the 200 million German marks expended annually on abortions by the federal health insurance program. The second alluded to the government's claim at the time of passage that the new law would reduce the number of abortions in West Germany.[116]

Beyond these editorial charges, several German bishops, including Cardinal Höffner, chair of the DBK (1976–1987), condemned the development of an "abortion mentality" in their Easter sermons. Höffner labeled it "scandalous" that in a welfare state like the Federal Republic, 67 percent of abortions fell under the "social justification." He called for a constitutional review of the new law. Höffner's Easter sermon received widespread coverage in the secular media, such as the *Süddeutsche Zeitung, Die Zeit, Die Welt*, and the *Westdeutsche Allgemeine Zeitung*.[117]

The conservative reaction to statistics indicating a significant increase in abortions placed the federal government and the SPD on the defensive.[118] In response, Johannes Rau, chair of the SPD in North Rhineland-Westphalia, launched a counteroffensive, denying allegations made by Cardinal Höffner against the SPD: "It is completely indisputable and must remain indisputable that pregnant women who find themselves in an economic crisis should and must be economically and financially supported in order to remedy this financial emergency." He also refuted Höffner's claim that the SPD endorsed a "right to abortion":

> I would like to assure you that the Social Democratic Party does not and will not support this ethically and legally untenable and false formulation. There is no "right to abortion." According to the law, an induced pregnancy termination is fundamentally illegal. Only if certain legal conditions are met, specifically the existence of a specific justification, is that not the case. That is the position of the law from which the Social Democrats will not deviate. . . . The SPD holds strictly to the law, however—a law that also recognizes the social justification.[119]

Rau ended the letter with a veiled attack on Cardinal Höffner's motives: "My party and I are prepared to search for improvements and to this end engage in pertinent discussions with the churches and social welfare associations; but surely the individual needs of pregnant women are not appropriate topics for controversy or polemical debates in the public sphere."[120]

The West German political climate had changed substantially since the abortion debate began in the early 1970s. Since then, the SPD-FDP coalition had grown more confident of public support for the reformed Paragraph 218. Unlike the situation in 1971, when some SPD officials abandoned the *Fristenlösung* because they feared antagonizing the Church, now SPD-FDP government officials no longer wavered, perhaps because they recognized that the abortion debate was a greater political liability and source of strife for the CDU-CSU and the Catholic Church than it was for them.

In fact, the CDU-CSU coalition had been deeply divided on abortion even in the early 1970s. Party members could not agree on the validity of the social and eugenic justifications or on the appropriate punishment for illegal abortions. Unable to resolve its differences, the Christian coalition submitted two reform proposals in 1974. The following year, the CDU-CSU remained divided and thus offered no counterproposal to the *Indikationslösung* proposed by the SPD. High-ranking Catholic leaders such as Bernhard Vogel worried that the CDU's "listlessness" on Paragraph 218 reform might alienate Catholics.[121]

In sum, the abortion debate exposed deep rifts in the CDU-CSU coalition, between the Catholic Church and the CDU, and between the CDU and women. In the 1976 Bundestag elections, the CDU experienced another drop in the "woman bonus." Only 1.6 percent more women than men voted for the CDU. Women's issues, such as abortion, had become a liability for the Christian parties, alienating their core constituency—women (see Appendix L). For conservative Catholic and Protestant women voters, the indecision of the CDU-CSU signaled the betrayal of traditional Christian values: "I sent a letter to our party, the CDU/CSU stating: 'If you keep delaying and cannot reach agreement on such important things, then you will never hold power again.'"[122] Conversely, for women influenced by the feminist movement, the party's stances on women's issues were no longer attractive. As Sara Elise Wiliarty noted, in the 1970s the CDU "found itself caught between loyal voters who preferred the party's traditional stance on women's issues and an emerging constituency with different policy preferences."[123]

These heated exchanges over Paragraph 218 marked only the beginning of a stormy year centered on the abortion debate. On July 14, 1979, Hartwig Holzgartner, the Catholic chair of the CSU's Working Committee for Health Policy (Gesundheitspolitischer Arbeitskreis der CSU), made national headlines when he stated, "The National Socialists killed the Jews, and International Socialists kill the unborn. What is taking place among our people is precisely the way back to Auschwitz." The SPD and FDP charged that Holzgartner had sunk to an "unsurpassable level of political squalor."[124] The CSU general secretary dismissed SPD reactions as "sanctimonious retorts."[125]

As he had in 1972, Cardinal Höffner added fuel to the fire, ensuring that the abortion debate dominated media coverage of the 1980 national elections. In late July 1979, Deutschlandfunk invited Cardinal Höffner and

Ingrid Mathäus-Maier, an FDP member of the Bundestag, to comment on Holzgartner's statements and the revised Paragraph 218. Although Höffner did not repeat Holzgartner's Nazi comparison, his remarks suggested that he sympathized with it: "Yes, I can understand why the Munich physician Dr. Holzgartner called abortions brutal mass murders—not the actual occurrences [of abortion] in the Federal Republic—but if abortion is murder, then 73,000 abortions is likewise mass murder."[126]

Höffner's remarks produced an immediate reaction that illustrated just how much the West German social and political climate had changed since the early 1970s. In 1972, the parliamentary secretary of state in the Justice Ministry, Alfons Bayerl, expressed "shock and concern" about the Vatican newspaper's statements, but made no accusations about the Church's Nazi past. Even Rudolf Augstein, known for his antagonistic relationship with the Catholic Church, had refrained in 1972 from attacking the Church's record under National Socialism. In the 1980s, the same rules no longer applied. On Deutschlandfunk, Matthäus-Maier responded to Höffner's remarks by attacking the Catholic Church's record under Nazism: "I must say that I find this comparison to mass murder committed during the Third Reich particularly astounding, given, for example, that the Catholic Church under the Nazi dictatorship did not likewise castigate such mass murders as it now thinks it must do for a reform reached through democratic processes."[127]

If Matthäus-Maier's 1980 remarks exemplified the erosion of political deference accorded the Catholic Church, Hans-Jochen Vogel's response illustrated the changed relationship between Catholics and the West German episcopate. Vogel—minister of justice, SPD party member, and practicing Catholic—spoke out against Höffner's intervention in an open letter:

> I am deeply disturbed by this situation, but considered whether it should be overlooked.... such silence seems to me dishonest and even irresponsible. Dishonest, because I have known you, Cardinal, for a long time and also respected you when we have represented different viewpoints.... Irresponsible, because by invoking you and the authority of your spiritual office, others have taken control of this topic and exploited it in gravely intolerable ways with the result that antagonism and hate have taken the place of serious discussion.
>
> So I decided on this letter. I write it not as federal minister of justice for the government. I write it as a Catholic member of the Bundestag who agrees with the existing version of § 218 StGB and is therefore responsible for its standards

and consequences. I write as a Social Democrat who finds it unbearable to be named in the same breath with the initiators of Auschwitz."[128]

Vogel's response was personal, political, and unabashedly Catholic. He spoke of his moral responsibility for the consequences of the revised law, for which he would have to answer to God. He acknowledged his disappointment with 1978 statistics that indicated an increase in abortions. He refused to abandon the current law, however, and argued that the focus should be "on further improvements to the system of counseling and assistance."[129] He warned against equating the social justification with financial need: "In truth, the social justification includes a large number of complex conflicts that cannot be resolved with money."[130] Vogel ended by suggesting that Cardinal Höffner emulate the example of Cardinal König of Vienna: "'Therefore I urgently request, Cardinal, that you rescind your avowal of understanding for an immoderate statement and instead caution prudence to those who due to blind fanaticism challenge the foundations for cooperation in our society. Cardinal König has provided an example of how discussion about the defense of nascent life can be led with great engagement but without reciprocal aberrances and demonization. I ask you: Follow this example."[131] Hans-Jochen Vogel's letter differed significantly from his brother's 1972 interview with *Der Spiegel*. Although disquieted by Höffner's intervention, his brother had avoided confrontation, stating that he was "no censor of cardinals." Seven years later, Hans-Jochen Vogel did not hesitate to advise a bishop on how to behave.

Although Höffner denied that he or any other bishop had ever accused Hans-Jochen Vogel "personally or the SPD in general of consciously choosing to rob the unborn child of adequate protection," he refused to rescind his assessment of abortion as murder, asserting, "If from the beginning a person grows inside the mother's womb, then the intentional killing of this unborn person must by definition be characterized legally as murder, as well as according to medical and biological reasoning."[132]

Höffner's second political intervention produced an even stronger reaction than the initial one, receiving coverage in major U.S. media outlets, such as the *New York Times* and the *Washington Post*.[133] The greater media attention reflected Cardinal Höffner's changed status within the Church hierarchy. In 1972, Höffner had not been chair of the DBK. His predecessor, Cardinal Döpfner, also condemned the revised law; however, Döpfner had refrained from intervening directly in electoral campaigns, never condemning a specific party platform or endorsing a particular political candidate in the post–Vatican II era. In contrast, Höffner had a long history of transgressing the boundary between church and state.[134]

No one should have been surprised, therefore, by the 1980 pre-election pastoral letter endorsed by the DBK under the leadership of Cardinal Höffner. Although the letter did not explicitly endorse Franz Josef Strauss, the CDU-CSU candidate for the chancellorship, its condemnation of current SPD-FDP government policy on abortion and divorce law, as well as its fiscal policies, left little room for conjecture; the DBK wanted Catholics to support the CDU-CSU coalition.

The 1980 pastoral letter deviated significantly from those issued by the DBK prior to the 1972 and 1976 federal elections, when Döpfner chaired the DBK. According to *Der Spiegel*, Bishop Hemmerle drafted a letter modeled on earlier election pastoral letters. His letter advised Catholics to vote in accordance with Christian beliefs but did not condemn any specific policies; thus, it did not give the impression of endorsing any particular political party. The DBK, however, had taken a conservative turn since the deaths of two influential moderates—Cardinal Döpfner in 1976 and Bishop Tenhumberg in 1979. Commission IV of the DBK (responsible for social and charitable issues) rejected Hemmerle's version and asked Anton Rauscher, a professor of Christian social teachings at the University of Augsburg, to revise it. Rauscher had close ties with Franz Josef Strauss and was an active member of the CSU's advisory committee on matters of church and state. *Der Spiegel* claimed that Josef Homeyer, secretary of the DBK, in conjunction with Rauscher strategically bypassed the Bonn leader of the Commissariat of German Bishops, Paul Bocklet, who in recent years had spearheaded efforts to improve the West German Catholic Church's relationship with the SPD.[135] In any case, the partisanship of the final pastoral letter ensured controversy in an otherwise dull election campaign. Chancellor Helmut Schmidt (SPD) reacted angrily: "A bishop or priest who wants to make policy should first take off his cassock."[136]

Catholic voters also reacted negatively to the letter. Catholic youth in the Diocese of Regensburg issued a six-page statement criticizing Höffner's partisan stance.[137] A survey of one thousand Catholics conducted by the Bielefeld-Emnid Institute for *Der Spiegel* showed that only 30 percent approved of the pastoral letter. The survey also noted that 32 percent of Catholics supported the existing abortion law, while 41 percent thought the current law was not liberal enough. In short, approximately 70 percent of West German

Catholics rejected the Church's position on birth control and Höffner's actions.[138] In all likelihood, the pastoral letter did more damage than good for the CDU-CSU's electoral prospects. As the sociologist Gerhard Schmidtchen noted, "The stronger the conflicts of value with the Church are, the more attractive the Social Democratic Party becomes for the churchgoer as well as for those who have distanced themselves from the Church."[139]

Although Höffner's actions were by no means the only reason for Franz Josef Strauss's failed bid for the chancellorship, his loss—one of the worst in the history of the West German Christian parties—made it clear that the CDU-CSU could not take an exclusionary approach; it had to pursue an alliance with the FDP. An alliance with the FDP necessitated establishing more distance between itself and the Catholic Church on the issue of abortion.

Christian Women, the Abortion Debate, and a New Call for Equality (1984)

With the CDU-CSU's return to power in 1982, the secular media immediately predicted a cultural turn (*Wende*), anticipating that the CDU-CSU would pursue a policy of legal and moral restoration. Nowhere was the expectation stronger than in the arena of abortion politics, and feminist groups reacted to the CDU-CSU victory by staging nationwide demonstrations in favor of women's right to self-determination.[140] Feminists' reaction was predictable. But what caught many by surprise was the emergence of Christian Democratic women as major actors in the abortion debate and their concerted opposition to the efforts of conservatives to turn back the legislative clock.

In the 1970s Christian women (Catholic and Protestant) within the CDU had been deeply divided on abortion and consequently exercised no significant influence on the political debate on Paragraph 218. Although most did not support feminist demands concerning abortion, the feminist movement had influenced CDU women. Prior to 1969, the Women's Union of the CDU (Frauen Union, FU) focused exclusively on organizing charity events and social functions; it did not address political issues. In 1969, the FU passed a new statute, announcing the group's intention to take political stances on issues concerning women. After Helene Wex (Protestant) became president of the FU in 1971, the organization slowly evolved into a serious political player in the CDU.[141]

However, the FU did not align with the feminist movement; instead, in the 1970s, it endeavored to provide women with an alternative to political feminism. It did so by championing programs intended to recognize the value of women's labor not only in the workforce but also in the home. For example, the group championed a work-family policy that would provide a parent with a small allowance to stay at home, the assumption being that this would be the mother, since she was more likely to have the lower salary. Unlike the SPD plan, the CDU plan would make funds available to both mothers in the workforce and stay-at-home mothers. Although this policy reinforced traditional gendered divisions of labor, it recognized the importance of parenting and thus assigned a higher value to women's conventional labor in the home. It also represented a tacit acknowledgment that not all children lived in traditional two-parent families. The debate on abortion had made it clear that many single mothers had abortions for financial reasons; CDU women believed that the child allowance would curtail such abortions. The policy also had the advantage of aligning with demands by feminist journals such as *Courage* that women be paid for housework. Yet despite the plan's emphasis on a gendered division of labor, conservatives within the party resisted for ideological and financial reasons. Some argued that women should not be paid to do what was their moral duty; others believed that the policy was too expensive. In the end, the FU succeeded in having its child allowance proposal incorporated into the 1975 CDU party platform.[142]

By 1982, when the CDU-CSU in conjunction with the FDP returned to power, the FU leadership was united in its support for the existing abortion law. Since the 1970s, the profile of its members and its officers had experienced significant change. The typical female CDU-CSU officer was no longer either a single women or an older woman in her late fifties or early sixties. Instead, she was more likely a young, married, and educated career woman—a doctor, a lawyer, a journalist, or an academic. In 1984, only two CDU Bundestag members were housewives and more than half were under the age of forty-five.[143] These career women did not feel obligated to defer to their male colleagues, especially on issues that had a direct impact on women. When in November 1983 seventy-four male, conservative CDU-CSU Bundestag representatives sponsored an initiative abolishing federal funding for socially justified abortions, eighteen CDU women spearheaded the opposition. The CDU parliamentary leader, Ingrid Roitzsch, expressed her frustration with renewed discussion of Paragraph 218: "It is terribly irrelevant. Men have no knowledge, but they exert pressure."[144]

At the 1984 CDU Party Congress in Stuttgart, CDU women went on the offensive. Roitzsch and her supporters argued that the changes proposed by the seventy-four men would not prevent abortions; instead, they would unfairly penalize poor women. Susanne Rahardt, a member of the CDU Hamburg executive board, and Editha Limbach underscored that women with financial means would continue to have socially justified abortions in private clinics, while poor women would have to resort to other means that placed their health in jeopardy. Both women argued that creating a more family-friendly environment in West Germany held the key to reducing the number of abortions in Germany.[145]

The FU in conjunction with the FDP and 190 of their more moderate male colleagues in the CDU created a commission responsible for drafting legislation that provided women with short, intermediate, and long-term assistance. Rowitha Verhülsdonk, chair of the Rhineland-Palatinate Women's Union and a Catholic, defended this alternative approach by drawing on the experience of Catholic counseling centers:

> The annual reports provide us with information on the counseling practices of the various counseling centers. It is very interesting and impressive that it is precisely the Church counseling centers—here I refer particularly to Catholic ones—that repeatedly note that they succeed in changing the path of desperate women who come to the center wanting an abortion only if they are able to provide not only assistance for having the child, but also psychological and material support well beyond this point in time.[146]

Since the 1970s, the position of CDU women had come to more closely approximate that of women in the SPD and FDP. Although they rejected the *Fristenlösung*, the FU leaders resisted efforts by their conservative colleagues to abolish federal funding for abortion. They even rejected the demands of more moderate colleagues, like Hermann Kroll-Schlüter and Peter Schröder, for a precise legal definition of "social emergency." Ingrid Roitzsch explained, "An emergency is a subjective perception. I do not want to play judge."[147] Finally, FU leaders argued that abortion law must recognize diverse values. Editha Limbach noted: "Personally, for reasons of conscience, I believe that abortion is justified only if it serves to save another life, namely that of the mother. But I accept that other women may examine their conscience and reach a different conclusion. I believe that we must respect different decisions of conscience and that in our policy we must take into account these differences."[148] The FU and its allies defeated their conservative colleagues. In doing so, they preserved the CDU-CSU alliance with the FDP, without which the CDU could not have maintained its hold on power.[149]

Like the FU, the kfd reconsidered its position on Paragraph 218. On May

24, 1984, the kfd national leadership announced its support for the FU initiative, stating that criminal punishment was not the best way to reduce the incidence of abortion. The kfd's new orientation reflected its growing awareness of the flight of young women from the Church. In an effort to counteract this trend, the kfd's national leadership in the 1980s championed equality for women in church and society, as well as a more moderate approach to questions of sexual morality. As noted in Chapter 2, many local kfd chapters did not welcome this new orientation. When the national kfd leadership repudiated the initiative of CDU-CSU conservatives, which was enthusiastically supported by the West German bishops, kfd members at the grassroots level expressed outrage. A priest in his capacity as spiritual adviser to the St. Joseph-Sythen parish chapter accused the kfd of defying the bishops: "I want to point out that Cardinal Höffner, in the name of the German Bishops' Conference, expressly welcomed the legal initiative of the 74 CDU/CSU Bundestag members. He deeply regretted the behavior of the 18 female CDU/CSU Bundestag members. If Catholic women's organizations do not speak out clearly for change, they are at odds, if not in confrontation, with the German bishops on this fundamental question."[150] The kfd's support for the FU position also placed the organization in conflict with the ZdK, which in 1982 had launched a lobbying campaign to end federal funding of abortion.[151]

The proposed revisions of Paragraph 218 figured prominently at the 1984 Catholic Congress held in Munich in early July 1984. The congress ended with a mass rally supporting the defense of unborn life. At the rally, which was attended by 65,000 Catholics, the ZdK president, Hans Maier, condemned the apathy toward unborn human life while many "cry out for baby seals." Maier's assertion that West Germany placed a higher value on baby seals than unborn human life was not without foundation. In February 1984, the *Rheinische Merkur/Christ und Welt* and the *Süddeutsche Zeitung* published the results of an Allensbach Institute survey that asked West Germans to rank a list of moral transgressions from most offensive to least offensive. A majority of Germans chose the following order: child abuse, cruelty to animals, world hunger, the killing of baby seals off the coast of Canada, the use of chemical pesticides, an abortion by an otherwise healthy woman, deceptive statements by a politician, noisy mopeds, and giving up a newborn child for adoption.[152]

The survey revealed the chasm between the moral values of West Germans and those of the institutional Church. Even more disturbing for

Church authorities, this gap also applied to Catholics. In a letter to the *Süddeutsche Zeitung*, a German Catholic woman attacked Maier's speech at the Catholic Congress: "To overlook cruelty to animals and, in particular, the murder of seals because abortion exists—does that even qualify as religion? My spontaneous reaction was to leave a church that does not value the entirety of creation."[153] Although this reaction was atypical, the disenchantment of many women with the Catholic Church was real. At the forum "Women in Church and Society" held during the 1984 Catholic Congress, Hanna-Renate Laurien, a member of the ZdK and a CDU politician, expressed her disappointment with the Church's continued silence on women's issues:

> Where does she [the Church] address the double standard employed by men? Where does she discuss the fact that today women are disenfranchised by means of their uterus, while men, as always, express their sexuality without consequences? Where is it discussed that the revolt against one's own corporality is often nothing other than a response to the historic contempt for women[?] ... Our Church, which advanced the human dignity of the servant, the poor, the woman, does not now venture to set an example on the matter of women and to recognize the consequences of its statements.[154]

Women's relationship to the Catholic Church was changing—a fact that did not go unnoticed by the secular or religious press. In the *Süddeutsche Zeitung*, Heidrun Graupner described the reception of Hanna-Renate Laurien's presentation:

> The presentation had, in any case, a catalytic effect on the audience, which applauded enthusiastically and at length. Some were unhappy with the proposed policy of small steps, and demanded a revolution—a female priesthood. The questions ranged from family politics on divorce, remarriage, and abortion to the different concepts of chasteness applied to men and women. Clearly there was touchiness about the many slights to women.... Yet many women turned to Hanna-Renate Laurien with perplexed statements like "I am happy as a full-time housewife and mother; I don't understand this presentation."[155]

Given women's greater engagement in the Catholic community than that of their male counterparts, the Church could not afford to ignore this changing relationship. The abortion debate placed Catholic women in conflict with the institutional Church and with male-dominated lay organizations, such as the ZdK. It also placed them in conflict with each other.

Mutter with a Lowercase "m"

In January 1988, the kfd introduced a change in the graphic design of the title page of its magazine, *Frau und Mutter*; the title now read *Frau & mutter*. This seemingly innocuous change instigated a polemical debate within the West German Catholic Church that touched on the interrelated subjects of abortion, motherhood, women's role in the Church, and the emergence of a smaller, more conservative West German Church.

In September 1988, Archbishop Johannes Dyba of Fulda published a statement in the diocesan newspaper *Bonifatiusbote* in which he expressed his concerns about the implications of the new title and called on women in his diocese to resist this change:

> The small "m" is not simply an orthographic error, but a conscious directional indicator about which women and mothers should be concerned. In an age in which every third child in our population is murdered in the mother's womb ... we write Mother in the lowercase. In an age in which the achievements of mothers, who through their children secure the future of our culture, people, and church, are violated, we write Mother in the lowercase. Motherhood is intrinsic to womanhood, and where it does not reach fruition, an emotional crippling begins; the degeneration in church, culture, and people begins.[156]

Dyba's letter received widespread distribution via the KNA; intense public interest in Dyba's statement was prompted in part by rumors that the pope planned to make Dyba a cardinal. The kfd national leadership responded immediately. The general secretary, Anneliese Lissner, released a statement that challenged Dyba's patriarchal understanding of womanhood: "Are women basically mothers? Are men basically fathers? Certainly, the latter has never been the societal or ecclesial position. Periodically, albeit not in all historical eras, women have been defined solely as mothers. Their world was limited to husband, house, and children. That is over and cannot be restored through incantation and suppression."[157] The *Frau & mutter* editors, Barbara Leckel and Anneliese Knippenkötter, also released a statement to the press; they attacked what they perceived as the letter's subtext:

> A Catholic association is totally against women if it uses a lowercase "m." It has no problem with killing unborn life; it has nothing against "every third child in the mother's womb" being murdered; and it disregards the "achievements of mothers, who secure the future of culture, the people, and the Church." That

is implied and it is demagogy ... the *Frau & mutter* editorial staff do want to support Dyba's statement that "the age calls for motherliness." Indeed, it does, but we want to make a fine distinction: The age calls for the motherliness of women and men.[158]

Increasingly, Catholic women rejected the Church's notion of motherhood and refused to suffer insults in silence.

The cult of motherly sacrifice, which defined womanhood in terms of a mother's willingness to sacrifice all for her children, was losing its sway over West German Catholic women. The Münster chapter of the kfd wrote the central office: "We are hurt and angered by Archbishop Dyba's statement, especially since this is not the first time that he has made such defamatory remarks. We believe that 'the Church as a model of living together in partnership—acted upon by men and women' should publicly, at least, attempt to interact fairly with women."[159] Ursula Männle, a kfd member and CDU parliamentarian, wrote Dyba directly. She accused him of trying "to mobilize women against the kfd"[160] and underscored the hypocritical, authoritarian, and misogynist character of his statements:

> If motherhood is intrinsic to woman, then fatherhood should be intrinsic to manhood. Yet neither our society nor our Church makes this claim; Pope John Paul I once said: "God is mother and father," and I found this comforting. But from your letter, I experience neither the paternal nor maternal dimension of God; I sense only the authoritarian magistracy. You want to mandate what womanhood is. Women are indeed different from men in that they have been blamed for every evil in the world.[161]

Another kfd member wrote the pope directly: "I fear that if Bishop Dyba is made cardinal of Cologne, many women and young people will take offense. It would not surprise me if they not only quietly but also officially left the Church."[162]

But the negative reactions of kfd members should not be overemphasized. In fact, most members rejected the national leadership's position. On October 4–5, 1988, the kfd central office reported forty-six responses to date—twelve supporting the kfd position, twenty-two rejecting it, and twelve "unclear."[163] This negative grassroots reaction underscored the increasingly conservative makeup of those who remained active in church life. For conservative women, the kfd's new title signaled an erosion of Christian values: "What has gotten into these women who deny the most beautiful and happiest dimension of their essence? Is it because Mary is so little venerated today? Is it because youth education in our Church does not stress purity? Does Catholic bridal and marriage counseling now mislead the conscience on contraception?"[164] For the kfd national leadership and for those women who wanted to redefine women's traditional relationship to the Church, these types of responses underscored the uphill battle that they faced—not only must they change the consciousness of the male hierarchy, they must foster a new understanding of womanhood among their conservative core constituency. In the form letter sent to supporters of the kfd position, the national leadership explained: "It aggrieves us how many women do not recognize that they are being manipulated when they allow their personhood to be reduced to motherhood. If their self-worth is determined by motherhood alone, then the inevitable separation from their children and the diverse lifestyles of other women becomes a profound injury. Some responses to our dispute with Archbishop Dyba can be understood only thus."[165] The kfd national leadership could not assume that its increasingly conservative base desired a new relationship between women and the Church hierarchy. Consequently, it tried to steer a middle course, which often proved unsatisfactory to women on both sides of the debate.

The national kfd leadership also could not assume the unconditional support of the ZdK. As in the 1984 legal debate on abortion, the ZdK did not unilaterally agree with the kfd. Although many in the ZdK, including the ZdK vice president, Dr. Walter Bayerlein, believed the kfd's reaction to Dyba's letter was justified and that Dyba intentionally suggested a connection between the kfd and mass killing of unborn children, the ZdK president, Hans Maier, did not. And it would be the more conservative Maier who acted as liaison between the kfd and Archbishop Dyba in a dispute that never reached a satisfactory resolution.[166]

Five years later, Archbishop Dyba served as chair of a meeting between representatives of the DBK and Catholic women's organizations. The meeting was prompted by the results of the 1993 Allensbach Institute survey commissioned by the DBK. The survey on women in the Church showed that 77 percent of Catholic women between the ages of sixteen and twenty-nine felt the Church did not understand them.[167] However, the survey also indicated that the women most active in the church were deeply committed to the values emphasized by the hierarchy (see Appendixes H and I). To the chagrin of the representatives of the women's organizations, Dyba described this small group of women who had no tolerance for "newfangled stuff" as embodying the future of the Church.[168] The smaller, more conservative Church predicted by Karl Rahner in the early 1970s was fast becoming a reality, but it was not one without significant political influence.

. . .

This chapter has focused on a select group of catalytic moments in the abortion debate and the events they set in motion. It has argued that the political influence exercised by Catholic politicians in the 1950s had long-term ramifications for political debates on abortion in the 1970s. The Constitutional Court drew on Christian principles, particularly Catholic ones, in reaching its decision in 1975 that the state had an obligation to protect prenatal life, even from the mother. This verdict gave the Catholic Church and other opponents of abortion law reform a significant discursive advantage in all subsequent debates on the defense of unborn life.

This advantage did not end with the fall of the Berlin Wall. The push for reunification reignited the legal and theological debate on abortion. In the former East German state, women from the Independent Workers' Association did not want West Germany's more conservative abortion law to become the law of the new unified state. Fearing the abortion issue might derail reunification, the unification treaty, signed in October 1990, postponed discussion, assigning future responsibility to the Bundestag for a law "that better guarantees the protection of unborn life and the constitutionally acceptable management of a conflict situation for women than is now the case in either part of Germany."[169] The treaty affirmed a fetus's right to life; however, it did not mention women's right to self-determination. Thus, it ensured that West German framing of the issue took precedence over East German framing in subsequent discussions. In June 1992, the new Bundestag approved a bill that required mandatory counseling and a waiting period but left the decision about whether to have an abortion in the first trimester to the woman. In May 1993, the Federal Constitutional Court overturned the new law in response to a suit brought by 249 Christian Democrats. They argued that abortion must remain a felony (with a penalty of one to three years in prison) unless extenuating circumstances existed—rape, incest, or endangerment of the mother's life. In June 1995, the Bundestag reached a compromise that maintained the illegality of abortion while providing for conditions of non-prosecution.[170]

But this discursive advantage came at a price for German Catholicism. As we saw in this chapter, the 1970s abortion debate failed to galvanize and reunite a Catholic community deeply divided by the 1968 papal encyclical, *Humanae Vitae*. The Catholic milieu was not restored as conservatives had hoped. Instead, the institutional Church became increasingly isolated in its condemnation of abortion as the abortion debate progressed. In the mid-1970s, the EKD broke with the Catholic Church, supporting a social-medical justification that took into consideration the pregnant woman's overall well-being rather than just her physical health. The CDU became reluctant to reopen a debate that proved a political liability. Young Catholic women turned their backs on Catholic pregnancy counseling centers and increasingly turned their backs on the Church.

In an effort to stop women's exodus from the Church, the national kfd leadership adopted in 1979 a new mission statement that placed greater emphasis on women's equality in church and society. In 1984, the kfd leadership defied the DBK and the ZdK by supporting the *Indikationslösung*. Like the FU, the kfd leadership argued that social assistance rather than legal sanctions provided the best means for protecting unborn life. This argument met with stiff resistance from the episcopate, male-dominated Catholic lay organizations, and even some local chapters of the kfd.

In fact, the issue of how best to protect unborn life—by means of social assistance or legal sanction—continues to divide Catholics. In September 1999, the pope condemned the German Catholic Church's involvement in a counseling program entitling women to non-prosecuted abortions. The German bishops tried to reach a compromise with the Vatican. However, John Paul II rejected all compromise proposals and pressed for compliance. In November 1999, the DBK acquiesced to the Vatican's demands, and the Church withdrew from the counseling process. However, Bishop Franz Kamphaus of Limburg refused to comply, stating, "No woman frivolously comes to a Catholic counseling center; no woman comes to pick up a license to kill."[171] German lay Catholics also rebelled, establishing Donum Vitae, an independent organization aimed at continuing Catholic involvement in the counseling process.

The Vatican responded swiftly to this open rebellion. In 2002, John Paul II stripped Bishop Kamphaus of his authority over the counseling center in his diocese.[172] The CDF demanded that the German bishops prohibit Catholics working for Donum Vitae from holding office in any official Church organization. In 2006, the DBK gave in to CDF demands.[173] Since Donum Vitae's staff consisted overwhelmingly of Catholic women who also held offices in Church-sponsored organizations, such as Caritas and Sozialer Dienst katholischer Frauen, the group's female staff now faced a choice between continued involvement in official Catholic organizations or working for Donum Vitae.[174] The Church's ultimatum undoubtedly exacerbated the ongoing departure of German women from the Catholic Church. A 1993 survey showed that approximately two-thirds of German Catholic women believed the Church's teachings on celibacy, divorce, contraception, and abortion were too rigid (see Appendix I).[175]

Yet it would be a mistake to view these developments only through the lens of decline. As the Church became smaller, those who remained faithful to the Church redoubled their efforts to protect unborn life. Recognizing the Church's altered position in German society and its loss of influence in the CDU, German Catholics sought out new alliances and strategies. These efforts first bore fruit in the context of debates on NRTs and genetic engineering. Confronted with this new threat to unborn life, German bishops overcame past differences with the EKD and embraced new arguments; the kfd formed an alliance with radical feminists affiliated with the Green Party. As we shall see in the next chapter, these efforts had an important influence on the Bundestag's decision to adopt stiffer regulations than those recommended by the Christian Democratic government. The arguments made in this debate would later be applied to the abortion debate. In 2009, Catholic parliamentarians garnered sufficient votes from women in the Green and Social Democratic Parties to mandate a three-day waiting period in late-term abortions when a fetal disability had been diagnosed. They did so by linking the traditional pro-life argument to a new argument that abortion violated the rights of the disabled—an argument the Church first embraced in the battle against NRTs. Slowly, a smaller Catholic Church was developing a new theological and political identity for a postsecular age.

CHAPTER 5

Assisted Reproduction
Changing Bedfellows

> Father and mother, is quite out of fashion.
> I've shown up pretty well that idle pother—
> The thought of child by no means implies mother:
> The tender point from which life sprang and started
> Is gone—clean gone—the glory all departed...
> No doubt the old views may still for the brute beast
> Answer, but man, high-gifted man at least,
> Will have a higher, purer form of birth.[1]

Johann Wolfgang von Goethe penned these lines more than one hundred years before the birth of the first test tube baby. Although we are accustomed to thinking of assisted reproduction as a relatively new phenomenon, artificial insemination (AI) was introduced as a treatment for human infertility more than two hundred years ago. In 1785, a Scottish doctor, John Hunter, advised a man suffering from hypospadias to collect his semen and have his wife inject it into her vagina; the woman later gave birth to a healthy child.[2] This first documented report of successful human AI quickly captured public attention and the imagination of European authors; the encroachment of science and the state on the sphere of human reproduction became a common trope in utopian and dystopian accounts of humanity's future.[3] Experts in medicine, law, and theology almost immediately began debating the acceptability and implications of these incursions.

This chapter offers a comparative analysis of three German debates on assisted reproduction—one that commenced in 1905, a second in 1958, and a third that began in earnest in 1984. The first and third debates witnessed intense public engagement. The second debate was largely confined to experts. Only the third debate resulted in changes in the German legal code. As this chapter will show, neither technological innovation nor an increase in the practice of assisted reproduction can account for the results of the third debate. In fact, unless one factors in the broader cultural, social, and political context, the timing of these debates makes little sense.

The chapter highlights continuities and discontinuities among the three debates with reference to framing, arguments, actors, and context. It demonstrates that secular and religious discourses on assisted reproduction actually became more entangled over time, despite Germany's growing secular orientation. This increased entanglement, I argue, resulted from the dynamic interplay of changes taking place in the Catholic Church and in German society.

As discussed in the preceding chapter, by the mid-1970s a growing awareness existed in the Church that traditional arguments on the defense of unborn life and on marital morality no longer resonated with the general public or with West German Catholics. In addition, the interests of the Catholic Church no longer always coincided with those of the two self-identified Christian parties. New arguments and new strategies were needed in order for the Church to remain a relevant actor in debates on NRTS and more generally in German debates on the defense of life. Against this backdrop, a new Catholic political and theological identity for a post-secular age slowly began to take shape in Germany. This smaller and more activist Church would achieve its first victory in 1990, when the Bundestag passed the Embryo Defense Act banning embryological research, egg donation, surrogacy, and preimplantation genetic diagnosis (PGD).

Moral Scruples in the Early Medico-Legal Debate on Artificial Insemination (1905)

In 1905, the German judicial system confronted its first case involving artificial insemination. In December 1904, a German husband challenged the legitimacy of a baby girl born to his wife on August 7, 1904. He claimed that he and his wife of six years had been unable to have sexual relations despite multiple attempts earlier in their marriage. Between October 10, 1903, and February 8, 1904, no attempt at sexual relations occurred. Consequently, the child could not be his. The wife denied having had any extramarital sexual relations. She explained that unbeknownst to her husband, she had "scooped up fresh semen ejaculated on the bedclothes" and used it to impregnate herself.[4] The case would make its way from the District Court in Koblenz (Landgericht Koblenz) to the Cologne Regional Appellate Court (Oberlandesgericht Köln) and finally to the Supreme Court of the German Reich (Reichsgericht).

The medico-legal issues were as follows: (1) Was AI medically possible? (2) If so, was the child born in this manner legitimate? (3) Did the husband's ignorance of the insemination mitigate his responsibility for the child? (4) Could doctors who performed AI, including female physicians, be sued for paternity? (5) Did homologous insemination (i.e., artificial insemination by the husband's sperm, AIH) violate the dignity of marriage? (6) Had advances in the medical sciences made existing paternity laws obsolete? To answer the first question, the courts sought out expert medical opinion, only to discover that German doctors disagreed on AI's feasibility. Professor Doutrelpont of Bonn, who testified at the first trial, implicitly accepted AI; rather than question the plausibility of the woman's account, he focused on determining the husband's virility. On the basis of his conclusion that the husband was not sterile, the court affirmed the child's legitimacy.

At the second trial, Professor Fritsch of Bonn testified that in his expert opinion AI was not medically feasible.[5] His viewpoint represented that of most German doctors, and in fact the second trial prompted several doctors to publish accounts of their failed attempts at AI as proof of its infeasibility, or at least its extreme rarity.[6] Given contemporary knowledge about human reproduction, it is not surprising that German doctors doubted the procedure's efficacy. Since the contemporary medical consensus was that ovulation coincided with menstruation, doctors performed inseminations at the least optimal point in the woman's cycle (immediately before or after ovulation).[7]

The procedure's low success rate was not the only reason that German doctors shied away from recommending AI to infertile couples. Although technically speaking AI was not difficult, it was logistically complex, since experts believed that insemination had to take place immediately after intercourse; the woman's sexual arousal, it was believed, facilitated fertilization. The German physician and sexologist Hermann Rohleder explained: "To my mind the absence of alkaline secretion in the cervix is the first unfavorable or retarding factor in artificial impregnation. In order to call forth such secretion in the woman artificially it would be necessary to excite her sexually, a step which no responsible physician would take. But of course, this excitation can be produced naturally by the husband through cohabitation (or at least attempts in case he should be suffering from impotence) a few moments before the entrance of the physician."[8] The procedure, therefore, was performed either at the doctor's home or in the patient's house with the doctor waiting outside the bedroom. After having sexual relations, the husband delivered the condom to the doctor, who aspirated sperm from it with a syringe. Accompanied by the husband, the doctor entered the bedroom and injected the sperm into the woman's uterus. Although in France and the United States, masturbation quickly replaced condom coitus as the preferred means of sperm collection, German doctors disavowed the practice for aesthetic, moral, and medical reasons. Catholic doctors often cited the Church's condemnation of masturbation; other physicians posited that masturbation decreased the potency of the sperm and thus lowered the chances of successful insemination. Alternatively, they opined that the method was too humiliating for the husband.[9]

In fact, moral discomfiture with the procedure rather than either its low success rate or the logistical issues involved accounted for AI's unpopularity in Germany. Walter Stoeckel, one of the founding fathers of gynecology in Germany, characterized the procedure in the early 1920s as a "perversity of thought, feeling, and action" and warned doctors "not to besmirch their hands with it."[10] In his 1921 history of AI, Hermann Rohleder countered this negative assessment by pointing to the role played by Italian Catholic doctors in developing AI and by emphasizing Catholic theology's emphasis on fecundity: "Now if the strictly observing Catholic physicians do not have moral scruples against artificial fecundation, then certainly no objections need be raised by the Protestant Church."[11] But few German doctors seemed to find this argument convincing; out of 35,000 doctors practicing in Germany, Rohleder estimated, perhaps 10 performed AI.[12]

Yet despite the medical community's overwhelming disavowal of AI, the Cologne court sustained the lower court's decision in 1907. For jurists, the fundamental question was not the feasibility of the procedure but the legitimacy of the child conceived via AI. According to Paragraph 1591 of the German Civil Code (Bürgerliches Gesetzbuch), marital cohabitation during the period of conception constituted a precondition of legitimacy. Did AIH meet the legal standard for marital cohabitation, and if so, should the courts treat paternity cases involving AI in the same way they dealt with cases involving alleged extramarital sexual relationships? In short, should the burden of proof remain on the husband challenging the child's legitimacy, or in cases of alleged AI should the burden of proof shift to the woman? By ignoring Dr. Fritsch's testimony and ruling in the wife's favor, the appellate court suggested that the same legal standard applied. Despite the improbability of the procedure, the child was deemed legitimate because the husband failed to present convincing evidence of his wife's infidelity.[13]

The Cologne court's decision prompted intense discussion in medical and legal journals, with critics of the decision interjecting moral arguments into legal and medical ones. In the *Deutsche Medizinische Wochenschrift*, Dr. Th. Olshausen opined:

> German legislators established strict criteria for challenging the legitimacy of the child for good reason; the relinquishment of the conjugal character of a child born within wedlock must be avoided if possible. The procedure followed by the appellate court, nevertheless, is unacceptable. It does not matter whether one finds artificial insemination medically feasible or treats it with skepticism, as most German experts do. When transferred from the realm of science into the realm of practice, artificial insemination is incompatible with the dignity of marriage.[14]

Dr. J. Schwalbe's rebuttal appeared in the same issue of *Deutsche Medizinische Wochenschrift*. Schwalbe questioned Olhausen's formalistic understanding of the law: "I do not wish to believe that the legislators placed as much emphasis on a literal interpretation of cohabitation as Mr. Olshausen supposes."[15] In the law journal *Das Recht*, Dr. Traumann took a similar position: "Not the state-sanctioned *copula carnalis*, but the certainty of filiation to the parents, who are joined in the bond of marriage, is the legal standard for paternity."[16] Others, such as Hermann Rohleder, countered Olshausen's moral argument with their own: "It seems to me that I have already demonstrated sufficiently that it is incompatible with the physician's dignity to refuse to alleviate the suffering caused by sterility."[17]

In June 1908, the decision of Germany's highest court superseded that of the Cologne appellate court. The Reichsgericht upheld the child's legitimacy; however, it shifted the burden of proof from the man to the woman. In cases of alleged AI, the court ruled that the woman must provide explicit testimony as to how the artificial fertilization occurred. On a case-by-case basis in consultation with medical experts, the court would rule on the feasibility of the particular insemination and decide the child's legitimacy accordingly.[18]

The German courts never addressed whether the husband's ignorance of the procedure mitigated his responsibility for the child. Yet in professional journals and in public lectures, doctors and lawyers debated the issue at length. Hermann Rohleder argued that the woman's subterfuge had to be taken under advisement, but legal experts, such as Eugen Wilhelm and Dr. Traumann, thought differently. Wilhelm acknowledged that the subterfuge was a moral offense, but it was not a criminal one.[19] Taking a natural law approach, Traumann reasoned, "Even in natural procreation, the will of the procreator often is not directed to procreation, but on the contrary strives most earnestly against it. When nature triumphs over the will of her subjugated people, they must surrender and acknowledge the legal consequences that they attached to the natural process."[20] For the purpose of establishing legitimacy, the husband's consent was inconsequential; however, the woman's consent was required.

The debate among the experts also touched upon whether a doctor who performed AI (with or without the consent of the woman) could be sued for paternity. Schwalbe argued that the method of impregnation was irrelevant to the determination of paternity: "The filial relationship of the child to the couple is determined only by whose ovum and whose sperm have supplied the germinal material. If it were possible to spawn a homunculus in a test tube by bringing together the ovum and the spermatozoon, even then the man and the woman who supplied the materials would have to be considered the child's parents."[21] The doctor facilitated the birth; he or she did not sire the child.

The experts avoided applying this rationale to artificial insemination by donor's sperm (AID). In fact, most jurists and physicians made no reference to AID. Doctors who did mention it mainly recounted the desperate pleas of childless women, whom they rebuffed for their willingness to transgress moral boundaries in their desperate pursuit of motherhood.[22] Even Hermann Rohleder expressed moral reservations about AID, although he did not rule it out: "I would undertake this step only where the sterility had engendered grave psychic disturbances and dangerous depressive states which threatened to become severe and incurable psychoses, or to eventuate in suicide or at least divorce."[23]

Practical considerations also more than likely informed the medical community's reluctance to engage the unpopular topic of AID. At the time of the trial, the German medical community was involved in a heated battle with the state over medical fees and doctors' rights. In an effort to safeguard the profession's autonomy, the Hartmann League organized doctors' strikes in which German physicians refused to treat any patient paying with state funds.[24] For a profession trying to maintain unity within its ranks while fending off an imminent challenge to its autonomy by the state, broaching the taboo topic of AID would have been a poor strategy.

The German AI debate was enmeshed in a broader transnational debate on population politics, racial hygiene, gender, and national identity. Childlessness—intended or unintended—was perceived as a symptom of an unhealthy gender system, moral degeneration, and national decline. Authors such as Hans Blüher and Paul Möbius in Germany, Edward C. Clarke in the United States, Émile Zola in France, and H. B. Marriot Watson in Great Britain railed against the masculinization of women and the emasculation of men, predicting civilization's collapse if the situation were not reversed. Access to educational and career opportunities, they maintained, impaired, limited, or destroyed women's reproductive organs. Women's growing independence, they argued, threatened the virility of men and of the nation.[25]

Against this backdrop, infertility and AI as a treatment for it captured the public imagination, which meant that eugenics and the preservation of gender hierarchies formed the persistent subtext of the debate. Medical treatises cautioned doctors against performing the procedure for couples with a familial history of disorders that they believed to be hereditary, such as alcoholism, tuberculosis, and mental defects. A few German doctors endorsed AI as a tool for improving the human race. A 1915 article in *Zeitschrift für Sexualwissenschaft* described AI as a "eugenic blessing."[26] However, most eugenicists expressed doubts about AI, warning that its use might lower the quality of offspring. According to Alfred Ploetz, the German physician who coined the term "racial hygiene," AI cut short the race of the spermatozoa to the egg, thereby increasing the chances that damaged or weak sperm would survive to fertilize the ovum.[27] Others feared that medical manipulation compromised the integrity of the sperm, increasing the risk of birth defects. Thus, most supporters acknowledged that the technique required refinement: "Regarding animals, artificial insemination is used with healthy individuals aiming at an amelioration of the race. With humans, it is used to bridge a pathological gap in the processes normally leading to conception. To use it for eugenic purposes is not yet possible."[28]

Experts also offered differing opinions on AI as a means of restoring the gendered order. AI's proponents argued that allowing an impotent man to father children would restore the self-confidence and virility of German men.[29] Opponents saw AI as part of a feminist conspiracy to eliminate men from the reproductive process. In German and Austrian journals, such as *Die Gegenwart* and *Die Fackel*, commentators warned of man's obsolescence and of the self-reproducing woman.[30] In response to these charges, lawyers and doctors tried to reassure the public of the rarity of the practice and thus its social, cultural, and legal insignificance: "The practical side of the matter is certainly of very little significance. The cases reported by reliable authors can be enumerated on one's fingers, and even with some of these reports an experienced critic still could raise doubts."[31]

Meanwhile, a parallel debate was taking place among Catholic theologians. In 1897, the Holy Office (today, the CDF) had issued a terse "non licere" in response to the following question: Can artificial fecundation be performed on a woman?" Almost immediately a theological debate erupted: What did the Holy Office mean? Did it mean that AI was immoral? Or was the Holy Office condemning only the means of sperm collection in this particular case—that is, masturbation? Some Catholic theologians in Germany and elsewhere in Europe argued the latter, prompting a very graphic debate on potentially licit methods of sperm collection.[32] This theological debate continued unabated until 1951, when Pope Pius XII left no doubt that regardless of the means of sperm collection, any form of artificial insemination violated the dignity of marriage: "To reduce the cohabitation of married persons and the conjugal act to a mere organic function for the transmission of gametes would be to convert the domestic hearth, sanctuary of the family, into nothing more than a biological laboratory."[33]

These two debates—one secular and one Catholic—on assisted reproduction had few points of intersection in the early 1900s. While lawyers and doctors made vague references to religious and moral reasons for condemning AI, Catholic theologians did not even mention the ongoing secular debate. As Charles Curran, a Catholic moral theologian and author of *Catholic Moral Theology in the United States: A History* explained, Catholic moral theology in Europe at the turn of the twentieth century operated in a world apart. Moral theologians wrote manuals in Latin aimed at guiding priests in their capacity as judges in the sacrament of penance. These manuals did not engage in secular thought; instead, they detailed a catalog of sins and provided extensive citations of past theologians to demonstrate precedence.[34] Those few European theologians who tried to accommodate or initiate a dialogue with the modern world were censured; on July 3, 1907, the Holy Office released *Lamentabili Sane* (Syllabus condemning the errors of modernists), detailing sixty-five "propositions to be condemned and prescribed," and on September 8 of that same year, Pius X issued the encyclical *Pascendi Dominici Gregis* censuring the doctrine of the modernists.[35]

Like German Catholic theologians, German Protestant theologians did not take part in this first debate; in fact, no Protestant treatises on the topic appeared until the 1950s. As late as 1954, John Francis Fletcher, a pioneer of Protestant bioethics, lamented in the preface of his *Morals and Medicine* the failure of Protestant theologians to develop an "ethics of medicine," in contrast to the "well-turned one, both explicit and implicit, in Catholic moral theology."[36] Thus, his 1954 text, which included a chapter on AI, represented one of the first efforts, if not the first, to develop a systematic Protestant theological approach to bioethics.

This lack of engagement in the first debate by the two largest religious communities in Germany meant that the question of AI's morality was only vaguely addressed. With the onset of World War I, the German public turned its attention to more pressing concerns, and the German Reich introduced no changes in its paternity law. Although AI continued to be discussed in medical journals throughout the 1920s and 1930s, the German public showed little interest. In 1923, Rohleder lamented, "If we waited until sterile mates demanded it, we could strike this technique from the tables of medical practice."[37]

Artificial Insemination and Penal Code Reform (1958)

On February 14, 1958, three members of the Bavarian Party and Dr. Sönning of the Christian Social Union (CSU) proposed to the Bavarian State Parliament (Bayerischer Landtag) the creation of a new law regulating AI: "In order to address the concerns of the Christian churches and the German medical community, artificial insemination of married women with foreign sperm is to be forbidden so that the right of children to know their familial lineage is safeguarded. The artificial insemination of unmarried women is prohibited categorically so as to prevent the artificial fabrication (*künstliche Erzeugung*) of illegitimate children."[38] They also requested that the Bavarian government push for federal regulation. The Social-Political Committee of the Bavarian State Parliament submitted a request to the federal government. On March 8, 1959, the Grand Commission on Penal Law (Große Strafrechtskommission)—created by the Federal Ministry of Justice in 1954 and charged with the task of drafting a new, more modern criminal code—addressed the question of AI. This discussion led to the commission's recommending legal sanctions.

Paragraph 203 of the 1960 and 1962 draft penal codes identified AID as a "crime against the moral order" and made it punishable by up to three years' imprisonment. Both drafts also imposed a minimum sentence of six months' imprisonment for anyone who performed artificial insemination (AIH or AID) without the woman's consent. AIH, performed by a doctor with a married couple's consent, was not subject to criminal prosecution. Both the CDU-CSU government and the Catholic Study Group for Penal Reform (Katholische Arbeitskreis für Strafrechtsreform) supported this formulation. The latter pointed out that although AIH might be morally reprehensible, it did not warrant criminal sanctions, since it jeopardized neither the marital community nor the child's well-being.[39]

Initially, a general consensus existed across the political spectrum that AID should be banned.[40] However, by the mid-1960s, support for Paragraph 203 had diminished substantially. At the Ninth International Criminal Law Congress held at The Hague in 1964, West German representatives received a strong reminder that the proposed ban was out of step with the international legal community.[41] Concomitantly, SPD and FDP members developed strong reservations, claiming that inclusion of the ban in the new criminal code would constitute the incorporation of a Christian category of sin into this secular document.[42] Even some members of the CDU-CSU began expressing doubts about the state's encroachment into such an intimate sphere.[43]

The German Medical Association (Bundesärztekammer) saw legal regulation as a threat to the profession's autonomy.[44] On March 8, 1958, at the 62nd Medical Assembly, the German medical community established professional guidelines for the practice of AI. The guidelines described AIH as a treatment of last resort and explicitly condemned AID on "moral grounds."[45] Self-regulation, the German Medical Association argued, made legal regulation "unwarranted."[46] The German Society for Forensic and Social Medicine (Deutsche Gesellschaft für gerichtliche und soziale Medizin) also supported self-regulation: "We believe that legal regulation is harmful. . . . It concerns a most delicate matter of the intimate sphere, which should be confidentially discussed and decided by the immediate participants, namely the wife, the husband, and the doctor."[47]

By the mid-1960s, the sense of legal urgency had passed. At a meeting of the Cologne CDU in 1967, Max Güde, chair of the Grand Commission, stated that he had no objections to abandoning Paragraph 203 if a majority of the Bundestag supported this action.[48] One year later, Güde acknowledged in an interview with *Der Spiegel* the unlikelihood that any ban on AI would be included in the final version of the revised criminal code.[49] Paragraph 203 disappeared from subsequent drafts; AID remained free of legal regulation.

Multiple parallels existed between the first and second debates. In the second debate, as in the first, contemporary understanding of gender relations informed medical discussions. In keeping with public discourses on domesticity and motherhood, doctors in the early 1960s emphasized a vulnerable and irrational feminine psyche in need of protection. For example, the German Association of Women Doctors (Deutscher Ärztinnenbund) warned, "There exists in fact the danger that the mother will seek out the unknown donor or embrace the known donor," thereby destabilizing the marital community.[50]

Like their early-twentieth-century counterparts, legal experts focused on the challenges AI posed to the legal understanding of paternity, legitimacy, adultery, and informed consent. Wilhelm Geiger, president of the Second Senate of the Constitutional Court, argued that biological parenthood was the determining factor for establishing paternity: "It is the woman who gave birth to the child and the man whose sperm made the child that determine parenthood. The method of impregnation—cohabitation, with medical assistance, by artificial insemination, within marriage or outside of marriage, or by a third party—is completely irrelevant."[51] Geiger also asserted that failure to obtain the consent of the biological mother or father for the insemination did not negatively affect the legitimacy of the child. In paternity/legitimacy cases involving allegations of AID, Geiger contended that the child's legitimacy must be upheld unless "strong evidence exists that the mother could not have been impregnated by the husband."[52]

However, this second debate's focus on AID did introduce two new issues: incest and male adultery. Doctors and lawyers feared that donor children might later unwittingly violate Paragraph 4 of the German Civil Code outlawing marriage between close blood relatives.[53] Jurists also asked whether a husband who had donated his semen for the impregnation of a woman other than his wife had committed adultery. Justice Geiger worried that donor insemination created a new category of adultery: "Are sexual relations really the only violation of fidelity? Is not marital fidelity also injured when the man deceives the woman or the woman deceives the man by pursuing insemination *ab alieno*?"[54] Consequently, he argued that the legal definition of adultery should be amended so that it included "insemination *artificialis ab alieno*."[55] Although Geiger recognized that by necessity "injustice and criminal injustice are two circles lacking congruence," he believed that AID required legal regulation in order to safeguard the sanctity of the marital community.[56]

The second debate also differed from the first in its overt incorporation of religious arguments. This reflected fundamental shifts in German society and in the German theological community. As noted in earlier chapters, the

Catholic Church gained considerable influence in postwar Germany. Authorities of the Allied occupation supported the active involvement of the Christian churches in the reconstruction of Germany, so that the democratization of Germany went hand in hand with efforts at re-Christianizing the nation. Moreover, with the division of Germany, Catholics lost their minority status, and in the early years of the Federal Republic, they occupied most leadership positions in the CDU-CSU.[57]

Numerous CDU-CSU government officials embraced Christian principles as the foundation of German law and maintained close connections with Catholic lay organizations. Thus, in arguing for a ban on AID, CDU-CSU officials often made explicit religious references. For example, Dr. Helene Große-Schönepauck, the only high-ranking female official in the Ministry of Family Affairs, argued before the Bundestag: "It is essential that the legislature support the federal government's initiative for regulation . . . so that man—the crown of God's creation—is not reduced to technological product. Rightly a Swiss moral theologian recently explained that this development is morally depraved and irreconcilable with the model of faith found in the New Testament."[58] Two pages of her speech were devoted to Pius XII's 1949 condemnation of AI.[59] Große-Schönepauck sent a copy of the speech to the leadership of the kfd and provided the organization with updates on legislative developments.

Religious arguments also found their way into German public discourse on AI via the active engagement of a new actor in contemporary moral-political debates—professional theologians, particularly Catholic theologians. The failure of the German Catholic Church to combat National Socialism had a profound impact on the direction of German theology. German theologians argued that the concept of the Church as standing above and separate from human societies (*societas perfectas*) had hindered the Church's efforts to provide moral leadership in resisting Nazism. Determined not to repeat this mistake, Catholic theologians in Germany championed social justice and dialogue with the secular world as critical elements of theology.[60] The move away from Latin as the language of moral theology, which had begun in the late 1920s, was now complete, and German Catholic theologians no longer hesitated to enter public discourses on political topics with moral implications.

Theologians such as Johannes Stelzenberger, Bernhard Häring, and Karl Rahner not only published theological treatises on AI intended for a general audience; they contributed essays to edited volumes that included perspectives from non-Catholic experts in the fields of science, medicine, law, and Protestant theology. Although Stelzenberger's contribution to the debate was limited to detailing prewar theological debates and postwar papal pronouncements,[61] Bernhard Häring's and Karl Rahner's contributions embodied the German Catholic theological community's new commitment to dialogue with the modern world, ecumenism, historicity, and an understanding of moral theology that moved beyond identifying and hierarchically ordering categories of sin.

Bernhard Häring first addressed AI in his 1954 three-volume manual of morality, *Das Gesetz Christi*, which received international acclaim for its conscious move away from a legalistic approach to morality and for its emphasis on Christian morality as a dialogue between God and man.[62] In rejecting AIH and AID, Häring did not quibble over means of sperm collection or draw distinctions between venial and mortal sins. Instead, he underscored two issues. First, he criticized the procedure's separation of the unitive and procreative aims of sexual intercourse, noting, "For marriage is a perfect fellowship of love, not merely a partnership of convenience for the production of offspring regardless of method or techniques."[63] AI robbed the child of his or her right to be born from "parents bound to each other by marriage."[64]

Häring also deplored the dehumanizing effects of the technology: "In its frightfully rapid diffusion, in part with state approval, it is a symptom of perverted nature, *which dreads attachment and submission in love and abandons itself to the fascination with technique.* In this nuclear age technical man has fashioned a weapon in the atomic bomb capable of destroying the human race by force from without. Artificial insemination, the substitute for fruitful marital love through technical fertilization, exposes his inner impoverishment."[65] He would later modify his position on AI. In 1972, Häring published *Heilender Dienst: Ethischer Probleme der Modernen Medizin*, in which he offered qualified support for AIH: "There are no convincing arguments to prove either the immorality of ejaculation by the husband in view of fatherhood nor the immorality of introducing that sperm into the wife's uterus."[66]

Like Häring, Karl Rahner drew attention in his treatment of assisted reproduction to the rapid transformation of society wrought by new technologies. Between 1966 and 1967, he wrote and revised two essays on the technological manipulation of human life—"Experiment Mensch: Theologisches über die Selbstmanipulation des Menschen" and "Zum Problem der genetische Manipulation aus der Sicht des Theologen." In the first essay,

Rahner warned against many of the self-manipulations so vividly depicted in Huxley's *Brave New World*—sperm banks of desirable genetic stock, mass brainwashing, and governments controlled by a genetically engineered Übermenschen. Christians must "oppose with utter resoluteness those kinds of self-manipulation which are the most recent form of barbarity, slavery, the totalitarian annihilation of personality and formation of a monochrome society."[67] However, he also cautioned the Catholic Church against rejecting all technological and genetic interventions: "But it would be symptomatic of a cowardly and comfortable conservatism hiding behind misunderstood Christian ideals and maxims . . . to simply condemn the approaching age of self-manipulation as such; to break out into lyrical laments on the theme of degrading barbarity, the cold, technological rationalism, the destruction of what is 'natural,' the rationalisation of love, . . . the levelled-down mass society, the end of history in a faceless fellahin society without a history, etc."[68] For Rahner, a direct correlation did not necessarily exist between the technical and the artificial, on the one hand, and dehumanization and alienation, on the other.

In the second essay, Rahner explicitly addressed the morality of AID, leaving no doubt that he did not consider it among the harmless self-manipulations that he outlined in the first essay. In disavowing AID, his second essay offered a much more negative assessment of genetic manipulation than his first: "What, in fact, is the driving force behind genetic manipulation? Who is driven to it? One would answer: hate for one's destiny; the person who, at the most profound level of his being, is in despair that he cannot dispose of his existence. In genetic manipulation such a man clearly oversteps every boundary between legitimate eugenic precautions and the realm, in which the desperate fear of destiny rules tyrannically."[69] Genetic manipulation, he opined, opened boundless possibilities to humanity, while at the same time closing off the possibility of transcendence: "This is clearly to be seen in our case, since the concrete genetic manipulation is ruled by the desire to eradicate the *fatum* from existence at a decisive point. Although this plan does not entirely succeed, it is contrary to the original desire, for this desire hates destiny and can only love—as the product of its own free action—what it has calculated and planned. It no longer desires to say, 'I have come by man from the Lord'—from *God*, who cannot be manipulated, who must be concretely present in man's existence."[70]

Rahner also reiterated Häring's concern about the harm done to a marriage and to a child when procreation occurred outside its proper context:

"Genetic manipulation, however, does two things: it fundamentally separates the procreation of a new person as the permanent manifestation of the unitive love of the married couple; and it transfers procreation, isolated and torn from its human matrix, to an area outside the intimate sphere of humanity to which sexual union properly belongs, and which at the same time implies the fundamental readiness of the marriage partners to allow their unity to manifest in the child."[71] This harm extended to society as well. Although in 1954 Häring vaguely alluded to broader social ramifications, Rahner detailed what he believed were the inevitable eugenic applications of reproductive technologies: "A *partial* genetic manipulation furthermore would create two new 'races' of mankind if it became recognized as normal practice in the public consciousness: technologically manipulated, super-bred 'test-tube humans,' who inevitably would have a special status in society, and 'ordinary,' unselected, mass-produced humans, procreated in the old-fashioned way."[72]

Rahner did not explicitly mention Germany's recent National Socialist past; nevertheless, his description left no doubt about the parallels and dangers of repeating that past. He ended the essay with a call to action: "Thus, here, as in many of cases in moral theology, we are faced today with a new, additional question of great importance: How can this no [to genetic manipulation] be established in modern society as society's own maxim, its own inner attitude and 'instinct,' in the face of society's pluralism?"[73]

German Protestant theologians tentatively entered the debate as well; as Dieter Giesen noted in his 1962 monograph on the German debate, "A Protestant ethics scarcely exists that comments in detail on artificial insemination."[74] The few Protestant theologians who did enter the fray usually distinguished between AIH and AID.[75] They described AIH as morally acceptable so long as it supported the marital community and was not used to circumvent conjugal relations. AIH, they argued, should be left to the discretion of the married couple. In 1960, Fedde Bloemhof wrote: "The married couple must make the decision together. . . . Christian ethics cannot establish general rules here if it wants to remain a Christian ethics, that is to say, an ethics that does not decrease their freedom and responsibility for making the decision themselves but that always underscores anew that freedom and responsibility belong to the couple."[76]

Although most Protestant leaders accepted AIH, there were at least two important exceptions: Otto Dibelius, bishop of Berlin and Brandenburg, and Hermann Dietzelbinger, bishop of Munich. Dibelius characterized AI as dehumanizing and linked its development to communism and American capitalism: "If artificial insemination were to gain the upper hand, the vilification of man to brute creature would be complete. It makes one think of the praise of artificial insemination that is being reported both from Communist Hungary and from the American world."[77] Protestant and Catholics agreed that AID was morally reprehensible.[78]

The concern expressed by Häring, Rahner, and Dibelius about the rapid transformation of society and its negative impact on the moral order found a receptive audience in Germany. Increased material prosperity and the emerging culture of mass consumption in late 1950s West Germany generated widespread fears about decadence and loosening morals.[79] Germans blamed these unsavory developments (whether real or imagined) on the "Americanization" of German culture. On a daily basis, Germans confronted a mental and physical landscape profoundly transformed by American influences. Building designs, advertisements, fashion styles, and music all pointed to the ubiquitous U.S. invasion of German consciousness. Admittedly, West Germans desired the prosperity that accompanied these transformations, but they also associated them with a threat to German identity and autonomy.[80] This cultural panic over "American capitalist disorder" and its threat to German values in the late 1950s, as Michael Geyer has convincingly argued, found "a political outlet with the mobilization against the atomic bomb."[81] Although West Germany's chancellor, Konrad Adenauer, and other members of the CDU-CSU leadership supported rearmament, the German populace, including CDU sympathizers and West German Catholics, had strong reservations.[82] Fear of "nuclear death" and concern about the United States' ability to safeguard German security resulted in the resurfacing of "cultural memories that had been repressed and frozen."[83] Lingering resentment of the Allied occupation, denial and self-pity about the National Socialist past, as well as dreams of *Heimat* and "the cult of noble Indians (and their good German friends)" found new life, as the clash over nuclear weapons and other technologies reached a crescendo between 1958 and 1962.[84]

Only against the backdrop of cultural panic and German fear of "nuclear death" does the apocalyptic and anti-American tone of the German experts' debate on AID make sense, since at the time of the proposed ban, the procedure had little or no support within the German medical, legal, or theological community. In fact, German doctors remained reluctant to recommend the procedure to their patients. At the time of the proposed ban, experts estimated that only 1,000 children living in Germany had been conceived by means of artificial insemination. In contrast, experts estimated that 100,000 children had been conceived by AI in the United States, 4,200 in Britain, and between 1,000 and 20,000 in France.[85] Although there are no statistics indicating how many of those 1,000 German children may have been conceived with donor sperm, experts agreed that the conservative German medical community did not share the U.S. and British acceptance of AID.[86]

In fact, German press coverage of foreign developments in reproductive medicine up until the time of the proposed ban verged on hostile. For example, *Der Spiegel* carried headlines such as "Test Tube Babies—Test Tube Adultery" and "The Anonymous Adultery."[87] The Hamburg newspaper *Die Zeit* opted for a more creative outlet for its disapproval. In 1949, it reprinted Goethe's account of the homunculus in *Faust, Part II* prefaced by a reference to scientific advancements in reproductive medicine and to George Bernard Shaw's *As Far as Thought Can Reach: A.D. 31,920*, the fifth of five plays in his *Back to Methuselah (A Metabiological Pentateuch)*. In the play, Pygmalion is murdered by the two seemingly perfect artificial human beings he created.[88] Thus, rather than addressing any immediate legal or medical challenge, the debate on legal sanctions against AI in the late 1950s and early 1960s seemed to serve as a discursive space onto which social conservatives and their opponents could displace fears of "nuclear death" and anti-American sentiment without betraying party alliances. A 1958 Allensbach survey indicated that 70 percent of CDU sympathizers supported a plebiscite on rearmament and that 54 percent of these sympathizers would not have supported the CDU position. Moreover, 62 percent of Catholic churchgoers and 67 percent of Protestant ones said they opposed nuclear weapons.

Both conservative Christian supporters of the ban and representatives of the liberal German press in the late 1950s and early 1960s depicted AI as a foreign invasion, a threat to the German moral order, and a looming disaster comparable to nuclear war. Like Häring, Rahner, and Dibelius, Margarethe Albrecht, chair of the Federation of German Women Doctors (Deutscher Ärztinnenbund), linked the inherent immorality of AI to the Cold War: "In the end, it is about whether we, as doctors, are of the opinion that in this much-praised, highly developed technological world with its atom bombs and moon rockets, artificial fabrication of humans is one of the corresponding requirements of the times, or whether we believe that this intervention in the mystery of creation is incompatible with our culture, with the dignity of humanity, and with our medical ethics."[89]

West Germans perceived advances in reproductive technologies, like those in nuclear weapons, as a foreign invasion from which West German society must be protected. At a 1962 meeting of the CDU, Professor Hirschmann explained: "We must at once begin to defend ourselves against these things. We already have seen the helplessness of Italian authorities in Padua. In the United States all along there have been experiments in which human and animal sperm have been mixed with one another."[90] While Hirschmann only implied U.S. responsibility for these heinous developments, the liberal German press was far less circumspect in its accusations. In a 1963 article entitled "Fatherhood: From the Freezer," *Der Spiegel* attributed the emerging "Brave New World" not to Aldous Huxley, but to American scientists.[91] In particular, *Der Spiegel* singled out the U.S. Nobel Prize winner Hermann J. Muller, who at a 1962 conference organized by the Ciba Foundation called for the creation of sperm banks in which the genetic material of geniuses would be preserved so that superior human offspring might result.[92] In outlining Muller's vision, *Der Spiegel* repeatedly highlighted not only the eugenic dimensions of Muller's plan but its relationship to a future nuclear holocaust: "Soldiers could preserve their genetic material in radiation-proof vaults before going off to a nuclear war."[93] Another U.S. scientist, Dr. Jerome Sherman, *Der Spiegel* explained, recently had taken steps to make Muller's dream a reality; Sherman announced at the 11th International Congress for Genetics the birth of two "deep-freeze children."[94] The father's sperm had been stored at −196 degrees Celsius, which according to *Der Spiegel* was the "same temperature at which some rocket fuels were preserved."[95] Two years previously, in response to an article by Muller on the same topic published in the journal *Science*, *Die Zeit* minced no words, labeling his futuristic vision "icebox fornication" (*Eisschrank-Unzucht*).[96] The line between immorality, nuclear apocalypse, and American culpability could not have been more blurred.

For Germans, AI represented an area in which Germans could assert their autonomy from and moral superiority over their former U.S. occupiers. For example, in explaining the proposed ban of AI to an American audience, Eduard Dreher, an officer of the Justice Ministry, underscored the moral and cultural differences between the two nations: "We had anticipated that the American critics would be opposed to the punishment provided in the Draft Code for artificial insemination (§ 203), which is widely practiced in the United States of America. Such a completely different judgment is traceable, I believe, to deep-seated differences in psychic makeup. Replacing love's mystery with medical intervention is more repulsive to us than adulterous lust."[97] At least for some West Germans, Paragraph 203 demarcated a distinct German legal and moral identity.

In taking the moral high ground on AI, some Germans also underscored that the Americans and the British, unlike the Germans, had failed to learn from National Socialism. Undoubtedly, the 1962 Ciba Foundation symposium gave some credence to this claim. The symposium, intended to facilitate communication between scientific communities across the globe, gained notoriety for the eugenic recommendations of several of the symposium's most prominent U.S. and British participants—including the already mentioned Nobel Prize winner Hermann J. Muller, Julian Huxley, Francis Crick, Albert Szent-Gyorgyi, Joshua Lederberg, Gregory Pincus, and J. B. S. Haldane. German and Austrian scientists, philosophers, and theologians immediately expressed harsh criticism of the eugenic proposals. For example, the Austrian biologist M. Klein equated Muller's approach to biology with that practiced under Hitler: "We have an example in the biology taught in Germany during the Hitler régime.... We must be very careful in teaching biology, and especially in teaching eugenics, not to teach a directed biology like that of Muller."[98] Following the 1966 publication of the German edition of *Man and His Future*,[99] the German geneticist Friedrich Vogel denounced the suggestion of the British Nobel Prize laureate Francis Crick that the state require couples to obtain licenses to reproduce: "The proposal, submitted by a leading natural scientist of the younger generation ... shows a shocking naïveté and inner apathy (*innere Unbetroffenheit*) about what we all have learned about the human capacity for inhumanity from the history of this century."[100] In a 1969 volume protesting the Ciba symposium, the German sociologist Friedrich Wagner warned against inaugurating a "new era of euthanasia," and Wilhelm Kütemeyer, a pioneer in medical anthropology, lamented, "Apparently National Socialism is only a precursor to what is now threatening to dictate the entire world."[101]

But by 1969 linking advances in human genetics to moral collapse, nuclear death, and National Socialism no longer prompted legal or medical sanctions against reproductive technologies; the CDU-CSU government had abandoned the campaign for legal regulation, recognizing that most Bundestag legislators no longer supported it. Four years later, at the 73rd Medical Assembly, West German doctors reversed their 1958 moral condemnation of AI, stating that it did not contradict professional ethics, although they did not go so far as to recommend the procedure, owing to unresolved legal issues.[102] One prominent Catholic moral theologian, Franz Böckle, now offered an even more positive reassessment of AID. At the 1970 Marburger Forum Philippinum, he stated: "I consider less critical the issue of heterologous insemination in a childless marriage. At least it is wrong here to speak of adultery, precisely because a breach in the intimate sexual community (*Geschlechtsgemeinschaft*) does not exist."[103]

The emergence of more moderate stances on AID in West Germany coincided with diminishing fears about imminent nuclear annihilation and the concomitant upsurge in West German support for the German–American alliance. The construction of the Berlin Wall in 1961 and the peaceful resolution of the Cuban Missile Crisis in 1962 increased German confidence in the United States' ability to safeguard West German security, leading to a much more positive assessment of the West German alliance with the United States by 1965.[104] As fears of a nuclear apocalypse receded in the German imagination, advances in science and technology met with a more positive reception. In 1966, polls showed that 72 percent of Germans now had a favorable view of science and technology.[105] Admittedly, entangled fears of genetic manipulation, nuclear war, moral degeneracy, and Americanization never completely disappeared. However, by the mid-1960s most West Germans were content to pursue the good life, no longer actively protesting nuclear rearmament or reproductive technologies. Not until the late 1970s and early 1980s, when new actors joined old ones, would both issues resurface and reproductive technologies become subject to state regulation.

Protests: Catholics, Environmentalists, and Radical Feminists (1980s)
In Vitro Fertilization: A Brave New World

On July 25, 1978, the ten-year anniversary of *Humanae Vitae*'s publication, Louise Brown—the first test tube baby—was born in England. In vitro fertilization/embryo transfer (IVF/ET) is defined as the fertilization of the egg outside the mother's womb; the fertilized egg is then surgically implanted in the woman's uterus. IVF/ET created the possibility of a new type of surrogacy—gestational surrogacy, in which the fertilized egg of one woman is implanted in the uterus of another woman. IVF/ET and gestational surrogacy raised a plethora of interlocking medical, legal, and ethical issues, of which AID had only scratched the surface.

First, the two interrelated procedures called into question traditional definitions of parenthood. They allowed lesbian and gay couples to have children without engaging in any heterosexual activity. Moreover, gestational surrogacy created a scenario in which a child could potentially have five parents—the intended or social parents, the egg and sperm donors, and the gestational surrogate. Overnight, the issues of paternity, legitimacy, and liability had become more complex. Did the gestational surrogate have a right to keep the child if she decided that she did not want to relinquish it? Did the social parents have a legal responsibility for the surrogate mother and her family if she developed serious complications or died during the pregnancy? Alternatively, who assumed legal and financial responsibility for the child if the child was born with a serious physical or mental disability?

Second, IVF gave the embryo, at least temporarily, an existence independent of the mother, raising several questions: What was the legal status of the extracorporeal embryo? Did it constitute a human life guaranteed protection under the law? If legislators took steps to safeguard the extracorporeal embryo's right to life, what were the implications for abortion law? Would this necessitate more stringent legal protection of the in utero embryo, effectively eliminating women's access to abortion? Since IVF treatment routinely involves stimulating hyperovulation (through the administration of drugs), more eggs are produced than can be implanted. Could these so-called surplus embryos be used for research purposes, or did they have a right to life?

Third, IVF and concomitant advances in preimplantation genetic diagnosis (PGD) and recombinant DNA technology opened the door to forms of eugenic selection that previously existed only in the realm of science fiction. PGD screening made it possible to identify extracorporeal embryos exhibiting signs of genetic disorders, the assumption being that these embryos would not be implanted. What should be the fate of damaged embryos, and did parents have a right to a "perfect child"? Did the pursuit of the "perfect child" infringe upon the rights of the disabled? Similarly, advances in recombinant DNA technology suggested that soon scientists would be able to manipulate genes in order to correct genetic disorders or create designer babies (selection of sex and eye color, genetically enhanced intelligence, etc.). Should scientists and patients be free to make such choices, or as the Austrian-born biochemist Erwin Chargaff alleged in 1987, did such choices represent the path to a "molecular Auschwitz"?[106]

Finally, the high cost and low success rate of IVF complicated matters further.[107] Beyond the question of medical insurance coverage, IVF's high cost and its use in conjunction with gestational surrogacy created numerous possibilities for coercion and exploitation of poor women acting as surrogates for those who could afford the procedure. As demand for egg donors and surrogates increased, international traffickers in domestic and sexual services moved quickly to fill the demand. IVF and gestational surrogacy created an international infertility industry that highlighted the inadequacy of national regulations and underscored the persistence of colonial relationships between the First and Third Worlds.

A Slow Start to the German Debate

As daunting as these issues were, the West German public at first showed little interest in the topic. Between 1978 and 1984, the German debate on the regulation of NRTs and genetic research remained largely confined to experts.

In response to news of Louise Brown's birth, the West German Federal Ministry of Research and Technology (Bundesministerium für Forschung und Technik, BMFT) created the Central Commission for Biological Security (Zentrale Kommission für Biologische Sicherheit, ZKBS) in 1978; it issued the first guidelines for experiments involving in vitro recombined nucleic acid. The guidelines were not legally binding and applied only to federal research institutes and private research projects receiving government funds.[108] That same year, the BMFT also drafted legislation outlining laboratory protocol and safety procedures for genetic engineering research. But the bill never passed; the scientific community blocked enactment by arguing that the proposed restrictions violated its constitutional right to conduct research free from state interference.[109]

The German public remained indifferent, prompting the ZKBS chair to comment to F. Cramer, a scientist at the Max Planck Institute, "The public certainly is unpredictable. It is inclined either to repression or to hysteria."[110] Even the provocative coverage of IVF in newspapers such as *Der Spiegel* and *Die Zeit* between 1978 and 1984 failed to spark widespread public interest.[111] For example, immediately following Louise Brown's birth, *Der Spiegel*'s cover showed a gloved hand pulling a fully formed baby by its feet from a test tube; the caption read: "Test Tube Children: Progress or Sacrilege (*Frevel*)?"

The accompanying article carried the headline "A Step in the Direction of Homunculus." The article highlighted the scientific community's trepidation and the procedure's commercial aspects. The reporter disdainfully noted that the doctors had sold the story's exclusive rights to the highest bidder—the *Daily Mail*.[112] In 1982, *Die Zeit* printed a story titled "Respect Down the Drain," in which the author quoted extensively from British news

Figure 5.1. "Test Tube Children: Progress or Sacrilege?" *Der Spiegel*, July 31, 1978. Used with the permission of SPIEGEL-Verlag. © 1978 DER SPIEGEL.

stories about the creation of "surplus children who are cannibalized in favor of other children" in the "chamber of horror" of the British physiologist Robert Edwards—the doctor in the Louise Brown case.[113]

Like the general public, German Catholics initially showed little interest, and West German Catholic organizations, such as the kfd, seemed reluctant to discuss either involuntary childlessness or advances in fertility treatment. In October 1979, a woman wrote a letter to the editors of *Frau und Mutter* asking when the organization planned to break its "deadly silence" on the topic; the woman reported that she had undergone "numerous medical procedures" for infertility but remained childless and felt isolated within the kfd.[114]

For Catholics, IVF/ET posed difficult questions. On the one hand, it seemed to align with Catholic theology's emphasis on procreation; given the

Church's understanding of women's primary role as mother, might IVF/ET represent a viable solution for Catholic women who, like the kfd reader just mentioned, felt isolated in their communities because they could not have children? On the other hand, the separation of procreation from the unitive function of marriage contradicted Catholic theology, as did the production of surplus embryos that never had the chance to achieve personhood.

Although Catholic lay organizations at first remained silent on the topic, German bishops and theologians did not. On July 29, 1978, three days after Louise Brown's birth, the moral theologian Franz Böckle spoke out in favor of IVF in a radio interview for the North German Radio Station series *Christianity in This Age* (*Christentum in dieser Zeit*); he argued that IVF merely represented a "shift in the site" of fertilization; therefore, it was not immoral.[115] On August 4, 1978, the Munich moral theologian Johannes Gründel echoed this assessment in a published essay.[116] Outraged, Cardinal Höffner, chair of the DBK, released a statement denouncing IVF and the misinformation provided by "certain" theologians. He noted that Pius XII explicitly had condemned any manipulation of human reproduction on multiple occasions. Höffner also enumerated four reasons IVF violated Christian morality: (1) The ends did not justify the means; countless embryos had been sacrificed in order to bring about the first test tube baby. (2) The eugenic implications of IVF made it a threat to humanity comparable to National Socialism. (3) It eroded the marital bond; a child created in the laboratory could never trust his or her paternity. (4) It separated the unitive and procreative purposes of the conjugal act.[117]

But neither the secular media's outrageous headlines nor Höffner's condemnation elicited much reaction from the German public or Catholics. Even the birth on April 16, 1982, of Oliver—the first German test tube baby—failed to generate any sustained public reaction, and the BMFT made no additional efforts to institute regulations. In fact, two years passed before the Justice Ministry established the Benda Commission (1984), tasked with assessing whether NRTs and genetic engineering required regulation. Concomitantly, the SPD and the Green Party demanded the creation of a Parliamentary Enquête Commission on Genetic Engineering. In calling for the commission, the two political parties had very different motives. The Green Party, particularly its female members, wanted to push for a unilateral ban on NRTs and genetic engineering. The SPD preferred a more neutral focus on the risks and benefits of genetic engineering; however, it too had strong reservations about new reproductive and genetic technologies.[118]

The creation of the two commissions opened the door for a much broader discussion of NRTs and genetic engineering, one in which the German public soon became embroiled. On November 25, 1985, the Benda Commission published its recommendations. Like the Grand Commission for Penal Code Reform in the 1960s, the Benda Commission saw no reason to regulate AIH. The report reminded physicians of their responsibility to consider the best interests of the future child before recommending AIH/IVF to infertile couples. The commission also underscored that physicians were under no legal obligation to provide this treatment; as with abortion, they could refuse treatment for reasons of conscience.

The Benda Commission asserted that every effort must be made to prevent the creation of surplus embryos. Doctors should harvest and fertilize only the number of eggs that could be implanted during one IVF treatment. If they did not implant all harvested eggs, they should be required to explain to the local medical board why they failed to do so. Although the commission expressed strong reservations about AID, it did not advise a unilateral ban; rather, AID procedures should be approved on a case-by-case basis. In AID procedures, the sperm donor had no right to anonymity; doctors should maintain detailed records on donors, and donor children on reaching the age of sixteen should be given access to these records. The commission recommended banning egg and embryo donation as well as gestational and traditional surrogacy. It also recommended that unwed couples and single women not have access to these procedures, although it did provide for some exceptions to this rule.

The Benda Commission was much more divided on embryological research, and the final report reflected the differing views of its members. A clear majority spoke out against the creation of embryos specifically for research purposes, arguing it violated human dignity since these embryos had never had the opportunity to realize personhood.[119] Although some members demanded a unilateral ban on embryological research, the commission recommended strict guidelines: "Experiments with human embryos are defensible only insofar as they serve the detection, prevention, or cure of a disease in the concerned embryo or advance a clearly defined and significant medical finding."[120] Prenatal diagnosis, the commission advised, should be used only if concrete reasons existed for suspecting disease or hereditary damage.[121] The CDU-CSU government drafted legislation in 1985 that closely adhered to the Benda Commission's recommendations.[122]

The 1985 proposed bill closely approximated a proposed bill before the

British Parliament at that time. The two bills had only one significant difference. The British draft allowed research on all embryos up to the fourteenth day after fertilization. The West German draft allowed research only on surplus embryos and banned the creation of embryos specifically for research purposes. If the Bundestag had passed the bill, both England and Germany would have been on the liberal end of the regulation spectrum in Europe. However, the German bill did not pass; instead, in 1989, West Germany amended its Adoption Placement Act (Adoptionsvermittlungsgesetz) to make gestational and traditional surrogacy illegal.[123] The following year, a newly reunified Germany adopted the Embryo Protection Act (Embryonenschutzgesetz, ESchG). The ESchG unconditionally banned all forms of research on embryos. Although the new law did not go so far as to transfer the regulation of IVF from the medical community to the state, it prohibited the harvesting of more eggs than could reasonably be implanted during one IVF cycle, outlawed the freezing of embryos, and criminalized egg/embryo donation, surrogate motherhood, postmortem insemination, nonmedical sex selection, and PGD. However, it left the regulation of AID to the medical community.[124] The two laws placed Germany on the conservative end of the European policy spectrum—alongside traditionally Catholic nations such as Austria, Italy, Ireland, and Portugal.

Catholic Politics in a Postsecular Age: The Unholy Alliance

Why did West Germany end up adopting stricter regulations than those originally proposed by the conservative CDU-CSU government? Why did Germany's path diverge from that of England, given that initially it was following a parallel track? Why did the regulation of reproductive technologies succeed now, when previous efforts had failed? And why did the call for regulation intensify rather than dissipate with the passage of time, as had been the case in the two previous debates? Germany's conservative turn does not make sense unless we take into account three developments: (1) renewed public hostility to science and technology; (2) the heterogeneity of the anti-research/NRT lobby; and (3) the new strategies and alliances pursued by Catholics. Political scientists and jurists such as Nicole Richardt and John A. Robertson have emphasized the importance of the first two developments.[125] But what scholars have left largely unexplored is the third. Christian conservatives, radical feminists, and disability rights activists did not just tolerate each other; they shared information and strategies. At times, they even coordinated protest actions. In short, an issue-specific alliance formed between these groups. This "unholy alliance"—as contemporary proponents of NRTs, such as the FDP legal expert Detlef Kleinert, labeled it—provided an additional impetus for strict regulation.[126] It also had long-term consequences for women's access to abortion in a reunified Germany and points to the emergence of a postsecular Catholic identity in Germany.

By the mid-1970s, Germans' distrust of science and technology was on the rise. The 1973 oil crisis had prompted the West German government to pursue nuclear power as the answer to economic decline, rising inflation, and energy supply.[127] This policy was not welcomed by most Germans. Having lost the economic security of the Miracle Years and seen the destruction done to the environment by years of unchecked economic growth, they responded by renewing their protests against nuclear weaponry and power. This hostility found expression in the German secular media. If one looks again at the 1978 *Spiegel* cover announcing Louise Brown's birth (see Figure 5.1), one sees a second headline concerning Klaus Traube, a West German engineer and former manager of a nuclear power plant, who became an outspoken critic of nuclear power and was the subject of an illegal wiretap by the Federal Office for the Protection of the Constitution (Bundesamt für Verfassungsschutz). The article criticized the unchecked power of the government and of the scientific community.[128] Beyond the cover, *Der Spiegel* made no direct connections between authoritarianism, nuclear technology, environmental destruction, and NRTs. But the juxtaposition of the two headlines foreshadowed the future strategy of Green Party feminists.

The Green Party had not existed at the time of the two earlier debates; it emerged in the late 1970s from citizen initiatives protesting nuclear energy and advocating environmental protection. By 1979, there were more than fifty thousand of these citizen initiative groups, and their total membership rivaled that of registered political party members (1.6 million). Leaders of these initiatives envisioned the founding of a new political party focused on environmental protection that would transcend the traditional conservative–liberal divide. These "green" parties formed first at the regional level and had a variety of orientations. Some were conservative, others were liberal, and some were even Marxist. For example, Herbert Gruhl, a former member of the CDU, founded the conservative environmental group Green Action Future (Grüne Aktion Zukunft). In October 1978, leftist radicals formed the Alternative List for Democracy and Environmental Protection (Alternative Liste für Demokratie und Umweltschutz).[129]

Joseph Beuys, Petra Kelly, Ossip K. Flechtheim, and Rudolf Bahro wanted to incorporate regional green parties from both sides of the political spectrum into one national green party. They tried to bridge the left–right divide among environmental activists, but their efforts ultimately failed. At the first Green Party platform convention in March 1980, conservatives, moderates, and radicals clashed on several issues. One of the most divisive issues was abortion. Conservatives wanted the party platform to advocate protecting unborn life; radicals wanted to eliminate Paragraph 218 from the criminal code. By the summer of 1980, conservative environmentalists, such as Herbert Gruhl, who had been instrumental in organizing the national Green Party, had resigned.[130] With the exodus of conservatives, moderates lost some influence in the party, and the Green Party's identity shifted farther to the left. In 1982, the Green Party adopted a list of eight conditions for any coalition with the Social Democratic Party. Among these were the stipulations that the SPD support the immediate shutdown of all nuclear power plants and that a ban be enforced on the installation of NATO cruise missiles and Pershing 2s on West German soil.[131] A new generation of Germans believed that the end of the world was near. According to a 1981 Allensbach survey, 76 percent of Green Party members anticipated the world's end through atomic warfare.[132]

By 1984, the Green Party's environmental and antinuclear politics had developed a new dimension, as feminists gained increased prominence within the party.[133] In addition to advocating for the abolition of Paragraph 218, Green women parliamentarians denounced reproductive and genetic technologies, linking their objections to environmental protection and fears of nuclear destruction. When in 1985 the Parliamentary Enquête Commission opted for a costs-benefits approach to NRTs and genetic research, Green Party women adjusted their strategy, augmenting their legislative campaign with a media campaign intended "to break the organized silence about genetic and reproductive technology" and to mobilize the public.[134]

In April 1985, Green Party women in conjunction with a local feminist group in Cologne organized the first national congress against reproductive and genetic technologies—Frauen gegen Gentechnik und Reproduktionstechnik. The congress adopted the motto "The Exploitation of Nature, Women, and the Third World" and aimed at catalyzing grassroots international opposition to NRTs and genetic engineering.[135] As Maria Mies made clear in her opening speech, the congress assumed the undesirability of these technologies: "We did not organize this congress in order to lead a pluralist discussion about the advantages and disadvantages of new reproductive technologies for women.... The aim of this congress is in fact to call on women for a discussion of and campaign against these newest inventions of the techno-patriarchy."[136] An estimated two thousand women from Germany and abroad attended.[137]

At the congress, Green feminists and members of the autonomous feminist movement outlined four reasons for condemning reproductive and genetic technologies. First, they contended that NRTs were inherently sexist, because the technologies forced women to relinquish control of their bodies to a male-dominated scientific community that showed little regard for women's health; they also reinforced the notion of womanhood as inextricably linked to motherhood. This exploitation of women they connected to the "techno-patriarchal" exploitation of the environment. Erika Hickel, a Green parliamentarian, explained, "My two years' experience in the Bundestag with commission experts has taught me the meaning of fear: It was a horror cabinet, exemplifying how human dignity is equated again and again with men's dignity, how fantasies of total domination over nature and over women prevail, how contempt for nature descends into contempt for women."[138] Thus, participants rejected the genetic manipulation of crops, animals, and humans. Dorothy Liers posited a link between rising infertility rates and destruction of the environment: "Of course, a connection exists between the increasing infertility of women and rising environmental contamination as a result of high doses of radioactive materials."[139]

Second, speakers at the congress revived the 1960s eugenics argument that associated assisted reproduction with National Socialism and U.S. capitalism. Maria Mies described NRTs as a "new eugenics on a global scale" that would make Hitler's racial politics seem like mere "child's play."[140] In the same talk, she criticized developments in the United States: "The genetic manipulation of animal and plant life is also about the same principle of selection and destruction. Life, even human life, should be adapted to the needs of the industrial system. What we have learned from the United States about developments in this area is sufficient to recognize the connection between sexism, racism, and these techniques."[141]

Third, the speakers viewed IVF as a threat to women's right to abortion because it reinforced equating womanhood with motherhood. Marina Steinbach explained: "Women who call for abortion are characterized in our society as antisocial, egoistic, etc., because they do not behave in a role-appropriate manner, while reproductive technologies are justified because they meet the demands of women and their need to beget children. With both arguments it is about the definition of woman as mother; it is about establishing the primary role of women, in which motherhood either is coerced or is made possible."[142]

Finally, the participants emphasized the colonial and class dimensions of NRTs. Promoting NRTs in the First World, they argued, represented one side of an international population policy that sought to control women's fertility in the Third World: "This technology is necessarily racist. We must take into account that practitioners support 'the right' of white women in rich nations 'to have a biological child' while using the same technologies to make Third World women sterile or at least subject them to rigid controls."[143]

The Catholic rationale for rejecting NRTs differed substantially from that of radical feminists. The Catholic rationale stemmed from its objections to abortion. Catholics believed that NRTs threatened the sanctity of life and of marriage. They argued that human life began at the moment of conception; thus, the extracorporeal embryo constituted a human life, and the West German state under Article 1 of the Basic Law had a positive duty to safeguard its life. This duty, they claimed, followed logically from the 1975 German Constitutional Court decision on abortion, which stated, "The life developing in the mother's womb has an independent legal value that stands under the protection of the Constitution."[144]

Given the different rationales and the fact that the ZdK banned the Green Party from the 1984 Catholic Congress, an alliance between Catholics and Greens seemed unlikely. Yet in the autumn of 1987, Marianne Dirks, the first postwar kfd president, made contact with several secular feminists of the Green Party, including Maria Mies, Mechthild Höflich, Brigitte Dorst, and Helga Fischer.[145] This unprecedented correspondence was prompted by the news that the American surrogacy broker Noel P. Keane had set up shop in Frankfurt. Keane planned to match childless West German couples with American surrogates; adoption of the resulting children would take place in the United States. Dirks believed that blocking Keane required the coordinated efforts of all opponents, and she convinced kfd leaders and radical feminists of the same. In October 1987, Anneliese Lissner, then the general secretary of the kfd, wrote Mechthild Höflich, "The kfd also has not been inactive in this matter.... In this initial round we seemed to have blocked it, but I will pursue further moves in this direction, and I am aware that in you I have found a sister-in-arms (*Mitstreiterin*)."[146]

This newly forged bond between Catholic women and radical feminists makes sense only if one recalls the staunch resistance of the Women's Union of the CDU and of the kfd in 1984 to the efforts of male conservatives in the CDU-CSU to impose stricter regulations on abortion (discussed in Chapter 4). In standing up against their conservative male colleagues, Catholic women leaders had demonstrated their independence and their more moderate stance on abortion. Their changed perspective created space for dialogue with secular feminists on shared concerns such as surrogacy, NRTs, and genetic engineering.

In addition, points of overlap did exist between Catholic and feminist arguments on NRTs. Both posited a slippery slope, with NRTs leading to a "new eugenics on a global scale."[147] Both emphasized the need to protect human dignity, even though they disagreed on whose dignity was being violated. Feminists claimed it was the woman's dignity, while Catholics considered it the dignity of the embryo. Still, in emphasizing "human dignity"—whether that of the woman or the embryo—Catholics and Green parliamentarians succeeded in shifting the terms of the debate from utilitarian arguments (cost-benefit analysis) to deontological ones. The utilitarian risk-benefit arguments of the early debate gave way to deontological arguments in the late 1980s.[148] The new emphasis on the ethics of NRTs meant that Germany's National Socialist past now figured prominently. This younger generation of protesters, having never lived under National Socialism, showed no hesitation in pointing out not only ideological similarities but also continuities in personnel.[149] Sara Jensen, a West German Green parliamentarian and scientist, asserted, "In the organizations that support pre-implantation genetic diagnosis, there is some continuity in personal [sic] with Nazi biological and racial hygiene programs."[150] These types of charges placed supporters of NRTs and embryological research on the defensive.

Nor was it just Catholic women who showed themselves capable of bridging ideological differences to advance a shared goal. West German bishops also demonstrated a new flexibility in the debate on NRTs and embryological research. To be sure, German bishops did not enter into an alliance with the Green Party. However, they made compromises and endorsed new arguments so that the German Christian communities could unite in their opposition. On November 30, 1989, chair of the DBK, Karl Lehmann, approved a 112-page joint declaration on the defense of life, *Gott ist ein Freund des Lebens*.

This ecumenical document, coauthored by Catholics and EKD members and endorsed by thirteen other Christian communities, differed in two key respects from previous declarations made by the West German Catholic Church. First, neither the German bishops nor the Vatican had ever linked the protection of unborn life to environmental protection, although German bishops and theologians had compared its impact to that of nuclear war. But the ecumenical declaration made the connection explicit: "What we need is a comprehensive joint effort by all to defend life. This is the guiding principle of the declaration of the churches. We need a comprehensive effort: therefore a declaration that addresses the challenges and responsibilities in protecting the living space of the earth as well as defending human life."[151] Given the vociferous reaction of West German Catholic officials to a 1983 Allensbach survey showing that Germans considered the killing of baby seals a more serious moral offense than abortion,[152] their willingness to advance an argument that tried to bridge the gap between abortion opponents and environmental activists constituted a fundamental departure.

Second, the German bishops had never framed their objection to abortion in terms of a violation of the rights of the disabled. Instead, they had underscored the need to protect the dignity of all life. In 1986, they wrote: "Every human is destined to give shape to his own life under the most varied of circumstances. This implies at the same time that the life of each is worth the same, regardless of one's social status, education, ability, economic situation, or even health."[153] In contrast, *Gott ist ein Freund des Lebens* specifically highlighted the negative impact that PGD had on the rights of the disabled: "Finally, we cannot overlook the mentality that could develop concerning the life of disabled persons and their acceptance by society as a result of the coupling of prenatal diagnosis and abortion.... Society could reach a point where it no longer accepts disabled children. They need not have been born. For the self-image of the disabled, the consequences would be incalculable, given such an assessment by the world around them."[154]

The united front of Christian communities, the resistance of radical feminists, and the alliance that formed between West German women with very different religious and political orientations resulted in substantial pressure being placed on the CDU government to change its position on NRTs and embryological research. On November 11, 1988, Bavaria introduced the Reproductive Medicine Bill (Fortpflanzungsmedizingesetz, FMG) in the Bundesrat; the bill proposed transferring regulatory authority from the medical community to the states, as well as banning all embryological research. Fearing a loss of professional autonomy as well as fundamental changes in the medical insurance system, the medical and scientific communities now adopted a defensive strategy. The Assembly of German doctors decided that unmarried couples should have access to NRTS, only if an ethics board gave them special permission. Additionally, the Max Planck Institute and the German Research Society (Deutsche Forschungsgemeinschaft) retreated from their earlier support for embryological research; they now called for a moratorium on such research. The final bill adopted by the Bundestag in 1990 represented a compromise between the more lenient legislation initially proposed by the CDU government and the FMG bill proposed by Bavaria.[155] For the moment, the "unholy alliance" had succeeded in limiting the practice of NRTs in Germany and in banning embryological research.

. . .

The battle did not end in 1990. Since then the pro-research lobby has succeeded in introducing several revisions to the 1990 law. In 2002, the Stem Cell Act (Stammzellgesetz) established criteria that allowed researchers to conduct some embryological research using stem cells imported from foreign countries.[156] In 2011, the Law for the Regulation of Pre-implantation Diagnosis (Gesetz zur Regelung der Präimplantationsdiagnostik) approved the use of PGD in cases where there is a high risk of severe genetic disease in the embryo owing to the genetic disposition of one or both parents. It can also be performed if there is a high probability of miscarriage or of stillbirth because of severe damage to the embryo.[157]

These modifications reflect a breakdown in the late 1980s coalition that transcended the left–right ideological divide. Since the 1990s, German women have become less united in their opposition to reproductive technologies as arguments favoring personal autonomy have gained supporters among female parliamentarians and in feminist circles.[158] Still, opponents of NRTS and embryological research continue to thwart some proposals of the pro-research lobby. The Embryo Defense Act has not been overturned; therefore, stem cells from surplus embryos created by IVF procedures performed in Germany may not be used for research purposes. Moreover, PGD cannot be utilized as a standard diagnostic test.[159] In sum, opponents have succeeded in keeping Germany on the conservative end of the European policy spectrum.

But the legacy of the "unholy alliance" extends beyond Germany's strict policy on NRTs and embryological research. In 2009, conservative Catholics applied the connection drawn between disability rights and reproductive medicine in the context of the debate on NRTs to the abortion debate. By doing so, they gained substantial support among Social Democrats and Greens, particularly female members, for a mandatory three-day waiting period for late-term abortions (i.e., after twenty-two weeks of pregnancy) when a fetal disability had been diagnosed. Green Party and Social Democratic women did not want to be seen as opponents of disability rights.

Catholic parlimentarians' successful appeal to disability rights in the debates on NRTs and on abortion is a victory that neither historians of Germany nor historians of gender can afford to ignore, because it points to an important development within political Catholicism. Out of the crisis years of the 1970s, a more activist, albeit smaller, Catholic Church emerged. This activist minority has proved both resilient and flexible, slowly developing new strategies for promoting the Church's message in a pluralist society. This learning process has not proceeded in a linear fashion, nor to date has it influenced all debates in which the Catholic Church is embroiled. Moreover, it has not meant abandoning Catholic doctrine on the defense of life championed by the Vatican. Rather, for Catholic leaders it has entailed a subtle shift from the promotion of the feminized piety of the nineteenth century aimed at filling the pews with women to a strategic deployment of an ideology of gender intended to safeguard contemporary Church teachings and mobilize a politically engaged, conservative core constituency. Fueled by significant financial resources and international connections, an insurgent German Catholic minority has experienced some political successes by stitching together political and cultural alliances for a postsecular world.

Epilogue

This book has detailed the crucial role played by gender politics in producing first a crisis in, and later a transformation of, German Catholicism. It has argued that both the crisis and the transformation resulted from the dynamic interplay of endogenous and exogenous forces. It has emphasized that it would be an oversimplification to equate this transformation with religious decline. Between 1959 and 1989, the West German Catholic Church experienced a significant decline in numbers, as moderates and liberals distanced themselves from the Church or left it (or both). With their departure, what remained was an increasingly unified and activist-oriented conservative core. This conservative core has proved both resilient and flexible, developing new strategies, issue-specific alliances, and arguments in order to promote its message in Germany's changed political climate.

In the immediate postwar period, the German Catholic milieu and political Catholicism experienced a brief period of restoration as the nation struggled to recover from the moral and economic ruin wrought by National Socialism. Catholic politicians dominated the CDU-CSU coalition and championed the creation of a Christian occident as a fourth way forward— one that not only represented a break from the nation's Nazi past, but also distinguished it from its former American occupiers and from neighboring East Germany. The CDU-CSU successfully advanced natural law as the appropriate foundation for German law, using Christian principles to justify policies that promoted youth defense measures and the breadwinner/housewife model. However, even in the 1950s, signs of growing public discontent with CDU policy existed, and by the 1960s, a secular and religious crisis of authority engulfed West Germany. Neither the Church nor the secular state emerged from this crisis unchanged. Both were ill prepared to confront the wave of secular and religious movements that, beginning in the 1960s, challenged institutional authority and made the politicization of sexual relations, albeit in very different ways, the focal point of their campaigns (e.g., the student movement, the feminist movement, and the women's ordination movement).

For the Catholic Church, the battle was waged on two fronts. Within the Church, an internal debate on marital morality and women's place in the

Church developed that continues to this day. The German Church also was and remains an active participant in secular debates on women's reproductive rights and the defense of unborn life. In the second half of the twentieth century, these two debates, one religious and the other secular, became increasingly entangled as a result of changes taking place in the Church and in German society. With the redrawing of the map in 1945, Catholics ceased to be an embattled minority. In fact, they dominated the leadership of the ruling CDU-CSU coalition government in the early years of the Federal Republic. The Church also underwent significant changes. Vatican II introduced a new orientation in Catholicism, calling upon laypersons and members of the institutional Church to engage with the modern world. Reform-minded theologians, priests, and laypersons took their message to the court of public opinion, and the institutional Church responded in kind. As a result of secular media coverage, internal Catholic debates became public debates in which non-Catholics became active participants. Conversely, secular debates on gender and sexuality witnessed an active Catholic engagement. In both debates, German bishops, theologians, and priests championed a wide range of positions; thus, the postwar institutional Catholic Church was never the monolithic actor that many pundits and scholars have assumed.

Moreover, the diversity of views on gender and sexuality in the German Catholic community did not result simply from the importation of ideas from outside the Church. In arguing in favor of married priests, women's ordination, birth control, and the liberalization of abortion law, reform-minded Catholics based their arguments on Catholic traditions, as did their opponents. This theological contestation, which highlighted latent contradictions and ambiguities in Church doctrine and pitted Catholics against Catholics, has received little attention from historians seeking to explain either the collapse of the Catholic milieu or the Church's subsequent transformation. Instead, the transformation of Catholicism has been depicted largely as the product of external forces beyond the Church's control—namely, secularization, urbanization, industrialization, and consumerization of German society. Certainly, these external factors played an important role; however, in ignoring the internal dynamics of institutional change, scholars have underestimated the Catholic Church's ability to learn from and adapt to changing social, cultural, and political circumstances.

As we have seen, Catholic women in the late 1980s collaborated with Green Party women, radical feminists, and disability rights activists to promote strict regulations governing NRTs and stem cell research. The German bishops also demonstrated a new willingness to compromise, overcoming past differences with the EKD on abortion, to issue a joint statement on the defense of life that gained the support of thirteen other Christian communities. These two actions played an important role in changing the terms of the political debate on NRTs and stem cell research. An early debate that focused on the costs and benefits of NRTs metamorphosed into one in which ethical considerations took center stage. The result was that the Bundestag adopted stricter regulations than those initially proposed by the conservative CDU-led government. In 2009, conservative Catholics won another political victory in the battle against the liberalization of German abortion law. By linking traditional pro-life arguments with a new argument that abortion violated the rights of the disabled, they were able to garner sufficient support from women in the Green and Social Democratic Parties to mandate a three-day waiting period for late-term abortions when a fetal disability had been diagnosed.

In highlighting these political victories, this study recognizes that the contemporary German Catholic Church has experienced multiple setbacks in recent years and that it faces significant challenges in the future. In January 2010, for example, news broke that there had been at least fifty cases of sexual abuse at a Jesuit high school in Berlin; the cases dated from the 1970s and 1980s, and the alleged perpetrators were two priests. Within weeks of this first report, a flood of victims came forward. More than 250 allegations of abuse were made, affecting twenty-two out of Germany's twenty-seven dioceses. The ZdK president, Alois Glück, described the scandal as "one of the worst crises that we've seen in the Catholic Church here in Germany."[1] An unprecedented 173,790 German Catholics separated from the Church that year—roughly a 40 percent increase over the previous year.[2] These events cast a pall over the Church in Germany.

The euphoria that many Germans experienced in 2005, when the first German pope was chosen by the College of Cardinals since 1523, had unequivocally ended. Gone were the banner headlines proclaiming "Wir sind Papst!" (We Are Pope!).[3] Rather than a source of national pride whose election proved that Germany was no longer a "pariah" among nations, Joseph Ratzinger, Pope Benedict XVI, became an embarrassment for some Germans and the symbol of everything wrong in the Church for many. *Der Spiegel* noted:

There is no lack of recommendations relating to the future of the Church, both from believers and non-believers. Suddenly everyone knows what the Church has done wrong in decades gone by: the celibacy and the exclusion of women from the priesthood; the hierarchy of old men and the persecution of any efforts to liberalize the theology; the blind condemnation of contraception and birth control in the poor regions of the world; the eternal lack of understanding of homosexuality; the mistrust of technology and modern culture; and the constant needling and provocation aimed at the Protestant churches, Judaism and Islam.[4]

This negative assessment of the Church was exacerbated by Benedict XVI's repeated failure to address the cases of abuse in Germany. On March 19, 2010, he issued a pastoral letter to Irish Catholics, apologizing for the clergy's abuse of children. The letter disappointed Irish Catholics because it did not directly address the Church's long history of concealing abuse. It disappointed German Catholics because it made no reference to the child abuse cases in Benedict's homeland; this failure became the subject of numerous headlines in the German press.[5] Christian Weiser, the German spokesperson for the reform movement Wir sind Kirche, noted: "The pope's silence doesn't look good. It certainly won't improve his authority and his esteem in the church here. Just a word of compassion for the victims would have won him sympathies."[6] News reports that linked Benedict XVI directly to the German child abuse scandal only made matters worse. First, his brother, Georg Ratzinger, was accused of physically abusing boys while he was the director of the Regensburger Domspatzen. Then, reports surfaced that a pedophile priest had been reinstated at a Catholic parish in Munich during Benedict's tenure as archbishop of Munich and Freising.

The pastoral letter also angered many reform-minded Catholics because it suggested that a "misinterpretation of the Second Vatican Council" was to blame for the current scandal, in that it had "contributed in no small measure to a weakening of faith and the loss of respect for the Church and her teachings."[7] On March 24, 2010, the international office of "Wir sind Kirche" responded to this accusation, declaring it "outrageous" and demanding that the Church admit the "culpability of its own structures."[8]

The pope's handling of the clerical abuse crisis in Germany was far from the first misstep that Benedict XVI had made in the eyes of the German public, but it was the most damaging. It prompted his old adversary, Hans Küng, to release an open letter in which he cataloged the failures of Benedict's papacy and implicated him in the conspiracy of silence:

There is no denying the fact that the Roman Congregation for the Doctrine of the Faith under Cardinal Ratzinger (1981–2005) engineered a worldwide system of covering up cases of sexual crimes committed by clerics. . . . On May 18, 2001, Ratzinger personally sent a solemn communication to all the bishops addressing severe crimes (*"epistula de delictis gravioribus"*). It sealed abuse cases under the *"secretum pontificium,"* the violation of which could entail grave ecclesiastical penalties. Rightly, therefore, many people have expected a personal mea culpa on the part of the former prefect and current pope. Yet unfortunately the pope passed up the opportunity afforded by Holy Week. Instead, on Easter Sunday, he had the dean of the College of Cardinals attest to his innocence *"urbi et orbi."*[9]

According to news reports, a few German Catholics were even calling for his resignation.[10]

Three years later, that resignation became a reality. In Germany, commentators immediately began debating whether Benedict's resignation would be good for the German Church and for the world Church. The left-leaning *Tageszeitung*'s headline read simply, "Thanks Be to God" (*Gott sei Dank*). Innes Pohl, the chief editor of the daily newspaper, wrote: "During his eight-year pontificate, Pope Benedict XVI succeeded in surpassing even the worst fears. As God's deputy, Benedict showed little interest in facing the numerous sexual abuse crimes within his own institution, or in confronting the fascist organization Opus Dei. Whether the topic was women, homosexuals, rape or human rights, it is hard to be more reactionary than this pope."[11] The conservative *Die Welt* also criticized Ratzinger, but not because he failed to reform Church teachings on sexuality. Instead, it noted that Ratzinger had succumbed to the individualism that he had opposed. It also championed the Church's stalwart defense of tradition:

> One should, however, recognize that there are good reasons for strengthening the earthly institution of the church as an antipode to the current *zeitgeist* and its unavoidable relativization of values. One should understand why he cannot say yes to gay marriage and why he cannot embrace Protestantism. The church's dilemma is simple: If it refuses to bend to the times, it will lose members; if it does bend, it will lose them anyway. Joseph Ratzinger, who once called himself a "servant to the truth," embodies and bears witness to the conviction that the church can only be healthy if it remains convinced of the unlimited possibilities opened up by complete faith.[12]

These two statements encapsulate the ongoing battle between conservative and progressive Catholics over the future direction of the Church. Progressives believe that renewal necessitates that the Church modify its teachings on gender and sexuality. In contrast, conservatives believe that the Church must hold firm, even if that means cultivating a smaller Church.

Under John Paul II and Benedict XVI, conservatives had the upper hand. In fact, following John Paul II's call for a "new evangelization" that would be "new in its ardor, its methods, and its expression," the Catholic Church experienced an upsurge in grassroots, evangelical organizations that emphasized papal loyalty, Marian devotion, and the defense of life.[13] In Germany, groups such as the Internationaler Marialogischer Arbeitskreis Kevalaer (1978), Jugend 2000 (1989), Initiativkreis katholischer Laien und Priester (1989), and Marianische Liga—Vereinigung Katholischer Frauen (1997) championed official Church teachings and billed themselves as representing authentic Catholicism. By 2011, there were seventy officially recognized evangelical Catholic communities operating in Germany.[14] At the international level, Catholic evangelical events such as World Youth Day and the annual meeting of the lay evangelical movement Communio e Liberazion in Rimini, Italy, regularly attract more than a million Catholics from around the world. True to John Paul II's vision, these events capitalize on modern methods to spread official teachings. For example, World Youth Day combines a celebration of papal authority with a rock concert atmosphere.

In addition to supporting these grassroots movements, the Vatican under John Paul II employed the strategy of marginalizing liberals and moderates. Where one stood on clerical celibacy, artificial contraception, abortion, homosexuality, and women's ordination served as a litmus test for advancement in the Church. While supporting the Vatican's position did not guarantee high office, failing to do so prevented promotion and possibly led to disciplinary action. In Germany, Catholic theologians, such as Bernhard Häring, Hans Küng, Uta Ranke-Heinemann, and Hubertus Mynarek, were investigated by the CDF because of their positions on gender and sexuality. Moderate cardinals and bishops such as Joseph Frings, Julius Döpfner, and Heinrich Tenhumberg, who supported the limited use of artificial contraception by married couples, were replaced after they died by individuals who did not—Joseph Höffner, Joseph Ratzinger, and Reinhard Lettmann, respectively. Even lay Catholics were not immune to this trend. As we saw in Chapter 4, German Catholic women were forced in 2006 to choose between continued involvement with Donum Vitae and holding office in official Catholic organizations.

This phenomenon was by no means peculiar to Germany. In the United States, Charles Curran and more recently Elizabeth McEnroy lost their teaching positions at Catholic universities because of their stances on sexual morality and women's ordination, respectively. The CDF also launched multiple investigations of the Belgian theologian Edward Schillebeeckx for, among other things, his views on celibacy and the sacramental nature of the clerical office.

This strategy of promoting a "creative minority" was not without merit. Some sociological studies have shown that the religions that have experienced the greatest growth in recent years are the ones that clearly demarcate themselves from the prevailing secular culture—the Church of Latter Day Saints, Pentecostal Christianity, and Islam. In *A Theory of Religion*, Rodney Stark and William Bainbridge labeled these types of religion "high tension religions." They argued that, in a secularized world, mainstream religions get lost in the secular melting pot. Youth gravitate toward high-tension religions because they offer a clear sense of identity in a rootless secularized world.[15] If high attendance at Catholic World Youth Days and the proliferation of Catholic pro-life youth group actions such as Jugend 2000 (1989), Totus Tuus—Evangelisation und mehr (1994), and Jugend für das Leben (1997) can be seen as indicators, this strategy has achieved at least partial success in attracting a dedicated cadre of German youth. But cultivating a "creative minority" based on strict adherence to official doctrine is not without its perils if, in addition to safeguarding doctrinal purity, its motive is that of recruitment and renewal. A smaller Church can be a more committed Church, but it also can lead to a poorer Church. Since evangelization costs money, the Church cannot ignore issues of retention entirely. It must somehow find the right balance between the enforcement of doctrinal purity and pastoral forgiveness for those who fall short in following the Church's teachings.

With the election of Jorge Mario Bergoglio of Argentina as Pope Francis I, moderate and reform-minded German Catholics hoped that the pendulum had swung back in their direction, and early informal statements made by the pope seemed to suggest that it had. In an interview conducted by Father Antonio Spadaro on behalf of *La Civiltà Cattolica*, *America*, and other major Jesuit journals in December 2013, Francis suggested that the Church in recent years had focused too much on sexual morality: "We cannot insist only on issues related to abortion, gay marriage and the use of contraceptive methods." This statement in conjunction with the new pope's off-the-cuff remark to a reporter concerning the acceptance of gay priests in the Church—"If someone is gay and seeks the Lord with goodwill, who am I to judge?"—created a new sense of possibility among reform-minded German Catholics. Christian Weisner of Wir sind Kirche commented, "It was a strong statement and an important signal that Francis is not afraid of reality."[16] This hope was reinforced by the pope's choice of Walter Kasper, the former bishop of Rottenburg-Stuttgart and president emeritus of the Pontifical Council for Promoting Christian Unity, to speak on the topic of family and marriage before a consistory on the family at the Vatican. In his two-hour address, Kasper argued in favor of allowing divorced and remarried Catholics to receive Communion after a period of penance.

This proposal prompted vehement protests from five prominent cardinals, including the German prefect for the CDF, Gerhard Cardinal Müller. In a January 2014 interview with *L'Osservatore*, Müller described Kasper's theology as "radically wrong."[17] And just one week before the Extraordinary General Assembly of the Synod of Bishops on "The Pastoral Challenges of the Family in the Context of Evangelization" (October 5–19, 2014), Muller's interview appeared simultaneously in book form in the United States, Italy, and Spain. At roughly the same time, an edited volume, *Remaining in the Truth of Christ*, also appeared in print. Its list of contributors read like a who's who of Vatican politics—Cardinal Gerhard Müller; Walter Brandmüller, president emeritus of the Pontifical Committee of Historical Sciences; Raymond Burke, prefect of the Supreme Tribunal of the Apostolic Signatura; Carlo Caffarra, archbishop of Bologna; and Velasio de Paolis, president emeritus of the Prefecture for Economic Affairs of the Holy See.[18]

The stage was set for an epic battle between conservatives and progressives at the synod. This battle captured the imagination of the secular and religious press to a degree not witnessed since Vatican II. It also pitted against each other two German theological heavyweights—Walter Kasper, backed by the German Bishops' Conference, and Gerhard Müller, backed by the Roman Curia.

Initially, it seemed that the pastoral approach of progressives would win the day. The interim report of the synod released on October 14, 2014, suggested that on a case-by-case basis, divorced and remarried Catholics might be given access to Communion. It stressed that priests should emphasize the "positive aspects" of lifestyles the Church considered gravely sinful, including homosexual unions.[19] Moreover, the report broke with earlier Church documents that labeled homosexuality "intrinsically disordered."[20] In doing so, the report was not recommending doctrinal change but a more forgiving approach in the application of doctrine to the pastoral setting.

The report generated banner headlines across the globe that contained words like "earthquake" and "radical about-face."[21] In Germany, the president of ZdK, Alois Glück, described the report as indicative of a significant change in Vatican attitudes and praised Pope Francis for acting as an "icebreaker for an anxiety-free discussion" on previously taboo topics; the DBK spoke of "significant change" in the Vatican's attitude toward divorced and homosexual persons.[22] In contrast, prominent conservatives labeled it "shameful" and a "betrayal"; in the German-speaking world, katholisches. info, the Arbeitskreis für Katholiken, and Gloria.tv provided German translations of conservative condemnations from around the world.[23] In the wake of the media frenzy and conservative backlash, most of the "welcoming language" found in the interim report disappeared from the final report.

The October 2014 synod was only the first of two planned synods on the family; the second was scheduled to take place in October 2015. But neither the progressive nor the conservative camp seemed willing to wait until then to resolve the issue. At a press conference on February 25, 2015, Reinhard Cardinal Marx, chair of the DBK, announced: "We are not a branch of Rome. Each conference of bishops is responsible for pastoral care in its cultural context and must preach the Gospel in its own, original way. We cannot wait for a synod to tell us how we have to shape pastoral care for marriage and family here."[24]

This statement prompted an immediate reaction from German members of the Curia. Cardinal Müller chastised the ZdK, stating that the idea of "delegating certain doctrinal or disciplinary decisions on marriage and family" to bishops' conferences was "absolutely anti-Catholic" and failed to "respect the church's Catholicity." In a letter to the editor of the German Catholic newspaper *Tagespost*, Paul Josef Cardinal Cordes, former president of the Pontifical Council Cor Unum, also rebuked Marx, noting that statements like "We are not a branch of Rome" demonstrated "theological blurriness."[25] Conservative German Catholic groups also protested; the Katholische Arbeitskreis wrote an open letter to the DBK, in which it reiterated Pope Benedict's repeated warning against "building a dictatorship of relativism."[26] As one commentator noted, the Church stands at a "precipice," and whether it can find a middle way between these two visions of renewal remains unknown.[27] The way forward into the future is not yet clear.

Appendixes

APPENDIX A
WEST GERMAN CHURCH ATTENDANCE, 1954–1965

Year	Diocese of Cologne	Diocese of Aachen	Diocese of Münster	Diocese of Trier	West Germany
1954	39.7	49.8	53.9	59.1	47.9
1955	39.9	49.1	52.9	58.4	47.2
1956	39.4	48.6	51.8	57.9	46.6
1957	39.6	48.5	51	57.8	46.4
1958	39.4	47.7	55.4	56.4	45.9
1959	39.6	47.2	54.9	56.6	45.6
1960	38.7	46.8	54.5	56.5	46.1
1964	35.5	43.8	51.2	53.8	43.3

Note: Data are percentages.
Source: Franz Gröner, *Kirchliches Handbuch: Amtliches statistisches Jahrbuch der katholischen Kirche Deutschlands*, vols. 24 and 25 (Cologne: Bachem, 1962 and 1969).

APPENDIX B
EASTER COMMUNION RATES FOR FOUR DIOCESES, 1954–1964

Year	Diocese of Cologne	Diocese of Aachen	Diocese of Münster	Diocese of Trier
1954	41.9	52	54.9	65
1955	41.8	51.9	54.2	64.3
1956	41.7	51.3	53.2	64
1957	42.1	52.6	52.7	63.7
1958	42.5	52.2	56.9	63.9
1959	42	51.9	56.3	64
1960	41.6	51	56.5	63.3
1964	39.3	48.5	53.8	61.5

Note: Data are percentages.
Source: Franz Gröner, *Kirchliches Handbuch: Amtliches statistisches Jahrbuch der katholischen Kirche Deutschlands*, vols. 25 and 26 (Cologne: Bachem, 1962 and 1969).

APPENDIX C
SECULAR PRIESTS IN GERMAN DIOCESES, 1915–1958

Diocese	Priests				
	1915	1921	1938	1952	1958
Aachen	—	—	8.5	7.5	7.3
Augsburg	15.5	15.2	15.6	9.5	8.7
Bamberg	10.3	10.3	10.8	7.3	7.2
Berlin	—	—	7.2	6.1	7.5
Breslau (Rest)	5.2	6.1	7.1	10.1	12.3
Eichstatt	18.1	18.3	13.0	13.3	13.2
Essen	—	—	—	—	4.8
Freiburg	10.9	10.8	11.3	13.3	13.2
Fulda	12.9	11.7	12.3	8.4	9.2
Hildesheim	10.8	11.0	12.7	6.4	7.0
Köln (Cologne)	7.7	7.0	8.1	6.9	6.9
Limburg	8.5	7.9	8.8	6.9	6.8
Mainz	8.1	8.6	9.3	7.7	7.4
Meißen	—	5.2	9.5	4.9	7.0
Munich-Freising	11.0	11.1	10.9	8.0	7.7
Münster	9.4	8.3	8.9	7.5	7.3
Osnabrück	13.5	12.0	10.7	7.8	8.4
Paderborn	8.7	8.4	9.5	7.3	7.8
Passau	15.9	15.0	15.4	10.8	10.8
Regensburg	12.7	12.6	13.0	10.3	10.3
Rottenburg	16.1	15.2	13.8	9.3	8.4
Speyer	8.7	8.4	9.4	8.8	8.6
Trier	8.9	8.6	9.1	7.9	7.5
Würzburg	13.8	12.8	13.0	9.5	9.7
National average by year	9.6	9.4	10.2	8.1	7.9

Note: Data represent number of priests per 10,000 Catholics.
Source: Jan Dellepoort, Norbert Greinacher, and Walter Menges, eds., *Die deutsche Priesterfrage: Eine soziologische Untersuchung über Klerus und Priesternachwuchs in Deutschland* (Mainz: Matthias-Grünewald, 1962), 186.

APPENDIX D

CELIBACY

SURVEY OF WEST CATHOLICS OVER THE AGE OF SIXTEEN FOR THE WÜRZBURG SYNOD

Question: As you know, Catholic priests cannot marry. What is your opinion: Should this rule be maintained? Should exceptions be allowed under special circumstances? Or should the requirement be abolished?

	All Catholics	10–9 (strong attachment to Church)	8–7	6–4	3–2	1–0 (minimal)
Abolished	62	31	51	73	83	91
Exceptions made	21	30	31	17	10	4
Celibate, no exceptions	16	37	17	6	5	3
No opinion	1	2	1	1	2	2

Note: Data are percentages. Results were reported for all Catholics, as well as delineated according to how participants rated their attachment to the Church.
Source: Gerhard Schmidtchen, *Zwischen Kirche und Gesellschaft: Forschungsbericht über die Umfragen zur Gemeinsamen Synode der Bistümer in der Bundesrepublik Deutschland* (Freiburg: Herder, 1972), 132. ©Verlag Herder GmbH, Freiburg im Breisgau.

APPENDIX E
SURVEY OF ALL WEST GERMAN PRIESTS ON CELIBACY FOR WÜRZBURG SYNOD

Question: Recently, there has been a discussion about changing the celibacy requirement. What is your opinion on the following two proposed changes?

Proposal I: Men in established marriages should be ordained as priests.

	All Priests	Ordained before 1921	Ordained, 1941–1945	Ordained, 1966–1970
Essential	28	10	22	43
Worth considering	51	48	58	43
Unnecessary	10	15	11	6
Indefensible	6	12	5	3
No opinion	5	15	4	5

Proposal II: The celibacy requirement should be abolished; the decision should be left to the priest.

Essential	28	6	18	54
Worth considering	23	9	25	25
Unnecessary	16	17	21	9
Indefensible	28	51	31	9
No opinion	5	17	5	3

Note: Data are percentages.
Source: Gerhard Schmidtchen, *Zwischen Kirche und Gesellschaft: Forschungsbericht über die Umfragen zur Gemeinsamen Synode der Bistümer in der Bundesrepublik Deutschland* (Freiburg: Herder, 1972), 135. © Verlag Herder GmbH, Freiburg im Breisgau.

APPENDIX F
CATHOLIC PRIESTS IN GERMANY, 1958–2008

Year	Number of Profane Priests	Absolute Change	Percentage
1958	19,916		
1959	19,931	15	0.08
1960	20,065	134	0.67
1961	19,997	−68	−0.34
1962	20,016	19	0.10
1963	20,098	82	0.41
1964	20,125	27	0.13
1965	20,204	79	0.39
1966	20,155	−49	−0.24
1967	20,171	16	0.08
1968	20,012	−159	−0.79
1969	19,855	−157	−0.78
1970	19,651	−204	−1.03
1971	19,485	−166	−0.84
1972	19,201	−284	−1.46
1973	18,975	−226	−1.18
1974	18,735	−240	−1.26
1975	18,542	−193	−1.03
1976*	18,351	−191	−1.03
1977	18,160	−191	−1.04
1978	17,886	−274	−1.51
1979**	17,827	−59	−0.33
1992	16,808	—	—
1993	16,669	−139	−0.083
1994	16,416	−253	−1.52
1995	16,172	−244	−1.49
1996	15,842	−330	−2.04
1997	15,577	−265	−1.67
1998	15,462	−115	−0.74
1999	15,115	−347	−2.24
2000	14,889	−226	−1.50
2001	14,722	−167	−1.12
2002	14,479	−243	−1.65
2003	14,244	−235	−1.62
2004	14,006	−238	−1.67
2005	13,924	−82	−0.59

2006	13,739	−185	−1.33
2007	13,552	−187	−1.36
2008	13,027	−525	−3.87

*1976–1979, estimated.
**1980–1991, no available figures.
Source: Forschungsgruppe Weltanschauungen in Deutschland, Katholische Weltpriester und evangelischen Theologen Deutschland 1953–2008, version from January 9, 2011/sfe, www.fowid.de.

APPENDIX G
GERMAN CATHOLICS ON CLERICAL CELIBACY, 1994

Should the Church preserve or abolish the celibacy requirement for priests?

	All Catholics	Opinion by Age Group				
		18–24	25–29	30–44	45–59	60 and Older
Preserve	12	10	23	6	13	12
Abolish	87	90	77	93	87	85
No opinion	1	0	0	1	0	3

Note: Data are percentages.
Source: Emnid survey for *Der Spiegel*; 500 surveyed; *Der Spiegel*, November 30, 1994. Reprinted by Forschungsgruppe Weltanschauungen in Deutschland, Erstellungsdatum, version of August 30, 2005, www.fowid.de.

APPENDIX H

GERMAN ATTITUDES ON ABORTION IN MARCH–APRIL 1971

Issue 1: Every woman should have the unconditional right to decide to have an abortion (Schwangerschaftsunterbrechung).

	Agree	Disagree	No Opinion
Total voting population	54	35	11
Potential voters for			
SPD-FDP	65	26	9
SPD	65	26	9
FDP	65	25	10
CDU-CSU	45	44	11
Men	56	32	12
Women	52	37	11
Catholics	51	39	10
Protestants	57	32	11
By Age Group			
Ages 16–21	73	20	7
Ages 22–25	61	26	13
Ages 26–29	66	24	10
Ages 30–39	63	30	7
Ages 40–59	51	36	13
Ages 60 and over	38	49	13

Issue 2: Every woman should have the right during the first trimester of her pregnancy to have an abortion (Schwangerschaftsunterbrechung).

	Agree	Disagree	No Opinion
Total voting population	58	31	11
Potential voters for			
SPD-FDP	69	22	9
SPD	68	22	10
FDP	71	19	10
CDU-CSU	49	40	11
Men	61	28	11
Women	56	34	10
Catholics	54	36	10
Protestants	61	27	12
By Age Group			
Ages 16–21	79	14	7
Ages 22–25	63	25	12
Ages 26–29	71	18	11
Ages 30–39	68	25	7
Ages 40–59	54	34	12
Ages 60 and over	42	46	12

Issue 3: A woman should be able to terminate a pregnancy if she lives in particularly difficult social and economic conditions.

	Agree	Disagree	No Opinion
Total voting population	58	31	11
Potential voters for			
SPD-FDP	69	22	9
SPD	68	22	10
FDP	71	19	10
CDU-CSU	49	40	11
Men	61	28	11
Women	56	34	10

Catholics	54	36	10
Protestants	61	27	12
By Age Group			
Ages 16–21	79	14	7
Ages 22–25	63	25	12
Ages 26–29	71	18	11
Ages 30–39	68	25	7
Ages 40–59	54	34	12
Ages 60 and over	42	46	12

Issue 4: After receiving medical advice, every woman should be allowed to terminate a pregnancy if a strong probability exists that the child will be born with a physical or mental defect.

	Agree	Disagree	No Opinion
Total voting Population	83	6	11
Potential voters for			
SPD-FDP	87	3	10
SPD	87	3	10
FDP	89	1	10
CDU-CSU	80	9	11
Men	83	6	11
Women	83	7	10
Catholics	80	10	10
Protestants	86	3	11
By Age Group			
Ages 16–21	87	6	7
Ages 22–25	86	1	13
Ages 26–29	88	1	11
Ages 30–39	87	6	7
Ages 40–59	82	6	12
Ages 60 and over	77	11	12

Issue 5: If medical opinion indicates that the pregnancy endangers the mother's life, the woman should be allowed to have an abortion.

	Agree	Disagree	No Opinion
Total voting Population	85	4	11
Potential voters for			
SPD-FDP	89	1	10
SPD	89	2	9
FDP	90	0	10
CDU-CSU	83	6	11
Men	85	4	11
Women	85	4	11
Catholics	84	6	10
Protestants	86	2	12
By Age Group			
Ages 16–21	93	1	6
Ages 22–25	87	0	13
Ages 26–29	87	2	11
Ages 30–39	90	3	7
Ages 40–59	83	4	13
Ages 60 and over	79	8	13

Note: Data are percentages.
Source: "Infratest Politikbarometer, March/April 1971," reprinted in Harald Pawlowski, *Krieg gegen die Kinder? Für und wider die Abtreibung mit einer Dokumentation* (Limburg: Lahn, 1971), 146–149.

APPENDIX I

CATHOLIC WOMEN'S PERCEPTION AND APPROVAL OF CHURCH POSITIONS, 1993

Question: Many issues are subject to debate in the Church; on others, the Church has a clear position. On each of these cards, a specific theme is given. Please mark those cards on which you believe the Church has a clear position that you understand.

	All Catholic Women	
	Clear position	In Agreement with Church Position
Abortion	91	37
Clerical celibacy	89	15
Role of the pope	81	34
Contraception	80	12
Divorce	77	20
Common law marriage	67	19
Sexuality	55	12
Religious instruction	52	34
Role of women in the Church	37	11

Note: Data are percentages.
Source: Institut für Demoskopie (Allensbach), *Frauen und Kirche: Eine Repräsentativbefragung von Katholikinnen: 1. Februar 1993* (Bonn: Sekretariat der Deutschen Bischofskonferenz, 1993), III.

APPENDIX J
CATHOLIC WOMEN AND ALIENATION FROM THE CHURCH, 1993

Question: In general, do you believe that the Church understands the concerns and problems of women today?

	By Age Group						By Relationship to the Church		
	All	16–29	30–44	45–59	60–65	Over 65	Close	Medium	Distant
Yes	20	10	17	21	26	30	39	11	1
No	62	77	70	61	46	48	37	72	87
Undecided	18	13	13	18	28	22	24	17	12

Note: Data are percentages.
Source: Institut für Demoskopie (Allensbach), *Frauen und Kirche: Eine Repräsentativbefragung von Katholikinnen: 1. Februar 1993* (Bonn: Sekretariat der Deutschen Bischofskonferenz), 102.

APPENDIX K
"MÄNNERKIRCHE ODER FRAUENKIRCHE"

Question: In this picture, two women are discussing the Catholic Church. Which woman best represents your view? The one in the top image or the bottom?

	Catholic Women		
	All	Under 30	Active in Church
Top: "Men exercise too much influence in the Church. Women have hardly any say. If anything, it is a man's church."	54	68	38
Bottom: "I disagree. Women, especially in community, are very influential. Women are the most active there. If anything, it is a woman's church."	20	10	36
Undecided	26	22	26

	By Attachment to Parish Community			
	Close	Medium	Only Loosely	Not at All
Top position	30	50	60	68
Bottom position	40	26	13	6
Undecided	30	24	27	26

Note: Data are percentages.
Source: Institut für Demoskopie (Allensbach), *Frauen und Kirche: Eine Repräsentativbefragung von Katholikinnen: 1. Februar 1993* (Bonn: Sekretariat der Deutschen Bischofskonferenz), 103.

APPENDIX L
CDU "WOMEN'S BONUS," 1953–1987

Year	Women Voting for CDU	Men Voting for CDU	Difference
1953	47.2	38.9	8.3
1957	53.5	44.6	8.9
1961	49.6	40.4	9.2
1965	51.7	42.1	9.6
1969	50.6	40.6	10.0
1972	46.0	43.0	3.0
1976	48.8	47.2	1.6
1980	43.7	44.2	−0.5
1983	49.2	47.7	1.5
1987	45.1	42.5	2.6

Note: Data are percentages.
Source: Sara Elise Wiliarty, *The CDU and the Politics of Gender in Germany: Bringing Women to the Party* (Cambridge: Cambridge University Press, 2010), 21.

APPENDIX M

OPINIONS ON WOMEN PRIESTS IN THE CATHOLIC CHURCH, 1992

Should the Catholic Church Allow Women Priests?	All Germans	Catholic Churchgoers
Yes	70	50
Indifferent	19	12
No	10	37

Note: Data are percentages. Two thousand surveyed in the former West German states.
Source: Data drawn from Priesterinnen Erwünscht, Emnid survey, in "Päpstin mit Recht auf Heirat," *Der Spiegel*, December 21, 1992.

APPENDIX N
GERMAN CATHOLIC CHURCH LIFE, 1960–2010

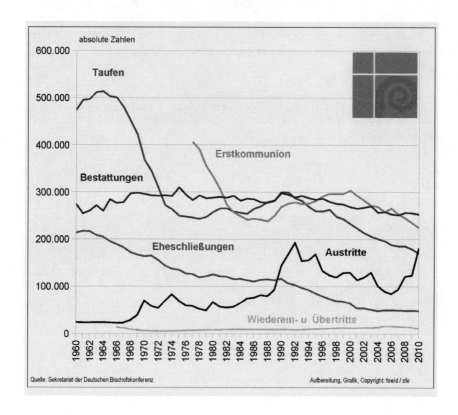

Absolute Zahlen, Absolute numbers
Austritte, Church separations
Bestattungen, Church burials
Eheschließungen, Church marriages
Erstkommunion, First Communions
Täuflinge, Baptisms

Source: Forschungsgruppe Weltanschauungen in Deutschland, Erstellungsdatum: Kirchliches Leben—Katholisches Deutschland (insgesamt), 1960–2010, version of November 7, 2011, www.fowid.de.

Notes

INTRODUCTION

1. ZdK, KT-Essen 1968, Presse-Echo, no. 30, "Opas Kirche ist tot," *Stern*, September 22, 1968.
2. ZdK, *Mitten in dieser Welt* (Paderborn: Bonifatius, 1968).
3. Dagmar Herzog, "Christianity, Disability, Abortion: Western Europe, 1960s–1980s," *Archiv für Sozialgeschichte* 51 (2011): 1–40, here 1.
4. Elizabeth D. Heineman, *What Difference Does a Husband Make? Women and Marital Status in Nazi and Postwar Germany* (Berkeley: University of California Press, 1999), 9.
5. Erwin Gatz, *Die katholische Kirche in Deutschland im 20. Jahrhundert* (Freiburg: Herder, 2009), 131.
6. Ibid., 133.
7. Ibid., 134.
8. Uta Poiger, *Jazz, Rock, and Rebels: Cold War Politics and American Culture in a Divided Germany* (Berkeley: University of California Press, 2000), 213.
9. Ibid., 218–219.
10. Letter to the editor, *Frau und Mutter*, August 1952.
11. Franz Gröner, ed., *Kirchliches Handbuch: Amtliches statistisches Jahrbuch der Katholischen Kirche Deutschlands*, vols. 25–26 (Cologne: Bachem, 1962, 1969).
12. Mark Edward Ruff, *The Wayward Flock: Catholic Youth in Postwar West Germany, 1945–1965* (Chapel Hill: University of North Carolina Press, 2005), 66.
13. Gatz, *Die katholische Kirche*, 166.
14. Quoted in John W. O'Malley, *What Happened at Vatican II* (Cambridge, MA: Belknap Press of Harvard University Press, 2008), 98.
15. Gatz, *Die katholische Kirche*, 177.
16. Although the quote's veracity cannot be confirmed, for many Catholics it became emblematic of the new direction taken by Vatican II.
17. "Roman Catholics: Authority under Fire," *Time*, March 19, 1965.
18. Marcel Lefebvre, "A Little Light on the Present Crisis in the Church (March 7, 1968)," in Marcel Lefebvre, *A Bishop Speaks: Writings and Addresses, 1963–1976*, trans. V. S. M. Fraser (Kansas City, MO: Angelus Press, 2007), 43.
19. Yves Congar, *La Crise dans l'Église et Mgr. Lefèbvre* (Paris: Cerf, 1976), 50.
20. Sybille Steinbacher, *Wie der Sex nach Deutschland kam: Der Kampf um Sittlichkeit und Anstand in der frühen Bundesrepublik* (Munich: Siedler, 2011), 19–21.
21. Clayton J. Whisnant, *Male Homosexuality in West Germany: Between Persecution and Freedom, 1945–69* (New York: Palgrave Macmillan, 2012), 4.
22. Mark Mazower, *Dark Continent: Europe's Twentieth Century* (New York: Vintage Books, 2000), 85.
23. On the multiple challenges launched by Germans in the 1940s and 1950s, see Steinbacher, *Wie der Sex nach Deutschland kam*.
24. Dagmar Herzog, *Sexuality in Europe: A Twentieth-Century History* (New York: Cambridge University Press, 2011), 134.
25. On different explanations for the sexual revolution, see ibid., 133–134.
26. In 1967, the French government did not provide legal guidelines for the sale and

manufacture of contraceptives; access to contraceptives remained limited until 1972. See Melanie Latham, *Regulating Reproduction: A Century of Conflict in Britain and in France* (New York: Manchester University Press, 2002), 38–39.

27. Herzog, *Sexuality in Europe*, 140–160.

28. Quoted in Konrad Jarausch, *After Hitler: Recivilizing Germans, 1945–1995* (New York: Oxford University Press, 2006), 166.

29. Dagmar Herzog, *Sex after Fascism: Memory and Morality in Twentieth-Century Germany* (Princeton, NJ: Princeton University Press, 2005), 141.

30. Poiger, *Jazz, Rock, and Rebels*, 46.

31. Ibid., 48.

32. On reform efforts in the 1960s and early 1970s, see, e.g., Tim Bush, *Die Deutsche Strafrechtsreform: Ein Rückblick auf die Sechs Reformen des deutschen Strafrechts, 1968–1998* (Baden-Baden: Nomos, 2005); for an account that contrasts the aims of the early reform movement with those of the reform movement in the 1990s, specifically with reference to sexual offenses, see Tatjana Hörnle, "Penal Law and Sexuality: Recent Reforms in German Criminal Law," *Buffalo Criminal Law Review* 3, no. 2 (2000): 639–685.

33. Quoted in Frederic Spotts, *The Churches and Politics in Germany* (Middleton, CT: Wesleyan University Press, 1973), 159–160.

34. The term "sheepfold" is referred to in *Catechism of the Catholic Church*, 2d. ed., no. 754, as follows: "The Church is, accordingly, a *sheepfold*, the sole and necessary gateway to which is Christ. It is also the flock of which God himself foretold that he would be the shepherd, and whose sheep, even though governed by human shepherds, are unfailingly nourished and led by Christ himself, the Good Shepherd and Prince of Shepherds, who gave his life for his sheep."

35. Simone Twents, *Frau sein ist mehr: Die Würde der Frau nach Johannes Paul II* (Buttenwiesen: Stella Maris, 2002), 200.

36. Joachim Meisner, "Vorwart," in ibid.

37. On the feminization of religion in Europe, see Irmtraud Götz von Olenhusen, ed., *Wunderbare Erscheinungen: Frauen und katholische Frömmigkeit im 19. und 20. Jahrhundert* (Paderborn: Schöningh, 1995); Claude Langlois, *Le catholicisme au feminin: Les congrégations françaises à supérieure Générale au XIXe siècle* (Paris: Cerf, 1984); Caroline Ford, *Divided Houses: Religion and Gender in Modern France* (Ithaca, NY: Cornell University Press, 2005).

38. Sara Elise Wiliarty, *The CDU and the Politics of Gender in Germany: Bringing Women to the Party* (New York: Cambridge University Press, 2010), 42.

39. For works with minimal or no coverage of religion's role in twentieth-century German debates on gender and sexuality, see Attina Grossmann, *Reforming Sex: The German Movement for Birth Control & Abortion Reform, 1920–1950* (New York: Oxford University Press, 1992); Ute Frevert, *Women in Modern Germany: From Bourgeois Emancipation to Sexual Liberation* (New York: Berg, 1989); Erica Carter, *How German Is She? Postwar West German Reconstruction and the Consuming Woman* (Ann Arbor: University of Michigan Press, 1997); Myra Ferree, *Varieties of Feminism: German Gender Politics in Global Perspective* (Stanford, CA: Stanford University Press, 2012).

40. Ann Taylor Allen, "Religion and Gender in Modern German History: A Historiographical Perspective," in *Gendering Modern German History: Rewriting Historiography*, ed. Karen Hagemann and Jean H. Quataert (New York: Berghahn Books, 2007), 194.

41. See "Strafrecht: Wahnhafte Beziehung," *Der Spiegel*, September 9, 1988.

42. See Allen, "Religion and Gender," 190–207.

43. Ibid., 203.

44. See Herzog, *Sex after Fascism*.

45. Herzog, "Post coitum triste est . . . ? Sexual Politics and Culture in Postunification Germany," *German Politics & Society* 28, no. 1 (2010): 111–140.

46. See Eva-Maria Silies, *Liebe, Lust und Last: Die Pille als weibliche Generationserfahrung in der Bundesrepublik, 1960–1980* (Göttingen: Wallstein, 2010).

47. Mark Ruff, "Review of *Zeitgeschichtliche Katholizismusforschung: Tatsachen, Deutungen, Fragen. Ein Zwischenbilanz*," *Catholic Historical Review* 91, no. 4 (2005): 852.

48. See Rainer M. Lepsius, "Parteiensystem und Sozialstruktur: Zum Problem der Demokratisierung der deutschen Gesellschaft," in *Wirtschaft, Geschichte und Wirtschaftsgeschichte*, ed. William Abel (Stuttgart: Fischer, 1966), 371–393.

49. See Wilfried Loth, *Katholiken im Kaiserreich: Der politische Katholizismus in der Krise des wilhelminischen Deutschlands* (Düsseldorf: Droste, 1984).

50. On the cohesiveness of the milieu during the Imperial, Weimar, and Nazi eras, see Antonius Liedhegener, *Christentum und Urbanisierung: Katholiken und Protestanten in Münster und Bochum, 1830–1930* (Paderborn: Schöningh, 1997); Christoph Kösters, "'Fest soll mein Taufbund immer steh'n . . .'—Demonstrationskatholizismus im Bistum Münster 1933—1945," in *Zwischen Loyalität und Resistenz: Soziale Konflikte und politische Repression während der NS-Herrschaft in Westfalen*, ed. Rudolf Schlögel and Hans-Ulrich Thamer (Münster: Aschendorff, 1996), 158–184; and Christoph Schank, "*Kölsch-Katholisch*": *Das katholische Milieu in Köln, 1871–1933* (Cologne: Böhlau, 2004); Maria-Anna Zumholz, *Volksfrömmigkeit und katholisches Milieu: Marienerscheinungen im Heede, 1937–1950, im Spannungsfeld von Volksfrömmigkeit, nationalsozialistischem Regime und kirchlicher Hierarchie* (Cloppenburg: Runge, 2004). For studies that identify signs of collapse during the Weimar era, see Oded Heilbronner, *Catholicism, Political Culture, and the Countryside: A Social History of the Nazi Party in South Germany* (Ann Arbor: University of Michigan Press, 1998); Thomas Nipperdey, *Religion im Umbruch: Deutschland, 1870–1918* (Munich: Beck, 1988); Gerhard Paul and Klaus-Michael Mallmann, *Milieus und Widerstand: Eine Verhaltensgeschichte der Gesellschaft im Nationalsozialismus, Widerstand und Verweigerung im Saarland, 1935–1945* (Bonn: Dietz, 1995). For studies that associate the collapse with the post–World War II era, see Wilhelm Damberg, *Abschied vom Milieu? Katholizismus im Bistum Münster und in den Niederlanden, 1945–1980* (Paderborn: Schöningh, 1997), and Mark Ruff, *Wayward Flock*.

51. See Benjamin Ziemann, "Der deutsche Katholizismus im späten 19. und 20. Jahrhundert: Forschungstendenzen auf dem Weg zu sozialgeschichtlicher Fundierung und Erweiterung," *Archiv für Sozialgeschichte* 40 (2000): 402–422.

52. See Benjamin Ziemann, *Katholische Kirche und Sozialwissenschaften, 1945–1975* (Göttingen: Vandenhoeck & Ruprecht, 2007).

53. Mark Ruff, "Integrating Religion into the Historical Mainstream: Recent Literature on Religion in the Federal Republic of Germany," *Central European History* 42 (2009): 328.

54. Ibid.

55. Ibid., 329.

56. See Michael Fellner, *Katholische Kirche in Bayern: Religion, Gesellschaft und Modernisierung in der Erzdiözese München und Freising* (Paderborn: Schöningh, 2008), and Christian Schmidtmann, *Katholische Studierende, 1945–1973: Ein Beitrag zur Kultur- und Sozialgeschichte der Bundesrepublik Deutschland* (Paderborn: Schöningh, 2006).

57. See Wilhelm Damberg and Frank Bösch, *Soziale Strukturen und Semantiken des Religiösen im Wandel: Transformationen in der Bundesrepublik Deutschland, 1949–1989* (Essen: Klartext, 2011).

58. Mark Ruff, "Conference Report: Catholicism in Germany—Contemporary History and the Present," *Contemporary Church History Quarterly* 19, no. 1 (March 2013), https://contemporarychurchhistory.org, accessed February 24, 2015.

59. Ruff, "Review of *Zeitgeschichtliche Katholizismusforschung*," 852.

60. See Derek K. Hastings, "Fears of a Feminized Church: Catholicism, Celibacy, and the Crisis of Masculinity in Wilhelmine Germany," *European History Quarterly* 38 (2008): 34–65, here 34.

61. See David Blackbourn, *Marpingen: Apparitions of the Virgin Mary in Nineteenth-Century Germany* (Ithaca, NY: Cornell University Press 1994).

62. See Damberg, *Abschied vom Milieu?*

63. See Lukas Rölli-Alkemper, *Familie im Wiederaufbau: Katholizismus und bürgerliches Familienideal in der Bundesrepublik Deutschland, 1945–1965* (Paderborn: Schöningh, 2000); Petra von der Osten, *Jugend- und Gefährdetenfürsorge im Sozialstaat: Auf dem Weg zum Sozialdienst katholischer Frauen, 1945–1968* (Cologne: Böhlau, 2003); and Ruff, *Wayward Flock*.

64. Gene Burns, *The Frontiers of Catholicism: The Politics of Ideology in a Liberal World* (Berkeley: University of California Press, 1992), 2.

65. See Myeong-Gu Seo and W. E. Douglas Creed, "Institutional Contradictions, Praxis, and Institutional Change: A Dialectical Perspective," *Academy of Management Review* 27, no. 2 (2002): 222–247. On this theoretical shift, see Aaron Smith and Fiona M. Graetz, *Philosophies of Organizational Change* (Northhampton, MA: Edward Elgar, 2011), 74–89.

66. Norbert Lüdecke, "*Humanae Vitae*," in *Erinnerungsorte des Christentums*, ed. Christoph Markschies and Herbert Wolf (Munich: Beck, 2010), 534–546, here 545.

67. Ibid.

68. Ibid.

69. Donald P. Kommers and Russell A. Miller, *The Constitutional Jurisprudence of the Federal Republic of Germany* (Durham, NC: Duke University Press, 2012), 539.

70. Ibid.

71. For the 1917 Code of Canon Law, see Charles Augustine, *A Commentary on the New Code of Canon Law*, 8 vols. (St. Louis Park, MO: Herder, 1918–1923). For the remaining three documents, citations were taken from the website of the Eternal Word Television Network, www.ewtn.com.

72. Listed by language are the Vatican website's documents for which I furnished the English translations. German: Pius XII, *Menti Nostrae*, September 23, 1950. Italian: CCE, *Orientamenti educativi per la formazione al celibato sacerdotale*, April 11, 1974; Paul VI, *Ad Pascendum*, August 15, 1972; Paul VI, *Pontificalis Romani*, June 18, 1968. Spanish: John Paul II, *Discurso a la Asamblea del CELAM*, March 9, 1983; Paul VI, *Ministeria Quadem*, August 15, 1972; Pius XII, *Discurso al Congreso de la Union Católica Italiana de Obstétricas con la colaboración de la Federatión Nacional de Colegios de Comadronas Católicas*, October 29, 1951; Pius XII, *Discurso al VII Congreso de la Sociedad Internacional de Hematología*, September 12, 1958; Pius XII, *Votre Présence*, September 29, 1949.

1. CELIBACY FOR THE KINGDOM OF HEAVEN AND EARTH

1. From the Latin *caelibātus*, "unmarried"; see *Oxford English Dictionary*, 2d ed., www.oxfordamericandictionary.com.

2. *Presbyterorum Ordinis*, December 7, 1965, no. 16.

3. Tina Beattie, *New Catholic Feminism: Theology and Theory* (London: Routledge, 2006), 143.

4. See Anthony K. W. McLaughlin, "The Obligation of Perfect and Perpetual Continence

and Married Deacons in the Church" (Ph.D. diss., Catholic University of America, 2010), 80.

5. See Thomas Aquinas, *Compendium of Theology*, trans. Cyril Vollert (St. Louis: Herder, 1947), ch. 192.

6. See Ibid., ch. 191.

7. See Aquinas, *Summa Theologica* II, part 2, q. 153 a. 2.

8. Georg Denzler, ed., *Lebensberichte verheirateter Priester: Autobiographische Zeugnisse zum Konflikt zwischen Ehe und Zölibat* (Munich: Piper, 1989), 30.

9. "Die Freiheit zur Ehe wird es nicht geben: Gespräch mit dem Kölner Weihbischof Dr. Augustin Frotz über den Zölibat," *Der Spiegel*, January 12, 1970.

10. Fritz Leist, ed., *Zum Thema Zölibat: Bekenntnisse von Betroffenen* (Munich: Kindler, 1973), 39.

11. John W. O'Malley, "A History of a Misunderstood Tradition: Some Basics about Celibacy," *America* 187, no. 13 (2002): 7–11.

12. Rölli-Alkemper, *Familie im Wiederaufbau*, 39–41.

13. Herbert Doms, *The Meaning of Marriage*, trans. George Sayer (New York: Sheed & Ward, 1939), 89.

14. Susan A. Ross, "The Bride of Christ and the Body Politic: Body and Gender in Pre-Vatican II Theology," *Journal of Religion* 71, no. 3 (1991): 345–361.

15. Ibid.

16. "Junge Christen befragen die Kirche: Gespräch u.a. mit Weihbischof Walther Kampe, München 1968," in *Der Zölibat: Geschichte und Gegenwart eines umstrittenen Gesetzes*, ed. Joachim Stephan Hohmann (Frankfurt: Lang, 1993), 308.

17. Priests in the Eastern rite may marry under the following conditions: (1) no marriage after ordination; (2) required periods of sexual continence; (3) only one marriage prior to ordination, and not to a widower. Priests cannot marry a woman the Church deems unfit. Bishops may not marry.

18. McLaughlin, "Obligation," 104–108, 265–268.

19. Jan Dellepoort, "Einige Gedanken über die europäische Priesterfrage," *Die Europäische Priesterfrage: Bericht der Internationalen Enquête in Wien, 10.–12. Oktober 1958*, ed. Franz Jachym et al. (Vienna: Internationales katholisches Institut für kirchliche Sozialforschung, 1959), 65–66.

20. Ibid., 60.

21. *Catechism of the Catholic Church*, 2d ed., no. 1234.

22. Richard A. Schoenherr, *Goodbye Father: The Celibate Male Priesthood and the Future of the Catholic Church* (Oxford: Oxford University Press, 2004), 12.

23. Dellepoort, "Einige Gedanken," 60–69.

24. AEK, CRII 13.2, 6/36–37.

25. AEK, CRII 13.2, 6/38–39.

26. Jan Dellepoort, Norbert Greinacher, and Walter Menges, eds., *Die deutsche Priesterfrage* (Mainz: Matthias-Grünewald, 1962), 88, 137.

27. Leist, ed., *Zum Thema Zölibat*, 12.

28. Ibid., 33.

29. See *Optatam Totius*, October 28, 1965, sec. 10; Paul VI, *Sacerdotalis Caelibatus*, June 24, 1967, secs. 62–63. CCE, *Orientamenti educativi per la formazione al celibato sacerdotale*, April 11, 1974.

30. "Roman Catholics against Celibacy," *Time*, August 28, 1964.

31. John XXIII, *Sacerdotii Nostri Primordia*, August 1, 1959.

32. O'Malley, *What Happened at Vatican II*, 270–271.

33. Georg Denzler, *Die Geschichte des Zölibats* (Freiburg: Herder, 1993), 170.
34. O'Malley, *What Happened at Vatican II*, 271.
35. AEK, CR 21.64, 2/136.
36. Letter to the editor, *Der Spiegel*, January 26, 1970.
37. Colleen McDannell, *The Spirit of Vatican II: The History of Catholic Reform in America* (New York: Basic Books, 2001), 304.
38. O'Malley, *What Happened at Vatican II*, 271.
39. See *Lumen Gentium*, November 21,1964, sec. 42; *Perfectae Caritatis*, October 28, 1965, sec. 12; *Optatam Totius*, October 28, 1965 sec. 10; *Presbyterorum Ordinis*, December 7, 1965, no. 16.
40. See, e.g., Fritz Leist, *Der Sexuelle Notstand und die Kirchen* (Freiberg: Herder, 1972); Leist, ed., *Zum Thema Zölibat*; Hubertus Mynarek, *Eros und Klerus* (Düsseldorf: Econ, 1978); Eugen Drewermann, *Kleriker: Psychogramm eines Ideals* (Olten: Walter, 1989).
41. Pius XII, *Sacra Virginitas*, March 25, 1954, sec. 32.
42. *Presbyterorum Ordinis*, December 7, 1965, no. 16.
43. Michael Schmaus and Rudolf Lange, *Das Priestertum: Sein Wesen und seine Aufgaben: Überlegungen zur kirchlichen Raumplanung* (Bamberg: Otto, 1969).
44. McLaughlin, "Obligation," 157–159.
45. O'Malley, *What Happened at Vatican II*, 175.
46. Ralph M. Wiltgen, *The Inside Story of Vatican II: A Firsthand Account of the Council's Inner Workings* (Charlotte, NC: Tan Books, 2014), 108. This book was first published in 1967 as *The Rhine Flows into the Tiber: A History of Vatican II* by Hawthorne books in New York, New York.
47. The council fathers did not establish any definitive norms for the permanent diaconate. On June 18, 1967, Paul VI issued the motu proprio *Sacrum Diaconatus Ordinem*, which set the age for mature candidates (married or unmarried) at thirty-five. See Paul VI, *Sacrum Diaconatus Ordinem*, June 18, 1967, part III, no. 12. In June 1968, the apostolic constitution, *Pontificalis Romani*, established official rites for diaconal ordination, and in 1972 Paul issued another motu proprio, *Ad Pascendum*, offering further clarification of the rules. With the promulgation of the new Code of Canon Law in 1983, additional regulations went into effect. See Paul VI, *Pontificalis Romani*, Sono approvati i nuovi riti per l'ordinazione dei Diaconi, Presbiteri e Vescovi, June 18, 1968; Paul VI, *Ad Pascendum*, August 15, 1972; and Code of Canon Law (1983), Title VI: Orders, 1008–1054.
48. The celibacy requirement applies to married deacons upon the death of their wife; they may not remarry. See McLaughlin, "Obligation," 232–247.
49. Josef Hernoga, *Das Priestertum: Zur nachkonziliaren Amtstheologie im deutschen Sprachraum* (Frankfurt: Lang, 1997), 15–29.
50. J. Waterworth, ed. and trans., *The Canons and Decrees of the Sacred and Ecumenical Council of Trent* (London: Dolman, 1848), 155.
51. Hernoga, *Das Priestertum*, 15–18.
52. O'Malley, *What Happened at Vatican II*, 50.
53. See *Presbyterorum Ordinis*, no. 2.
54. O'Malley, *What Happened at Vatican II*, 245.
55. Hernoga, *Das Priestertum*, December 7, 1965, 60–63.
56. Elizabeth McEnroy, *Guests in Their Own House: The Women of Vatican II* (New York: Crossroad, 1996), 34–35.
57. Ibid., 126–127.
58. *Gaudium et Spes*, December 7, 1965, sec. 29.

59. IMWAC, "Manifesto of the International Movement We Are Church," http://www.we-are-church.org, accessed March 10, 2012.

60. Walter Goddijn, quoted in "Massenflucht aus dem Joch Christus," *Der Spiegel*, October 18, 1971.

61. See Pierre de Locht, "Conjugal Spirituality, 1930–1960," *Concilium* (1976): 34–37. The author describes how, as part of the Catholic Action Movement, some French priests began questioning their celibacy after extensive contact with families; however, at this point, no public challenge to the celibacy requirement developed.

62. Denzler, *Die Geschichte des Zölibats*, 110–115.

63. Pius XII, *Menti Nostrae*, September 23, 1950, no. 141.

64. O'Malley, *What Happened at Vatican II*, 188.

65. Ibid., 246.

66. See Gerhard Schmidtchen, *Zwischen Kirche und Gesellschaft: Forschungsbericht über die Umfrage zur Gemeinsamen Synode der Bistümer in der Bundesrepublik Deutschland* (Freiburg: Herder, 1972), 184.

67. See Edward Schillebeeckx and Catharina Halkes, *Mary: Yesterday, Today and Tomorrow* (New York: Crossroad, 1993), and Uta Ranke-Heinemann, *Eunuchs for the Kingdom of Heaven: Women, Sexuality and the Catholic Church*, trans. Peter Heinegg (New York: Doubleday, 1990).

68. Giuseppe Alberigo, ed., *The Council and the Transition: The Fourth Period and the End of the Council, September 1965–December 1965*, vol. 5 of *A History of Vatican II*, trans. Matthew J. O'Connell (Maryknoll, NY: Orbis, 2006), 234–235.

69. The encyclical addressed only clerical celibacy, and not the vow of chastity taken by consecrated religious. *Sacerdotalis Caelibatus*, June 24, 1967, secs. 2–13.

70. Hans Küng, *Disputed Truth: Memoirs*, trans. John Bowden (New York: Continuum, 2007), 36.

71. "Zölibat: Quelle der Freude," *Der Spiegel*, July 10, 1967.

72. Karl Rahner, "Celibacy of the Secular Priest," *Furrow* 19, no. 2 (1968): 60.

73. Ibid., 61–62.

74. Ibid., 62.

75. Ibid., 64.

76. Ibid., 72.

77. "Zölibat: Quelle der Freude."

78. Denzler, *Die Geschichte des Zölibats*, 85.

79. Thomas Sartory and Gertrude Sartory, *Strukturkrise einer Kirche: Vor und nach der Enzyklika "Humanae Vitae"* (Munich: Deutscher Taschenbuch, 1969), 141–143.

80. "Wort der deutschen Bischöfe zur seelsorglichen Lage nach dem Erscheinen der Enzyklika 'Humanae Vitae,'" *Nachkonziliare Dokumentation*, vol. 14 (Trier: Paulinus, 1968).

81. Franz-Maria Elsner, "Essen war anders," in *Mitten in dieser Welt: 82nd Deutscher Katholikentag Essen 1968*, ed. ZdK (Bonn: Bonifatius, 1968), 15.

82. "Opas Kirche ist tot."

83. ZdK, KT-Essen 1968, Presse-Echo, no. 11, "3000 Katholiken fordern Revision des Pillen-Verbots," *Hamburger Abendblatt*, September 7, 1968; ZdK, KT-Essen 1968, Presse-Echo, no. 11, Heinz Schweden, "Gewissen gegen Gehorsam," *Rheinische Post*, September 5, 1968.

84. Elsner, "Essen war anders," 16.

85. ZdK, KT-Essen 1968, Presse-Echo, no. 9, Vilma Sturm, "Wir sind die linken Frommen: Die Opposition auf dem Katholikentag in Essen," *FAZ*, September 5, 1968.

86. ZdK, KT-Essen 1968, Presse-Echo, no. 9, Ulrich Schwarz, "Der Priester darf kein Patriarch mehr sein," *Ruhr-Nachrichten*, September 15, 1968.

87. ZdK, KT-Essen 1968, Presse-Echo, no. 9, Günter Streich, "Kritischen Katholiken künden Aktionen an: Prof. Rahner versuchte Brückenschlag zwischen Konservativen und 'Rebellen,'" *Neue Rheinzeitung*, September 5, 1968.

88. ZdK, KT-Essen 1968, Presse-Echo, no. 9, Hans Schulte, "Hochwurden muß gehen: Priester nicht mehr heilige Außenseiter," *Düsseldorfer Nachrichten*, September 5, 1968.

89. Schweden, "Gewissen gegen Gehorsam."

90. Letter to the editor, *Der Spiegel*, January 26, 1970.

91. JHD, Würzburger Synode—ZDF Postfach Synode, 2.1/012–037.

92. Ibid.

93. Schmidtchen, *Zwischen Kirche und Gesellschaft*, 132.

94. Gerhard Schmidtchen, *Priester in Deutschland: Forschungsbericht über die im Auftrag der Deutschen Bischofskonferenz durchgeführte Umfrage unter allen Welt- und Ordenspriestern in der Bundesrepublik Deutschland* (Freiburg: Herder, 1973), 69.

95. Thomas G. Feuchtmann, "'Uncoupling' Celibacy: Dutch Pastoral Council V," *America*, January 31, 1970.

96. Georg Denzler, *Das Papsttum und der Amtszölibat*, vol. 2. (Stuttgart: Hiersemann, 1976), 355.

97. See "Zölibat: Zerrütte Ehe," *Der Spiegel*, January 26, 1970.

98. Küng, *Disputed Truth*, 93.

99. Denzler, *Die Geschichte des Zölibats*, 137.

100. "Eingabe des Vereins katholischer deutscher Lehrerinnen (VkdL) an die Deutsche Bischofskonferenz in Essen-Heidhausen zur Frage des Religionsunterrichts und zur Zölibatsfrage von 7.2.1970," in *Der Zölibat*, ed. Hohmann, 323.

101. Denzler, *Die Geschichte des Zölibats*, 137.

102. AEK, CRII 13.2, 6/64–65.

103. Denzler, *Das Papsttum und der Amtszölibat*, vol. 2, 358–359.

104. Hans Urs von Balthasar, ed., *Bischofssynode 1971: Das Priesteramt* (Einsiedeln: Johannes, 1972), 74.

105. Ibid., 77.

106. See JHD, Würzburger Synode, 2.61012–033, Westdeutscher Rundfunk, "Erwartungen an die westdeutsche Pastoralsynode (II)," Sendung: Sonntag, den 10 August 1969, 1900–19.30 Uhr II. Programm; Westdeutscher Rundfunk, "Erwägungen zur westdeutschen Pastoralsynode. Christliche Gedanken zu unserer Zeit," Sendung: Donnerstag, den 23. Oktober. 1969, 19.45–20.00 Uhr, II. Programm; Norddeutscher Rundfunk, "Synode '72: Aufbruch zu einer neuen Kirche?," Sendung: 11. April 1970, 18.00–18.30 Uhr, 2. Programm.

107. JHD, Würzburger Synode, 2.11012–061, Ergebnisprotokoll der 7. Sitzung der K VII "Charismen, Dienste, Ämter" von 9.12 bis 10.12.71, Anlage 2: Protokoll AG 2.

108. JHD, Würzburger Synode, 2.11012–061, Ergebnisprotokoll der 9. Sitzung der K VII "Charismen, Dienste, Ämter" vom 13.3 bis 14.3.72.

109. JHD, Würzburger Synode, 2.11012–061, Ergebnisprotokoll der 4. Sitzung der K VII "Charismen, Dienste, Ämter" vom 30.6.71 bis 1.7.71.

110. AEK, Archiv der DBK, Würzburger Synode, 291, Letter from Gustav Vogel, contact person for *Priester ohne Amt*, to Bishop Tenhumberg.

111. AEK, Archiv der DBK, Würzburger Synode 539, Ergebnisprotokoll der 10. Sitzung der KVII vom 12.6 bis 13.6.1972.

112. AEK, Archiv der DBK, Würzburger Synode, 289, "Überlegungen zum priesterlichen Dienst in der Kirche."

113. Schmidtchen, *Zwischen Kirche und Gesellschaft*, 127.

114. AEK, Archiv der DBK, Würzburger Synode 290, Protokollauszug der Aprilsitzung 1972 der Deutschen Bischofskonferenz in Essen.

115. Ibid.

116. L. Bertsch et al., eds., *Gemeinsame Synode der Bistümer in der Bundesrepublik Deutschland*, vol. 1 (Freiburg: Herder, 1976), 591.

117. Hubertus Mynarek, "Der Ausstieg oder Opportunisten haben es leichter," in *Lebensberichte verheirateter Priester: Autobiographische Zeugnisse zum Konflikt zwischen Ehe und Zölibat*, ed. Georg Denzler (Munich: Piper, 1989), 99–112.

118. "Kirchenaustritt: Küß mich, Priester," *Der Spiegel*, November 13, 1972.

119. Mynarek, "Der Ausstieg oder Opportunisten haben es leichter," 100.

120. "Priester: Totale Tröstung," *Der Spiegel*, February 20, 1978.

121. "Der Spiegel berichtete," *Der Spiegel*, January 15, 1979.

122. "Reformation durch Schlüsselloch," *Die Zeit*, January 25, 1974.

123. "Immer mehr ein Zentrum der Unordnung," *Der Spiegel*, October 8, 1973.

124. Ibid.

125. "Negative Polizei," *Der Spiegel*, October 8, 1973; "Ungeschickter Gesandter," *Die Zeit*, October 12, 1973.

126. ZdK, 2103, 1854, no. 1, Josef Altrogge's letter protesting the statement of solidarity issued by the ZdK in support of Bishop Kempf on October 17, 1973; letter from Bernhard Vogel, ZdK president, to Cardinal Döpfner reiterating the organization's solidarity with the German bishops and with Bishop Kempf in particular, October 19, 1973.

127. See "Negative Polizei"; "Ungeschickter Gesandter."

128. AEK, Archiv der DBK, Würzburger Synode, 289, Helmut Link, "Zur Situation der ehemaligen Priester und Ordensleute in der BRD." The paper was made available to members of Subcommission VII of the Wurzburg Synod. In the report, the author noted the lack of comprehensive data on clerical defections. Efforts by Subcommission VII to obtain statistical data from the CDF on the number of priests in the world Church and in Germany who left office because of the celibacy requirement met with failure. On June 20, 1973, Hanspeter Heinz, secretary of Subcommission VII, received word from a friend working for the CDF that access had been denied. See letter from Hermann Schwedt to Hanspeter Heinz, AEK, Archiv der DBK, 289. Estimates of the total number of departures from the priesthood during Paul VI's papacy range as high as 46,000. See George Weigel, *God's Choice: Pope Benedict XVI and the Future of the Catholic Church* (New York: HarperCollins, 2005), 52.

129. CDF, *Letter to All Local Ordinaries and General Moderators of Clerical Religious Communities Regarding the Dispensation of Priests from Celibacy*, October 14, 1970, no. 5.

130. Anne Lueg, *Wenn Frauen Priester lieben: Der Zölibat und seine Folgen* (Munich: Kösel, 1994), 17–21.

131. For a contemporary account of women's ghettoization in a male-dominated Church, see Teresa Bock, "Aufgaben und Mitarbeit der Frauen in der Kirche," in *Die Frau in Gesellschaft und Kirche: Analysen und Perspektiven*, ed. Anton Rauscher (Berlin: Duncker & Humblot, 1986), 202–211. On the suppression of female theologians in the 1960s, 1970s, and 1980s, see Iris Müller, "Katholische Theologinnen: Unterdrückt, aber dennoch angepaßt und ergeben," in *Zur Priesterin berufen: Gott sieht nicht auf das Geschlecht. Zeugnisse römischer-katholischer Frauen*, ed. Ida Raming et al. (Thaur: Dr.-und-Verl.-Haus Thau, 1998), 43–52.

132. kfd-1175, Gesprächskreises zwischen Vertreterinnen der katholischen Frauenverbände und Mitgliedern der Pastoralkommission, February 4, 1984.

2. WOMEN'S ORDINATION

1. Catholic theologians trace this metaphor to the covenantal relationship between Yahweh and Israel, as well as to New Testament writings in Ephesians and Revelations. On this point, Catholic theologians who support women's ordination and those who reject it agree.

2. Manfred Hauke, *Women in the Priesthood? A Systematic Analysis in the Light of the Order of Creation and Redemption*, trans. David Kipp (San Francisco: Ignatius Press, 1988), 115.

3. CDF, *Inter Insigniores*, October 15, 1976, par. 30–31.

4. Beattie, *New Catholic Feminism*, 131.

5. On medieval arguments against women's ordination, see Bernard Cooke and Gary Macy, *Ordination of Women in the Medieval Context* (New York: Lexington Books, 2002).

6. Joseph Mausbach, *Die Stellung der Frau im Menschheitsleben: Eine Anwendung katholischer Grundsätze auf die Frauenfrage* (Munich: Zentralstelle des Volksvereins für das katholische Deutschland, 1906), 59.

7. On women's ordination in the Church of Sweden, see Christina Odenberg, "Ordination and Consecration of Women in the Church of Sweden," in *Women and Ordination in the Christian Churches: International Perspectives*, ed. Ian Jones, Janet Wootton, and Kirsty Thorpe (New York: T & T Clark, 2008), 113–122.

8. In 1964, the Synod of Thuringia decided that women pastors "could be used only in private services for women, children, and the handicapped." This law remained in effect until 1978, when at least on paper women pastors were accorded the same rights as male pastors. However, in Bavaria, as a concession to opponents of women's ordination, men were given veto power—meaning a male pastor could veto the installation of a female pastor in his parish; this provision remained in effect until 1998. Today, women hold an estimated one-third of all ministerial positions in the EKD and account for approximately one-half of all theological students. See www.ekd.de, accessed January 25, 2014.

9. Deborah Halter, *The Papal 'No': A Comprehensive Guide to the Vatican's Rejection of Women's Ordination* (New York: Crossroad, 2004), 67–73.

10. For a brief history of the WOC, see Michele Dillon, *Catholic Identity: Balancing Reason, Faith and Power* (Cambridge: Cambridge University Press, 1999), 77–114.

11. For a history of women's ordination in the Anglican Communion in England, see Clare Walsh, *Gender and Discourse: Language and Power in Politics, the Church and Organizations* (New York: Longman, 2001), 164–209.

12. John XXIII, *Pacem in Terris*, April 11, 1963, no. 41.

13. Richard L. Camp, "From Passive Subordination to Complementary Partnership," *Catholic Historical Review* 76, no. 3 (1990): 512.

14. The 1917 Code of Canon Law (Canon 813, Paragraph 2) prohibited female altar servers; however, if no man was available, a woman could assist if she "answers from a distance and does not approach the altar." See C. Augustine, *On the Sacraments (Except Matrimony) and Sacramentals*, vol. 4 of *Commentary*, 150–151. Canon 118 reserved major and minor orders for men. See C. Augustine, *Clergy and Hierarchy*, vol. 2 of *Commentary*, 56–58.

15. Anthony K. W. McLaughlin, "The Obligation of Perfect and Perpetual Continence and Married Deacons in the Church" (Ph.D. diss., Catholic University of America, 2010), 132.

16. C. Augustine, *Administrative Law*, vol. 6 of *Commentary*, 205.

17. Gertrud Heinzelmann, "Woman and the Council—Hopes and Expectations: A Petition Addressed to the Preparatory Commission of Vatican Council II Concerning the Place of Woman in the Roman Catholic Church," in *Wir schweigen nicht länger! Frauen äußern sich zum II Vatikanischen Konzil*, ed. Gertrud Heinzelmann (Zurich: Interfeminas, 1964), 79. The text

includes Gertrud Heinzelmann's petition in German and in English. Citations are taken from the English text.

18. Ibid., 87.
19. Ibid.
20. Ibid., 92.
21. Ibid., 97.
22. Iris Müller and Ida Raming, "Kritische Auseinandersetzung mit den Gründen der katholischen Theologie betreffend den Ausschluß der Frau vom sakramentalen Priestertum," in *Wir schweigen nicht länger!*, ed. Heinzelmann, 61.
23. Ibid., 66.
24. Ibid.
25. Josefa Theresia Münch, "My Letters to the Pope," *Catholic Citizen: Journal of St. Joan's International Alliance* 72, no. 1 (1991): 18–29, www.womenpriests.org, accessed February 5, 2015.
26. Ibid.
27. Ibid.
28. Ibid.
29. Gino Concetti, "Die Frau und das Priestertum," *L'Osservatore Romano*, November 8–12, 1965, reprinted in Iris Müller and Ida Raming, *Unser Leben im Einsatz für Menschenrechte in der römisch-katholischen Kirche* (Münster: LIT, 2007), 183.
30. Ibid.
31. kfd-273, Statistische Auswertung der Umfrage unter kfd-Mitgliedern zur Liturgiereform, 1960/61; kfd-618, Leserzuschriften mit Anregungen für die Konzilseingabe "Wünsche katholischer Frauen…"; kfd-633, Leservorschläge für die Konzilseingabe, 1961; Marianne Dirks and Anneliese Lissner, "Wünsche katholischer Frauen, Mütter und Ehepaare an das Konzil," in *Konkrete Wünsche an das Konzil*, ed. Viktor Schurr (Kevelaer: Butzon & Becker, 1961), 57–93.
32. Ida Friederike Görres attacked the motives of the contributors to *Wir schweigen nicht länger!* in the German Catholic journal *Der Christliche Sonntag*. A heated debate ensued between Friederike Görres and Josefa Theresia Münch. See Ida Friederike Görres, "Über die Weihe von Frauen zu Priestern," *Der Christliche Sonntag*, June 20, 1965; Josefa Theresia Münch, "Sollen Frauen in der Kirche schweigen sein?," *Der Christliche Sonntag*, August 15, 1965; Münch, "Katholische Priesterinnen?," *Der Christliche Sonntag*, October 10, 1965.
33. For an excerpt, see Gertrud Heinzelmann, *Die getrennten Schwester: Frauen nach dem Konzil* (Zurich: Interfeminas, 1967), 78–79.
34. McDannell, *Spirit of Vatican II*, 108–109.
35. *Gaudium et Spes*, December 7, 1965, no. 29.
36. Jean Galot, *Theology of the Priesthood*, trans. Roger Balducelli (San Francisco: Ignatius Press, 1984), 183–187.
37. Richard P. McBrien, ed., *The HarperCollins Encyclopedia of Catholicism*, 6th ed. (New York: HarperCollins, 1995), 866.
38. Paul VI, *Ministeria Quadem*, August 15, 1972, par. 4 and 6.
39. Proponents and opponents of women's ordination accept that female deacons existed in the early Church but disagree on whether this early office constituted an ordained ministry. For a positive assessment, see John Wijngaards, *The Ordination of Women in the Catholic Church: Unmasking a Cuckoo's Egg Tradition* (London: Darton, Longman & Todd, 2001), 138–155; Peter Hünermann, ed., *Diakonat: Ein Amt für Frauen in der Kirche—Ein frauengerechtes Amt?* (Ostfildern: Schwabenverlag, 1999); for a negative assessment, see Hauke, *Women in the Priest-*

hood?, 440–444; and Aimé-Georges Martimort, *Deaconesses: An Historical Study*, trans. K. D. Whitehead (San Francisco: Ignatius Press, 1986).

40. kfd-767, Marianne Dirks, "Status und Aufgabe" (1967), 5.

41. Hildegard Harmsen, *Die Frau heute: Fragen an die Kirche* (Frankfurt: Kafke, 1967), 85.

42. 1983 Code of Canon Law, Canon 230, Paragraph 3.

43. Opponents and supporters of altar girls interpreted the omission differently. Opponents noted that Canon 2 stated that any law not specifically abrogated remained in effect. Supporters argued that Canon 203, Paragraph 2 implied that females could receive temporary deputation to act as altar servers. See John P. Beal, James A. Coriden, and Thomas J. Green, *New Commentary on the Code of Canon Law* (New York: Paulist Press, 2000), 1103.

44. kfd-730, Marianne Dirks, "Forderungen der Gegenwart an die Frauen- und Müttergemeinschaften" (November 24, 1953), 13.

45. kfd-612, Marianne Dirks, "Die Frau als Trägerin und Vermittlerin des eucharistisches Lebens" (lecture transcript), Eucharist World Congress (Munich, 1960), 2.

46. kfd-737, Marianne Dirks, "Priester und Frau" (lecture manuscript), Königstein, 1967.

47. kfd-592, Marianne Dirks, " Gedanken zur apostolischen und fürsorgerischen Arbeit in Kirche und Gesellschaft," *Korrespondenzblatt* (March 1965): 54–68.

48. kfd-742, Letter of Marianne Dirks to Rusche, February 10, 1969; kfd-767, "Status und Aufgabe der Frau und Kirche heute" (lecture manuscript), 2.

49. Heinzelmann, *Schwester*, 39.

50. Ibid., 20–21.

51. kfd-737, Marianne Dirks, "Zur Situation der Frau in der Kirche" (manuscript), *Diakonia* (May 1967): 4.

52. kfd-737, Marianne Dirks, "Priester und Frau" (lecture manuscript), Königstein, 1967.

53. kfd-1127, Letter of Marianne Dirks to Dr. Hildegard Harmsen, June 15, 1967.

54. kfd-746.1, 2. Europäischer Kongress für das Laienapostolat, 1966.

55. Ibid.

56. kfd-1127, Harmsen to Dirks, August 4, 1967.

57. kfd-1127, Dirks to Harmsen, August 7, 1967.

58. AEK, Archiv der DBK, Würzburger Synode 290, Letter from Dr. Barbara Wilk to Bishop Tenhumberg, May 4, 1971.

59. AEK, Archiv der DBK, Würzburger Synode 290, Letter from Bishop Tenhumberg to Dr. Barbara Wilk, May 26, 1971.

60. L. Bertsch et al., eds., *Gemeinsame Synode*, 595.

61. Experts disagreed on whether the New Testament alone substantiated the existence of an ordained female diaconate. Hünermann argued that biblical evidence was inconclusive, but he found the evidence in combination with other early documents of the Church convincing. See Peter Hünermann, "Conclusions Regarding the Female Diaconate," *Theological Studies* 36, no. 2 (June 1975): 326.

62. Bertsch et al., eds., *Gemeinsame Synode*, 595.

63. AEK, Archiv der DBK, Würzburger Synode 289, "Überlegungen zum priesterlichen Dienst in der Kirche," Working paper of Speyer theological students on the priesthood sent to the commission on October 3, 1971, by Leo Zirker on the recommendation of the priest Erich Ramstetter.

64. Müller and Raming, *Unser Leben im Einsatz*, 210.

65. AEK, Archiv der DBK, Würzburger Synode 539, SK VII, Protokoll der AG 3, September 15, 1971.

66. AEK, Archiv der DBK, Würzburger Synode 290, Letter from Barbara Bredlow to Bishop Klaus Hemmerle, November 12, 1972.

67. AEK, Archiv der DBK, Würzburger Synode 539, SK VII, Protokoll der AG 3, September 15, 1971.

68. The survey results were prefaced by the following remarks: "A few months ago, the KDFB conducted a survey on women's role in church and society. The following remarks are indicative of members' response, based on station in life (*Lebensstand*), career, and age." See JHD D0.5.7, 1973–1992, Marianne Pünder, "Die Frau in Kirche und Gesellschaft: Ergebnis einer Umfrage," *Die Christliche Frau* 62, no. 6 (1973): 167–173. In the section "Position in the Church," no distinctions are made except according to age.

69. JHD D0.5.7, 1973–1992, Marianne Pünder, 171.

70. Letter to the editor, *Frau und Mutter*, September 1973.

71. Ingebourg Rocholl-Gärtner, ed., *Anwalt der Frauen: Hermann Klens, Leben und Werk* (Düsseldorf: Klens, 1978), 93–95.

72. The 1920s secular women's movement in Germany addressed women's ordination. Works by Catholic authors supporting women's ordination include Ilse von Stach, *Die Frauen von Korinth: Dialoge* (Breslau: Bergstadt, 1929), and Engelbert Krebs, "Vom Priestertum der Frau," *Hochland* 19 (1922): 196–215. The 1920s women's ordination movement in Germany ended with Hitler's rise to power. For a brief history, see Ida Raming, *Frauenbewegung und Kirche: Bilanz eines 25-jährigen Kampfes für Gleichberechtigung und Befreiung der Frau seit dem 2. Vatikanischen Konzil* (Weinheim: Deutscher Studien, 1989), 38–39, and Hauke, *Women in the Priesthood?*, 60–61.

73. E. F. Sheridan, ed., *Love Kindness! The Social Teachings of the Canadian Bishops (1958–1989)—A Second Collection* (Sherbrooke: Éditions Paulines and the Jesuit Centre for Social Faith and Justice, 1991), 499.

74. Permanent Committee for International Congresses of the Lay Apostolate, *Man Today: Proceedings of the Third World Congress for the Lay Apostolate*, vol. 2 (Rome: Permanent Committee for International Congresses of the Lay Apostolate, 1968), 229–230. Hauke, *Women in the Priesthood?*, 72.

75. Betty Friedan, *It Changed My Life: Writings on the Women's Movement* (New York: Random House, 1976), 370.

76. Ibid., 292.

77. Ibid.

78. Ibid., 297.

79. Ibid.

80. Ibid.

81. Paul VI, *Address to the General Secretary of the "International Women's Year,"* November 6, 1974.

82. *Inter Insigniores*, October 15, 1976, par. 28.

83. Pirjo Markkola, "Patriarchy and Women's Emancipation," in *World Christianities, c. 1914–c. 2000*, ed. Hugh McLeod (New York: Cambridge University Press, 2006), 561–562.

84. Paula D. Nesbitt, *Feminization of the Clergy in America: Occupational and Organizational Perspectives* (New York: Oxford University Press, 1999), 30–32.

85. Halter, *The Papal 'No,'* 69–73.

86. Correspondence between Canterbury and Rome, first letter of Donald Coggan to Paul VI, July 9, 1975, http://www.womenpriests.org, accessed December 12, 2012.

87. Paul VI to Donald Coggan, November 25, 1975, http://www.womenpriests.org, accessed December 12, 2012.

88. Mary J. Henold, *Catholic and Feminist: The Surprising History of the American Catholic Feminist Movement* (Chapel Hill: University of North Carolina Press, 2008), 120.

89. Ibid., 121.

90. Raming, *Frauenbewegung und Kirche*, 100. See also "Ich tue mich schwer, meinen Papst zu lieben," *Der Spiegel*, July 30, 1984.

91. Henold, *Catholic and Feminist*, 123.

92. Ibid., 123–124.

93. Ibid., 124.

94. Ibid., 125.

95. Ibid., 136.

96. Pontifical Bible Commission, "Report: Can Women Be Priests?" *Origins* 6, no. 6 (July 1976): 92.

97. Leonard Swidler, "Introduction: Roma Locuta, Causa Finita?," in *Women Priests: A Catholic Commentary on the Vatican Declaration*, ed. Leonard and Arlene Swidler (New York: Paulist Press, 1976), 3.

98. Karl-Heinz Weger, "Endgültig keine Ordination der Frau?" *Orientierung* 41, no. 6 (1977): 64.

99. *Inter Insigniores*, October 15, 1976, par. 4.

100. Ibid., par. 5.

101. Ibid., par. 6.

102. Ibid.

103. Ibid.

104. Ibid., par. 10.

105. Ibid.

106. Ibid., par. 13.

107. Ibid., par. 17.

108. Ibid., par. 21.

109. Ibid., par. 27.

110. Ibid., par. 28.

111. Ibid., par. 31.

112. Raimondo Spiazzi, "The Advancement of Women according to the Church," *L'Osservatore Romano*, February 10, 1977.

113. Ibid.

114. Numerous scholars have underscored Balthasar's influence on John Paul II's "theology of the body." See, e.g., Susan Rakoczy, "Mixed Messages: John Paul II's Writings on Women," in *The Vision of John Paul II: Assessing His Thought and Influence*, ed. Gerard Mannion (Collegeville, MN: Liturgical Press, 2008), 159–183; Agneta Sutton, "Complementarity of the Sexes: Karl Barth, Hans Urs von Balthasar, and John Paul II," *New Blackfriars* 87, no. 1010 (2006): 418–433; Brendan Leahy, "John Paul II and Hans Urs von Balthasar," in *The Legacy of John Paul II*, ed. Gerald O'Collins and Michael A. Hays (New York: Burns & Oates, 2008), 31–50.

115. Hans Urs von Balthasar, "The Uninterrupted Tradition of the Church," *L'Osservatore Romano*, February 24, 1977.

116. Ibid.

117. Ibid.

118. Albert Ebneter, "Keine Frauen im Priesteramt." *Orientierung*, no. 1 (1977): 26.

119. Ibid.

120. Ibid.

121. Hans Küng and Gerhard Lohfink, "Keine Priestertum der Frau?," *Theologische Quartalschrift*, no. 157 (1977): 146.

122. Karl Rahner, "Priestertum der Frau?," *Stimmen der Zeit*, no. 195 (1977): 293.

123. Ibid.

124. Carroll Stuhlmueller, "Internal Indecisiveness," in *Women Priests: A Catholic Commentary on the Vatican Declaration*, ed. Leonard Swidler and Arlene Swidler (New York: Paulist Press, 1977), 23.

125. Ibid.

126. *Inter Insigniores*, October 15, 1976, par. 8.

127. Heinzelmann, ed., *Wir schweigen nicht länger!*, 84.

128. "Orientierungs- und Arbeitsprogramm der kfd 1979," *Frau und Mutter*, no. 9, 1979.

129. Wilhelm Kempf, "Frauen in der christlichen Kirche," *Frau und Mutter*, no. 7–8, 1981.

130. CDWDS, *Inaestimabile Donum*, April 3, 1980, no. 18, http://www.ewtn.com, accessed April 2, 2012.

131. kfd-1335, Messedienerinnen-Aktion, Reader responses, June 1980–June 1981.

132. Ibid.

133. kfd-1335, Messedienerinnen-Aktion, Reader responses, October 1980.

134. kfd-1335, Messedienerinnen-Aktion, Letter from Anneliese Lissner to Cardinal Höffner, June 13, 1980.

135. Letter to the editor, *Frau und Mutter*, September 1983.

136. Hildegard Lüning, "Frauen verändern die Gotteslehre," *Orientierung* 44, no. 14/15 (1980): 150.

137. kfd-1175, Letter from the Kreis katholischer Frauen im Heliand-Bund to kfd President, Irmgard Jalowy, November 1987.

138. kfd-1335, Messedienerinnen-Aktion, Reader responses, June 1980–June 1981.

139. The Traditionalisten-Bewegung, later renamed the Liga katholischer Traditionalisten, was founded in 1965 in France; Elisabeth Gerster launched the German chapter in 1967. The guiding principle was that "the Church needed no reform." See Elisabeth Gerster, *Die katholische Traditionalisten-Bewegung: Eine Selbstdarstellung* (Cologne: Benziger, 1970), 9. Hans Milch, Walter Hoeres, and Fritz Feuling founded Bewegung für Papst und Kirche in 1969 in protest against Vatican II theological innovations; the group supported priestly celibacy and *Humanae Vitae*. Marienkinder (Children of Mary)—established in 1983 in Augsburg, Germany—focused on Marian devotion. The group made headlines in 1985 when its founders were excommunicated after conducting a Corpus Christi procession at the same time as the official diocesan procession. In 1996, one of the group's founders, Joseph Zanker, received a three-year prison sentence after being found guilty of twenty-one counts of coercion and assault against youth members. In 2009, the group regained its status as an official Catholic organization. On the excommunication and later rehabilitation of the group, see Barbara Hans, "Bishop Mixa buhlt um Sektierer," *Der Spiegel*, March 6, 2009; and Stefan Mayr, "Mixa holt Sektierer in die Kirche," *SZ*, March 4, 2009. For a brief account of the other groups, see Barbara Hans and Christian Wiesel, "Christlicher Fundamentalismus: Kirche der Extreme," *Spiegel Online*, February 5, 2009, http://www.spiegel.de, accessed March 12, 2013.

140. Hanna-Renate Laurien, "Die Frau als mündiger Christ," *Orientierung* 45, no. 3 (1981): 33.

141. kfd-1335, Letter from Auxiliary Bishop Walther Kampe to Cardinal Höffner, June 10, 1980.

142. Ibid.

143. Ibid.

144. CDWDS, "Vatican Communication on Female Altar Servers," March 15, 1994, no. 4, http://www.etwn.com, accessed January 13, 2013.

145. "SPD-Frauen: Lob für Bischöfe, Kritik am ZdK": KNA, October 29, 1981.

146. Ibid.

147. kfd-1170, Letter from the kfd central office to Cardinal Höffner, DBK chair, November 26, 1981.

148. Ibid.

149. "Ich hoffe, daß nicht noch mehr Frauen aus der Kirche ausziehen," BDKJ-Informationsdienst, December 19, 1984.

150. kfd-1188, Letter from Anneliese Lissner to a local kfd chapter, April 9, 1984.

151. Letter from T.S. of Weener/Ems to Secretary-General of the kfd, Anneliese Lissner, May 21, 1984.

152. "BDKJ Münster: Offener Brief an den Papst," BDKJ-Informationsdienst, June 15, 1987.

153. "Päpstin mit Recht auf Heirat," Der Spiegel, December 21, 1992.

154. In 1970, Ida Raming completed her habilitation, "Der Ausschluß der Frau vom priesterlichen Amt—gottgewollte Tradition oder Diskriminierung?," under Karl Rahner. However, it was not published until 1973.

155. Raming, Frauenbewegung und Kirche, 92–93. See also Angelika Strotmann, "Arbeitsgemeinschaft Feminismus und Kirchen," in Handbuch Feministische Theologie, ed. Christine Schaumberger and Monika Maaßen (Münster: Morgana, 1986), 158; Magdalene Bußmann, "Männer, Mitren und Macht," in Beten allein genügt nicht: Briefe an den Papst, ed. Thomas Seiterlich (Hamburg: Rowolt, 1987), 105.

156. J. M. Potter in New Woman—New Church 7, no. 2 (April 1974): 5, cited in Raming, Frauenbewegung und Kirche, 95.

157. Raming, Frauenbewegung und Kirche, 94.

158. Ibid., 97.

159. For a brief organization history, see the website of Maria von Magdala: Initiative Gleichberechtigung der Frauen in der Kirche, "Die Chronik," http://www.mariavonmagdala.de, accessed December 12, 2012.

160. Ibid.

161. "Papst und Päpstin," Die Zeit, February 3, 1989.

162. See Ida Raming, "Relevanz und Stellenwert des Kirchenrechts in der feministischen Theologie," in Theologiefeministisch: Disziplinen, Schwerpunkte, Richtungen (Düsseldorf: Patmos, 1988), 120–121. For the ecumenical approach, see, e.g., Luise Schottroff, Silvia Schroer, and Marie-Theres Wacker, eds., Feministische Exegese: Forschungserträge zur Bibel aus der Perspektive von Frauen (Darmstadt: Wissenschaftliche Buchgesellschaft, 1995); Renate Jost and Eveline Valtink, eds., Ihr aber, für wen haltet ihr mich? Auf dem Weg zu einer feministisch-befreiungstheologischen Revision von Christologie (Gütersloh: Kaiser, 1996); Michael N. Ebertz, a sociologist of religion, reached a similar conclusion in 2006, noting that many women in the Catholic Church stayed active in the Church by creating "spaces within the Church free of patriarchal structures" or by finding "a place within Catholic organizations, particularly those oriented towards women, where they can vent their frustrations." See Michael N. Ebertz, "Exodus? Frauen und die katholische Kirche in Deutschland," in Katholiken in den USA und Deutschland: Kirche, Gesellschaft und Politik, ed. Wilhelm Damberg and Antonius Liedhegener (Münster: Aschendorff, 2006), 269.

163. Rosemary Radford Ruether, "Should Women Want Women Priests or Women-Church?," Feminist Theology 20, no. 63 (2011): 68.

164. Mary Hunter, cited in ibid.

165. Ulrike Wagner-Rau, *Zwischen Vaterwelt und Feminismus: Eine Studie zur pastoralen Identität von Frauen* (Gütersloh: Gütersloher Verlagshaus, 1992), 202–205.

166. Ibid., 164–169.

167. kfd-1175, "Die Bischöfe und die Frauen: Man kommt sich näher," KNA, July 16, 1987.

168. Of the 103 Episcopal conferences represented, 34 were from Africa, 24 from America, 24 from Europe, 17 from Asia, and 4 from Oceania. Also present were 23 heads of dicasteries of the Roman Curia and leaders of various *movimenti*, such as Opus Dei, the Emmanuelites, Focolare, and Charismatics.

169. Roberto Suro, "Pope Opens Synod of Bishops on Role of the Laity," *NYT*, October 2, 1987.

170. Ludwig Kaufmann, "Bischofssynode: Die verdrängte Frauenfrage—Dritter Bericht zur Bischofssynode," *Orientierung* 51, no. 21 (1987): 226.

171. Ibid.

172. John Paul II, *Christifideles Laici*, December 30, 1988, no. 49.

173. "Katholische Frauengemeinschaft Deutschlands: Pressemitteilung," KNA, November 5, 1987.

174. John Paul II, *Mulieris Dignitatem*, August 15, 1988, no. 1, par. 3.

175. See, e.g., Kimberly A. Kennedy, "*Totus Tuus Sum*, Maria: Pope John Paul II's Framing of the Feminine Genius," in *The Rhetoric of Pope John Paul II*, ed. Joseph R. Blaney and Joseph P. Zompetti (New York: Lexington Books, 2009), 103–150.

176. *Mulieris Dignitatem*, August 15, 1988, no. 3, par. 4.

177. Ibid., no. 4, par. 1.

178. Ibid., no. 11, par. 6.

179. Ibid., no. 10, par. 4.

180. Ibid., no. 7, par. 8.

181. Ibid., no. 6, par. 5; emphasis in original.

182. In *Evangelium Vitae*, John Paul II cited *Mulieris Dignitatem* twice. He did so the first time to establish the coresponsibility of the father for the child. He made the second reference to *Mulieris Dignitatem* when he reasserted woman's primary contribution to church and society as mother; through motherhood, she taught humanity the authenticity of human relations. See John Paul II, *Evangelium Vitae*, March 25, 1995, nn. 55, 134.

183. "New feminists" supported John Paul's II's views on women's place in the Church; they did not champion gender equality.

184. See, e.g., Prudence Allen, "*Mulieris Dignitatem* Twenty Years Later: An Overview of the Document and Challenges," *Ave Maria Law Review* 13, no. 8 (2007): 13–47; Michele M. Schumaker, "John Paul II's Theology of the Body on Trial: Responding to the Accusation of the Biological Reduction of Women," *Nova et Vetera* (Engl. ed.) 10, no. 2 (2012): 463–484.

185. *Mulieris Dignitatem*, August 15, 1988, no. 7, par. 1.

186. Ibid., no. 6, par. 1.

187. Ibid., no. 21, par. 3.

188. Ibid., no. 20, par. 5.

189. Ibid., no. 25, par. 5; emphasis in original.

190. Ibid., no. 25, par. 4.

191. Ibid., no. 25, par. 6 and no. 26, par. 1; emphasis in original.

192. Gregory Baum, "Bulletin: The Apostolic Letter Mulieris Dignitatem," *Concilium* 206 (1989): 147.

193. Ibid.

194. Ibid.

195. Elisabeth Gössmann, "Kommentar," in *Die Zeit der Frau: Apostolisches Schreiben "Mulieris Dignitatem"* (Freiburg: Herder, 1988), 145–146. Like the feminist theologian Elisabeth Schüssler-Fiorenza, Gössmann had difficulty securing a university teaching post in West Germany. From 1956 to 1989, she taught in Japan; since 1990, she has been an extraordinary professor in the Faculty of Philosophy, Philosophy of Science and Religious Studies at the Ludwig Maximillian University in Munich. See her curriculum vitae at http://www.philosophie.uni-muenchen.de, accessed April 10, 2015.

196. Irene Willig, KNA, October 4, 1988, cited in ibid., 146.

197. Maria von Magdala, "'Gleiche Würde'—aber keine gleichen Rechte: Stellungsnahme der Frauengruppe Maria von Magdala zum Apostolischen Schreiben Johannes Pauls II. *Mulieris Dignitatem*," cited in Raming, *Frauenbewegung und Kirche*, 99. In 1995, Monika Kringels-Kemen also made the comparison. See Monika Kringels-Kemen, "Wider die Apartheid am Altar," in *Nennt uns nicht Brüder: Frauen in der Kirche durchbrechen das Schweigen*, ed. Norbert Sommer (Stuttgart: Kreuz, 1985), 221–228.

198. Susan A. Ross, "The Bridegroom and the Bride: The Theological Anthropology of John Paul II and Its Relation to the Bible and Homosexuality," in *Sexual Diversity and Catholicism: Toward the Development of Moral Theology*, ed. Patricia Beattie Jung and Joseph Andrew Coray (Collegeville, MN: Liturgical Press, 1989), 53.

199. Beattie, *New Catholic Feminism*, 110.

200. Ibid., 111.

201. Ibid.,13.

202. Ibid.,105.

203. In fact, the kfd editorial staff declined to make any claims about the percentage of supporters and opponents for this very reason. See Letter to the editor, *Frau und Mutter*, July–August 1989.

204. Letter to the editor, *Frau und Mutter*, July–August 1989.

205. kfd-1170, Reader responses concerning *Mulieris Dignitatem*, January 23, 1990.

206. Letter to the editor, *Frau und Mutter*, March 1989.

207. kfd-1170, *Frauen und Kirche*, 1993 Allensbach survey commissioned by the DBK.

208. John Paul II, *Veritatis Splendor*, August 6, 1993, no. 67.

209. Ibid., no. 116.

210. John Paul II, *Sacerdotalis Ordinatio*, May 22, 1994, no. 4, par. 2.

211. Thomas J. Reese, *Inside the Vatican: The Politics and Organization of the Catholic Church* (Cambridge, MA: Harvard University Press, 1996), 276.

212. Commission on Woman in the Church created by the Belgian Bishops' Conference, "Who May Dwell within Your Tent?" (Wie Mag Toeven Binnen Uw Tent?), translated from the Flemish by John Wijngaards and reprinted with permission of the commission on the website Women Can Be Priests: The International Catholic Online Authority on Women Ministries, http://www.womenpriests.org, accessed December 12, 2012.

213. CDF, "Responsum ad Propositum Dubium Concerning the Teaching Contained in *Ordinatio Sacerdotalis*," October 28, 1995.

214. "Päpstin mit Recht auf Heirat," *Der Spiegel*, December 21, 1992.

215. John Paul II, "Address to the German Bishops on the Occasion of their *ad Limina* Visit," November 20, 1999, no. 10, par. 1. *Ad limina* visit refers to the visit to Rome that bishops make every five years to report on their dioceses.

216. Halter, *The Papal 'No,'* 146.

217. See, e.g., Sophie de Ravinel, "Sept Femmes 'ordonnées' prêtre sur le Danube," *Le Figaro*, July 2, 2002; Kate Connolly and Philip Willan, "Vatican Casts Out 'Ordained' Women:

Excommunicated Danube Seven Remain Defiant in the Name of Religious Equal Rights," *Guardian* (London), August 6, 2002; Matthias Stolz, "Sieben Tage mit Ida Raming," *Die Zeit*, August 15, 2002.

218. Halter, *The Papal 'No,'* 147. For an extensive list of irregularly ordained Catholic women, see the website of the international organization Roman Catholic Womenpriests, http://www.romancatholicwomenpriests.org, accessed December 11, 2012.

219. Halter, *The Papal 'No,'* 106. McEnroy sued for breach of contract. The Indiana State Supreme Court ruled that it lacked jurisdiction because of the First Amendment's guarantee of religious freedom. A copy of the decision can be found at http://law.justia.com, accessed December 11, 2012.

220. Manfred Hauke, *God or Goddess? Feminist Theology: What Is it? Where Does It Lead?*, trans. David Kipp (San Francisco: Ignatius Press, 1995), 116.

221. Ibid., 115.

222. Donna Steichen, *Ungodly Rage: The Hidden Face of Catholic Feminism* (San Francisco: Ignatius Press, 1991), 371.

3. ARTIFICIAL CONTRACEPTION

1. For a comprehensive history of Catholic theological discourses on contraception from 50 AD to 1965, see John T. Noonan, Jr., *Contraception: A History of Its Treatment by the Catholic Theologians and Canonists* (Cambridge, MA: Belknap Press of Harvard University Press, 1965).

2. Herzog, *Sexuality in Europe*, 98.

3. Ibid., 96–106.

4. The pros and cons of a smaller Catholic Church became the subject of heated Catholic debate under John Paul II and Benedict XVI. See Ian Fisher, "Benedict XVI and the Church That May Shrink or May Not," *NYT*, May 29, 2005, http://www.nytimes.com, accessed May 14, 2012.

5. Pius XII, *Discurso al Congreso de la Union Católica Italiana de Obstétricas con la colaboración de la Federación Nacional de Colegios de Comadronas Católicas*, October 29, 1951. In his 1930 encyclical *Casti Connubii*, Pius XI noted that sexual relations between married couples during the "sterile time" was lawful so long as the intention was procreation. However, he did not address the deliberate use of these days as a means of limiting family size; this omission led to conflicting theological interpretations. See Pius XI, *Casti Connubii* December 31, 1930, no 59.

6. Noonan, *Contraception*, 446.

7. Lynch quoted in ibid., 446–447.

8. See, e.g., Augustine, *Of the Good of Marriage*, no. 1, www.newadvent.org, accessed October 28, 2011, and Thomas Aquinas, *On Love and Charity: Commentary on the Sentences of Peter Lombard*, trans. Peter A. Kwasniewski, Thomas Bolin, and Joseph Bolin (Washington, DC: Catholic University of America Press, 2008), 4.31.1.1.

9. Noonan, *Contraception*, 495.

10. Herbert Doms, *The Meaning of Marriage*, trans. George Sayer (New York: Sheed & Ward, 1939), 185–189.

11. Ibid., 165–197.

12. Rölli-Alkemper, *Familie im Wiederaufbau*, 132.

13. See *Casti Connubii*, December 31, 1930, no. 7.

14. Ibid., no. 55.

15. Ibid., no. 56.

16. Ibid., no. 57.

17. Ibid., no. 61.

18. Ibid., no. 26. Pius XI did place limits on the woman's subordination to her husband. He held that subordination could not compromise the dignity owing a woman as a human being.

19. Quoted in Heineman, *What Difference Does a Husband Make?*, 128.

20. Quoted in ibid.

21. Ibid.

22. Ibid., 130.

23. Silies, *Liebe, Lust und Last*, 40.

24. Heineman, *What Difference Does a Husband Make?*, 128–130. For a more in-depth account of West Germans' embrace of alternative family forms in the late 1940s, see Robert G. Moeller, *Protecting Motherhood: Women and the Family in the Politics of Postwar West Germany* (Berkeley: University of California Press, 1993); Silies, *Liebe, Lust und Last*, 36–45.

25. Herzog, *Sex after Fascism*, 103.

26. See Silies, *Liebe, Lust und Last*, 40, and Heineman, *What Difference Does a Husband Make?*, 136.

27. "Die Mutter-die Seele der Familie," *Frau und Mutter*, January 1951.

28. CDU draft quoted in Heineman, *What Difference Does a Husband Make?*, 143.

29. Ibid., 148.

30. Moeller, *Protecting Motherhood*, 102.

31. Maria D. Mitchell, *The Origins of Christian Democracy: Politics and Confession in Modern Germany* (Ann Arbor: University of Michigan Press), 171–173.

32. Heineman, *What Difference Does a Husband Make?*, 147–150.

33. Moeller, *Protecting Motherhood*, 137.

34. Hanna Schissler, "German and American Women between Domesticity and the Workplace," in *The United States and Germany in the Era of the Cold War 1945–1968: A Handbook*, vol. 1, ed. Detlev Junker (Cambridge: Cambridge University Press, 2004), 564.

35. Heineman, *What Difference Does a Husband Make?*, 157–158.

36. Ibid., 158.

37. Moeller, *Protecting Motherhood*, 138.

38. Ludwig Erhard, *Deutsche Wirtschaftspolitik: Der Weg der sozialen Marktwirtschaft* (Düsseldorf: Econ, 1962).

39. Erica Carter, *How German Is She? Postwar Reconstruction and the Consuming Woman* (Ann Arbor: University of Michigan Press, 1997), 43.

40. Ibid., 59–65.

41. Moeller, *Protecting Womanhood*, 140.

42. Quoted in Mitchell, *Origins of Christian Democracy*, 109.

43. Ibid.

44. Ibid., 82.

45. Moeller, *Protecting Motherhood*, 43–44.

46. Silies, *Liebe, Lust und Last*, 42.

47. Christine von Oertzen, *The Pleasure of a Surplus Income: Part-time Work, Gender Politics, and Social Change in West Germany, 1955–1969*, trans. Pamela Selwyn (New York: Berghahn Books, 2007), 4.

48. Ibid., 47–48.

49. Silies, *Liebe, Lust und Last*, 56–57.

50. Herzog, *Sex after Fascism*, 101.

51. Elizabeth Heineman, *Before Porn Was Legal: The Erotic Empire of Beate Uhse* (Chicago: University of Chicago Press, 2011), 61–86.

52. "Wenige aber gute . . . und die Antwort," *Frau und Mutter*, February 1951.

53. Idamarie Solltmann, "Zum großen Frauentag," *Frau und Mutter*, August 1954.

54. See Georg Volk, " . . . und was sagt der Artzt dazu?," *Frau und Mutter*, February 1951; Georg Volk, " . . . und was sagt der Artzt dazu?," *Frau und Mutter*, June 1951.

55. Letter to the editor, *Frau und Mutter*, August 1959.

56. Anneliese Lissner, "Probleme der Ehemoral," *Frau und Mutter*, April 1965.

57. B189/6180–71, *Rheinische Merkur*, May 19, 1975.

58. Gertrud von Le Fort, *Die ewige Frau; Die Frau in der Zeit; Die zeitlose Frau* (Munich: Josef Kösel & Friedrich Pustet, 1934).

59. Ibid., 84–95.

60. E. R. Maexie, *Die Frau vor der Zukunft* (Vienna: Herold, 1961), 95–96.

61. Hans March, "Zur Sexual-Ethik," *Stimmen der Zeit: Monatsschrift für das Geistesleben der Gegenwart* 157, no. 19 (1954–1955): 289–301.

62. See Marina Warner, *Alone of All Her Sex: The Myth and the Cult of the Virgin Mary* (New York: Alfred A. Knopf, 1976), 58.

63. Ibid., 337.

64. ZdK, *Arbeitstagung Freiburg*, April 10–14, 1962 (Paderborn: Bonifatius Press, 1962), 32. Prior to 1966, ZdK publications called the biennial congresses "workshops" (*Arbeitstagung*). The eighty-first meeting in 1966 was the first to be designated a Catholic congress (Katholikentag).

65. Australian public resistance amounted to two Catholic doctors. See Sabine Sieg, "'Anovlar': Die erste europäische Pille: Zur Geschichte eines Medikaments," in *Die Pille: Von der Lust und von der Liebe*, ed. Gisela Staupe and Lisa Vieth (Berlin: Rowohlt, 1996), 139.

66. Ibid., 138–140.

67. Anne-Marie Durand-Wever, "Eine Pille reguliert die Fruchtbarkeit." *Stern*, June 20, 1961.

68. Silies, *Liebe, Lust und Last*, 80.

69. Ibid.

70. On theological disapproval prior to 1968, see Noonan, *Contraception*, and Ambroggio Valsecchi, *Controversy: The Birth Control Debate, 1958–1968*, trans. Dorothy White (Washington, DC: Corpus Books, 1968).

71. According to this doctrine, a harmful action is permissible if it is the side effect (i.e., the "double effect") of an action that produces a greater good. The harmful effect may be a foreseen effect, but the person may not will the bad act as a means of pursuing a greater good.

72. Pius XII, *Discurso al VII Congreso de la Sociedad Internacional de Hematología*, September 12, 1958.

73. Valsecchi, *Controversy*, 28.

74. Lambruschini, quoted in ibid., 29.

75. Prior to 1963, both Häring and Böckle endorsed the use of progestational drugs for therapeutic purposes only. See Bernhard Häring, "Verantwortete Elternschaft: Aber wie?," *Theologischer Digest* 2 (1959): 153–159; Franz Böckle, "Die sittliche Beurteilung sterilisierender Medikamente," *Herder Korrespondenz* 16 (1962): 354–371.

76. Doms supported using the rhythm method if serious reasons existed for not having a child. See Doms, *Meaning of Marriage*, 196.

77. J. M. Reuss, "Eheliche Hingabe und Zeugung: Ein Diskussionsbeitrag zu einem differenzierten Problem," *Tübinger Theologische Quartalschrift* 143 (1963): 454–476.

78. See Dietrich von Hildebrand, *Das trojanische Pferd in der Stadt Gottes* (Regensburg: Habbel, 1968). Hildebrand left Germany for the United States in 1941 but remained an active participant in German theological debates during the postwar era.

79. Wiltgen, *Inside Story*, 305–306. The commission was composed of members of the

Theological Commission and the Commission of the Lay Apostolate. This "mixed" commission was formed in 1962 after the council fathers rejected the schema on the Church drafted by the Preparatory Commission. Each subcommission of the "mixed" commission was assigned responsibility for revising one chapter of the schema.

80. Ibid., 306–307.

81. *Lumen Gentium*, November 21, 1964, no. 31; see also *Apostolicam Actuositatem*, November 18, 1965, no. 2; *Presbyterorum Ordinis*, December 7, 1965, no. 9; *Ad Gentes*, December 7, 1965, no. 21.

82. Ottaviani quoted in Wiltgen, *Inside Story*, 307.

83. Thomas Fox, *Sexuality and Catholicism* (New York: George Braziller, 1995), 46–48.

84. Peter Hebblethwaite, *Paul VI: The First Modern Pope* (London: HarperCollins, 1993), 443.

85. Published first in John C. Ford and J. J. Lynch, "Contraception: A Matter of Practical Doubt," *Homiletic and Pastoral Review* (April 1968): 563, reprinted in Hebblethwaite, *Paul VI*, 444.

86. Bernhard Häring, *My Witness for the Church*, trans. Leonard Swidler (New York: Paulist Press, 1992), 67.

87. Hebblethwaite, *Paul VI*, 445.

88. *Gaudium et Spes*, December 7, 1965, pt. II, ch. 1, n. 14.

89. On Vatican I, see John M. Bellito, *The General Councils: A History of Twenty-one Councils from Nicaea to Vatican II* (New York: Paulist Press, 2002), 117–125.

90. *The HarperCollins Encyclopedia of Catholicism* noted that the two documents contained fifteen references to episcopal governance as "collegial" and thirty-seven references to the hierarchy being united as a "collegium." See McBrien, ed., *HarperCollins Encyclopedia of Catholicism*, 330. See also *Lumen Gentium*, November 21, 1964, no. 22.

91. M. T. Litonjua, *Creative Fractures: Sociology and Theology* (Bloomington, IN: Author House, 2011), 237.

92. The commission initially consisted of six members; by its final meeting in May 1966, it had seventy-five members. See Kaiser, *Politics of Sex*, 46–47.

93. Ibid., 46–56.

94. *Casti Connubii*, December 31, 1930, no. 5.

95. Auxiliary Bishop Reuss of Mainz in a letter to Pope Paul VI, January 1965, quoted in Kaiser, *Politics of Sex*, 76.

96. Ibid., 69–76.

97. Hebblethwaite, *Paul VI*, 468.

98. Ibid., 469.

99. "Majority Papal Commission Report," 162.

100. Hebblethwaite, *Paul VI*, 487.

101. B189/1176–6. In a letter to Käte Strobel, the minister of Family (SPD), dated January 2, 1970, a West German man accused the minister of being "deeply influenced by the papal encyclical." The man believed that papal influence had been the reason Strobel had not supported making oral contraception available over the counter.

102. B189/1178–223, "Die Pille ist noch kein Geschäft," *Handelsblatt*, October 22, 1964.

103. B189/1178–132, "Deutsche Frauen an dritter Stelle im Antibabypillen-Verbrauch?," Deutsche Presse-Agentur, August 1968.

104. Silies, *Liebe, Lust und Last*, 103.

105. Roughly 40 percent of "thalidomide babies" died before their first birthday; those who did live had severe defects, including missing limbs and internal organs. See *Webster's New World Medical Dictionary*, 3d ed. (New York: Wiley, 2008), 420.

106. B189/11766-197-98, Letter from Dr. Bernhardt, Federal Ministry of Health to M.S., September 21, 1962.

107. Sieg, "'Anovlar,'" 132.

108. Katholischen Sozialwissenschaftlichen Zentralstelle Mönchengladbach, ed., "Religion ohne Kirche? Eine Herausforderung für Glaube und Kirche," *Kirche und Gesellschaft*, no. 30 (1977): 13.

109. Dagmar Herzog, "Between Secularization, Postfascism, and the Rise of Liberation Theology," in *Die Gegenwart Gottes in der modernen Gesellschaft: Transzendenz und religiöse Vergemeinschaftung in Deutschland*, ed. Michael Geyer and Lucian Hölscher (Göttingen: Wallstein, 2006), 433.

110. Quoted in Jarausch, *After Hitler*, 166.

111. Julius Döpfner, "Instruction to the Confessors of the Munich Archdiocese (1965)," in *The Church and Contraception*, ed. John T. Noonan, Jr. (New York: Paulist Press, 1967), 74.

112. Letter to the editor, *Der Spiegel*, August 12, 1968.

113. Walter Dirks, "Der Papst gegen die Kirche," *Frankfurter Hefte* 23, no. 9 (1968): 625.

114. Sartory and Sartory, *Strukturkrise einer Kirche*, 139.

115. Ibid., 147-148.

116. ZdK, 2103-1864, Letter from Karl Furst zu Löwenstein to Cardinal Döpfner, August 12, 1968.

117. Jaeger quoted in Sartory and Sartory, *Strukturkrise einer Kirche*, 143-144.

118. DBK, *Wort der deutschen Bischöfe zur seelsorglichen Lage nach dem Erscheinen der Enzyklika "Humanae Vitae,"* www.dbk.de, accessed May 12, 2011.

119. ZdK, KT-Essen 1968, Presse-Echo, no. 8. See, e.g., "Heftige Opposition auf dem 82. Katholikentag," *Nordwest Zeitung Oldenburg*, September 4, 1968; "Radikale Katholiken: Papst soll Abtreten!" *Fränkische Landeszeitung* (Ansbach), September 5, 1968.

120. ZdK, KT-Essen 1968, Presse-Echo, no. 10, "Auf der Empore knipst die politische Polizei," *Schwäbisches Tagblatt*, September 6, 1968.

121. ZdK, KT-Essen 1968, Presse-Echo, no. 10, Wilhelm Kirchner, "APO ist gefährlicher als NPD," *WAZ*, September 6, 1968.

122. ZdK, KT-Essen 1968, Presse-Echo, no. 9, Reinhold Noll, "Was muß der gute Katholik tun?," *Fränkische Nachrichten*, September 5, 1968. Heinz Schweden, editor of the *Rheinische Post*, reached the same conclusion. See ZdK, KT-Essen, 1968, Presse-Echo, no. 11, Heinz Schweden, "Gewissen gegen Gehorsam," *Rheinische Post*, September 7, 1968.

123. ZdK, KT-Essen 1968, Presse-Echo, no. 11. "Ehe = 2 × 1—sonst nichts?," *Schwäbische Donau Zeitung*, September 7, 1968.

124. See, e.g., the "Postfach Synode" results: Catholics identified celibacy as the most critical issue, and interconfessional marriage was a distant second. JHD, Würzburger Synode: ZDF Postfach Synode, 2.1/012-037.

125. "Halbe Wahrheit," *Der Spiegel*, March 6, 1972.

126. ZdK 2103, 1854, no. 2, Präsidium Generalsekretariat—Pres. Bernhard Vogel, Letter from a pariah priest to Bernhard Vogel, June 5, 1974.

127. B189/2820-0026, Katholische Ärztearbeit Deutschlands, Ärztliche Stellungnahme zu medizinischen Fragen der Enzyklika 'Humanae Vitae.'

128. B189/2819-0124-125, Protokoll über die 5. Zusammenkunft zur Erörterung von Grundsatzfragen der Geschlechterziehung und Familienplanung am 2. Oktober 1968 in Bundesministerium für Familie und Jugend.

129. B189/6180-12, Gertrud Zimmermann, Internal memo concerning *Stellungnahme des*

Deutschen Caritasverbandes zum 'Bericht der Kommission zur Auswertung der Erfahrungen mit dem reformierten § 218 StGB (entspr. 24./25.06.1980), July 23, 1980.

130. kfd-746, World Union of Catholic Women's Organizations (WUCWO) meeting, October 31–November 5, 1968.

131. kfd-1914, Geschichte der Katholischen Frauengemeinschaft Deutschlands.

132. See Katholische Frauengemeinschaft Deutschlands, *Auf dem Weg in die Zukunft: Orientierungs- und Arbeitsprogramm 1979*, http://www.kfd-bundesverband.de, accessed November 4, 2014.

133. kfd-1332, Anneliese Lissner, "Feministische Theologie als Befreiungstheologie," 1980 Catholic Congress in Berlin.

134. kfd-1170, Papal visit to Germany, November 1980.

135. kfd-1170, Letter from H.K. to the kfd central office, December 14, 1980.

136. kfd-1170, Letter from the St. Maria Magdalena Rheinbreitbach chapter to the kfd central office, December 16, 1980.

137. 1985 Allensbach survey, quoted in "Eine 'dramatische' Abkehr junger Frauen von der Kirche," *Frau und Mutter*, April 1986.

138. ZdK, KT-78, 82, and 84, 8000/1077, "Berichterstattung: 'Frauen: Kinder, Küche, Kirche,'" *Die Zeit*, September 10, 1982.

139. ZdK, KT-Aachen 1986, Zeitungsausschnitte, box 1, Harald Biskup, "Höffner verlangt Glaubensgehorsam," *Kölner Stadt-Anzeiger*, September 28–29, 1985.

140. Alois Rummel, "Familienplanung ohne Besserwisserei: Joseph Kardinal Höffner definiert die Königsteiner Erklärung der deutschen Bischöfe," *Rheinische Merkur/Christ und Welt*, February 8, 1986.

141. kfd-842.1, Letter from Ria Pechel to Joseph Höffner, February 17, 1986.

142. kfd-842.1, Letter from Irma Jalowy to Joseph Höffner, February 21, 1986.

143. kfd-1175, "Protokollauszug: Sitzung der Pastoralkommission am 7./8. Juli 1987."

4. THE ABORTION DEBATE

1. On shifts in canon law, see Sabine Demel, *Abtreibung zwischen Straffreiheit und Exkommunikation: Weltliches und kirchliches Strafrecht auf dem Prüfstand* (Stuttgart: Kohlhammer, 1995).

2. Exod. 21:21–22 (New American Bible, 1970).

3. Fox, *Sexuality and Catholicism*, 91–95.

4. Demel, *Abtreibung zwischen Straffreiheit*, 80–81, 86–88.

5. Fox, *Sexuality and Catholicism*, 94.

6. See Thomas Aquinas, *Summa Theologica*, q. 78, art. 1. On early Church fathers' views on delayed hominization, see David Albert Jones, *The Soul of the Embryo: An Inquiry into the Status of the Human Embryo in the Christian Tradition* (New York: Continuum, 2004).

7. Jones, *Soul of the Embryo*, 171–193.

8. Ranke-Heinemann, *Eunuchs for the Kingdom*, 304.

9. Sister Margaret McBride's excommunication received widespread coverage in the American press. See, e.g., "Sister Margaret McBride: Don't Confess," *National Public Radio*, May 21, 2012, http://www.npr.org. See also Catholic News Service, "Arizona Mercy Nun reinstated," *Dialog*, http://thedialog.org, both accessed May 12, 2012.

10. The Brazilian excommunications received international press coverage. See, e.g., Gary Duffy, "Abortion Row Shakes Brazilian Opinion," *BBC News*, April 2, 2009, http://news.bbc.co.uk; "Katholische Kirche exkommuniziert Mutter von vergewaltigter Neunjähriger," *Der Spiegel*, March 5, 2009, www.spiegel.de; "L'Avortement d'une fillette de 9 ans bouleverse le Brésil," *Le Figaro*, March 9, 2009, http://www.lefigaro.fr; and Andrew Downie, "Nine-Year-Old's

Abortion Outrages Brazil's Catholic Church," *Time*, March 6, 2009, time.com; all accessed May 12, 2012.

11. Demel, *Abtreibung zwischen Straffreiheit*, 94–100.

12. CDF, *On Procured Abortions*, November 18, 1974, no. 13.

13. McBrien, ed., *HarperCollins Encyclopedia of Catholicism*, 5–7.

14. Ranke-Heinemann, *Eunuchs for the Kingdom*, 300. In 1970, she became the first woman to hold a Catholic teaching chair in Germany. In 1987, she lost the chair for having rejected the virgin birth of Mary; during a live television debate, she described it as insulting to ordinary women.

15. Ibid.

16. Bernhard Häring, *Das Gesetz Christi: Moraltheologie*, vol. 3 (Freiburg: Wewel, 1961), 225.

17. Ibid.

18. Ranke-Heinemann, *Eunuchs for the Kingdom*, 299.

19. On the different theological perspectives, see David Smith, "Abortion: A Moral Controversy," *Dialogue: A Journal for Religious Studies and Philosophy*, no. 8 (April 1997): 13–18.

20. Rahner, quoted in Ranke-Heinemann, *Eunuchs for the Kingdom*, 306.

21. Anton Antweiler, "Dürfen Katholiken abtreiben?," *Stern*, July 18, 1971; see also "Kirche: Halbe Wahrheit," *Der Spiegel*, March 6, 1972.

22. D. Smith, "Abortion," 18. Like Antweiler, Böckle was Swiss but taught in West Germany.

23. B189/6311-61-62, Horst Hermann, "Achtung statt Achtung: Die Folgen des §218 und das kirchliche Unehelichenrecht," *Publik*, July 9, 1971. Hermann lost his teaching authorization in 1975 due to his outspoken criticism of Catholic doctrine on marriage, as well as his negative comments about the close relationship between church and state in Germany.

24. *Gaudium et Spes*, December 7, 1965, no. 76.

25. For a detailed history, see, e.g., Atina Grossmann, *Reforming Sex: The German Movement for Birth Control and Abortion Reform, 1920–1950* (New York: Oxford University Press, 1992); Michael Gante, § 218 in der Diskussion: Meinungs- und Willensbildung, 1945–1976 (Düsseldorf: Droste, 1991).

26. Grossmann, *Reforming Sex*, 136–166.

27. Articles 1 and 2 of the Basic Law, http://www.bundestag.de, accessed March 15, 2015.

28. Herzog, *Sex after Fascism*, 222.

29. For a brief summary of abortion reform efforts in Great Britain, France, Italy, and Belgium in the early 1970s, see ibid., 156–160. For the American abortion debate, see, e.g., David Garrow, *Liberty and Sexuality: The Right to Privacy and the Making of* Roe v. Wade (New York: Macmillan, 1994).

30. On East German abortion policy, see Donna Harsh, "Society, the State, and Abortion in East Germany, 1950–1972," *American Historical Review* 102, no. 1 (1997): 53–84.

31. See Myra Marx Ferree et al., *Shaping Abortion Discourse: Democracy and the Public Sphere in Germany and the United States* (New York: Cambridge University Press, 2002).

32. "Das Gesetz des Staates und die sittliche Ordnung," Joint Statement of the EKD and Catholic Church (1970) reproduced in Harald Pawlowski, *Krieg gegen die Kinder? Für und wider die Abtreibung—Mit einer Dokumentation* (Limburg: Lahn, 1971), 129. See also Simone Mantei, *Na und Ja zur Abtreibung: Die Evangelische Kirche in der Reformdebatte um [Paragraph] 218 StGB, 1970–1976* (Göttingen: Vandenhoeck & Ruprecht, 2004), 62–82.

33. For an excerpt from "Verlautbarung der deutschen Bischöfe zur Strafrechtsreform, insbesondere zum Schutz des werdenden Lebens" released by the DBK on September 24, 1970, and the complete official statement of the BDKJ board of directors of December 3, 1971, see JHD, *218: Ein Paragraph und seine Probleme* (Düsseldorf: Schriftenreihe des Jugendhauses

Düsseldorf, 1972). For the text of the ZdK declaration of October 30, 1970, see ZdK, "Erkärung des Zentralkomitees der Deutschen Katholiken zum Schutz des werdenden Lebens," *Berichte und Dokumente*, no. 11 (1970): 5–6.

34. "Erklärung des Verbandes der niedergelassenen Ärzte Deutschlands," June 24, 1971, in Pawlowski, *Krieg gegen die Kinder?*, 155.

35. ACDP, VIII-005-040/3, Letter from the Berufverband der Frauenärzte to Reiner Barzel, February 8, 1973.

36. Rudolf Augstein, "Grundgesetz und 218," *Der Spiegel*, September 13, 1971.

37. Ibid.

38. "Wir haben gegen den §218 verstossen," *Stern*, June 3, 1971. The actual number of illegal abortions in Germany was unknown, with estimates ranging from 100,000 to 1,000,000.

39. Pawlowski, *Krieg gegen die Kinder?*, 19.

40. "Infratest-Politikbarometer" of March–April 1971 in ibid., 146–150.

41. Wiliarty, *CDU and the Politics of Gender*, 82.

42. For a comparative analysis of German and American feminism, see Ferree, *Varieties of Feminism*.

43. "Aktionsprogramm gegen Abtreibung: CAJ und 'Junge Gemeinschaft' wollen Öffentlichkeit informieren," BDKJ-Informationsdienst, July 16, 1971.

44. Ibid.

45. The Speyer and the Hildesheim kfd diocesan chapters sent letters to every member of the Bundestag in September 1971; the letters condemned any law allowing abortion except when the mother's life was endangered. See ACDP VIII-005-040/3, Letter from the Diözesanverband Speyer (kfd) to Bundestag members, September 30, 1971, and Letter from the Diözesanverband Hildesheim to Bundestag members, September 24, 1971. In February 1971, the *Deutsche Tagespost* published an exchange of letters between Franz Graf von Magnis, the founder of the German chapter of the Community of the Lady of All Nations, Federal Justice Minister Jahn, and Willy Brandt. See Franz Graf von Magnis, ed., *Pornographie-Ehescheidung-Abtreibung: Gedanken, Analysen, Dokumente* (Aschaffenburg: Pattloch, 1971), 83–88.

46. Jaeger, quoted in Pawlowski, *Krieg gegen die Kinder?*, 92.

47. Pawlowski, *Krieg gegen die Kinder?*, 127.

48. B189/6311–549, "Wortlauf der Stellungnahme," *Die Welt*, February 15, 1972.

49. B189/6311–526, quoted in Horst Schlitter, "Scharfer Angriff des Vatikans gegen Bonn," *Frankfurter Rundschau*, February 13, 1972.

50. B189/6311–549, F. M. Rum, "Wer kommentierte im 'Osservatore' den § 218?," *Die Welt*, February 15, 1972.

51. Otto B. Roegele, "Wächteramt oder Herrschaftsanspruch? Die Bischöfe, der § 218 und die Politik," *Communio: Internationale Katholische Zeitschrift* 3 (1972): 272.

52. Ibid.

53. Ibid.

54. "Ich bin nicht Zensor von Kardinal," *Der Spiegel*, March 13, 1972.

55. Ibid.

56. Roegele, "Wächteramt oder Herrschaftsanspruch?," 277.

57. Ibid., 274–277.

58. "Sowieso allein," *Der Spiegel*, December 11, 1972.

59. Wiliarty, *CDU and the Politics of Gender*, 81.

60. "Das ist geistliche Nötigung."

61. See ZdK, Großkundgebun der Arbeitsgemeinschaft der katholischen Verbände Deutschlands: Für das Leben, 29. September 1973, *Berichte und Dokumente* 20 (1973). The is-

sue was dedicated to the mass rally in Bonn on September 29, 1973, and included all official speeches delivered at the rally.

62. At a ZdK plenary meeting at which the upcoming rally was discussed, Aenne Brauksiepe repeatedly referred to the Nazi parallels drawn by the British doctor. See Aenne Brauksiepe, "Einführung in den Tagesordnungspunkt, 23–24 March 1973," *Berichte und Dokumente* 18 (1973): 39–40. However, at the rally, the two speakers did not. See ZdK, "Zur den Erfahrungen in anderen Ländern," *Berichte und Dokumente* 20, (1973): 23–24. The speakers are not identified by name in the report.

63. See, e.g., the speech of Barbara Schmid-Egger, chair of the BDKJ, "Menschenrechte und Menschenwürde," in ZdK, *Berichte und Dokumente* 20, (1973): 11–15.

64. Karl Rahner, *Strukturwandel der Kirche als Aufgabe und Chance* (Freiburg: Herder, 1971), 29.

65. Ibid., 69.

66. Ibid., 90.

67. Ibid., 74–75.

68. Ibid., 24.

69. ZdK, KT-1974, in Mönchengladbach, Presseausschnitte, no. 23, Hannes Burger, "Kirche ohne Konflikte" *Stuttgarter Zeitung*, September 16, 1974.

70. Ibid.

71. Mantei, *Na und Ja zur Abtreibung*, 403.

72. Friedrich Karl Fromme, "Kompromiß über den Paragraphen 218 nach dem Ärzte-Konzept?," *FAZ*, May 20, 1974.

73. Mantei, *Na und Ja zur Abtreibung*, 412–413.

74. "Wir nehmen die Herausforderung an: Erklärung des Präsidenten des Zentralkomitees der Katholiken," KNA, June 6, 1974.

75. "Noch hat die Fristenregelung keine Gesetzeskraft: Erklärung des Vorsitzenden der Bischofskonferenz, Kardinal Döpfner," KNA, June 6, 1974.

76. "Schwieriger Test," *Die Zeit*, June 21, 1974.

77. BVerfGE 39, 1—Schwangerschaftsabbruch 39, 1, A I 8.

78. Unlike the U.S. Supreme Court, the German Constitutional Court under Article 93 of the Basic Law can rule on questions of constitutionality without having a case involving litigants who claim to have been injured by the law. In legal parlance, this means that it can determine the constitutionality of a statute "in the abstract." See Kommers and Miller, *Constitutional Jurisprudence*, 374.

79. The 1951 Federal Constitutional Court Act (Article 14, pt. 1, par. 1) gave the First Senate responsibility for reviewing the constitutionality of laws and for resolving constitutional debates arising out of ordinary litigation. The Second Senate had authority over political disputes between branches and levels of government. It could also settle election disputes and rule on the constitutionality of political parties. In 1956, the Bundestag amended the FCCA in order to distribute the caseload between the two courts more evenly. The Second Senate, in addition to political cases, gained jurisdiction over constitutional complaints involving civil and criminal procedures. The First Senate maintained jurisdiction over all cases involving issues of substantive law. See Kommers and Miller, *Constitutional Jurisprudence*, 19.

80. BVerfGE 39, 1—Schwangerschaftsabbruch, A II 2. The CDU also argued that the Bundestag could not act without the concurrence of the Bundesrat. See sec. A, pt. II, no. 1. All translations of the decision are my own.

81. BVerfGE 39, 1, A III 1b and 1c.

82. BVerfGE 39, 1, A, III, 2.

83. Ibid.
84. Ibid.
85. BVerfGE 39, 1, C I 1b.
86. BVerfGE 39, 1, C I 1c.
87. BVerfGE 39, 1, C, II 2.
88. BVerfGE 39, 1, C III 3.
89. BVerfGE 39, 1, C II, 3 and D II 1 and 2a.
90. "218-Protest: Von hinten gegriffen," *Der Spiegel*, February 24, 1975. This protest action took place before the decision's release. The decision had been leaked to the secular press.
91. Ferree, *Varieties of Feminism*, 65.
92. Hans Schueler, "Die Sittenwächter der Nation: Karlsruhe entschied wider die Fristenlösung," *Die Zeit*, February 28, 1975.
93. Roderich Reifenrath, "Die-Karlsruhe Enzyklika," *Frankfurter Rundschau*, February 26, 1975.
94. Rudolph Augstein, "Zuchtmeister für Bonn und Bürger," *Der Spiegel*, March 3, 1975.
95. BVerfGE 39, 1, "Abweichende Meinung der Richterin Rupp-v. Brünneck und des Richters Dr. Simon zum Urteil des Ersten Senats des Bundesverfassungsgerichts vom 25.Februar 1975," B II 2.
96. See BVerfGE 1, 14—Südweststaat, October 23, 1951, no. 27; BVerfGE 3, 225—Gleichberechtigung, December 18, 1953, B II 2b. On the role of natural law in early high court decisions, see James E. Heget, *Contemporary German Legal Philosophy* (Philadelphia: University of Pennsylvania Press, 1996); Samuel Moyn, "Personalism, Community, and the Origins of Human Rights," in *Human Rights in the Twentieth Century*, ed. Stefan-Ludwig Hoffmann (Cambridge: Cambridge University Press, 2011), 85–106. On German legal experts who rejected the revival of Catholic natural law, see Lora Wildenthal, "Rudolf Laun and the Human Rights of Germans in Occupied and Early West Germany," in *Human Rights in the Twentieth Century*, ed. Stefan-Ludwig Hoffmann (Cambridge: Cambridge University Press, 2011), 125–146. For a 1960s German legal study expressing concern about Catholic influence on German law, see Helmut Simon, *Katholisierung des Rechtes? Zum Einfluß katholischen Rechtsdenken auf die gegenwärtige deutsche Gesetzgebung und Rechtsprechung* (Göttingen: Vandenhoeck & Ruprecht, 1962).
97. BGHZ 3, 107 referenced in Simon, *Katholisierung des Rechtes?*, 16.
98. Gottfried Dietze, "Natural Law in Modern European Countries," *Natural Law Forum* 73 (1956): 74–75.
99. On its widespread acceptance in postwar Germany, see Freiherr von der Heydte, "Natural Law Tendencies in Contemporary German Jurisprudence," *Natural Law Forum* (1956): 115–121.
100. At this time, Hans-Christoph Seebohm (Protestant) belonged to the conservative Deutschepartei. In 1960, he joined the CDU. For a short biography, see "Geschichte der CDU, Konrad-Adenauer-Stiftung," http://www.kas.de, accessed March 13, 2015.
101. BVerfGE 39, 1, C I 1d.
102. Gante, § 218 in der Diskussion, 54–55.
103. Ferree et al., *Shaping Abortion Discourse*, 154–178.
104. Bernhard Vogel, "Bericht zur Lage in der Vollersammlung des Zentralkomitees der Deutschen Katholiken am 7. März, 1975," in ZDK, *Berichte und Dokumente*, no. 25 (1976): 7.
105. B189/18194, KNA, no. 61, March 13, 1976.
106. DBK, "Empfehlungen für Seelsorger und Religionslehrer nach der Änderung des § 218 StGB," May 7, 1976, http://www.dbk.de, accessed March 8, 2013.
107. DBK, "Empfehlungen für Ärzte und medizinische Fachkräfte in Krankenhäusern

nach der Änderung des § 218 StGB," May 7, 1976, http://www.dbk-shop.de, accessed March 15, 2015.

108. Bernhard Vogel was the ZdK president from 1972 to 1976. In March 1976, Hans Maier assumed the presidency.

109. B189/6180, 79–80, Hans-Jochen Vogel, "Zum Wort der Bischöfe erklärt Bundesminister Dr. Hans-Jochen Vogel," *Das Recht*, May 20, 1976.

110. ZdK, 2103, 1869, Letter from Militia Sanctae Mariae to Bernhard Vogel, May 25, 1976. Militia Sanctae Mariae is the "militant company of the Knights of Our Lady," an international Catholic confraternity founded in France. In 1968, Bishop Graber of Regensburg established the German chapter. In the 1970s, it actively campaigned against abortion law reform in Germany, France, and Italy. For more information, see its website, www.militia-sanctae-mariae.org, accessed March 12, 2015.

111. ZdK, 2103, 1869, Letter from a Catholic man to Bernhard Vogel, September 6, 1976.

112. ZdK, 2103, 1869, Letter from a parish priest to Bernhard Vogel, November 14, 1975.

113. ZdK-2103, 1869, Letter from a Catholic constituent to Bernhard Vogel, September 5, 1976. Marcel Lefebvre founded the International Society of Saint Pius X (SSPX) in 1970; its mission is the preservation of traditional Catholic values. In 1988, Lefebvre was excommunicated after ordaining four SSPX priests as bishops without papal approval. In September 2011, the Vatican pursued reconciliation with the SSPX, offering it the status of personal prelature (the status held by Opus Dei); in February 2012, the group rejected the reconciliation proposal.

114. kfd-1158, Sitzung des Ständigen Rates in Würzburg, "Erklärung der deutschen Bischöfe zum Jahr des Kindes 1979" (revised draft).

115. B189/6180, "Zum Jahr des Kindes," *Abendzeitung München*, February 10, 1979. The Cartell-Rupert Mayer, founded in 1946 as the Cartel of Christian Lodges, changed its name in 1954. To this day, it works in conjunction with the Hilfe für Mutter und Kind e. V. to provide women with alternatives to abortion. See the group's website, http://cartell-rupert-mayer.de, accessed May 12, 2012.

116. B189/6180-149, "Für Mord sind Riesensummen da! Regierung—wie belügst du uns!" *Neue Bildpost*, April 15, 1979.

117. This brief list of newspapers covering Höffner's sermon is by no means exhaustive; see BA 189/6180-144–149.

118. Government statistics indicated that the number of legal abortions increased by almost 30 percent between 1977 and 1978.

119. B189/6180-151–153, Letter from the SPD chair of North Rhineland-Westphalia to Höffner, April 23, 1979.

120. Ibid.

121. ZdK 2103, 1854, no. 1, Letter from Bernhard Vogel to Helmut Kohl, April 11, 1974.

122. ZdK, 2103, 1854, no. 1, Letter from a Catholic woman to Bernhard Vogel, May 7, 1974.

123. Wiliarty, *CDU and the Politics of Gender*, 22.

124. "Die Diskussion um den Paragraphen 218 ist in Deutschland aufs neue entbrannt," *Die Welt*, August 6, 1979.

125. Ibid.

126. B189/6180-173, Joseph Höffner, "Kein Anspruch auf Schwangerschaft," reprinted in *Die Welt*, August 6, 1979.

127. Ibid.

128. B189/6180-182, Letter from Hans-Jochen Vogel to Joseph Höffner, September 4, 1979.

129. B189/6180-187–188, Letter from Vogel to Höffner, September 4, 1979.

130. B189/6180-188, Letter from Vogel to Höffner, September 4, 1979.

131. B189/6180-189, Letter from Vogel to Höffner, September 4, 1979.

132. B189/6180-193, Letter from Höffner to Vogel, September 12, 1980.

133. Höffner's intervention received substantial coverage from several major American news outlets. See, e.g., John Vinocur, "Bishops Criticize Schmidt's Policy as Election Nears," *NYT*, September 12, 1980; Elizabeth Pond, "Roman Catholic Church Causes Election Furor in W. Germany," *Christian Science Monitor*, September 18, 1980; John Vinocur, "How Dumb Can Politics Get? In Bonn, They Wonder Aloud," *NYT*, September 21, 1980; Bradley Graham, "Schmidt and Catholics Clash," *Washington Post*, September 26, 1980.

134. "Das ist geistliche Nötigung," *Der Spiegel*, September 22, 1980.

135. Ibid.

136. Helmut Schmidt, quoted in "Worte der Woche," *Die Zeit*, September 19, 1980.

137. "Das ist geistliche Nötigung," *Der Spiegel*, September 22, 1980.

138. "Die Herde denkt anders," *Der Spiegel*, September 22, 1980.

139. "Das ist geistliche Nötigung."

140. Hanno Kühnert, "Wie im alten Rom," *Die Zeit*, March 4, 1983.

141. See Frank Bösch, *Macht und Machtverlust: Die Geschichte der CDU* (Munich: DVA, 2002), 240–245, and Petra Holz, *Zwischen Tradition und Emanzipation: Politikerinnen in der CDU in der Zeit von 1945 bis 1957* (Sulzbach-Taunus: Ulrike Helmer, 2004).

142. Wiliarty, *CDU and the Politics of Gender*, 79–108.

143. "Das Fähnlein der Einundfünfzig," *Die Zeit*, December 28, 1984.

144. Margrit Gerste, "Männer in Not," *Die Zeit*, February 17, 1984.

145. See "Tagesprotokoll: 32. Bundesparteitag der Christlichen Demokratischen Union Deutschlands, 10. Mai 1984," 205–208. The protocol is available online via the Konrad-Adenauer Stiftung, www.kas.de, accessed May 12, 2012.

146. See "Tagesprotokoll: 32. Bundesparteitag der Christlichen Demokratischen Union Deutschlands, 10. Mai 1984," 222.

147. Margrit Gerste, "Was will Heiner Geißler? Der Angriff auf Pro Familia war nur ein Vorgefecht," *Die Zeit*, July 20, 1984.

148. See "Tagesprotokoll: 32. Bundesparteitag der Christlichen Demokratischen Union Deutschlands, 10. Mai 1984," 205.

149. See kfd-1169, Letter from Dorothee Wilms to AG aller katholischen Frauenverbände in der Diözese Hildesheim, May 21, 1984.

150. kfd-1831, Letter from W. W. of the Catholic parish office of St. Joseph, Sythen in the Diocese of Münster to the kfd central office, July 11, 1984.

151. "ZdK zur Neuregelung des § 218," *ZdK-Mitteilungen*, no. 221, December 6, 1982.

152. In July, the *Rheinische Merkur/Christ und Welt* published a series on abortion reform and changing German attitudes; the referenced article was the third in the series. JHD, 2.110238-002, "Robben schützen, Menschen töten?," *Rheinische Merkur/Christ und Welt*, February 24, 1984. The SZ also prominently featured the results of the study; see Hans Heigert, "Robben ja-Kinder nein," *SZ*, July 16, 1984.

153. Letter to the editor from Helga B., "Kein Zusammenhang mit Robben," *SZ*, July 21, 1984.

154. Hanna-Renate Laurien's speech at the forum addressing women in church and society quoted in "Frauen—von der Kirche nur 'halbherzig' begleitet," *Südkurier Konstanz*, July 10, 1984.

155. ZdK, KT-Aachen 1984, Presseausschnitte, Heidrun Graupner, "Die Frauen setzen neue Signale," *SZ*, July 9, 1984.

156. kfd-1138, Johannes Dyba, "Das Wort des Bischofs," *Bonifatiusbote*, September 3–4, 1988.

157. kfd-1138, Press release, Anneliese Lissner, "Gott schuf die Frau nach seinem Bild—als Frau: Eine Erwiderung auf den Erzbischof von Fulda," September 1, 1988.

158. kfd-1138, Press release, Barbara Leckel and Anneliese Knippenkötter, September 1, 1988.

159. kfd-1138, Letter from the kfd Münster diocesan chapter to Lehmann, September 9, 1988.

160. kfd-1138, Letter from Ursula Männle to Dyba, September 21, 1988.

161. Ibid.

162. kfd-1138, Letter from a kfd local chapter to John Paul II, October 29, 1988.

163. kfd-1342, Protokoll der Sitzung des Hauptausschusses (kfd), Mainz, October 4–5, 1988.

164. kfd-1138, Catholic woman's letter to the editor of *Bonifatiusbote*, September 9, 1988.

165. kfd-1138, Anneliese Lissner, Form letter for positive responses to *Frau & mutter*.

166. kfd-1138, Aktennotiz: Bericht zur Lage des Präsidenten Prof. Maier vor dem Geschäftsführenden Ausschuß ZdK. Following this controversy, the title graphics were changed to *frau und mutter*.

167. kfd-1170, 1993 Allensbach survey, *Frauen und Kirche*.

168. kfd-1175, Aktennotiz für Frau Casel, Frau Dr. Tiemann und Herrn Gordz—über das Gespräch zwischen Vertreterinnen katholischer Frauenverbände und Mitgliedern der DBK am 4. März 1993.

169. Ferree et al., *Shaping Abortion Discourse*, 41.

170. Ibid., 40–43.

171. "Kirche: Mir kann nichts passieren," *Der Spiegel*, January 15, 2001.

172. "Pope Strips Some Authority from German Bishop," *Catholic World News*, March 11, 2002.

173. Enforcement of Vatican stipulations could take extreme forms. For example, in 2008, the bishop of Regensburg would not allow the diocesan choir to sing at the sixtieth birthday party of the CSU Bundestag member Maria Eichhorn because she had donated money to Donum Vitae. See "Protest wegen Donum Vitae: Kirche verbietet Regensburger Domspatzen das Singen," *Der Spiegel*, September 5, 2008.

174. "'Donum Vitae': Bischöfe untersagen Angestellten Mitarbeit," June 26, 2006, webpage for the diocese of Münster. http://kirchensite.de, accessed March 14, 2013.

175. kfd-1170, Allensbach survey, *Frau und Kirche*.

5. ASSISTED REPRODUCTION

1. Johann Wolfgang von Goethe, *The Second Part of Goethe's Faust*, trans. John Anster (London: Routledge, 1886), 90.

2. Hypospadias is a condition in which the urethral opening is on the underside of the penis rather than at the tip. Men with this condition may be able to have sexual intercourse; however, it is less likely that the sperm will be delivered deep enough into the vagina for fertilization to occur. Although many later accounts attributed the injection to Dr. Hunter, the earliest accounts did not. On the growing number of variations on the account, see William Kevin Glover, *Artificial Insemination among Human Beings* (Washington, DC: Catholic University of America Press, 1948), 4–5.

3. Examples of nineteenth- and early-twentieth-century literary treatments include Mary Shelly, *Frankenstein* (1815); Johann Wolfgang von Goethe, *Faust*, part 2 (1832); Jean-Louis Dubut de LaForest, *Le faiseur d'hommes* (1894); and Jules Hoch, *Le faiseur d'hommes et sa formule* (1906). On how French and British literary treatments of AI and sterilization reflected contemporary concerns about the nature and locus of feminine desire and population decline, see Mi-

chael Finn, "Female Sterilization and Artificial Insemination at the French Fin de Siècle: Facts and Fictions," *Journal of the History of Sexuality* 18, no. 1 (2009): 26–43, and Angus McLaren, *Reproduction by Design: Sex, Robots, Trees, and Test Tube Babies in Interwar Britain* (Chicago: University of Chicago Press, 2012).

    4. Hermann Rohleder, *Test Tube Babies: A History of Artificial Impregnation of Human Beings*, trans. John Hill (New York: Panurge Press, 1934), 184. Rohleder first broached the topic of AI in 1901 when he published *Vorlesungen über Geschlechtstrieb und gesamtes Geschlechtsleben des Menschen* (Berlin: Fischer, 1901).

    5. Glover, *Artificial Insemination*, 45.

    6. In his gynecological handbook of 1905, H. Fritsch made one reference to AI, recounting the story of a Parisian doctor who injected the husband's sperm into the woman's uterus; a severe infection resulted. H. Fritsch, *Die Krankheit der Frauen, für Ärzte und Studenten*, 11th ed. (Berlin: Wreden, 1905), 600. Dr. P. Fraenkel reported in 1909 on as yet unverified AI experiments. See P. Fraenkel, "Über künstliche Befruchtung beim Menschen und ihre gerichtsärztliche Beurteilung," *Ärztliche Sachverständigen-Zeitung* 15, no. 9 (1909): 169–175.

    7. Paul A. David, "Path-Dependent Learning and the Evolution of Beliefs and Behaviors: Implications of Bayesian Adaptation under Computationally Bounded Rationality," in *The Evolution of Economic Diversity*, ed. Antonio Nicita and Ugo Pagano (New York: Routledge, 2001), 87–88.

    8. Rohleder, *Test Tube Babies*, 57–58.

    9. Ibid., 113–114.

    10. Stoeckel, quoted in Ernst Fromm, "Artifizielle Insemination," in *Die künstliche Befruchtung beim Menschen: Diskussionsbeiträge aus medizinischer, juristischer und theologischer Sicht* (Cologne: Otto Schmidt, 1960), 26.

    11. Rohleder, *Test Tube Babies*, 142.

    12. Hermann Rohleder, *Künstliche Zeugung und Anthropogenie (Menschwerdung)* (Leipzig: Thieme, 1918), 2.

    13. Th. Olshausen, "Künstliche Befruchtung und eheliche Abstammung," *Deutsche Medizinische Wochenschrift* 38, no. 12 (1908): 515.

    14. Ibid., 516.

    15. J. Schwalbe, "Bemerkungen zu dem vorstehenden Aufsatz," *Deutsche Medizinische Wochenschrift* 38, no. 12 (1908): 516.

    16. Traumann, "Künstliche Befruchtung und Vaterschaft," *Das Recht* 13, no. 22 (1909): 765.

    17. Rohleder, *Test Tube Babies*, 186.

    18. Olshausen, "Das Reichsgericht zur Frage der künstlichen Befruchtung," 1636.

    19. Rohleder, *Test Tube Babies*, 186–187.

    20. Traumann, "Künstliche Befruchtung und Vaterschaft," 765.

    21. Schwalbe, "Bemerkungen zu dem vorstehenden Aufsatz," 516.

    22. Rohleder, *Test Tube Babies*, 166–167.

    23. Ibid., 172.

    24. On the German medical profession's struggle for autonomy, see Charles E. McClelland, *The German Experience of Professionalization: Modern Learned Professions and Their Organization from the Early Nineteenth Century to the Hitler Era* (New York: Cambridge University Press, 1991), 131–142.

    25. See, e.g., the British author H. P. Marriot Watson's "The Deleterious Effect of Americanisation on Women," *Nineteenth Century and After* (November 1903): 782–792; Émile Zola's novel *Fécondité* (Fruitfulness), first published in 1899, contrasted idyllic images of domestic tranquility with those of selfish couples deliberately limiting family size and the debauched

life of Séraphine; see also Hans Blüher, *Frauenbewegung und Antifeminismus* (Lauenburg/Elbe, 1921). For a brief discussion of the association drawn by Germans authors between the new woman and sterility, see Ute Frevert, *Men of Honour: A Social and Cultural History of the Duel*, trans. Anthony Williams (Cambridge: Polity Press, 1995), 223–224; and Ute Planert, *Antifeminismus im Kaiserreich: Diskurs, soziale Formation und politische Mentalität* (Göttingen: Vandenhoeck & Ruprecht, 1998), 171.

26. Christina Benninghaus, "Great Expectations: German Debates about Artificial Insemination in Humans around 1912," *Studies in History and Philosophy of Biological and Biomedical Sciences* 38 (2007): 385.

27. Ibid., 384.

28. Hans Meyer-Rügg, "Über künstliche Befruchtung beim Menschen," *Münchener Medizinische Wochenschrift* 63 (1916): 1416–1418.

29. Some doctors suggested that AI might cure male impotency. See H. W. Meier, "Zur Kasuistik der psychischen Impotenz," *Münchener Medizinischer Wochenschrift* 63 (1915), 1415–1416; Meyer-Rügg, "Über künstliche Befruchtung beim Menschen," 1416–1418.

30. Benninghaus, "Great Expectations," 385.

31. Schwalbe, "Bemerkungen zu dem vorstehenden Aufsatz," 516.

32. The Belgian theologian Arthur Vermeersch (1858–1936), for example, proposed six methods of sperm collection that he believed were aligned with Catholic doctrine: (1) involuntary nocturnal secretion of semen; (2) sexual relations with a punctured condom; (3) aspiration by needle; (4) prostate/rectal massage; (5) use of a syringe to extract sperm from the vagina after normal sexual relations; and (6) placement of a container in the vagina immediately after intercourse. As an involuntary act, nocturnal emission did not violate the Church's condemnation of masturbation. The second method—the use of a punctured condom—he argued, was permissible since it did not interfere with the normal means of conception (provided that the hole in the condom was sufficiently large). The third and fourth methods he justified on grounds that, unlike masturbation, they induced pain. Both the fifth and sixth methods presupposed normal intercourse and thus required no special moral disposition. See Dieter Giesen, *Die künstliche Insemination als ethisches und rechtliches Problem* (Bielefeld: Gieseking, 1962), 85–87.

33. Pius XII, *Discurso al Congreso de la Unión Católica Italiana de Obstétricas con la colaboración de la Federación Nacional de Colegios de Comadronas Católicas*, October 29,1951, pt. IV, par. 9.

34. On European moral theology and its intellectual isolation at the turn of the century, see Charles E. Curran, *Catholic Moral Theology in the United States: A History* (Washington, DC: Georgetown University Press, 2008), 1–34.

35. Holy Office, *Lamentabili Sane Exitu*, July 3, 1907. English translation available at http://www.papalencyclicals.net, accessed April 1, 2015; see also Pius X, *Pascendi Dominici Gregis*, September 8, 1907.

36. Joseph Fletcher, *Morals and Medicine: The Moral Problems of the Patient's Right to Know the Truth, Contraception, Artificial Insemination, Sterilization, and Euthanasia* (Princeton, NJ: Princeton University Press, 1954), xi.

37. Rohleder, *Test Tube Babies*, 162.

38. Giesen, *Die künstliche Insemination*, 234.

39. Ibid., 251.

40. Ute Helling, *Zu den Problemen der künstlichen Insemination unter besonderer Berücksichtigung des § 203 E 1962* (Berlin: Walter de Gruyter, 1970), 145.

41. Manfred Balz, *Heterologe künstliche Samenübertragung beim Menschen: Rechtliche und politische Überlegungen zu einem Vorhaben des Europarats* (Tübingen: Mohr, 1980), 7.

42. "Vorerst gar nichts," *Der Spiegel*, January 17, 1966.

43. Helling, *Zu den Problemen*, 145–146.

44. I have used "German Medical Association" rather than "National Chamber of Doctors" because the Bundesärztkammer uses the former on its English webpage. See http://www.bundesaerztekammer.de, accessed February 12, 2015.

45. Fromm, "Artifizielle Insemination," 31.

46. Ibid., 30.

47. Resolution of the Deutsche Gesellschaft für gerichtliche und soziale Medizin, quoted in ibid., 29.

48. Helling, *Zu den Problemen*, 146.

49. Rolf S. Müller and Axel Jeschke, "Man darf den Souverän Reizen: Spiegel-Gespräch mit dem CDU-Juristen Dr. Max Güde über Sexualstrafrecht," *Der Spiegel*, September 16, 1968.

50. Resolution of the Deutscher Ärztinnenbund from 1955, quoted in Fromm, "Artifizielle Insemination," 26.

51. Wilhelm Geiger, "Rechtsfragen der Insemination," in *Die Künstliche Befruchtung beim Menschen: Diskussionsbeiträge aus medizinischer, juristischer und theologischer Sicht*, ed. Alan F. Guttmacher (Cologne: Schmidt, 1960), 44.

52. Ibid., 46.

53. Ibid., 45.

54. Ibid., 53.

55. Ibid., 53–54.

56. Ibid., 54.

57. See Mitchell, *Origins of Christian Democracy*, 43–46.

58. B189/6320, 46–47, "Zur Strafrechtsreform," attached to a letter addressed to Elisabeth Reichstätter, kfd, May 2, 1963.

59. B189/6320, "Zur Strafrechtsreform," 48–50.

60. See Jerome-Michael Vereb, *"Because He Was German!" Cardinal Bea and the Origins of Roman Catholic Engagement in the Ecumenical Movement* (Grand Rapids, MI: Eerdmans, 2006); and Robert A. Krieg, *Catholic Theologians in Nazi Germany* (New York: Continuum, 2004), 156–160.

61. See Johannes Stelzenberger, "Die moraltheologische Beurteilung der künstliche Insemination," in *Die künstliche Befruchtung beim Menschen: Diskussionsbeiträge aus medizinischer, juristischer, und theologischer Sicht* (Cologne: Schmidt, 1960), 91–118.

62. On the innovative nature of Häring's *Gesetz Christi* and the international acclaim it received, see Kathleen A. Cahalan, *Formed in the Image of Christ: The Sacramental-Moral Theology of Bernhard Häring C.Ss.R.* (Collegeville, MN: Liturgical Press, 2004).

63. Häring, *Gesetz Christi*, vol. 3, 367.

64. Ibid.

65. Ibid.; emphasis in original.

66. Bernhard Häring, *Medical Ethics*, trans. Gabrielle L. Jean (Slough: St. Paul Publications, 1972), 93.

67. In 1965, Karl Rahner gave a lecture entitled "Experiment Mensch: Theologisches über die Selbstmanipulation des Menschen." Between 1965 and 1967, Rahner revised the text several times. In 1968, *Theological Digest* published the essay as "Experiment Man" (translated by W. Dych). In 1972, the series Theological Investigations offered a new translation of the essay. All citations are taken from the 1972 translation. Karl Rahner, "The Experiment with Man: Theological Observations on Man's Self-Manipulation," trans. Graham Harrison, in *Theological Investigations*, vol. 9: *Writings of 1965–1967* (New York: Herder, 1972), 211.

68. Ibid.

69. Like his first essay, the second essay underwent multiple revisions between 1966 and 1967 and appeared in several publications. It was reprinted in 1969 in the edited volume *Menschenzüchtung*. See Karl Rahner, "Zum Problem der genetischen Manipulation aus der Sicht des Theologen," in *Menschenzüchtung: Das Problem der genetischen Manipulierung des Menschen*, ed. Friedrich Wagner (Munich: Beck, 1969), 158.

70. Ibid.

71. Rahner, "Zum Problem der genetischen Manipulation," 159.

72. Ibid., 161.

73. Ibid., 166.

74. Giesen, *Die künstliche Insemination*, 64. The dearth of Protestant articles is also noted in a 1970 issue of *Der Spiegel*. See "Kirche/Künstliche Befruchtung: Der dritte Mann," *Der Spiegel*, March 23, 1970.

75. Other German Protestant theologians and church officials who shared this view include Helmut Thielicke, Guido N. Groeger, the director for the Center of the Evangelical Church in the Rhineland for Issues of Marriage and Family, and Bornikoel. See Helmut Thielicke, "Die künstliche Befruchtung: Ein Modellfall christlicher Ethik," *Sonntagsblatt*, January 19, 1957, 13–14, and January 29, 1957, 15–16. Guido N. Groeger, "Die Verantwortung des Einzeln," in *Die künstliche Befruchtung beim Menschen*, 137–146, and Bernhard Bornikoel, "Zum Problem der künstlichen Befruchtung," in *Geburtenregelung und Eugenik: Stellungnahmen zu sexual-ethischen Gegenwartsfragen*, ed. Bernhard Bornikoel and Hans Harmsen (Hamburg: Agentur des Rauhen Hauses, 1959), 13–16.

76. Fedde Bloemhof, "Entmenschlichung des Menschen und Mißbrauch der Wissenschaft," in *Die künstliche Befruchtung beim Menschen*, 128.

77. Bishop Otto Dibelius, *Rheinische Post*, December 28, 1949, quoted in Giesen, *Die künstliche Insemination*, 67.

78. Bloemhof, "Entmenschlichung des Menschen," 134–135; Helmut Thielicke, "Die künstliche Befruchtung," Part II, *Sonntagsblatt*, January 20, 1957, 15.

79. On East and West German responses to Americanization, see Uta G. Poiger, *Jazz, Rock, and Rebels*.

80. Michael Geyer, "America in Germany: Power and the Pursuit of Americanization," in *The German–American Encounter: Conflict and Cooperation between Two Cultures, 1800–2000*, ed. Frank Trommler and Elliott Shore (New York: Berghahn Books, 2001), 127–128.

81. Ibid., 129.

82. Michael Geyer, "Cold War Angst: The Case of West-German Opposition to Rearmament and Nuclear Weapons," in *The Miracle Years: A Cultural History of West Germany, 1949–1968*, ed. Hanna Schissler (Princeton, NJ: Princeton University Press, 2001) 393, 407 n. 129.

83. Geyer, "America in Germany," 129.

84. Ibid., 130. On the revitalization of the *Heimat* ideal and its successful deployment in early postwar conservation campaigns, see Sandra Chaney, *Nature of the Miracle Years: Conservation in West Germany, 1945–1975* (New York: Berghahn Books, 2008); on 1950s *Heimat* films that offered German viewers idealized depictions of nature, motherhood and femininity, and German identity, see Elizabeth Boa and Rachel Palfreyman, *Heimat—A German Dream: Regional Loyalties and National Identity in German Culture, 1890–1990* (Oxford: Oxford University Press, 2000), 86–129.

85. Helling, *Zu den Problemen*, 4–6.

86. See "Reagenzglas-Babys: Ehebruch in der Retorte," *Der Spiegel*, November 8, 1950, and "Der anonyme Ehebruch," *Der Spiegel*, February 5, 1958.

87. See, "Reagenglas-Babies: Ehebruch in der Retort," *Der Spiegel*, November 8, 1950, and "Der Anonyme Ehebruch," *Der Spiegel*, February 5, 1958.

88. Johann Wolfgang Goethe, "Künstliche Mensch," *Die Zeit*, December 12, 1949. No author's name is given; only Goethe's name appears in the byline. The introductory remarks allude to the George Bernard Shaw play; they do not explicitly reference Pygmalion's murder by his two creations.

89. Margarethe Albrecht, quoted in Giesen, *Die künstliche Insemination*, 41.

90. B 189/6311, Niederschrift über die 4. Sitzung ... CDU.

91. "Vaterschaft: Aus der Truhe," *Der Spiegel*, September 25, 1963.

92. Muller received the Nobel Prize in Medicine in 1946 for his research on genetic mutations caused by radiation. For his 1963 lecture, see Hermann J. Muller, "Genetic Progress by Voluntarily Conducted Germinal Choice," in *Man and His Future: A Ciba Foundation Volume*, ed. Gordon Wolstenholme (Boston: Little, Brown, 1963), 247–263.

93. "Vaterschaft," *Der Spiegel*, September 25, 1963.

94. Ibid.

95. Ibid.

96. V. G., "Kinder aus dem Katalog: Elitezüchtung durch künstliche Befruchtung?," *Die Zeit*, October 13, 1961.

97. Eduard Dreher, "Introduction," *German Draft Penal Code E 1962*, trans. Neville Ross (South Hackensack, NJ: Rothman, 1966), 19.

98. Remarks of M. Klein, "Discussion: Eugenics and Genetics," in *Man and His Future*, ed. Wolstenholme, 282.

99. Ciba Foundation, *Das umstrittene Experiment: Der Mensch—27 Wissenschaftler diskutieren die Elemente einer biologischer Revolution*, trans. Klaus Prost (Munich: Desch, 1966). The new title, "The Controversial Experiment: Man—27 Scientists Discuss the Elements of a Biological Revolution," hints at the book's negative reception in Germany. On this reception, see Heike Petermann, "Die biologische Zukunft der Menschheit: Der Kontext des CIBA Symposiums 'Man and His Future' (1962) und seine Rezeption," in *Ursprünge, Arten und Folgen des Konstrukts "Bevölkerung" vor, im und nach dem "Dritten Reich": Zur Geschichte der deutschen Bevölkerungswissenschaft*, ed. Rainer Mackensen, Jürgen Reulecke, and Josef Ehmer (Wiesbaden: VS, 2009), 393–414.

100. Friedrich Vogel, "Ist mit einer Manipulierbarkeit auf dem Gebiet der Humangenetik zu rechnen?—Können und dürfen wir Menschen züchten?," *Hippokrates* 38, no. 16 (1967): 642.

101. Friedrich Wagner, "Die Manipulierung des Menschen durch Genwissenschaft: Geschichte, Methoden, Ziele und Folgen," in *Menschenzüchtung*, ed. Wagner, 46; Wilhelm Kütemeyer, "Wissenschaft, Methode und Mensch, von der Medizin aus gesehen," in *Menschenzüchtung*, ed. Wagner, 128.

102. "Kirche/Künstliche Befruchtung: Der dritte Mann," *Der Spiegel*, March 23, 1970.

103. Franz Böckle, "Ethik unk Genetik: Podiumsgespräch und Diskussion," *Genetik und Gesellschaft: Marburger Forum Philippinum*, ed. G. Gerhard Wendt (Stuttgart: Wissenschaftliche Verlagsgesellschaft, 1970), 136.

104. Geyer, "America in Germany," 132.

105. Gerd Langguth, *The Green Factor in German Politics: From Protest Movement to Political Party*, trans. Richard Straus (London: Westview Press, 1984), 6.

106. Erwin Chargaff, "Engineering a Molecular Nightmare," *Nature* (May 1987): 199–200, here 199.

107. In the early 1980s, no standard method existed for reporting IVF success rates. On the different standards used, see Douglas T. Carrell and C. Matthew Peterson, ed., *Reproductive*

Endocrinology and Infertility: Integrating Modern Clinical and Laboratory Practice (New York: Springer, 2010), 103. In 1983, one IVF cycle cost approximately 5,000 DM in West Germany. On the costs, see "Kasse und künstliche Zeugung," *Die Zeit*, September 16, 1983; in 1984, infertility was reclassified as a disease in Germany; most German insurance companies now provide coverage for up to six IVF cycles.

108. Bernhard Gill, *Gentechnik ohne Politik: Wie die Brisanz der Synthetischen Biologie von wissenschaftlichen Institutionen, Ethik- und anderen Kommissionen systematisch verdrängt wird* (Frankfurt: Campus, 1991), 101.

109. Jürgen Hampel et al., "Germany," in *Biotechnology in the Public Sphere: A European Sourcebook*, ed. John Durant, Martin W. Bauer, and George Gaskell (London: Cromwell, 1998), 65. See also Article 5 of the Basic Law, which specifies, "Arts and sciences, research and teaching shall be free."

110. Gill, *Gentechnik ohne Politik*, 104.

111. Hampel et al., "Germany," 67. The authors contend that German media coverage from 1972 to 1984 was not as negative as some authors have argued. However, in compiling their data, they do not differentiate between different types of biotechnology (e.g., genetic manipulation of crops, of livestock, and of humans). Media coverage of IVF, surrogacy, and AID was overwhelmingly negative. A quantitative/qualitative analysis found that 80 percent of German media coverage of NRTs was negative between 1983 and 1990. See Irene Johanna Barnett, "Assisted Reproductive Technology Policy: A Comparative Case Study of Policy Outcomes in Germany and the United States" (Ph.D. diss., Kent State University, 2003), 145–153.

112. "Ein Schritt in Richtung Homunkulus," *Der Spiegel*, July 31, 1978.

113. "Respektvoll in den Ausguß," *Die Zeit*, October 8, 1978.

114. Letter to the editor, *Frau und Mutter*, October 1979.

115. B141/49460, 82, Böckle, quoted in "Stellungnahme des Vorsitzenden der Deutschen Bischofskonferenz, Kardinal Joseph Höffner, zum sogenannten 'Retorten-Baby,'" Pressedienst des Sekretariats der Deutschen Bischofskonferenz, August 10, 1978.

116. B141/49460, 83, Johannes Gründel, "Künstlich, aber nicht unsittlich. In Deutsche Zeitung vom 4. August 1978, note 4 in "Stellungnahme . . . zum sogenannten 'Retorten-Baby,'" Pressedienst, August 10, 1978.

117. B141/49460, 83–86.

118. Hampel et al., "Germany," 65.

119. Albin Eser, Hans-Georg Koch, and Thomas Wisenbart, *Regelungen der Fortpflanzungsmedizin und Humangenetik: Eine international Dokumentation gesetzlicher und berufsständischer Rechtsquellen* (Frankfurt: Campus, 1990), 41–47.

120. *Bericht der gemeinsamen Arbeitsgruppe in-Vitro-Fertilisation, Genomanalyse und Gentherapie* (Benda-Kommission), cited in ibid., 44.

121. Eser, Koch, and Wiesenbart, *Regelungen der Fortpflanzungsmedizin*, 45.

122. See Bundesminister der Justiz, "Diskussionsentwurf eines Gesetzes zum Schutz von Embryonen (Embryonenschutzgesetz-ESchG) vom 29.4.1986," in Ibid., 90–92.

123. Paragraph 13 of the revised adoption law addressed the surrogacy ban. See the excerpt of Gesetz zur Änderung des Adoptionsvermittlungsgesetzes (1989) in Eser, Koch, and Wiesenbart, *Regelungen der Fortpflanzungsmedizin*, 98.

124. See Embryonenschutzgesetz, in Eser, Koch, and Wiesenbart, *Regelungen der Fortpflanzungsmedizin*, 90.

125. See Nicole Richardt, "A Comparative Analysis of the Embryological Research Debate in Great Britain and Germany," *Social Politics: International Studies in Gender, State and Society* 10, no. 1 (2003): 86–128, and John A. Robertson, "Reproductive Technology in Germany and

the United States: An Essay in Comparative Law and Bioethics," *Columbia Journal of Transnational Law* 43 (2004): 189–227.

126. Kleinert, quoted in "Strafrecht: Wahnhafte Beziehung," *Der Spiegel*, September 9, 1988.

127. Horst Mewes, "A Brief History of the German Green Party," in *The German Greens: Paradox between Movement and Party*, ed. Margit Mayer and John Ely (Philadelphia: Temple University Press, 1998), 31.

128. "Die Unheimliche Macht der Selbstschützer," *Der Spiegel*, July 31, 1978.

129. Mewes, "Brief History," 33–36.

130. Langguth, *Green Factor*, 13–14.

131. Mewes, "Brief History," 37.

132. Langguth, *Green Factor*, 33.

133. On feminists' rise to power in the Green Party, see Claudia Pinl, "Green Feminism in Parliamentary Politics," in *German Greens*, ed. Mayer and Ely, 128–140.

134. Sara Jansen, "National Report on West Germany," FINNRET/FINRRAGE Conference, July 3–8, 1985, Lund, Sweden, http://www.finrrage.org, accessed January 15, 2013.

135. Heidi Hofmann, *Die feministischen Diskurse über Reproduktionstechnologien: Positionen und Kontroversen in der BRD und den USA* (Frankfurt: Campus, 1999), 104.

136. Maria Mies, "Reproduktionstechnik als sexistische und rassistische Bevölkerungspolitik," in *Frauen gegen Gentechnik und Reproduktionstechnik: Dokumentation zum Kongreß vom 19.–21. 4, 1985 in Bonn*, ed. Die Grünen im Bundestag, AK Frauenpolitik & Sozialwissenschaftliche Forschung und Praxis für Frauen (Cologne: Kölner Volksblatt, 1986), 44.

137. Hofmann, *Die feministischen Diskurse*, 103.

138. Erika Hickel, "Menschenwürde statt Männerwürde," in *Frauen gegen Gentechnik*, 38.

139. Dorothy Liers, "Familienpolitik, Gen- und Reproduktionstechnologie," in *Frauen gegen Gentechnik*, 86. See also the presentation of Maria Mies, "Argumente wider den Bio-Krieg," 114–118.

140. Mies, "Reproduktionstechnik als sexistische," 44.

141. Ibid., 45.

142. Marina Steinbach, "Der Mythos der Entscheidungsfreiheit," in *Frauen gegen Gentechnik*, 111.

143. Mies, "Reproduktionstechnik als sexistische," 45.

144. Bundesverfassungsgericht, BVerfGE 39, 1—Schwangerschaftsabbruch 1, February 25, 1975.

145. kfd-1177, Letter from Anneliese Lissner to Mechthild Höflich, October 19, 1987.

146. Ibid.

147. Mies, "Reproduktionstechnik als sexistische," 44.

148. On the cost-benefit emphasis of the early debate, see Hampel et al., "Germany," 63–76.

149. On Germany's changing relationship to its Nazi past, see Aleida Assmann, *Der lange Schatten der Vergangenheit: Erinnerungskultur und Geschichtspolitik* (Munich: Beck, 2006), and Norbert Frei, *1945 und wir: Das Dritte Reich im Bewusstsein der Deutschen* (Munich: Beck, 2005).

150. Sara Jansen, "National Report on West Germany," FINNRET/FINRRAGE Conference, July 3–8, 1985, Lund, Sweden, http://www.finrrage.org, accessed March 15, 2013.

151. Rat der Evangelischen Kirche Deutschland und Sekretariat der Deutschen Bischofskonferenz, *Gott ist ein Freund des Lebens*, November 30, 1989, 11.

152. For the survey and Maier's reaction, see, respectively, Hans Heigert, "Robben ja-Kinder nein," *SZ*, July 16, 1984, and "ZdK: 200.000 Abtreibungen jährlich sind unerträglich: For-

derungskatalog des ZdK an Parteien, Fraktionen und Regierungen," *ZdK-Mitteilungen*, no. 248, November 26, 1984.

153. Deutsche Bischofskonferenz, *Für das Leben: Pastorales Wort zur Schutz der ungeborenen Kinder* (November 24, 1986), 11, http://www.dbk.de, accessed August 24, 2015.

154. *Gott ist ein Freund des Lebens*, 100.

155. Richardt, "Comparative Analysis," 101–112.

156. Research using imported stem cells had to meet three criteria: (1) high priority, (2) previous successful results in animal experiments, and (3) detailed explanation of why embryonic stem cells would be required. The law also specified that imported stem cell lines must have been produced prior to May 7, 2007, and that the Central Ethics Commission must approve. See "Gesetz zur Sicherstellung des Embryonenschutzes im Zusammenhang mit Einfuhr und Verwendung menschlicher embryonaler Stammzellen (Stammzellgesetz) StZG," in Manuela Brewe, *Embryonenschutz und Stammzellgesetz: Rechtliche Aspekte der Forschung mit embryonalen Stammzellen* (Berlin: Springer, 2006), 300–306.

157. Kirsten Kullmann, "Genetic Risks: The Implications of Genetic Screening," *Spiegel Online International*, February 8, 2013, http://www.spiegel.de, accessed February 12, 2013.

158. On the emergence of differing feminist perspectives in the 1990s, see Kathrin Braun, "Women, Embryos, and the Good Society: Gendering the Bioethics Debate in Germany," in *Gendering the State in the Age of Globalization: Women's Movements and State Feminism in Postindustrial Democracies*, ed. Melissa Haussman and Birgit Sauer (Lanham, MD: Rowman & Littlefield, 2007), 147–168.

159. Kullmann, "Genetic Risks."

EPILOGUE

1. Glück, quoted in Tristana Moore, "German Priests' Sex Abuse Scandalizes Church," *Time*, March 15, 2010.

2. Kirchenaustritte, 1953–2010/2011, Forschungsgruppe Weltanschauungen in Deutschland, fowid.de, accessed April 14, 2015.

3. On April 25, 2005, *Die Bild-Zeitung* proclaimed, "We Are Pope." On the loss of euphoria, see, e.g., Elisabeth Zoll, "Benedikt versteht die Moderne nicht," *Neue Württembergische Zeitung*, April 15, 2010.

4. "Helpless in the Vatican: The Failed Papacy of Benedict XVI," *Spiegel Online International*, April 6, 2010, www.spiegel.de, accessed April 12, 2015.

5. See, e.g., Stephan Hebel, "Worüber der Papst schweigt," *Frankfurter Rundschau*, March 21, 2010; "Papst Benedikt schweigt weiter," *Handelsblatt*, April 4, 2010; "Missbrauch in der katholischen Kirche: Papst Benedikt XVI. schweigt," *Stern*, March 14, 2010.

6. Weiser, quoted in Thomas C. Fox, "After Abuse Letter, German Catholics Want More," *National Catholic Reporter*, March 22, 2010.

7. Benedict XVI, *Pastoral Letter to the Catholics of Ireland*, March 19, 2010.

8. IMWAC press release, March 24, 2010, www.wir-sind-kirche.de, accessed April 13, 2015.

9. Hans Küng, "Offener Brief: Historischer Vertrauensverlust," *SZ*, April 15, 2010. The letter also appeared in *Neue Zürcher Zeitung*, *La Repubblica*, *El País*, and *Le Monde* and was distributed via New York Times Syndication.

10. See "Helpless in the Vatican."

11. Ines Pohl, "Noch Schlimmer als erwartet," *TAZ*, February 11, 2013.

12. *Die Welt* editorial, quoted in Charles Hawley, "The World from Berlin: 'It Is Good That Benedict Is Gone,'" *Spiegel Online International*, February 12, 2013, www.spiegel.de, accessed April 13, 2015.

13. John Paul II, *Discurso a la Asamblea del CELAM*, March 9, 1983, pt. III, par. 5.

14. For a complete list, see Neue katholische geistliche Gemeinschaften und Bewegungen website, http://www.geistliche-gemeinschaften.de, accessed April 15, 2015.

15. See Rodney Stark and William Sims Bainbridge, *A Theory of Religion* (New Brunswick, NJ: Rutgers University Press, 1996).

16. Weisner, quoted in "'Not Afraid of Reality': Pope Praised for New Stance on Gays," *Spiegel Online International*, July 30, 2013, www.spiegel.de, accessed August 19, 2015.

17. "Archbishop Müller Affirms Doctrine, Pastoral Care for Divorced," *Catholic News Agency*, January 3, 2014, http://www.catholicnewsagency, accessed January 12, 2014.

18. See Roberto Dodaro, ed., *Remaining in the Truth of Christ: Marriage and Communion in the Catholic Church* (San Francisco: Ignatius Press, 2014).

19. For an English translation, see "Synod on Family: Midterm Report Presented, 2015 Synod Announced," *Vatican Radio*, October 14, 2014, http://en.radiovaticana.va; for the original Italian report, see http://press.vatican.va; both accessed January 12, 2015.

20. See *Catechism of the Catholic Church*, 2d ed., no. 2357; see also CDF, *Persona Humana*, December 29, 1975, sec. 8.

21. See, e.g., Mark Greaves, "Family Synod: Mid-term Report Is Hailed as a 'Pastoral Earthquake,'" *Catholic Herald*, October 13, 2014; Matteo Matzuzzi, "Il sesso squassa la vigna," *Il Foglio*, October 15, 2014; Adrienne Siegel, "Eglise: Un synode aux airs de séisme," BFMTV, March 19, 2014.

22. "ZdK und Bischofskonferenz reagieren auf Synoden-Zwischenbericht," October 14, 2014, domradio.de, accessed April 15, 2015.

23. For a summary from a conservative perspective, see Patrick B. Craine, "'Unacceptable': Numerous Vatican Synod Fathers Lining Up against Interim Report," October 15, 2014, www.lifesitenews.com, accessed April 13, 2015.

24. "DBK Vorsitzender Marx: 'Wir sind keine Filialen von Rom,'" *Katholische Nachrichten*, February 26, 2015, www.kath.net, accessed April 15, 2015.

25. See Jonathan Luxmoore, "Cardinal Says Bishops' Conferences Cannot Go It Alone," *National Catholic Reporter*, March 27, 2015, www.ncronline.org, accessed April 15, 2015.

26. "Offener Brief des Arbeitskreises von Katholiken im Raum Frankfurt am Main an Herrn Kardinal Marx und in Durchschrift an die Mitglieder der Deutschen Bischofskonferenz," March 15, 2015, www.katholikenkreis.de, accessed April 17, 2015.

27. Ross Douthat, "The Pope and the Precipice," *NYT Sunday Review*, October 25, 2014, www.nytimes.com, accessed April 12, 2015.

Selected Bibliography

ARCHIVES

Archiv für Christlich-Demokratische Politik, Konrad-Adenauer Stiftung (ACDP)
Archive of the Katholische Frauengemeinschaft Deutschlands, Düsseldorf (kfd)
Bund der Deutschen Katholischen Jugend, Düsseldorf, Jugendhaus Düsseldorf (JHD)
Bundesarchiv Deutschland (B)
Historisches Archiv des Erzbistums Köln (AEK)
Historisches Archiv des Erzbistums Köln, Archiv der Deutschen Bischofskonferenz
Historisches Archiv des Erzbistums Köln, Archiv der Deutschen Bischofskonferenz, Würzburger Synode
Zentralkomitee der deutschen Katholiken—Archiv (ZdK)

NEWSPAPERS AND PERIODICALS
RELIGIOUS

America Magazine
BDKJ-Informationsdienst
Bonifatiusbote: Kirchen Zeitung für das Bistum Fulda
Catholic World News
Communio: Internationale Katholische Zeitschrift
Concilium
Die Deutsche Tagespost
Dialog
Frankfurter Hefte
Frau und Mutter
Furrow
Herder Korrespondenz: Monatshefte für Gesellschaft und Religion
Kirche und Gesellschaft
Neue Bildpost
Orientierung
L'Osservatore Romano
Publik
Publik-Forum
Sonntagsblatt
Stimmen der Zeit: Monatsschrift für das Geistesleben der Gegenwart
Theologischer Digest
Tübinger Theologische Quartalschrift
ZdK-Mitteilungen

SECULAR

Abendzeitung München (Munich)
Ärztliche Sachverständigen-Zeitung (Berlin)
Deutsche Medizinische Wochenschrift (Leipzig)
Deutsche Presse-Agentur (Hamburg)
Düsseldorfer Nachrichten (Düsseldorf)

Le Figaro (Paris)
Frankfurter Allgemeine Zeitung (Frankfurt)
Frankfurter Rundschau (Frankfurt)
Fränkische Landeszeitung (Ansbach)
Guardian (Manchester)
Handelsblatt (Düsseldorf)
Hippokrates (Stuttgart)
Kölner Stadt-Anzeiger (Cologne)
Münchener Medizinische Wochenschrift (Munich)
Nature (Baltimore)
Neue Rheinzeitung (Koblenz)
Neue Württembergische Zeitung (Göppingen)
New York Times
Nordwest Zeitung Oldenburg (Oldenburg)
Das Recht: Rundschau für den deutschen Juristenstand (Munich)
Rheinische Merkur/Christ und Welt (Hamburg)
Rheinische Post (Düsseldorf)
Ruhr Nachrichten (Dortmund)
Schwäbische Donau Zeitung (Augsburg)
Schwäbisches Tagblatt (Tübingen)
Der Spiegel (Hamburg)
Spiegel Online International (Hamburg)
Stern (Hamburg)
Stuttgarter Zeitung (Stuttgart)
Süddeutsche Zeitung (Munich)
Südkurier Konstanz (Konstanz)
Time (New York)
Die Welt (Hamburg)
Westdeutsche Allgemeine Zeitung (Essen)
Die Zeit (Hamburg)
Zentralblatt für Gynäkologie (Leipzig)

PUBLISHED PRIMARY SOURCES

Allen, Prudence. "*Mulieris Dignitatem* Twenty Years Later: An Overview of the Document and Challenges." *Ave Maria Law Review* 13, no. 8 (2007): 13–47.

Aquinas, Thomas. *Compendium of Theology*. Translated by Cyril Vollert. St. Louis: Herder, 1947.

———. *On Love and Charity: Commentary on the Sentences of Peter Lombard*. Translated by Peter A. Kwasniewski, Thomas Bolin, and Joseph Bolin. Washington, DC: Catholic University of America Press, 2008.

———. *Summa Theologica*, 3 vols. English translation by the Fathers of the English Dominican Province. New York: Benziger, 1947.

Augustine. *Of the Good of Marriage*. Translated by C. L. Cornish. In *Nicene and Post-Nicene Fathers, First Series*, vol. 3. Edited by Philip Schaff. Buffalo, NY: Christian Literature Publishing, 1887. Revised and edited for New Advent by Kevin Knight. http://www.newadvent.org.

Augustine, Charles. *A Commentary on the New Code of Canon Law*, 8 vols. St. Louis Park, MO: B. Herder, 1918–1923.

Balthasar, Hans Urs von, ed. *Bischofssynode 1971: Das Priesteramt*. Freiburg: Johannes, 1972.
Benedict XVI. *Pastoral Letter to the Catholics of Ireland*. March 19, 2010.
Bertsch, L. et al., eds. *Gemeinsame Synode der Bistümer in der Bundesrepublik Deutschland*, vol. 1. Freiburg: Herder, 1976.
Bloemhof, Fedde. "Entmenschlichung des Menschen und Mißbrauch der Wissenschaft." *Die künstliche Befruchtung beim Menschen: Diskussionsbeiträge aus medizinischer, juristischer und theologischer Sicht*, 119–136. Cologne: Otto Schmidt, 1960.
Bock, Teresa. "Aufgaben und Mitarbeit der Frauen in der Kirche." In *Die Frau in Gesellschaft und Kirche: Analysen und Perspektiven*. Edited by Anton Rauscher, 202–211. Berlin: Duncker & Humblot, 1986.
Böckle, Franz. "Die sittliche Beurteilung sterilisierender Medikamente." *Herder Korrespondenz* 16 (1962): 354–371.
———. "Ethik und Genetik: Podiumsgespräch und Diskussion." *Genetik und Gesellschaft: Marburger Forum Philippinum*. Edited by G. Gerhard Wendt, 135–145. Stuttgart: Wissenschaftliche Verlagsgesellschaft, 1970.
Brauksiepe, Aenne. "Einführung in den Tagesordnungspunkt, 23–24 March 1973." *Berichte und Dokumente* 18 (1973): 36–48.
Chargaff, Erwin. "Engineering a Molecular Nightmare." *Nature* 327 (May 1987): 199–200.
Commission on Woman in the Church, Belgian Bishops' Conference. "Who May Dwell within Your Tent?" (Wie Mag Toeven Binnen Uw Tent?). Translated by John Wijngaards. Women Can Be Priests: The International Catholic Online Authority on Women Ministries. http://www.womenpriests.org.
Congregation for Catholic Education. *Orientamenti educativi per la formazione al celibato sacerdotale*. April 11, 1974.
Congregation for Divine Worship and the Discipline of the Sacraments. *Inaestimabile Donum*. Instruction Concerning Worship of the Eucharist Mystery. April 3, 1980. http://www.ewtn.com.
———. "Vatican Communication on Female Altar Servers." March 15, 1994. http://www.ewtn.com.
Congregation for the Doctrine of the Faith. *Declaration on Procured Abortion*. November 18, 1974.
———. *Donum Vitae*. Instruction on Respect for Human Life in Its Origin and on the Dignity of Procreation. February 22, 1987.
———. *Inter Insigniores*. Declaration on the Question of Admission of Women to the Ministerial Priesthood. October 15, 1976.
———. *Letter to all Local Ordinaries and General Moderators of Clerical Religious Communities Regarding the Dispensation of Priests from Celibacy*. October 14, 1980.
———. "Responsum ad Propositum Dubium Concerning the Teaching Contained in *Ordinatio Sacerdotalis*." October 28, 1995.
Dellepoort, Jan. "Einige Gedanken über die europäische Priesterfrage." In *Die Europäische Priesterfrage: Bericht der Internationalen Enquête in Wien, 10.–12. Oktober 1958*. Edited by Franz Jachym, 60–85. Vienna: Internationales katholisches Institut für kirchliche Sozialforschung, 1959.
Dellepoort, Jan, Norbert Greinacher, and Walter Menges, eds., *Die deutsche Priesterfrage: Eine soziologische Untersuchung über Klerus und Priesternachwuchs in Deutschland*. Mainz: Matthias-Grünewald, 1962.
Denzler, Georg, ed. *Lebensberichte verheirateter Priester: Autobiographische Zeugnisse zum Konflikt zwischen Ehe und Zölibat*. Munich: Piper, 1989.

Deutsche Bischofskonferenz. *Empfehlungen für Ärzte und medizinische Fachkräfte in Krankenhäusern nach der Änderung des § 218 StGB.* May 7, 1976. http://wwwdbk.de.

———. *Für das Leben: Pastorales Wort zum Schutz der ungeborenen Kinder.* 24 November 1986. http://www.dbk.de.

———. *Wort der deutschen Bischöfe zur seelsorglichen Lage nach dem Erscheinen der Enzyklika "Humanae Vitae."* August 30, 1968. http://www.dbk.de.

———. *Zu Fragen der Stellung der Frau in Kirche und Gesellschaft.* 21 September 1981. http://www.dbk.de.

Die Grünen im Bundestag, AK Frauenpolitik & Sozialwissenschaftliche Forschung und Praxis für Frauen, ed. *Frauen gegen Gentechnik und Reproduktionstechnik: Dokumentation zum Kongreß vom 19.–21. 4, 1985 in Bonn.* Cologne: Kölner Volksblatt, 1986.

Dietze, Gottfried. "Natural Law in Modern European Countries." *Natural Law Forum* 73 (1956): 73–91.

Dirks, Marianne and Anneliese Lissner. "Wünsche katholischer Frauen, Mütter und Ehepaare an das Konzil." In *Konkrete Wünsche an das Konzil.* Edited by Viktor Schurr, 57–93. Kevelaer: Butzon & Becker, 1961.

Doms, Herbert. *The Meaning of Marriage.* Translated by George Sayer. New York: Sheed & Ward, 1939.

Döpfner, Julius. "Instruction to the Confessors of the Munich Archdiocese (1965)." In *The Church and Contraception.* Edited by John T. Noonan Jr., 74. New York: Paulist Press, 1967.

Dreher, Eduard. "Introduction." *German Draft Penal Code E 1962.* Translated by Neville Ross. South Hackensack, NJ: Rothman, 1966.

Drewermann, Eugen. *Kleriker: Psychogramm eines Ideals.* Olten: Walter, 1989.

Elsner, Maria-Franz, "Essen war anders." In *Mitten in dieser Welt: 82. Deutscher Katholikentag Essen 1968.* Edited by Zentralkomitee der deutschen Katholiken, 15–39. Bonn: Bonifatius, 1968.

Eser, Albin. "Germany." *American Journal of Comparative Law* 21, no. 2 (1973): 245–262.

Eser, Albin, Hans-Georg Koch, and Thomas Wiesenbart, eds. *Regelungen der Fortpflanzungsmedizin und Humangenetik: Eine internationale Dokumentation gesetzlicher und berufsständischer Rechtsquellen.* Frankfurt: Campus, 1990.

Feld, Gerburgis, ed. *Wie wir wurden, was wir sind: Gespräche mit feministischen Theologinnen der ersten Generation.* Gütersloh: Gütersloher, 1998.

Fletcher, Joseph. *Morals and Medicine: The Moral Problems of the Patient's Right to Know the Truth—Contraception, Artificial Insemination, Sterilization, and Euthanasia.* Princeton, NJ: Princeton University Press, 1954.

Fraenkel, P. "Über künstliche Befruchtung beim Menschen und ihre gerichtsärztliche Beurteilung." *Ärztliche Sachverständigen-Zeitung* 15, no. 9 (1909): 169–175.

Friedan, Betty. *It Changed My Life: Writings on the Women's Movement.* New York: Random House, 1976.

Fritsch, H. *Die Krankheit der Frauen, für Ärzte und Studenten,* 11th ed. Berlin: Wreden, 1905.

Fromm, Ernst. "Artifizielle Insemination." In *Die künstliche Befruchtung beim Menschen: Diskussionsbeiträge aus medizinischer, juristischer und theologischer Sicht,* 25–36. Cologne: Dr. Otto Schmidt, 1960.

Giesen, Dieter. *Die künstliche Insemination als ethisches und rechtliches Problem.* Bielefeld: Ernst und Werner Gieseking, 1962.

Glover, William Kevin. *Artificial Insemination among Human Beings.* Washington, DC: Catholic University of America Press, 1948.

Gorby, John D. "Introduction to the Translation of the Abortion Decision of the Constitutional Court of the Federal Republic of Germany." *John Marshall Journal of Practice and Procedure* 9, no. 3 (1976): 557–594.

Gössmann, Elisabeth. "Kommentar." In *Die Zeit der Frau: Apostolisches Schreiben "Mulieris Dignitatem" Papst Johannes Pauls II*, 121–150. Freiburg: Herder, 1988.

Groeger, Guido N. "Die Verantwortung des Einzeln." In *Die künstliche Befruchtung beim Menschen Diskussionsbeiträge aus medizinischer, juristischer und theologischer Sicht*, 137–146. Cologne: Schmidt, 1960.

Gröner, Franz, ed. *Kirchliches Handbuch: Amtliches statistisches Jahrbuch der katholischen Kirche Deutschlands*, vol. 25. Cologne: Bachem, 1962.

———. *Kirchliches Handbuch: Amtliches statistisches Jahrbuch der katholischen Kirche Deutschlands*, vol. 26. Cologne: Bachem, 1969.

Häring, Bernhard. *Das Gesetz Christi: Moraltheologie*, 2d ed., vol. 3. Freiburg: Wewel, 1961.

———. "Die sittliche Beurteilung sterilisierender Medikamente." *Herder Korrespondenz* 16 (1962): 354–371.

———. *Medical Ethics*. Translated by Gabrielle L. Jean. Slough: St. Paul Publications, 1972.

———. *My Witness for the Church*. Translated by Leonard Swidler. New York: Paulist Books, 1992.

———. "Verantwortete Elternschaft: Aber wie?" *Theologischer Digest* 2 (1959): 153–159.

Harmsen, Hildegard. *Die Frau heute: Fragen an die Kirche*. Theologische Brennpunkte. Frankfurt: Gerhard Kafke, 1967.

Hauke, Manfred. *God or Goddess? Feminist Theology: What Is it? Where Does It Lead?* Translated by David Kipp. San Francisco: Ignatius Press, 1995.

———. *Women in the Priesthood? A Systematic Analysis in Light of Creation and Redemption*. Translated by David Kipp. San Francisco: Ignatius Press, 1988.

Heinzelmann, Gertrud. *Die getrennten Schwester: Frauen nach dem Konzil*. Zurich: Interfeminas, 1967.

———, ed. *Wir schweigen nicht länger! Frauen äußern sich zum II Vatikan Konzil*. Zurich: Interfeminas, 1964.

Helling, Ute. *Zu den Problemen der künstlichen Insemination unter besonderer Berücksichtigung des § 203 E 1962*. Berlin: Walter de Gruyter, 1970.

Hertel, Peter. *Glaubenswächter: Katholische Traditionalisten im deutschsprachigen Raum: Allianzen, Instanzen, Finanzen*. Würzburg: Echter, 2000.

Heydte, Freiherr von der. "Natural Law Tendencies in Modern European Countries." *Natural Law Forum* 73 (1956): 115–121.

Hildebrand, Dietrich von. *Das trojanische Pferd in der Stadt Gottes*. Regensburg: Habbel, 1968.

Höfer, Josef and Karl Rahner, eds. *Lexikon für Theologie und Kirche*. Freiburg: Herder, 1957.

Hohmann, Joachim Stephan. *Der Zölibat: Geschichte und Gegenwart eines umstrittenen Gesetzes: Mit einem Anhang wichtiger kirchlicher Quellentexte*. Frankfurt: Lang, 1993.

Holy Office [Congregation for the Doctrine of the Faith]. *Lamentabili Sane Exitu*. Syllabus Condemning the Errors of Modernists. July 3, 1907. http://www.ewtn.com.

Jansen, Sara. "National Report on West Germany." FINNRET/FINRRAGE Conference, July 3–8, 1985, Lund, Sweden, http://www.finrrage.org.

John XXIII. *Pacem in Terris*. Encyclical Letter on Peace on Earth. April 11, 1963.

———. *Sacerdotii Nostri Primordia*. Encyclical Letter on St. John Vianney. August 1, 1959.

John Paul II. *Address to the German Bishops on the Occasion of Their Ad Limina Visit*. November 20, 1999.

———. *Christifideles Laici*. Apostolic Exhortation on the Vocation and Mission of Laity in the Church and in the World. December 30, 1988.

———. *Discurso a la Asamblea del CELAM*. March 9, 1983.

———. *Evangelium Vitae*. Encyclical Letter on the Value and Inviolability of Human Life. March 15, 1995.

———. *Mulieris Dignitatem*. Apostolic Letter on the Dignity and Vocation of Being Woman on the Occasion of the Marian Year. August 15, 1988.

———. *Sacerdotalis Ordinatio*. Apostolic Letter on Reserving Priestly Ordination to Men Alone. May 22, 1994.

———. *Veritatis Splendor*. Encyclical Letter on Certain Fundamental Questions of the Church's Moral Teachings. August 6, 1993.

Jost, Renate and Eveline Valtink, eds., *Ihr aber, für wen haltet ihr mich? Auf dem Weg zu einer feministisch-befreiungstheologischen Revision von Christologie*. Gütersloh: Kaiser, 1996.

Katholische Frauengemeinschaft Deutschlands. *Auf dem Weg in die Zukunft: Orientierungs- und Arbeitsprogramm, 1979.*

Küng, Hans. *Disputed Truth: Memoirs*. Translated by John Bowden. New York: Continuum, 2007.

Kütemeyer, Wilhelm. "Wissenschaft, Methoden und Mensch, von der Medizin aus gesehen." In *Menschenzüchtung: Das Problem der genetischen Manipulierung des Menschen*. Edited by Friedrich Wagner, 113–134. Munich: Beck, 1969.

Le Fort, Gertrud von. *Die ewige Frau, Die Frau in der Zeit, Die zeitlose Frau*. Munich: Herold, 1961.

Leist, Fritz. *Der Sexuelle Notstand und die Kirchen*. Freiburg: Herder, 1972.

———, ed. *Zum Thema Zölibat: Bekenntnisse von Betroffenen*. Munich: Kindler, 1973.

Lueg, Anne. *Wenn Frauen Priester lieben: Der Zölibat und seine Folgen*. Munich: Kösel, 1994.

Maexie, E. R. *Die Frau vor der Zukunft*. Vienna: Herold, 1964.

Magnis, Franz Graf von, ed. *Pornographie—Ehescheidung—Abtreibung: Gedanken, Analysen, Dokumente*. Aschaffenburg: Pattloch, 1971.

Mausbach, Joseph. *Die Stellung der Frau im Menschheitsleben: Eine Anwendung katholischer Grundsätze auf die Frauenfrage*. Mönchengladbach: Zentralstelle des Volksvereins für das katholische Deutschland, 1906.

Meier, H. W. "Zur Kasuistik der psychischen Impotenz." *Münchener Medizinischer Wochenschrift* 63 (1915): 1415–1416.

Meyer-Rügg, Hans. "Über künstliche Befruchtung beim Menschen." *Münchener Medizinische Wochenschrift* 63 (1916): 1416–1418.

Müller, Iris. "Katholische Theologinnen: Unterdrückt, aber dennoch angepaßt und ergeben." In *Zur Priesterin berufen: Gott sieht nicht auf das Geschlecht. Zeugnisse römischer-katholischer Frauen*. Edited by Ida Raming et al., 43–52. Munich: Dr.-und-Verl.-Haus Thau, 1998.

Müller, Iris and Ida Raming. *Unser Leben im Einsatz für Menschenrechte in der römisch-katholischen Kirche*. Münster: LIT, 2007.

Münch, Josef Theresia. "My Letters to the Pope," *Catholic Citizen: Journal of St. Joan's International Alliance* 72, no. 1 (1991): 18–29. Reprinted on the website Women Can be Priests: The International Catholic Online Authority on Women's Ministries. http://www.womenpriests.org.

Mynarek, Hubertus. *Eros und Klerus*. Düsseldorf: Econ, 1978.

Olshausen, Th. "Das Reichsgericht zur Frage der künstlichen Befruchtung." *Deutsche Medizinische Wochenschrift* 34 no. 38 (1908): 1636.

———. "Künstliche Befruchtung und eheliche Abstammung." *Deutsche Medizinische Wochenschrift* 38, no. 12 (1908): 515–516.

Paul VI. *Address to the General Secretary of the "International Women's Year."* 6 November 1974.

———. *Ad Pascendum*. Motu Proprio. August 15, 1972.
———. *Humanae Vitae*. Encyclical Letter on the Regulation of Birth. July 25, 1968.
———. *Ministeria Quadem*. Carta Apostólica en forma de Motu Proprio por la que se reforma en la Iglesia Latina la disciplina relativa a la primera tonsura a las Órdenes Menores y al Subdiaconado. August 15, 1972.
———. *Pontificalis Romani*. Sono approvati i nuovi riti per l'ordinazione dei Diaconi, Presbiteri e Vescovi, June 18, 1968.
———. *Sacerdotalis Caelibatus*. Encyclical Letter on the Celibacy of the Priest. June 24, 1967.
———. *Sacrum Diaconatus Ordinem*. General Norms for Restoring the Permanent Diaconate in the Latin Church, June 18, 1967.
Pawlowski, Harald. *Krieg gegen die Kinder? Für und wider die Abtreibung—Mit einer Dokumentation*. Limburg: Lahn, 1971.
Permanent Committee for International Congresses of the Lay Apostolate. *Man Today: Proceedings of the Third World Congress for the Lay Apostolate*, vol. 2. Rome: Permanent Committee for International Congresses of the Lay Apostolate, 1968.
Pius X. *Pascendi Dominici Gregis*. Encyclical Letter on the Doctrine of the Modernists. September 8, 1907.
Pius XI. *Casti Connubii*. Encyclical Letter on Christian Marriage. December 31, 1930.
Pius XII. *Discurso al Congreso de la Unión Católica Italiana de Obstétricas con la colaboración de la Federación Nacional de Colegios de Comadronas Católicas*. October 29, 1951.
———. *Discurso al VII Congreso de la Sociedad Internacional de Hematología*. September 12 1958.
———. *Menti Nostrae*. Apostolisches Mahnwort über die Heiligkeit des Priesterlebens. September 23, 1950.
———. *Sacra Virginitas*. Encyclical Letter on Consecrated Virginity. March 25, 1954.
———. *Votre Présence*. Discurso a los participantes en el IV Congreso Internacional de Médicos Católicos. September 29, 1949.
Pontifical Bible Commission. "Report: Can Women be Priests?" *Origins* 6, no. 6 (July 1976): 92–96.
Prochownick, L. "Ein Beitrag zu den Versuchen künstlicher Befruchtung beim Menschen." *Zentralblatt für Gynäkologie* 39 (1915): 147–150.
Rahner, Karl. "Celibacy of the Secular Priest," *Furrow* 19, no. 2 (1968): 59–73.
———. *Strukturwandel der Kirche als Aufgabe und Chance*. Freiburg: Herder, 1971.
———. "The Experiment with Man: Theological Observations on Man's Self-Manipulation." Translated by Graham Harrison. In *Theological Investigations*, vol. 9: *Writings of 1965–1967*, 205–224. New York: Herder and Herder, 1972.
———. "Zum Problem der genetischen Manipulation aus der Sicht des Theologen." In *Menschenzüchtung: Das Problem der genetischen Manipulierung des Menschen*. Edited by Friedrich Wagner, 135–166. Munich: Beck, 1969.
Raming, Ida. *Frauenbewegung und Kirche: Bilanz eines 25-jährigen Kampfes für Gleichberechtigung und Befreiung der Frau seit dem 2. Vatikanische Konzil*. Weinheim: Deutscher Studien, 1989.
———. "Relevanz und Stellenwert des Kirchenrechts in der feministischen Theologie." In *Theologiefeministisch: Disziplinen—Schwerpunkte—Richtungen*. Edited by Mary Wacker, 115–142. Düsseldorf: Patmos, 1988.
Ranke-Heinemann, Uta. *Eunuchs for the Kingdom of Heaven: Women, Sexuality, and the Catholic Church*. Translated by Peter Heinegg. New York: Doubleday, 1990.
Rat der Evangelischen Kirche Deutschlands und Sekretariat der Deutschen Bischofskonfe-

renz, *Gott ist ein Freund des Lebens: Herausforderungen und Aufgaben beim Schutz des Lebens*, November 30, 1989. http://www.sterbehilfedeutschland.de.

Reuss, J. M. "Eheliche Hingabe und Zeugung: Ein Diskussionsbeitrag zu einem differenzierten Problem." *Tübinger Theologische Quartalschrift* 143 (1963): 454–476.

Roegele, Otto B. "Wächteramt oder Herrschaftsanspruch? Die Bischöfe, der §218 und die Politik." *Communio: Internationale Katholische Zeitschrift* 3 (1972): 269–277.

Rohleder, Hermann. *Test Tube Babies: A History of Artificial Impregnation of Human Beings.* Translated by John Hill. New York: Panurge Press, 1934.

———. *Vorlesungen über Geschlechtstrieb und gesamtes Geschlechtsleben des Menschen.* Berlin: Fischer, 1901.

Ruether, Rosemary Radford. "Should Women Want Women Priests or Women-Church?" *Feminist Theology* 20, no. 63 (2011): 63–72.

Sartory, Thomas and Gertrude Sartory. *Strukturkrise einer Kirche: Vor und nach der Enzyklika "Humanae Vitae."* Munich: Deutscher Taschenbuch, 1969.

Schaumberger, Kristine. *Weil wir nicht vergessen wollen: Zu einer feministischen Theologie im deutschen Kontext.* Münster: Morgana, 1987.

Schaumberger, Kristine and Luise Schottroff. *Schuld und Macht: Studien zu einer feministischen Befreiungstheologie.* Munich: Kaiser, 1988.

Schmaus, Michael and Rudolf Lange. *Das Priestertum: Sein Wesen und seine Aufgaben: Überlegungen zur kirchlichen Raumplanung.* Bamberg: St. Otto, 1969.

Schmidtchen, Gerhard. *Priester in Deutschland: Forschungsbericht über die im Auftrag der Deutschen Bischofskonferenz durchgeführte Umfrage unter allen Welt- und Ordenspriestern in der Bundesrepublik Deutschland.* Freiburg: Herder, 1973.

———. *Zwischen Kirche und Gesellschaft: Forschungsbericht über die Umfrage zur Gemeinsamen Synode der Bistümer in der Bundesrepublik Deutschland.* Freiburg: Herder, 1972.

Schottroff, Luise, Silvia Schroer, and Marie-Theres Wacker, eds. *Feministische Exegese: Forschungserträge zur Bibel aus der Perspektive von Frauen.* Darmstadt: Wissenschaftliche Buchgesellschaft, 1995.

Schumaker, Michele M. "John Paul II's Theology of the Body on Trial: Responding to the Accusation of the Biological Reduction of Women." *Nova et Vetera*, English ed., 10, no. 2 (2012): 463–484.

Schwalbe, J. "Bemerkungen zu dem vorstehenden Aufsatz." *Deutsche Medizinische Wochenschrift* 38, no. 12 (1908): 516.

Sheridan, E. F., ed. *Love Kindness! The Social Teachings of the Canadian Bishops (1958–1989)—A Second Collection.* Sherbrooke: Éditions Paulines and the Jesuit Centre for Social Faith and Justice, 1991.

Simon, Helmut. *Katholisierung des Rechtes? Zum Einfluß katholischen Rechtsdenken auf die gegenwärtige deutsche Gesetzgebung und Rechtsprechung.* Göttingen: Vandenhoeck & Ruprecht, 1962.

Sims, James Marion. *Clinical Notes on Uterine Surgery: With Special Reference to the Treatment of the Sterile Condition.* New York: William Wood, 1866.

Sommer, Norbert, ed. *Nennt uns nicht Brüder! Frauen in der Kirche durchbrechen das Schweigen.* Stuttgart: Kreuz, 1985.

Stach, Ilse von. *Die Frauen von Korinth: Dialoge.* Breslau: Bergstadt, 1929.

Steichen, Donna. *Ungodly Rage: The Hidden Face of Catholic Feminism.* San Francisco: St. Ignatius, 1991.

Stelzenberger, Johannes. "Die moraltheologische Beurteilung der künstliche Insemination." In

Die künstliche Befruchtung beim Menschen: Diskussionsbeiträge aus medizinischer, juristischer und theologischer Sicht. 91–118. Cologne: Dr. Otto Schmidt, 1960.

Sullerot, Evelyne and Odette Thiebault. *Die Wirklichkeit der Frau.* Munich: Steinhausen, 1979.

Swidler, Leonard and Arlene Swidler, ed. *Women Priests: A Catholic Commentary on the Vatican Declaration.* New York: Paulist Press, 1976.

Traumann, "Künstliche Befruchtung und Vaterschaft." *Das Recht: Rundschau für den deutschen Juristenstand* 13, no. 22 (1909): 761–765.

Wagner, Friedrich. "Die Manipulierung des Menschen durch Genwissenschaft: Geschichte, Methoden, Ziele und Folgen." In *Menschenzüchtung.* Edited by Friedrich Wagner, 13–50. Munich: Beck, 1969.

Waterworth, J., ed. and trans. *The Canons and Decrees of the Sacred and Ecumenical Council of Trent.* London: Dolman, 1848.

Wolstenholme, Gordon, ed. *Man and His Future: A Ciba Foundation Volume.* Boston: Little, Brown, 1963.

Vatican II Council. *Ad Gentes.* Decree on the Mission Activity of the Church, December 7, 1965.

———. *Apostolicam Actuositatem.* Decree on the Apostolate of the Laity, November 18, 1965.

———. *Christus Dominus.* Decree Concerning the Pastoral Office of Bishops, October 28, 1965.

———. *Gaudium et Spes.* Pastoral Constitution on the Church in the Modern World, December 7, 1965.

———. *Lumen Gentium.* Dogmatic Constitution on the Church, November 21,1964.

———. *Optatam Totius.* Decree on Priestly Training, October 28, 1965.

———. *Perfectae Caritatis.* Decree on Adaptation and Renewal of Religious Life, October 28, 1965.

———. *Presbyterorum Ordinis.* Decree on the Ministry and Life of Priests, December 7, 1965.

———. *Sacrosanctum Concilium.* Constitution on the Sacred Liturgy, December 4, 1963.

Vogel, Friedrich. "Ist mit einer Manipulierbarkeit auf dem Gebiet der Humangenetik zu rechnen? Können und dürfen wir Menschen züchten?" *Hippokrates* 38, no. 16 (1967): 640–650.

Wuermeling, Hans-Bernhard. "Bringt die katholische Lehre zur 'künstliche Befruchtung' neue Gesichtspunkte?" In *Lebensbeginn und menschliche Würde: Stellungnahme zur Instruktion der Kongregation für die Glaubenslehre vom 22.2.1987.* Edited by Stephan Wehowsky, 157–161. Frankfurt: Schweitzer, 1987.

Zentralkomitee der deutschen Katholiken. *Arbeitstagung Freiburg, 10–14 April 1962.* Paderborn: Bonifatius, 1962.

———. "Erklärung des Zentralkomitees der deutschen Katholiken zum Schutz des werdenden Lebens." *Berichte und Dokumente*, no. 11(1970): 5–6.

———. "Großkundgebung der Arbeitsgemeinschaft der katholischen Verbände Deutschlands: Für Das Leben, 29. September 1973." *Berichte und Dokumente*, no. 20 (1973): 1–19.

PUBLISHED SECONDARY SOURCES

Alberigo, Giuseppe, ed. *The Council and the Transition: The Fourth Period and the End of the Council, September 1965–December 1965.* Vol. 5 of *A History of Vatican II.* Translated by Matthew J. O'Connell. Maryknoll, NY: Orbis, 2006.

Allen, John, Jr. *The Future Church: How Ten Trends Are Revolutionizing the Catholic Church.* New York: Doubleday, 2009.

Anderson, Margaret Levina. "Piety and Politics: Recent Work on German Catholicism." *Journal of Modern History* 63 (1991): 681–716.

Arbeitskreis für kirchliche Zeitgeschichte Münster. "Katholiken zwischen Tradition und Moderne: Das katholische Milieu als Forschungsaufgabe." *Westfälische Forschungen* 43 (1993): 588–654.

Assmann, Aleida. *Der lange Schatten der Vergangenheit: Erinnerungskultur und Geschichtspolitik.* Munich: Beck, 2006.

Balz, Manfred. *Heterologe künstliche Samenübertragung beim Menschen: Rechtliche und politische Überlegungen zu einem Vorhaben des Europarats.* Tübingen: Mohr, 1980.

Beal, John P., James A. Coriden, and Thomas J. Green. *New Commentary on the Code of Canon Law.* New York: Paulist Press, 2000.

Beattie, Tina. *New Catholic Feminism: Theology and Theory.* New York: Routledge, 2007.

Bellito, John. *The General Councils: A History of Twenty-One Councils from Nicaea to Vatican II.* New York: Paulist Press, 2002.

Benninghaus, Christina. "Great Expectations: German Debates about Artificial Insemination in Humans around 1912." *Studies in History and Philosophy of Biological and Biomedical Sciences* 38 (2007): 374–392.

Blackbourn, David. *Marpingen: Apparitions of the Virgin Mary in Nineteenth-Century Germany.* Ithaca, NY: Cornell University Press 1994.

Boa, Elizabeth and Rachel Palfreyman. *Heimat—A German Dream: Regional Loyalties, and National Identity in German Culture, 1890–1990.* Oxford: Oxford University Press, 2000.

Bösch, Frank. *Macht und Machtverlust: Die Geschichte der CDU.* Munich: DVA, 2002.

Braun, Kathrin. "Women, Embryos, and the Good Society: Gendering the Bioethics Debate in Germany." In *Gendering the State in the Age of Globalization: Women's Movements and State Feminism in Postindustrial Democracies.* Edited by Melissa Haussman and Birgit Sauer, 147–168. Lanham, MD: Rowman & Littlefield, 2007.

Brewe, Manuela. *Embryonenschutz und Stammzellgesetz: Rechtliche Aspekte der Forschung mit embryonalen Stammzellen.* Berlin: Springer, 2006.

Bush, Tim. *Die deutsche Strafrechtsreform: Ein Rückblick auf die Sechs Reformen des deutschen Strafrechts, 1968–1998.* Baden-Baden: Nomos, 2005.

Cahalan, Kathleen A. *Formed in the Image of Christ: The Sacramental-Moral Theology of Bernhard Häring C.Ss.R.* Collegeville, MN: Liturgical Press, 2004.

Camp, Richard L. "From Passive Subordination to Complementary Partnership: The Papal Conception of a Woman's Place in Church and Society since 1878." *Catholic Historical Review* 76, no. 3 (1990): 506–525.

Carrell, Douglas T. and C. Matthew Peterson, eds. *Reproductive Endocrinology and Infertility: Integrating Modern Clinical and Laboratory Practice.* New York: Springer, 2010.

Carter, Erica. *How German Is She? Postwar Reconstruction and the Consuming Woman.* Ann Arbor: University of Michigan Press, 1997.

Chaney, Sandra. *Nature of the Miracle Years: Conservation in West Germany, 1945–1975.* New York: Berghahn Books, 2008.

Cooke, Bernard and Gary Macy. *Ordination of Women in the Medieval Context.* Vol. 1 of *A History of Women and Ordination.* New York: Lexington Books, 2002.

Curran, Charles E. *Catholic Moral Theology in the United States: A History.* Washington, DC: Georgetown University Press, 2008.

Damberg, Wilhelm. *Abschied von Milieu? Katholizismus im Bistum Münster und in den Niederlanden, 1945–1980.* Veröffentlichungen der Kommission für Zeitgeschichte. Paderborn: Schöningh, 1997.

Damberg, Wilhelm and Frank Bösch. *Soziale Strukturen und Semantiken des Religiösen im Wandel: Transformationen in der Bundesrepublik Deutschland, 1949–1989*. Essen: Klartext, 2011.

David, Paul A. "Path-Dependent Learning and the Evolution of Beliefs and Behaviors: Implications of Bayesian Adaptation under Computationally Bounded Rationality." In *The Evolution of Economic Diversity*. Edited by Antonio Nicita and Ugo Pagano, 85–132. New York: Routledge, 2001.

Demel, Sabine. *Abtreibung zwischen Straffreiheit und Exkommunikation: Weltliches und kirchliches Strafrecht auf dem Prüfstand*. Stuttgart: Kohlhammer, 1995.

Denzler, Georg. *Das Papsttum und der Amtszölibat*, vol. 2. Stuttgart: Hiersemann, 1976.

———. *Die Geschichte des Zölibats*. Freiburg: Herder, 1993.

Dillon, Michele. *Catholic Identity: Balancing Reason, and Power*. Cambridge: Cambridge University Press, 1999.

Dose, Ralf. *Die Durchsetzung der chemisch-hormonellen Kontrazeption in der Bundesrepublik Deutschland*. Berlin: Wissenschaftszentrum Berlin, 1989.

Ebertz, Michael. "Exodus: Frauen und die katholische Kirche in Deutschland." In *Katholiken in den USA und Deutschland: Kirche, Gesellschaft und Politik*. Edited by Wilhelm Damberg and Antonius Liedhegener, 260–72. Münster: Aschendorff, 2006.

Ferree, Myra Marx, *Varieties of Feminism: German Gender Politics in Global Perspective*. Stanford, CA: Stanford University Press, 2012.

Ferree, Myra Marx et al. *Shaping Abortion Discourse: Democracy and the Public Sphere in Germany and United States*. Cambridge: Cambridge University Press, 2002.

Finn, Michael. "Female Sterilization and Artificial Insemination at the French Fin de Siècle: Facts and Fictions," *Journal of the History of Sexuality* 18, no. 1 (2009): 26–43.

Fox, Thomas C. *Sexuality and Catholicism*. New York: George Braziller, 1995.

Frei, Norbert. *1945 und wir: Das Dritte Reich im Bewußtsein der Deutschen*. Munich: Beck, 2005.

Frevert, Ute. *Men of Honour: A Social and Cultural History of the Duel*. Translated by Anthony Williams. Cambridge: Polity Press, 1995.

———. *Women in Modern Germany: From Bourgeois Emancipation to Sexual Liberation*. New York: Berg, 1989.

Galot, Jean. *Theology of the Priesthood*. Translated by Roger Balducelli. San Francisco: Ignatius Press, 1984.

Gante, Michael. *§ 218 in der Diskussion: Meinungs- und Willensbildung, 1945–1976*. Düsseldorf: Droste, 1991.

Garrow, David. *Liberty and Sexuality: The Right to Privacy and the Making of* Roe v. Wade. New York: Macmillan, 1994.

Gatz, Erwin. *Die katholische Kirche in Deutschland im 20. Jahrhundert*. Freiburg: Herder, 2009.

Geyer, Michael. "America in Germany: Power and the Pursuit of Americanization." In *The German–American Encounter: Conflict and Cooperation between Two Cultures, 1800–2000*. Edited by Frank Trommler and Elliott Shore, 121–144. New York: Berghahn Books, 2001.

———. "Cold War Angst: The Case of West-German Opposition to Rearmament and Nuclear Weapons." In *The Miracle Years: A Cultural History of West Germany*. Edited by Hanna Schissler, 376–408. Princeton, NJ: Princeton University Press, 2001.

Geyer, Michael and Lucian Hölscher, eds. *Die Gegenwart Gottes in der modernen Gesellschaft: Transzendenz und religiöse Vergemeinschaftung in Deutschland*. Göttingen: Wallstein, 2006.

Gill, Bernhard. *Gentechnik ohne Politik: Wie die Brisanz der synthetischen Biologie von wissenschaftlichen Institutionen, Ethik- und anderen Kommissionen systematisch verdrängt wird*. Frankfurt: Campus, 1991.

Grossmann, Atina. *Reforming Sex: The German Movement for Birth Control and Abortion Reform, 1920–1950*. New York: Oxford University Press, 1995.

Halter, Deborah. *The Papal No: A Comprehensive Guide to the Vatican's Rejection of Women's Ordination*. New York: Crossroad, 2004.

Hampel, Jürgen et al. "Germany." In *Biotechnology in the Public Sphere: A European Sourcebook*. Edited by John Durant, Martin W. Bauer, and George Gaskell, 63–76. London: Cromwell, 1998.

Harsh, Donna. "Society, the State, and Abortion in East Germany, 1950–1972." *American Historical Review* 102, no. 1 (1997): 53–84.

Hastings, Derek K. "Fears of a Feminized Church: Catholicism, Celibacy, and the Crisis of Masculinity in Wilhelmine Germany." *European History Quarterly* 38 (2008): 34–65.

Hebblethwaite, Peter. *Paul VI: The First Modern Pope*. London: HarperCollins, 1993.

Heget, James E. *Contemporary German Legal Philosophy*. Philadelphia: University of Pennsylvania Press, 1996.

Heilbronner, Oded. *Catholicism, Political Culture, and the Countryside: A Social History of the Nazi Party in South Germany*. Ann Arbor: University of Michigan Press, 1998.

Heineman, Elizabeth D. *Before Porn Was Legal: The Erotic Empire of Beate Uhse*. Chicago: University of Chicago Press, 2011.

———. *What Difference Does a Husband Make? Women and Marital Status in Nazi and Postwar Germany*. Berkeley: University of California Press, 2004.

Henold, Mary J. *Catholic and Feminist: The Surprising History of the American Catholic Feminist Movement*. Chapel Hill: University of North Carolina Press, 2008.

Hernoga, Josef. *Das Priestertum: Zur nachkonziliaren Amtstheologie im deutschen Sprachraum*. Frankfurt: Lang, 1997.

Herzog, Dagmar. "Between Coitus and Commodification: Young West German Women and the Impact of the Pill." In *Between Marx and Coca-Cola: Youth Cultures in Changing European Societies Between 1960 and 1980*. Edited by Axel Schildt and Detlef Siegfried. 261–286. New York: Berghahn Books, 2006.

———. "Christianity, Disability, Abortion: Western Europe, 1960s–1980s." *Archiv für Sozialgeschichte* 51 (2011): 1–40.

———. "Post Coitum Triste Est . . . ? Sexual Politics and Culture in Postunification Germany." *German Politics and Society* 28, no. 1 (2010): 111–140.

———. *Sex after Fascism: Memory and Morality in Twentieth Century Germany*. Princeton, NJ: Princeton University Press, 2005.

———. *Sexuality in Europe: A Twentieth-Century History*. New York: Cambridge University Press, 2011.

Hofmann, Heidi. *Die feministischen Diskurse über Reproduktionstechnologien: Positionen und Kontroversen in der BRD und den USA*. Frankfurt: Campus, 1999.

Holz, Petra. *Zwischen Tradition und Emanzipation: Politikerinnen in der CDU in der Zeit von 1945 bis 1957*. Sulzbach-Taunus: Ulrike Helmer, 2004.

Hörnle, Tatjana. "Penal Law and Sexuality: Recent Reforms in German Criminal Law." *Buffalo Criminal Law Review* 3, no. 2 (2000): 639–685.

Hünermann, Peter, ed. *Diakonat: Ein Amt für Frauen in der Kirche: Eine frauengerechtes Amt*. Ostfildern: Schwabenverlag, 1999.

Jarausch, Konrad. *After Hitler: Recivilizing Germans, 1945–1995*. New York: Oxford University Press, 2006.

Jones, David Albert. *The Soul of the Embryo: An Inquiry into the Status of the Human Embryo in the Christian Tradition*. New York: Continuum, 2004.

Kaiser, Robert Blair. *The Politics of Sex and Religion*. Kansas City, MO: Leaven Press, 1986.

Kennedy, Kimberly A. "*Totus Tuus Sum*, Maria: Pope John Paul II's Framing of the Feminine Genius." In *The Rhetoric of Pope John Paul II*. Edited by Joseph R. Blaney and Joseph P. Zompetti, 199–210. Lanham, MD: Lexington Books, 2009.

Kösters, Christoph. "'Fest soll mein Taufbund immer steh'n . . .': Demonstrationskatholizismus im Bistum Münster, 1933–1945." In *Zwischen Loyalität und Resistenz*. Edited by Rudolf Schlögel and Hans-Ulrich Thamer, 158–184. Münster: Aschendorff, 1996.

Langguth, Gerd. *The Green Factor in German Politics: From Protest Movement to Political Party*. Translated by Richard Strauss. Boulder, CO: Westview Press, 1984.

Leahy, Brenden. "John Paul II and Hans Urs von Balthasar." In *The Legacy of John Paul II*. Edited by Gerald O'Collins and Michael A. Hays, 31–50. New York: Burns & Oates, 2008.

Lepsius, Rainer M. "Parteiensystem und Sozialstruktur: Zum Problem der Demokratisierung der deutschen Gesellschaft." In *Wirtschaft, Geschichte und Wirtschaftsgeschichte*. Edited by William Abel, 371–393. Stuttgart: Fischer, 1966.

Liedhegener, Antonius. *Christentum und Urbanisierung: Katholiken und Protestanten in Münster und Bochum 1830–1930*. Paderborn: Schöningh, 1997.

Litonjua, M. T. *Creative Fractures: Sociology and Religion*. Bloomington, IN: Author House, 2011.

Locht, Pierre de. "Conjugal Spirituality between 1930 and1960." *Concilium* (1976): 34–33.

Loth, Wilfried. *Katholiken im Kaiserreich: Der politische Katholizismus in der Krise des wilhelminischen Deutschlands*. Düsseldorf: Droste, 1984.

Lüdecke, Norbert. "*Humanae Vitae*." In *Erinnerungsorte des Christentums*. Edited by Christoph Markschies and Herbert Wolf, 534–546. Munich: Beck, 2010.

Mantei, Simone. *Na und Ja zur Abtreibung: Die Evangelische Kirche in der Reformdebatte um [Paragraph] 218 StGB, 1970–1976*. Göttingen: Vandenhoeck & Ruprecht, 2004.

Markkola, Pirjo. "Patriarchy and Women's Emancipation." In *World Christianities, c. 1914–2000*. Edited by Hugh McLeod, 555–562. New York: Cambridge University Press, 2006.

Mazower, Mark. *Dark Continent: Europe's Twentieth Century*. New York: Vintage Books, 2000.

Martimort, Áime Georges. *Deaconesses: A Historical Study*. Translated by K. D. Whitehead. San Francisco: St. Ignatius Press, 1986.

McBrien, Richard P., ed. *HarperCollins Encyclopedia of Catholicism*. New York: HarperCollins, 1995.

McClelland, Charles E. *The German Experience of Professionalization: Modern Learned Professions and Their Organization from the Early Nineteenth Century to the Hitler Era*. Cambridge: Cambridge University Press, 1991.

McDannell, Colleen. *The Spirit of Vatican II: The History of Catholic Reform in America*. New York: Basic Books, 2001.

McEnroy, Elizabeth. *Guests in Their Own House: The Women of Vatican II*. New York: Crossroad, 1996.

McLaren, Angus. *Reproduction by Design: Sex, Robots, Trees, and Test Tube Babies in Interwar Britain*. Chicago: University of Chicago Press, 2012.

McLaughlin, Anthony K. W. "The Obligation of Perfect and Perpetual Continence and Married Deacons in the Church." Ph.D. diss., Catholic University of America, 2010.

Mewes, Horst. "A Brief History of the German Green Party." In *The German Greens: Paradox between Movement and Party*. Edited by Margit Mayer and John Ely, 29–48. Philadelphia: Temple University Press, 1998.

Mitchell, Maria D. *The Origins of Christian Democracy: Politics and Confession in Modern Germany*. Ann Arbor: University of Michigan Press, 2012.

Moeller, Robert. *Protecting Motherhood: Women and Family in the Politics of Postwar West Germany.* Berkeley: University of California Press, 1993.

Moyn, Samuel, "Personalism, Community, and the Origins of Human Rights." In *Human Rights in the Twentieth Century.* Edited by Stefan-Ludwig Hoffmann, 85–106. Cambridge: Cambridge University Press, 2011.

Nesbitt, Paula D. *Feminization of the Clergy in America: Occupational and Organizational Perspectives.* New York: Oxford University Press, 1999.

Nipperdey, Thomas. *Religion im Umbruch: Deutschland, 1870–1918.* Munich: Beck, 1988.

Noonan, John T., Jr. *Contraception: A History of Its Treatment by Catholic Theologians and Canonists.* Cambridge, MA: Belknap Press of Harvard University Press, 1965.

Odenberg, Christina. "Ordination and Consecration of Women in the Church of Sweden." In *Women and Ordination in the Christian Churches.* Edited by Ian Jones, Janet Wootton, and Kirsty Thorpe, 113–122. New York: T & T Clark, 2008.

Oertzen, Christine von. *The Pleasure of a Surplus Income: Part-Time Work, Gender Politics, and Social Change in West Germany, 1955–1969.* Translated by Pamela Selwyn. New York: Berghahn Books, 2007.

O'Malley, John W. *What Happened at Vatican II.* Cambridge, MA: Belknap Press of Harvard University Press, 2008.

Osten, Petra von der. *Jugend- und Gefährdetenfürsorge im Sozialstaat: Auf dem Weg zum Sozialdienst katholischer Frauen, 1945–1968.* Cologne: Böhlau, 2003.

Palfreyman, Rachel. "Links and Chains: Trauma between the Generations in the Heimat Mode." In *Screening War: Perspectives on German Suffering.* Edited by Paul Cooke and Robert Silberman, 145–164. New York: Camden House, 2008.

Paul, Gerhard and Klaus-Michael Mallmann, *Milieus und Widerstand: Eine Verhaltensgeschichte der Gesellschaft im Nationalsozialismus, Widerstand und Verweigerung im Saarland, 1935–1945.* Bonn: Dietz, 1995.

Petermann, Heike. "Die biologische Zukunft der Menschheit: Der Kontext des CIBA Symposiums 'Man and his Future' (1962) und seine Rezeption." In *Ursprünge, Arten und Folgen des Konstrukts "Bevölkerung" vor, im und nach dem "Dritten Reich": Zur Geschichte der deutschen Bevölkerungswissenschaft.* Edited by Rainer Mackensen, Jürgen Reulecke, and Josef Ehmer, 393–414. Wiesbaden: Sozialwissenschaften, 2009.

Pinl, Claudia. "Green Feminism in Parliamentary Politics." In *The German Greens: Paradox between Movement and Party.* Edited by Margit Mayer and John Ely, 128–140. Philadelphia: Temple University Press, 1998.

Planert, Ute. *Antifeminismus im Kaiserreich: Diskurs, soziale Formation und politische Mentalität.* Göttingen: Vandenhoeck & Ruprecht, 1998.

Poiger, Uta. *Jazz, Rock, and Rebels: Cold War Politics and American Culture in a Divided Germany.* Berkeley: University of California Press, 2000.

Rakoczy, Susan. "Mixed Messages: John Paul II's Writings on Women." In *The Vision of John Paul II: Assessing His Thought and Influence.* Edited by Gerard Mannion, 159–183. Collegeville, MN: Liturgical Press, 2008.

Reese, Thomas J. *Inside the Vatican: The Politics and Organization of the Catholic Church.* Cambridge, MA: Harvard University Press, 1996.

Richardt, Nicole. "A Comparative Analysis of the Embryological Research Debate in Great Britain and Germany," *Social Politics: International Studies in Gender, State, and Society* 10, no. 1 (2003): 86–128.

Robertson, John A. "Reproductive Technology in Germany and the United States: An Essay in Comparative Law and Bioethics." *Columbia Journal of Transnational Law* 43 (2004): 189–227.

Rocholl-Gärtner, Ingebourg, ed. *Anwalt der Frauen: Hermann Klens, Leben und Werk*. Düsseldorf: Klens, 1978.

Rölli-Alkemper, Lukas. *Familie in Wiederaufbau: Katholizismus und bürgerliches Familienideal in der Bundesrepublik Deutschland, 1945–65*. Paderborn: Schöningh, 2000.

Ross, Susan A. "The Bridegroom and the Bride: The Theological Anthropology of John Paul II and Its Relation to the Bible and Homosexuality." In *Sexual Diversity and Catholicism: Toward the Development of Moral Theology*. Edited by Patricia Beattie Jung and Joseph Andrew Coray, 39–59. Collegeville, MN: Liturgical Press, 1989.

———. "The Bride of Christ and the Body Politic." *Journal of Religion* 71, no. 3 (1991): 345–361.

Ruff, Mark Edward. "Conference Report: Catholicism in Germany—Contemporary History and the Present." *Contemporary Church History Quarterly* 19, no. 1 (March 2013), https://contemporarychurchhistory.org.

———. "Integrating Religion into the Historical Mainstream: Recent Literature on Religion in the Federal Republic of Germany." *Central European History* 42 (2009): 307–337.

———. "Review of *Zeitgeschichtliche Katholizismusforschung: Tatsachen, Deutungen, Fragen. Ein Zwischenbilanz*." *Catholic Historical Review* 91, no. 4 (2005): 852.

———. *The Wayward Flock: Catholic Youth Organizations in the Federal Republic of Germany, 1945–1965*. Chapel Hill: University of North Carolina Press, 2005.

Schank, Christoph. *"Kölsch-Katholisch": Das katholische Milieu in Köln, 1871–1933*. Cologne: Böhlau, 2004.

Schillebeeckx, Edward and Catharina Halkes. *Mary: Yesterday, Today, and Tomorrow*. New York: Crossroad, 1993.

Schissler, Hanna. "German and American Women: Between Domesticity and the Workplace." In *United States and Germany in the Era of the Cold War: A Handbook*, vol. 1. Edited by Detlev Junker, 559–565. New York: Cambridge University Press, 2004.

Schmidtmann, Christian, *Katholische Studierende, 1945–1973: Eine Studie zur Kultur- und Sozialgeschichte der Bundesrepublik Deutschland*. Veröffentlichungen der Kommission für Zeitgeschichte. Paderborn: Schöningh, 2006.

Schoenherr, Richard A. *Goodbye Father: The Celibate Male Priesthood and the Future of the Catholic Church*. Oxford: Oxford University Press, 2004.

Silies, Eva-Maria. *Liebe, Lust und Last: Die Pille als weibliche Generationserfahrung in der Bundesrepublik, 1960–1980*. Göttingen: Wallstein, 2010.

Smith, David. "Abortion: A Moral Controversy." *Dialogue: A Journal for Religious Studies and Philosophy*, no. 8 (April 1997): 13–18.

Stark, Rodney and William Sims Bainbridge, *A Theory of Religion*. New Brunswick, NJ: Rutgers University Press, 1996.

Staupe Gisela and Lisa Vieth, ed. *Die Pille: Von der Lust und von der Liebe*. Berlin: Rowohlt, 1996.

Sutton, Agneta. "Complementarity of the Sexes: Karl Barth, Hans Urs von Balthasar and John Paul II." *New Blackfriars* 87, no. 1010 (2006): 418–433.

Valsecchi, Ambroggio. *Controversy: The Birth Control Debate, 1958–1968*. Translated by Dorothy White. Washington, DC: Corpus Books, 1968.

Wagner-Rau, Ulrike. *Zwischen Vaterwelt und Feminismus: Eine Studie zur pastoralen Identität von Frauen*. Gütersloh: Gütersloh Mohn, 1992.

Walsh, Clare. *Gender and Discourse: Language and Power in Politics, the Church, and Organizations*. New York: Longman, 2001.

Warner, Marina. *Alone of All Her Sex: The Myth and the Cult of the Virgin Mary.* New York: Alfred A. Knopf, 1976.
Webster's New World Medical Dictionary, 3d ed. New York: Wiley, 2008.
Weigel, George. *God's Choice: Pope Benedict XVI and the Future of the Catholic Church.* New York: HarperCollins, 2005.
Whisnant, Clayton J. *Male Homosexuality in West Germany: Between Persecution and Freedom, 1945–69.* New York: Palgrave Macmillan, 2012.
Wijngaards, John. *The Ordination of Women in the Catholic Church: Unmasking a Cuckoo's Egg Tradition.* London: Darton, Longman & Todd, 2001.
Wildenthal, Lora, "Rudolf Laun and the Human Rights of Germans in Occupied and Early West Germany." In *Human Rights in the Twentieth Century.* Edited by Stefan-Ludwig Hoffmann, 125–146. Cambridge: Cambridge University Press, 2011.
Wiliarty, Sara Elise. *The CDU and the Politics of Gender in Germany: Bringing Women to the Party.* Cambridge: Cambridge University Press, 2010.
Wiltgen, Ralph M. *The Inside Story of Vatican II: A Firsthand Account of the Council's Inner Workings.* Charlotte, NC: Tan Books, 2014.
Ziemann, Benjamin. "Der deutsche Katholizismus im späten 19. und 20. Jahrhundert: Forschungstendenzen auf dem Weg zu sozialgeschichtlicher Fundierung und Erweiterung," *Archiv für Sozialgeschichte* 40 (2000): 402–422.
———. *Katholische Kirche und Sozialwissenschaften, 1945–1975.* Göttingen: Vandenhoeck & Ruprecht 2007.
Zumholz, Maria-Anna. *Volksfrömmigkeit und katholisches Milieu: Marienerscheinungen im Heede, 1937–1950, im Spannungsfeld von Volksfrömmigkeit, nationalsozialistischem Regime und kirchlicher Hierarchie.* Cloppenburg: Runge 2004.

Index

abortion, 8–9, 13, 24–25, 109, 117; birth control as form of, 133; and Catholic doctrine, 19, 30, 63, 87–89, 128–129, 137–141; and Catholic lay organizations; 21, 93, 129–130, 134, 136; and clerical sexual abuse; 57; German attitudes about, 225–228; and German medical community, 144; legal regulation in Western Europe and United States, 7, 143, 145. *See also* Paragraph 218
Adenauer, Konrad, 10, 141, 189
adoption, 156, 166, 199, 203
adultery, 9, 138, 184, 190, 193
Albrecht, Margarethe, 190
Alfrink, Johannes, 50. *See also* Dutch Pastoral Council (1969)
Allen, Ann Taylor, 12
Allensbach Institute for Public Opinion Research, 22, 106–107, 132, 148, 166, 170, 190, 201, 205
Allied occupation, 2, 185, 189
Allocution to Midwives, 102–103
altar girls, 81–84, 246n43
Americanization, 3, 9, 189, 193
Anglican Communion, 63–64, 75–76, 93, 105
Anovlar: and German sexual mores, 123–125; introduction in Germany, 115–117. *See also* birth control
apostolic succession, 63
Aquinas, Thomas, 31, 65, 103, 138. *See also* natural law
artificial contraception. *See* Anovlar; birth control
artificial insemination: early medico-legal debate, 175–181; and penal code reform, 182–192. *See also* infertility; in vitro fertilization (IVF)
assisted reproduction. *See* artificial insemination; in vitro fertilization (IVF)
Association of Established Doctors in Germany, 144
Association of Young Christian Workers (CAJ), 146

Augstein, Rudolf, 145, 153, 160
Augustine of Hippo, 103, 105, 138
Auschwitz, 8, 146, 159, 161, 194. *See also* National Socialism

Balthasar, Hans Urs von, 79
Basic Law, 3, 20, 107, 261n78; and abortion, 151–155; and assisted reproduction, 203
Baum, Gregory, 91
Beattie, Tina, 31, 92
Belgian Bishops' Commission on Women and the Church, 94
Benda Commission, 197–199
Benedict XVI, 210–213. *See also* Ratzinger, Joseph
Bergoglio, Jorge Mario. *See* Francis I
Bielefeld-Emnid Institute, 22, 94, 162
birth control, 24, 33; and Anglican Church, 105; Catholic doctrine, 75, 102–104, 119–121; and German Catholic debate on, 102; and German law, 110–111; influence on celibacy debate, 47–49, 52, 128. *See also* Anovlar; rhythm method
Böckle, Franz: and abortion, 128, 141; and assisted reproduction, 193, 197; and birth control, 118, 255n75, 259n22
Bocklet, Paul, 162
Bothmer, Lenelotte von, 147
Brandmüller, Walter, 215
Brown, Louise, 195–197, 200
Bund der Deutschen Katholischen Jugend. *See* League of German Catholic Youth
Bundesärztekammer. *See* German Medical Association
Bundesrat, 150–151, 205
Bundestag, 12, 108; and assisted reproduction, 174, 183, 185, 192, 199, 202, 206, 210; and Paragraph 218, 145, 147, 150–153, 156, 159–160, 164, 166, 171, 173

calendar method. *See* rhythm method
campaign of self-incrimination, 145. *See also* Paragraph 218

291

canon law, 23, 31–32, 34, 52, 64, 67–68, 85, 137–138, 141
Caritas, 130, 172
Carter, Erica, 109
Casti Connubii, 33, 104–105, 120–122, 125, 253n5. *See also* birth control; rhythm method
Catholic milieu, 1, 101, 172, 208; historiography of, 14–18, 209
Catholic womanhood: Church's ideal of, 69–73, 130–132; women's rejection of, 168–170. *See also* marriage; motherhood
Catholic Women's Association in Germany (kfd), 21; and abortion, 136–137, 146, 155, 165–167; and altar girls, 81–84; and assisted reproduction, 173, 185, 196–197, 203; and birth control, 126, 133; and conflict with Archbishop Dyba, 168–171; and women's ordination, 68–70, 72–73, 87, 92; and women's relationship with the Church, 60, 130–132, 135
celibacy, 220–221, 224; and canon law, 31; and clerical shortage, 32, 34–36; dispensations from, 37, 59; and Eastern rite, 239n17; and the media, 55–59; and neoconservatism in the Church, 64; and Second Vatican Council, 38–45; theology of, 30, 33; and women's response to, 60
CDU-CSU coalition: and abortion, 143, 151; and Catholic Church, 1–2, 141; and Catholic voters, 148; family politics, 101, 107–110. *See also* Christian Democratic Union (CDU); Christian Socialist Union (CSU)
Center Party, 2, 15, 111
Central Association of Catholic Communities of Women and Mothers, 69. *See also* Catholic Women's Association in Germany (kfd)
Central Commission for Biological Security (ZKBS), 195
Central Committee of German Catholics (ZdK), 21, 58, 82, 84, 136, 203; and abortion, 144, 147–148, 151, 155–156, 166–168, 170–172; and birth control, 126, 129; and clerical abuse scandal, 210, 216
Central Preparatory Commission, 37, 40, 64. *See also* Second Vatican Council

Chargaff, Erwin, 194
Christian Democratic Union (CDU), 2, 10–11, 153, 159; women in the party, 137
Christian Socialist Union (CSU), 2, 159, 162, 182
Christifideles Laici, 87
Christliche Arbeiterjugend. *See* Association of Young Christian Workers (CAJ)
christliche Frau, Die, 72–73. *See also* League of German Catholic Women (KDFB)
Christus Dominus, 121
church attendance, 4, 22, 217
church separations, 10, 131, 234
CIBA symposium, 190–192
clerical shortage, 34, 36, 38, 50, 53, 63, 65, 75, 131, 222–223
Cold War, 20, 100, 190
collegiality, 6, 46, 121
Commission for Contemporary History, 14, 16
Communion, 4, 22, 67, 113, 125, 149, 215, 218
communism: and defections from Protestant churches, 34; in discourse on assisted reproduction, 189; and postwar West German identity 3, 108–109, 111;
Concilium, 82, 91
Congar, Yves, 6, 71
Congregation for Divine Worship and the Discipline of the Sacraments (CDWDS), 23, 81, 84
Congregation for the Doctrine of the Faith (CDF), 58–59, 212
Constanze, 106–107, 111
Council of Trent, 40–42; 67, 122
Crowley, Patricia and Patrick, 122
Curran, Charles, 181, 214

Damberg, Wilhelm, 16–17
Danube Seven, 94–95
Declaration on Procured Abortions, 139
Declaration on the Position of Women in the Church and Society, 10, 20, 84–85
delayed hominization, 138–140
Deutsche Bischofskonferenz. *See* German Bishops' Conference (DBK)
diaconate, 52; and admission of women, 10, 20, 30, 55, 68, 70–72, 81, 84, 87, 246n61;

and Protestant churches, 64; and *viri probati*, 39–41, 68, 240n47
Dibelius, Otto, 188–190
Dietzelbinger, Hermann, 144, 188
Dirks, Marianne, 68–71, 126, 130, 203
Dirks, Walter, 126
Doms, Herbert, 33, 103–104, 119, 255n76
Donum Vitae, 172–173, 214
Döpfner, Julius, 58, 213; and abortion 144–146, 151, 155–156, 161–162; and birth control, 119–120, 122, 125–126; and female diaconate, 70–71
Dördelmann-Lueg, Anne, 59
Dreher, Eduard, 191
Durand-Wever, Anne Marie, 116
Dutch Pastoral Council (1969), 17, 50–51, 74
Dyba, Johannes, 136, 168–170

Eastern Orthodox Church, 63
East Germany. *See* German Democratic Republic
Ehmke, Horst, 152
Embryo Defense Act (ESchG), 175, 199, 206
Engl, Barbara, 131
Erhard, Ludwig, 109
Eros und Klerus, 57
Essen Catholic Congress, 1, 48–49, 127–128, 149
eugenics, 180, 187–188, 191–192, 194, 197, 202, 204
euthanasia, 146, 192
evangelical Catholicism, 83, 135, 213
Evangelical Church in Germany (EKD), 3, 8, 52, 63, 144, 172–173, 204, 210
Evangelium Vitae, 89, 251n182
ewige Frau, Die, 113–114

family planning. *See* birth control
fascism, 3, 13, 100–101, 125. *See also* National Socialism
Federal Constitutional Court: and abortion, 130, 146, 150–155, 172; and assisted reproduction, 184, 203; jurisdiction of, 151, 261nn78–79
Federal High Court of Justice: and natural law, 154
Federation of German Women Doctors, 190

feminism, 10, 19, 20, 83, 85–86, 96, 130, 163. *See also* new feminism
feminist theology, 82, 85; critiques of, 96
feminized piety, 2, 10–11, 207
fertility. *See* infertility
fetus, 147; and Catholic theology, 138–141; legal status of, 152–155, 171
First Vatican Council, 121
Francis I, 25, 214–215
Frankfurter Allgemeine Zeitung, 150
Frankfurt Guiding Principles, 110
Frauenaktion 218, 144–145
Frauenfrage, 19
Frauen gegen Gentechnik und Reproduktionstechnik (congress), 201–203
Frau und Mutter, 107, 196; and altar girls, 81; and birth control, 112, 130; and feminist theology, 82, 92; and Second Vatican Council, 67; title change of, 136, 168; and women's ordination, 73
Free Democratic Party (FDP), 12, 145–147, 154, 160, 200; and alliance with CDU, 163–165; and alliance with SPD, 136, 143, 150, 158–159, 162, 183
Friedan, Betty, 74
Frings, Josef, 5, 35, 37, 52, 213
Fristenlösung. *See* Paragraph 218
Funcke, Liselotte, 145
Für das Leben rally, 148

Gante, Michael, 155
Gaudium et Spes, 67, 119
Geiger, Wilhelm, 184
genetic engineering, 173, 195, 197–198, 201, 204
German Bishops' Conference (DBK), 22; and abortion, 140, 142, 144, 155, 157–158, 161–162, 172; and altar girls, 82–84; and assisted reproduction, 197, 204; and birth control, 125, 133–134; and celibacy, 49, 51, 53–55, 57–60; and female diaconate, 70–71; and Francis I's papacy, 216; and women's exodus from the Church, 86, 93
German Democratic Republic, 8, 143, 208
German Medical Association, 150, 183, 268n44
Gesetz Christi, Das, 186
Geyer, Michael, 189

Glück, Alois, 210, 216
Goddess movement, 86
Görres, Ida Friederike, 67, 245n32
Gössmann, Elisabeth, 91, 255n195
Gott ist ein Freund des Lebens, 204–205
Grand Commission on Penal Reform, 182–183, 198
Green Party, 12; and abortion, 207; and assisted reproduction, 173, 197, 203–204, 209; history of, 200–201
Greinacher, Norbert, 51, 58, 147–148
Greve, Heinrich, 155
Große-Schönepauck, Helene, 185
Große Strafrechtskommission. *See* Grand Commission on Penal Reform
Gruhl, Herbert, 200–201
Grundgesetz. *See* Basic Law
Güde, Max, 183

Halkes, Catharina, 45, 132
Häring, Bernhard: and birth control, 113, 118, 140–141; and assisted reproduction, 185–190; disciplinary action against, 213; and Second Vatican Council, 43
Harmsen, Hildegard, 68, 70
Hartmann League, 179
Hauke, Manfred, 62, 96
Heineman, Elizabeth, 3, 106, 112
Heinzelmann, Gertrud, 64–66, 69–70, 80–81, 95
Hemmerle, Klaus, 72, 162
Herren und Knechte der Kirche, 57
Herzog, Dagmar, 1, 8, 13, 99, 107, 142
Heuss, Theodor, 154–155
Hickel, Erika, 202
Hildebrand, Dietrich von, 33, 103, 119, 255n78
Höffner, Joseph, 213; and abortion, 144, 146–149, 158–163, 166; and altar girls, 82–83; and assisted reproduction, 197; and birth control, 132–133; celibacy, 57
Hollander, Walther von, 106
Holy Office. *See* Congregation for the Doctrine of the Faith (CDF)
Holzgartner, Hartwig, 159–160
Homeyer, Josef, 162
homosexuality, 57, 63, 87, 91, 211
Humanae Vitae, 1, 13, 19, 29, 193; and collegiality, 121–122; and German debate on, 47–48, 100, 123, 125–126, 128–130, 133, 172
Hünermann, Peter, 71, 246n61
Hunt, Mary, 86
Hürth, Franz, 117–118

illegitimacy. *See* legitimacy (of child)
Indikationslösung. *See* Paragraph 218
infallibility, 94, 122, 128
infertility: causes of, 202; treatment of, 174, 176, 180, 271n107. *See also* artificial insemination; in vitro fertilization (IVF)
Initiative Group for Women Affected by Celibacy, 59
Initiativ Kirche von unten, 95
inner migration, 60, 85, 102, 135
Inter Insigniores, 62, 77–80, 93–95
in vitro fertilization (IVF), 193–196; and Catholic theology, 197; ecumenical opposition to, 204–206; feminist and kfd rejection of, 201–204; regulation of, 198–199, 206–207

Jaeger, Lorenz, 127, 146
Jahn, Gerhard, 145
Jensen, Sara, 204
John Paul II, 10, 30, 37, 131, 213; and abortion, 172; and Anglican Church, 64; and birth control, 128, 133; dispensations from celibacy, 59; and women's ordination, 63, 79, 87–91, 93–95. *See also* nuptial symbolism; theology of the body
John XXIII, 5, 36–37, 39, 58, 64, 122

Kampe, Walther, 33, 66, 83–84
Kamphaus, Franz, 172
Kasper, Walter, 215
Katholische Frauengemeinschaft Deutschlands. *See* Catholic Women's Association in Germany
Katholischer Deutscher Frauenbund. *See* League of German Catholic Women (KDFB)
Keane, Noel P., 203
Kempf, Wilhelm, 10, 56, 58, 81
Kindergeld, 108
Kirchenkampf, 110. *See also* National Socialism

Kleinert, Detlef, 12, 200
Klug, Ulrich, 147
Kommission für Zeitgeschichte. *See* Commission for Contemporary History
König, Franz, 37, 56, 161
Königstein Declaration, 20, 48, 101, 127–128, 133–134. See also *Humanae Vitae*
Kritischer Katholizismus, 127–128
Kühn, Heinz, 147
Kulturkampf, 1–2, 14, 47. *See also* Catholic milieu
Küng, Hans: and celibacy, 46–47, 51; and clerical abuse crisis, 211–212; disciplinary action against, 213; and women's ordination, 80
Kütemeyer, Wilhelm, 192

laicization, 32, 54, 58–59
Lambeth Conference, 105
Lambruschini, Ferdinando, 117–118
Laurien, Hanna-Renate, 83, 167
League of German Catholic Women (KDFB), 60, 72–73, 133, 247n68
League of German Catholic Youth (BDKJ), 4, 131
Lefebvre, Marcel, 6, 156–157, 263n113
Le Fort, Gertrud von, 113
legitimacy (of child), 106, 175–179, 184, 194
Lehmann, Karl, 204
Leist, Fritz, 36, 39
Lepsius, Rainier M., 14
Liénart, Achille, 5
Limbach, Editha, 165
Lissner, Anneliese, 131, 168, 203
liturgy, 40, 44, 67–68, 82
Lohfink, Gerhard, 80
Loi Neuwirth, 7
Lüdecke, Norbert, 19
Lumen Gentium, 38, 40, 42, 44, 68, 121

Maexie, E. R., 114
Maier, Hans, 166–167, 170, 263n108
March, Hans, 114
Marian devotion, 15, 17, 22; and Catholic womanhood, 113; and celibacy, 39, 44; and grassroots Catholicism, 213, 249n139; religious feminist critiques of, 45

Maria von Magdala: Initiative Gleichberechtigung für Frauen in der Kirche, 146
Mariology, 87
marriage, 115; in arguments against women priests, 87–92; Catholic understanding of, 2–4, 17, 19, 33; and contraception, 102–104, 113–114, 119, 254n18; and evangelical Catholicism, 83; and German law, 3, 105–108; and homosexuality, 214; and popular discourse, 109–111, 117; and priesthood, 23, 30–32, 37, 46, 52–53, 62–63, 239n17
Marx, Reinhard, 216
Mathäus-Maier, Ingrid, 160
Mausbach, Joseph, 63
McBride, Margaret, 138
McEnroy, Elizabeth, 95, 214, 253n219
Meisner, Joachim, 10
Mies, Maria, 201–203
Militia Sanctae Mariae, 156, 263n110. *See also* evangelical Catholicism
Ministry of Family Affairs, 108, 185
Ministry of Justice, 160, 182, 191, 197
Ministry of Research and Technology (BMFT), 195, 197
motherhood: and Catholic feminine ideal, 62–63, 69, 88–91, 104, 113–115, 140, 168, 252n182; in secular discourse, 106–110, 179, 184, 202–203; and surrogacy, 199 *See also* Catholic womanhood; marriage
Mothers' Schools, 113
Mulieris Dignitatem, 87–90, 93, 95; responses to, 91–92
Müller, Gerhard, 215
Muller, Hermann J., 191–192
Müller, Iris, 95
Münch, Josefa Theresia, 65–66
Mynarek, Hubertus, 39, 56–58, 213

National Socialism, 14, 37; and abortion debate, 148, 152, 160; and assisted reproduction, 25, 192, 197, 202, 204, 208; Catholic Church under, 101, 185; role in student rebellion, 125, 127–128, 141; and West German identity, 8–10, 107–110
natural family planning. *See* birth control; rhythm method
natural law: and assisted reproduction, 178; and Catholic marriage theology, 104;

and Catholic teaching on birth control, 102–103, 105, 128, 131; and German law, 109–110, 153–154, 204
new feminism, 10–11, 88. *See also* feminism
new reproductive technologies (NRT). *See* artificial insemination; in vitro fertilization (IVF)
nuptial symbolism, 63, 78–79, 87, 91, 95. *See also* John Paul II; theology of the body

Oertzen, Christine von, 111
O'Malley, John, 41–42
Optatam Totius, 38–39
Oraison, Marc, 47
oral contraception. *See* Anovlar
Orientierung, 77, 82
Osservatore Romano, L', 215; and abortion, 146–147; and celibacy, 50; on women's ordination, 66, 78
Osten, Petra von der, 17–18
Ottaviani, Alfredo, 40, 120

Pacem in Terris, 64
Papal Study Commission on Women in the Church and Society, 74
Paragraph 203: and German identity, 204; and penal reform, 182–184
Paragraph 218: Catholic opposition to, 146, 151, 156, 159, 166; and CDU women, 160, 164; feminist campaign against, 145, 201; history of, 142; kfd support of, 166; and SPD, 24, 136, 143, 158, 160; post-unification changes to, 2, 173, 206, 210
Parliamentary Enquête Commission on Genetic Engineering, 197, 201
Pascendi Dominici Gregis, 181
Paul VI, 10, 37, 44, 58; and abortion, 146; and birth control, 20, 47, 100, 120–123, 127, 133–134; and celibacy 45, 50, 52; and diaconate, 240n47; and women's ordination, 64, 67–68, 73–76
personalism, 33. *See also Casti Connubii*; Doms, Herbert
pill. *See* Anovlar; birth control
Pius XI, 120. *See also Casti Connubii*
Pius XII: and assisted reproduction 181, 185, 197; and birth control, 99–100, 102–103, 105, 117, 122; and celibacy, 39, 44; and diaconate, 40
Poiger, Uta, 3, 8
political Catholicism, 1–3, 15, 111, 207–208
Pontifical Bible Commission, 76
Pontifical Commission for the Revision of Canon Law, 68. *See also* canon law
Pontifical Study Commission on Family, Population, and Birth Problems, 121. *See also* birth control
pornography, 7–9
preimplantation genetic diagnosis (PGD), 175, 194
Presbyterorum Ordinis, 38–39
priesthood: defections from, 243n128; theology of, 42. *See also* celibacy; clerical shortage
Priests without Office, 54
principle of double effect, 117, 139–141, 255n71
Protestantism, 19, 110, 212. *See also* Evangelical Church in Germany (EKD)

Rahner, Karl: and abortion, 140; and assisted reproduction, 185–187; and celibacy, 46–49; and future of the Catholic Church, 149, 171; and women's ordination, 80
Raming, Ida, 65, 69–70, 76, 85–86, 95, 250n154
Ranke-Heinemann, Elisabeth, 45, 139–140, 213, 259n13
Ratzinger, Georg, 211
Ratzinger, Joseph, 51. *See also* Benedict XVI; Congregation for the Doctrine of the Faith (CDF)
Rau, Johannes, 158
Rauscher, Anton, 162
Reese, Thomas J., 94
Reproductive Medicine Bill (FMG), 205–206
Reuss, Joseph, 118–119, 122
Rheinische Merkur/Christ und Welt, 133
rhythm method, 47; and Catholic couples' experience with, 112–113; as licit method of birth control, 99–100, 102–103, 105
Richardt, Nicole, 199
Robertson, John A., 199
Rock, John, 125

Roegele, Otto, 148
Rohleder, Hermann, 176–179, 182
Roitzsch, Ingrid, 164–165
Rölli-Alkemper, Lukas, 17
Roman Curia, 5, 19, 40, 50, 87, 120, 215–216
Ross, Susan A., 33, 91–92
Ruether, Rosemary Radford, 76
Ruff, Mark, 4, 16–18

Sacerdotalis Caelibatus, 45–46
Sacerdotalis Ordinatio, 93–94
Sartory, Thomas and Gertrude, 126
Schillebeeckx, Edward, 214
Schissler, Hanna, 108
Schmidt, Helmut, 150, 162
Schmidtchen, Gerhard, 163
Schüssler-Fiorenza, Elisabeth, 76, 252n195
Schwenzer, Gerhard, 87
Second Vatican Council: and impact on postconciliar birth control debate, 119–123; and impact on postconciliar celibacy debate, 41–45; and impact on postconciliar women's ordination debate, 64–69
secularization, 15–18, 100, 209
Seebohm, Hans-Christoph, 154, 262n100
self-determination: women's right of, 142, 153, 163, 171
Sex after Fascism, 13, 142
sexual complementarity, 62, 79, 88–89, 95, 104
sexual revolution, 5, 39, 123. See also student movement
Silies, Eva-Maria, 13
Social Democratic Party (SPD), 9–10, 24, 84; and abortion, 136, 143, 145–148, 150–152, 155–156, 158–162, 164–165; and antinuclear politics, 201; and assisted reproduction, 183, 197; and the Basic Law, 107–108
Society of Saint Pius (SSPX), 20
Sommer, Norbert, 76
Sozialer Dienst katholischer Frauen, 172
Spadero, Antonio, 214
sperm collection, 176–177; and Catholic theology, 181, 186, 267n32
Spiazzi, Raimondo, 78–79
Spiegel, Der: and abortion, 141, 145–147,
161–162; and assisted reproduction, 183, 190–191, 195–196, 200; and Benedict XVI, 210–211; and birth control, 126, 128; and celibacy, 38, 47, 56–58; and women's ordination, 94; and women's place in the Catholic Church; 76, 82 161–162
Steffensky, Edmund, 57
Steichen, Donna, 96
Steinbacher, Sybille, 7
Stelzenberger, Johannes, 185–186
Stem Cell Act, 206, 273n156
sterilization: and Catholic theology, 117–118, 133, 138; under National Socialism, 142; and West German abortion debate, 146
Stern: and abortion, 141, 145–146; and birth control, 124–125
Stimmen der Zeit, 82, 114
Stoeckel, Walter, 177
Strauss, Franz Josef, 162–163
Strotmann, Angelika, 85
student movement, 8, 12–13, 19, 125, 143, 208. See also sexual revolution
Stuhlmueller, Carroll, 80
Subcommission VII, "Charismas, Ministries, Offices," 52–56, 70–72. See also Würzburg Synod
Süddeutsche Zeitung, Die, 158, 167
Suenens, Leo Joseph, 37–38, 42–43, 119–120, 122
surrogacy, 175, 193–195, 198–199, 203–204, 271n111
Swidler, Leonard, 77
Sztuka, Alfred, 37

Tenhumberg, Heinrich, 54–55, 70–72, 162, 213
test tube babies. See in vitro fertilization (IVF)
thalidomide, 124, 256n105
theology of the body, 63, 79, 87–90; theological criticism of, 91–92. See also John Paul II
Twents, Simone, 10

unification treaty, 171

Vatican I, 121

Vatican II. *See* Second Vatican Council
Vereinigung katholischer Priester und ihrer Frauen, 59
Verhülsdonk, Rowitha, 165
Veritatis Splendor, 93
viri probati, 52–55. *See also* diaconate
Vogel, Bernhard, 147, 151, 155–156, 159. *See also* Central Committee of German Catholics (ZdK)
Vogel, Hans-Jochen, 156, 160–161

Warner, Marina, 115
Weakland, Rembert G., 87
We Are Church (*Wir Sind Kirche*), 43, 95, 210–211, 215
Welt, Die, 147, 158, 212
Wiliarty, Sara Elise, 11, 159
Willig, Irene, 91
Wojtyla, Karol, 37. *See also* John Paul II
Women-Church Movement, 86
women's bonus, 10, 148, 232. *See also* Christian Democratic Union (CDU)
women's ordination, 21, 23–24, 60, 208–209, 213–214; and mainstream Catholic women's groups, 67, 69–70, 72–73, 81–84; movement for, 13, 76, 85–86; and Protestantism, 63–64, 75, 244n8; and secular feminism, 247n72; theological arguments against, 62, 66, 77–78, 87–90, 94; theological arguments for, 55–56, 79–80, 91–93. *See also* diaconate
Women's Ordination Conference (WOC), 63, 75–76, 86, 95

women's reproductive rights, 1, 6, 9, 24, 209
Women's Union (FU), 163–166, 172, 204. *See also* Christian Democratic Union (CDU)
World Congresses of the Lay Apostolate, 40, 74
World Synod of Bishops, 52–53; 75, 86–87, 216
Wuermeling, Josef, 108
Würzburg Synod, 17, 21–22, 73; and celibacy, 49, 54, 70, 128, 243n128; criticism of, 53, 55; and female diaconate, 70–71, 84; press coverage of, 56; survey results from, 44, 50–51, 220–221

youth culture, 3. *See also* student movement
youth defense laws, 8–9, 100, 208

Zeit, Die, 132, 151, 153, 190–191, 195
Zentralkomitee der deutschen Katholiken. *See* Central Committee of German Catholics (ZdK)
Zentrale Kommission für Biologische Sicherheit. *See* Central Commission for Biological Security (ZKBS)
Zentralverband der katholischen Frauen- und Müttergemeinschaften. *See* Central Association of Catholic Communities of Women and Mothers; Catholic Women's Association in Germany (kfd)
Ziemann, Benjamin, 15–16